The Marine Corps Reserve

Reserve

—

A History

by

RESERVE OFFICERS OF PUBLIC AFFAIRS UNIT 4-1

Division of Reserve, Headquarters, U.S. Marine Corps

Washington, D.C. : 1966

A Tribute to

MAJOR GENERAL MELVIN J. MAAS, USMCR

And all other Reserve Marines

who fought and died for God,

Country, and Corps from 1916 to 1966

Library of Congress Catalogue Number 66–62598

For sale by the Superintendent of Documents, U.S. Government Printing Office
Washington, D.C. 20402 - Price $3.50 (cloth)

III

Foreword

This book will close a curious gap in Marine history. It is hard to believe that no other volume anywhere tells the story of the Marine Corps Reserve. This Golden Anniversary edition covers the 50 crucial years from 1916, when Congress first authorized a Marine Corps Reserve, to 1966 when the 4th Marine Division/Aircraft Wing Team is an integral part of the muscle of American armed strength.

Unlike many of their fellow countrymen, Marine Reserves understand the importance of our current fight in Southeast Asia. The young blood we have in our Reserve can take the gaff and are ready to go on 30 days' notice if called. But, they won't be called unless there is a specific mission for them. Unlike 1950, when the Reserves helped turn the tide in Korea, our Regular Marine Corps was beefed up and could move into Vietnam on orders from the President. With 30,000 more Regular Marines in 1965 and another third of a billion dollars from the Congress, we were able this time to discharge our mission in Southeast Asia without calling up our "Sunday Punch," the Organized Reserve.

The Marine Reserve of today, like his father in World War II, his brother in Korea, or his grandfather in World War I, knows that the Marine Corps exists for a greater purpose than to kill or destroy. Reserves know that along with our military action we are building peace where there has been no peace, security where it hasn't existed and order where there is no order.

The Navy-Marine team depends upon the Reserves as never before. The Purple Hearts, the decorations, and the wires to next of kin are going to Reserves and their families today just as they have for 50 years. I visited Vietnam in January of 1966 at a time when four sons of Marine general officers were fighting there as lieutenants. One of these fine young men was a Reserve, just as are hundreds of other young ground officers and aviators and enlisted men in air and ground units there. Our Reserves are not Reserves in isolation, they are part of the team.

Today's Reserve is better, more efficient and better trained than ever before thanks to Congressional support which has made it possible for the Regular Marine Corps to supply teachers, training, and equipment in depth. The Six Months Training Program and back-to-back and multiple drills have truly given us a professional Reserve. This is far different from the earlier years so well reported in this history. The Regulars have come to know and understand the Reserve and to work aggressively to help solve its problems. Similarly, in the evolution of half a century, the reservist has taken full advantage of the training and equipment and now considers himself a Marine, period.

In talking with officers and men in Vietnam this year, I had difficulty in finding anyone who could point out any Reserves, and yet we know there were large numbers of junior officers completing three years active duty after college and some noncommissioned officers who volunteered for active duty late in 1965.

It is most fitting that this volume is a tribute to the late Major General Melvin J. Maas who was so much a part of this 50 years. His dedication, his perseverance, his courage, and his brillance in all matters affecting the Marine Corps and its Reserve are well chronicled here. His contribution was distinctly outstanding because of his great gifts, but his ardor in all things Marine was typical of hundreds of thousands of other Reserves then and now.

The officers who worked diligently over a three-year period to research and write this volume have performed a real service. I hope that this history will be read by Marines and their friends. I started reading it as a duty and soon became very interested in the story itself. I enjoyed the book and hope that it will better inform the American people concerning the role and mission of the Marine Corps Reserve.

WALLACE M. GREENE, JR.
GENERAL, U.S. MARINE CORPS
COMMANDANT OF THE MARINE CORPS

Introduction

Someone once said that a camel was a horse put together by a committee. This story was written by a committee from the Washington, D.C. Marine Corps Reserve Public Affairs Unit 4–1. We hope the book resembles neither a horse nor a camel. Professor Samuel Eliot Morrison has advised young historians to remember only that they have a story to tell and that the only way to tell it is to write. This we did.

If we have succeeded in being factual, informative, and interesting, it will be due in large measure to our wives, families, and office staffs who shouldered additional burdens while we were writing long hours at home or office. Any defects, however, are the responsibility of the commanding officer of the project.

Writing about the Corps in 1927, the late Colonel John W. Thomason, Jr., in my mind the greatest Marine writer, concluded his piece thus: "Being a Marine, I have tried to set forth simple tales without comment. It is unnecessary to write what I think of my own people, nor, would it be, perhaps, in the best taste." Subconsciously, we each felt this way when we wrote.

We have not cluttered up the book with footnotes, but have provided a modest index and bibliographical note. We hope the book will appeal to reservists and their families and that libraries will make it available to high school and college students. Recruiters should find it useful and all Marine units will have copies. There is no story of the Marine Corps Reserve otherwise available at this writing.

This book began when General Wallace M. Greene, Jr., was Chief of Staff and was completed during his term as Commandant. His confidence and his personal interest were all-important to our efforts.

Special thanks are also due to successive information officers in the Division of Reserve, Lieutenant Colonels Bill Blackwell and Larry Eskell and to Majors Glenn Stevens and Jim Maher and to their associates, particularly Miss Mary Lou Price, Miss Betty Krause, and Miss Sue Faulkner. The entire staff of the Marine Corps Historical Reference Section helped us in every possible manner and Mr. Henry I. Shaw, Jr., Chief Historian of the Marine Corps, gave us most valuable personal encouragement and guidance. Basic research by Lieutenant Colonel Guy Richards and monthly issues of *Leatherneck* Magazine during the long editorship of Reserve Colonel Donald L. Dickson were important sources of information as was *The Reserve Marine*.

We regret our inability to include mention of all Reserve units. We included those on which facts were readily available or those which seemed to be most interesting. We also regret our inability to tell the parallel story of the dedicated, devoted, and selfless Navy doctors, dentists, chaplains, and corpsmen who served us ashore and afloat and the Navy nurses who cared for our wounds and our ills. They were as much a part of us as the Marines whose uniforms they proudly wore and wear today with honor. We can never repay the debt we owe them or tell of the love we bear them. May God bless them all, the men and women of the medical department and chaplains' corps of the U.S. Navy and Naval Reserve.

These 50 years are not even a fly speck in the eyes of God, barely a fourth of Marine history itself. But, happily this story may come to life on film, in magazines, possibly in song, thanks to our working partners, the other two Public Affairs Units in New York and Los Angeles under Colonels Ray Henri and Bill Hendricks respectively.

These 50 years cover the life span of almost all the writing committee. And we have had a small part in history ourselves. Major Dick Kriegel who did much of the early writing and basic research flew to Vietnam in June 1965 as a Provincial Officer for AID. Major Russell Davis who had scheduled the printing of the book died suddenly at his desk at the Navy Department. Some of the general officers who helped us have died since we started the book, including the remarkable William P. T. (Petie) Hill. We are most grateful to Generals Silverthorn, Craig, McQueen, Stewart, Day, Woods, and Tomlinson who helped bring these pages to life with their recollections.

Most of the senior officers in this history began as enlisted men and advanced on merit, so this is their half century story. If we are pro-Marine it is because we Reserves are but part of a larger whole. Thoreau once said: "How vain it is to sit down to write when you have not stood up to live." We sat down to write because others before us had stood up to live, and die. We wrote not under the stern discipline of combat as did Brigadier General Robert L. Denig's World War II Combat Correspondents, but under the equally stern calendar which day by day moved toward 29 August 1966 and publication.

As the project director, it is a pleasure to pay tribute to the fine work of Colonel Sylvan J. Kaplan in the early planning, assigning and writing, to Lieutenant Colonels Ruth Broe, Henry Stevenson, Helen Wilson, and William Rodd who did much of the actual writing and to Majors Pat Meid and Dick Kriegel and Captain Dick Truitt who wrote entire chapters. Majors Duane Packard and Norm Hatch did the photo folios and Colonel Barry Zorthian and Captain Ken Coffey helped digest material for inclusion. Major Frances Jackson and Lieutenant Colonel Bill Merkel handled early historical research and contacts. Others who helped in a variety of ways were Colonel A. A. Gunnels, Lieutenant Colonels Crozet Duplantier and Russ Hendrickson and Majors Joe Bartlett and Emile Bourg and Captain Dave Dichter. Major "Eddie" Smith, first WR to retire under Public Law 810 helped considerably with the editing. Without Ruth Broe, Pat Meid, and Dick Kriegel, however, there would have been no book.

Writing in 1912, four years before our story began, historian H. G. Wells said: "Versatility, alert adaptability, these are urgent needs. In peace and war alike the unimaginative, uninventive man is a burthen and a retardation, as he never was before in the world's history." These pages tell the story of a group of remarkable men and women who served in war and in peace with the versatility and adaptability which has become the mark of America's secret weapon, the Reserve Marine.

If we Reserves are accepted as partners by the Regulars, and we are, it is because we have tried our best to be the Marines they are. It may have taken us almost 50 years, but the 4th Marine Division/Aircraft Wing Reserve Team proves we made it.

WILLIAM P. McCAHILL
COLONEL, USMCR
CO, PUBLIC AFFAIRS UNIT 4–1

Contents

Illustrations

Three 16-page sections of photographs follow pages 90, 156, and 218

Section I
Marine Reserves, Brooklyn, 1916—World War I, Air and Ground—Women Reservists (F)—Summer Training, Quantico, 1919–39 Era—On Parade, Decoration Day, 1927—Rifle Team Wins Roumanian Cup, 1939—Women Marines—World War II Campaigns: Guadalcanal, Tarawa, Cape Gloucester, New Britain

Section II
World War II: Saipan, Guam, Tinian, Peleliu, Iwo Jima, Okinawa—Woman Marine Reserve Band—First Women Reservists Sworn Into Regular Marine Corps—Reserve Hometown Training, 1945–50 Era—MCROA and Colonel Maas—Combat Correspondents Plaque—Summer Training, Lejeune—Korea Callup

Section III
Korea—WM Reserve Platoons—General Maas Retirement Ceremony—Marine Reservists' Training: Cold Weather, Deep Sea, Jets and 'Copters Into the Air, Artillery, Combat Exercises—Toys for Tots—Vietnam

The Marine Corps Reserve

—

A History

CHAPTER ONE

The Inception

"To be prepared for war is one of the most effectual means of preserving peace." George Washington.

Since the Marine Corps owes much of its success in developing its Reserve to the Navy, a brief look at the origins of the Naval Reserve is appropriate. The struggle for a Marine Corps Reserve was a part of the struggle for the Nation's early Naval Reserve. Indeed, the underlying philosophy appears to have been, to borrow from a popular song of our day: "You can't have one without the other."

From Civil War days, the need for a Naval Reserve was recognized by many Congressional and Naval leaders. Foremost among these was Admiral J. G. Walker, Chief of the Bureau of Navigation, Navy Department, who wrote to the Secretary of the Navy on 15 October 1889:

> Naval Reserves—I again repeat my former opinion, that the subject of speedily establishing a system of naval reserves, to meet the demands of the country, for rapidly manning and increasing its fleet upon the outbreak of war, is vitally important; and I beg to invite your favorable attention to the effort which has been made in Congress and in several of the States to effect the practicable and efficient solution of this problem. I presented the following arguments in my report of last year:
>
> At present no means exist for providing the fleet with a single trained man, beyond the number prescribed by law for the peace establishment, and it would seem that no argument should be necessary to secure the required legislative authority.
>
> The study and energy of maritime nations is being devoted to placing the reserves of men, as well as materials, in such a state of training and readiness as to make them available for effective service on 24-hour notice.
>
> Rapid mobilization may be said to be the leading naval question of the day, and the recent naval maneuvers abroad have given occasion for the frequent statement of the opinion that to readiness of ships and guns must be joined an equal readiness of men, to make any system of mobilization complete and effective.
>
> The bill presented by Mr. Whitthorne of Tennessee, and known throughout the country by his name, is a carefully framed and comprehensive measure which authorizes the enrollment of a naval militia and the formation of a naval reserve in the several sea and lake board States and provides government aid in supplying arms and equipment and facilities for training and drills.
>
> This bill has been received with much favor and would doubtless have passed the last Congress but for Mr. Whitthorne's serious illness. I am informed that it will again be presented, and I urge upon the Department its hearty support. Massachusetts, Rhode Island, New York, and Pennsylvania have already placed upon their statute books laws which anticipate and supplement the provisions of this national measure.
>
> It would be most unfortunate for the Navy and for coast defense should Congress fail to take advantage of the favorable state of public opinion of the subject of creating a naval reserve and pass an act to encourage, utilize, and bind together the State and individual effort, which has been made and is being made toward this end.

Despite the efforts of those who wanted a Reserve under the operational control of the Navy, the politics of the next 30 years dictated otherwise. Emphasis was placed, instead, on State-controlled naval militia organizations, supplied and assisted by the Navy Department.

On 23 August 1892 B. F. Tracy, Secretary of the Navy, reported that the naval appropriation act, approved 19 July 1892, had the following provision: "For arms and equipment connected therewith for naval militia of various States, under such regulations as the Secretary of the Navy may prescribe, $25,000 . . . ." Shortly after this Act was passed, 7 states mustered into their respective Naval Militia 148 officers, 160 petty officers, and 1,486 enlisted men for a total of 1,794 personnel.

From the beginning, it was evident that the Naval Militias could not fill the need for a second or inner line of defense. They were State organizations, organized and controlled by the various State laws. The Federal Government, represented by the Navy Department, had no direct control in Naval Militia matters. In effect, Congressional appropriations and Navy vessels and equipment were used by the Naval Militia units of the several States as the States saw fit.

The weaknesses of the Naval Militia were carefully examined by Lieutenant Commander William H. Southerland, Officer in Charge of the Naval Militia Office. On 1 November 1900 he wrote:

> I call your attention to these facts to show the absolute necessity for the creation, in addition to the naval militia organizations, of a government or national reserve force, which should be organized entirely under the control of the Navy Department.

Progress in establishing a Naval Reserved continued very slowly. Nearly 6 years later, George V. L. Meyer, Secretary of the Navy, wrote:

> In every foreign country possessing a first-class navy, provision is made for a large reserve of trained men, to be added to the enlisted personnel of the navy at the outbreak of war. Our provision for this contingency is inadequate. Beyond a few men on the retired list, for the most part too old to render effective service, we have no other reserve than the officers and men of the Naval Militia of the several States . . . we have about 6,000 naval militia organized by the different States bordering on the sea and on the Great Lakes. These small groups, while enthusiastic and generally efficient, are not under central control and training. The formation of a national naval militia, on the lines of the land militia, is a necessity and legislation is required to accomplish this.

Two years later, on 1 December 1911, Mr. Meyer reported:

> The department submitted to the 61st Congress a draft of a bill embodying its ideas for the legal establishment of a naval reserve of officers and men (introduced as S. 7644 and H.R. 24942) entitled: A bill to provide for a reserve of personnel for the U.S. Navy and Marine Corps and for its enrollment. . . .

On 4 October 1913, Admiral Victor Blue, Chief of the Bureau of Navigation, reported to the Secretary of the Navy:

> The importance of having a regularly enrolled and organized Naval Reserve for service in time of war cannot be too forcibly impressed upon the country . . . . Within the last year there has been established under the Bureau of Navigation, an Office of Naval Reserve. . . . To date it has a list of upwards of 2,600 men who have volunteered for enrollment. No doubt if Congress should authorize the formation of a national reserve in a manner that would make the proposition attractive, there would be no difficulty in recruiting the full quota in a very short time.

The next step toward an improved Naval Militia was the 12 April 1914 publication of Navy Department General Order No. 93, which established a Division of Naval Militia Affairs in the Navy Department.

Marines in the Naval Militia

Although a few Marine detachments had long been organized within several of the Naval Militias, their status as Marine Corps units was obscure. After nearly 30 years of ambiguity, the stage was finally set for clear definition of the role of Marines in the Naval Militia. Navy Department General Order No. 153, of 10 July 1915, provided this definition.

Significant among its several general provisions was the statement that the Navy Department was to: "so organize, arm, uniform, equip the Naval Militia that it may be eligible to be called forth by the President of the United States to serve the United States in the event of war . . . ." Of even greater import to this narrative is what the Order said about *members of the Marine Corps Branch, Naval Militia:*

> Officers—Marine Companies.
>
> For each Marine company of 60 or less enlisted men, there will be allowed the following officers:
>
> 1 Captain.
> 1 First Lieutenant.
> 1 Second Lieutenant.
>
> For a Marine company of more than 60 enlisted men, there will be allowed an additional second lieutenant.
>
> Noncommissioned Officers and Other Enlisted Men.
>
> For each Marine company of 48 enlisted men, there will be allowed noncommissioned officers and other enlisted men as follows:
>
> (a) 1 First Sergeant, 1 Gunnery Sergeant, 4 Sergeants, 5 Corporals, 1 Drummer, 1 Trumpeter.
> (b) 35 Privates.
>
> For each additional 8 privates over 35, an additional corporal may be appointed; and for each additional 16 privates over 35, an additional sergeant may be appointed.
>
> In Marine sections, the following officers will be allowed:
>
> 1 First Lieutenant; and the following officers and other enlisted men:
>
> 1 First Sergeant.
> 2 Sergeants.
> 1 Trumpeter.
> 17 Privates.
>
> Whenever a Marine company increases in size to 12 squads, it will be divided into 2 companies.

To encourage former enlisted men of the Navy and Marine Corps to enter the Naval Militia, and avoid interfering with the promotion of enlisted men of the Naval Militia who had no previous Navy or Marine Corps service, the Order further provided:

> Any former enlisted man of the U.S. Navy or Marine Corps who is in good standing in the community and who was honorably discharged will be allowed to enter the Naval Militia without professional examination in any unit of organization or headquarters of a brigade or of a battalion, with such rate or rank as he last held in the U.S. Navy or Marine Corps. . . .

The Order also authorized the formation of Marine Corps units up to and including battalions and brigades—when sufficient Marines and units were available—and established qualifications for the Marine Corps Branch.

Thus did Navy General Order No. 153 create a significant role for members of the Marine Corps Branch, Naval Militia.

Historically, Marines had been participating in the Naval Militia of some States almost from the inception of the Naval Militia program in 1892. Particularly colorful was the 1st Marine Corps Reserve Company of the New York State Naval Militia. Many members of this company, initially established in 1893, were later to give good account of themselves during World War I. Within the early Naval Militia of Massachusetts and Louisiana, too, Marine branches were active. An early photograph of the New York Naval Militia at Albany indicated Marines were present.

In effect, therefore, our modern Reserves are the successors of their brothers of 50 to 70 years ago who "trooped and stomped" essentially as Reserves—in deed, if not in name. For, in the final analysis, these early Marines were not classified as "Reserves" simply because there was no formal Reserve program in their day.

Passage of the Naval Militia Act of 16 February 1914 finally gave the Navy Department virtual control of the Naval Militia. From that time forward, the colorful Secretary of the Navy, Josephus Daniels, concentrated his efforts on expanding the Navy and creating a bona fide Naval Reserve. At the same time, Major General Commandant George Barnett was seeking to strengthen the Marine Corps and to create an operative Marine Corps Reserve. From a series of Daniels-Barnett conferences, came a coordinated plan of action: the Navy would suggest a Reserve in 1914 and try to get it into law during 1915; the Marine Corps would propose a Reserve in 1915 and try to get it authorized in 1916. This combined strategem, given added impetus by ominous events in Europe and elsewhere throughout the world, succeeded more or less according to plan. On 3 March 1915, the 63d Congress passed an Act providing for a larger Navy and creating a Naval Reserve. Seven months later, in his Annual Report for Fiscal Year 1915, the Commandant fired his opening barrage, declaring:

> The Marine Corps has no reserves. During the last session of Congress a naval reserve, consisting of men who have seen service in the Navy, was created. The adoption of a similar proviso for the Marine Corps is recommended.

Birth of the Marine Corps Reserve

On 29 August 1916, Congress passed "An Act making appropriations for the naval service for the fiscal year ending June 30th, 1917, and for other purposes." One of those "other purposes" was the Marine Corps Reserve.

The Act of 29 August 1916 was the statutory authority under which Navy Department General Order No. 231, issued 2 days later, informed "all persons belonging to the Navy":

> A U.S. Marine Corps Reserve, to be a consitituent part of the Marine Corps and in addition to the authorized strength thereof, is hereby established under the same provisions in all respects (except as may be necessary to adapt the said provisions to the Marine Corps) as those providing for the Naval Reserve Force . . .; *Provided*, That the Marine Corps Reserve may consist of not more than five classes, corresponding as near as may be, to the Fleet Naval Reserve, the Naval Reserve, the Naval Coast Defense Reserve, the Volunteer Reserve, and the Naval Reserve Flying Corps, respectively.

Thus, a Marine Corps Reserve—patterned after the Naval Reserve Force—was officially created. It consisted of 5 classes or types of personnel: Fleet Marine Corps Reserve, the Marine Corps Reserve A, the Marine Corps Reserve B, the Volunteer Marine Reserve, and the Marine Corps Flying Corps.

In addition to these 5 classes of reservists, both Naval and Marine, the Act also contained provisions regarding the Naval Milita and the National Naval Volunteers.

In retrospect, it would appear that at

this time both the Navy and Marine Corps had, in effect, *two* Reserves; for the same Act of 29 August provided for continuation of the Naval Militia and the National Naval Volunteers, with their included Marine Corps Branches. This ambiguity was eliminated on 1 July 1918 when, under Navy Department General Order No. 400, the National Naval Volunteers were transferred to the Naval Reserve Force, and the Marine Corps Branch was made a part of the Marine Corps Reserve. How far the pendulum had swung from the old days of the State-controlled, Navy-supported Militia is borne out by the fact that the Navy could, on its own authority, order this transfer of Volunteers who were actually members of State military forces.

Certainly, among the most interesting observations on the origin of the Marine Corps Reserve are the colorful recollections of Marine Reserve Major Edward B. Irving. In 1964, 13 years after his retirement, Major Irving recalled:

The Tap Root of the Marine Corps Reserve

The issue may be in doubt as to the birth of the Marine Corps Reserve in the minds of many who are searching the files for the tap root, but not in my mind. Yes, at age 68, I remember when. That was before I enlisted in the Marine Corps Reserve 3 days after the declaration of war in World War I. Here, I tasted from the cup of the old Marine Corps, when enlisted men were paid $30.00 a month, such pittance in pay attracting only remittance men, the rawest of adventures, and ne'er-do-wells. But, they all were welded-melded to solid nerve in a Corps that was proud of its heritage and determined above all to find a place in the sun in World War I.

Then, the Corps was a mere 5,000 men; its exploits . . . belied the token given them by the Army and Navy, "Seagoing bell hops!" These Regulars gave a proud meaning to the then prevalent slur, "Tell it to the Marines!" Issued two khaki uniforms, one to be washed and starched each day, and pressed on the 16-pound company iron before reporting for duty, these soldiers-of-the-sea were spit and polish personified, murderers on good behavior.

In Philadelphia, this high caliber reputation of the Corps seeped out into the minds of the populace intermittently, to be focused with high emphasis in the mind of one well-bred gentleman, A. J. Drexel Biddle, better known far and wide as Tony for his sporting prowess as an outstanding boxer of his day. But Tony had a great patriotic urge as well. He sensed, as did many others, that war with Germany was inevitable. And, being a fighting man at heart, he championed the Marines for what he knew them to be—the elite among fighting men in the American armed forces.

Therefore, single-handedly he set up a drill brigade in Philadelphia, borrowing Marine Corps non-coms as drill instructors. A goodly number of Philadelphia aristocrats joined his unit, as did adventurers from the not-so-prominent younger citizens. Additionally, he formed a voluntary secret service among older men, principally, each appointing two others to seek out German spies, they in turn reporting to only one person. Thus, no man knew more than three others in this secret service organization. There were some younger men who joined this latter outfit—I among them since my business activities were out of town in Chester, Pa.

Shortly thereafter, he recalled, uniforms were issued and a month or two of basic training followed. "I can still hear Sergeant Trimble's caustic observation, 'Twentieth Century Marines!'" he said, at having to "treat the cream of Philadelphia citizenry with kid gloves." Irving continued:

One day Major Killgore sent for me and asked if I would like to be his orderly. Anything was better than boot training so I said, Yes, sir, with considerable pleasure, whereupon I was transferred from the 1st

Company Reserve to the Barracks Detachment. In the capacity of orderly, I watched hundreds of other Marine Corps Reservists arrive from all parts of the country, together with regular Marines from outlying detachments. These were formed into a regiment christened the 5th Marines, with the 2 original Reserve Companies being transferred to this now famous organization.

Tears filled my eyes as I watched this regiment depart on a transport to endless glory at Chateau Thierry and Belleau Wood. Later, Tony Biddle was commissioned a Major in the Marine Corps Reserve to teach bayonet fighting, as a master boxer, the length and breadth of the Corps. Repeatedly, unarmed, he would taunt a recruit to attack him angrily with a bared bayonet on his rifle. Then, quickly, Tony would disarm the attacker—again and again. What guts! So, for my money, the tap root of the Marine Corps Reserve was Major A. J. Drexel Biddle, USMCR. May God rest his ardent soul.

Retired Major General William A. Worton, a charter member of the Marine Detachment, Massachusetts Naval Militia, who enlisted 29 May 1913 at the age of 16 while still a student at Boston Latin School, and later entered the Regular Marine Corps, suggests a different tap root in a 1964 letter:

> The Marine Detachment, Massachusetts Naval Militia (MNM) was the *first reserve organization of Marines* [his emphasis] in the United States, and consisted of one officer (First Lieutenant Walter A. Powers), and 36 enlisted men. Our armory was the old U.S.S. *Chicago* of the White Fleet which was tied up on the Boston end of the Charlestown Bridge. We drilled once a week and had our first 2-week tour of duty in 1913 with other elements of the Massachusetts Naval Militia in the U.S.S. *Chicago*, firing her old broadside battery off Block Island. About November 1914, the detachment was reorganized as the 1st Marine Company, M.N.M., and authorized an increase to 65 officers and enlisted; Lieutenant Powers was commissioned and subsequently Stewart

Chaffee was appointed Second Lieutenant. We moved to a hall at Mechanics Building which served as our Armory until mobilization day in 1917. During the years 1915 and 1916, we conducted our summer tours of duty with the Naval Militia in the U.S. *Kearsage* (Captain Gelm, U.S.N. Commanding).

> The Company voluntarily spent many weekends at the Wakefield Rifle Range under canvas learning the rudiments of field service.

General Worton recalled that officers attended the Training School for officers of the Massachusetts National Guard held in the 5th Massachusetts Infantry Armory at Charlestown, Massachusetts. Continuing, he wrote:

> The 1st Marine Company, M.N.M., and its predecessor, the Marine Detachment, M.N.M., were proud organizations; a high standard of discipline and training was immediately instituted and constantly maintained. We were fortunate in having Captain F. H. Delano, U.S. Marine Corps, as our first U.S. Inspector-Instructor; he immediately developed the love of Corps that has consistently been the heritage of the Boston Reserve Marine.

> About January 1917, Captain Powers resigned and Captain George H. Manks, formerly of the 9th Massachusetts Infantry, was appointed Captain of the 1st Marine Company, M.N.M.

> The 1st Marine Company, M.N.M., was ordered to extended active duty on 10 March 1917 by the Governor of the Commonwealth of Massachusetts, and, under the command of First Lieutenant W. A. Worton, proceeded to the Boston Navy Yard, marching from the Mechanics Building, via Washington Street to the Marine Barracks whereupon Lieutenant Worton reported to Colonel Newt Hall, U.S. Marine Corps, with the Company for Federal Duty. I was a boy of 20 years of age and have had many happy and proud experiences during a lifetime of service to my Corps, yet I still remember that day with much pride. It has always been my proud boast to say I was privileged to wear the insignia of the Common-

wealth of Massachusetts on my collar; for, in those days we wore the Massachusetts insignia just in rear of the Marine Corps emblems.

Who or what should be credited as being the tap root of the Marine Corps Reserve, the significant thing is that a Marine Corps Reserve *did* come into being in time to make its contribution to World War I. Because it was young, and because much confusion and doubt existed as to its future role and activities, the Marine Corps Reserve was subordinated to the rigorous recruiting campaigns of the Regular Establishment. Yet, thousands of America's best young men became Reserves and their blood mingled with that of the Regulars on every battlefield where Marines fought in France.

Mobilization of the Marine Corps

The role of the Marine Corps in World War I changed and expanded as the politics of the War Department and the Navy Department adjusted to the serious matter of providing trained personnel on land and sea.

Traditionally, Marines h a d served aboard ship, guarded naval installations, engaged in operations to protect the lives and property of Americans wherever and whenever threatened by forces which duly constituted authorities could not handle. On 29 August 1916, when the Marine Corps Reserve was created, the authorized strength of the Marine Corps was raised from 344 officers and 9,921 enlisted to 597 officers and 14,981 enlisted. On 26 March 1917, the President issued an executive order further increasing the Marine Corps to 693 officers and 17,000 enlisted. The Act of 1 July 1918 temporarily increased the Marine Corps to 3,017 commissioned

officers, 324 warrant officers, and 75,000 enlisted.

Recruiting to fill these increased quotas was naturally aided by growing concern over the war in Europe. The Regular Establishment had 2 basic types of enlistments: a 4-year hitch and an enlistment "for the duration." Because of its relatively small size and the large number of young men eager to get "over there," the Marine Corps had little trouble getting enough recruits. Most enlistments were for the duration. Basically, these volunteers joined the Marine Corps expressly to help win the war and then planned to go back to their civilian pursuits—they were not career-minded Marines.

Lieutenant General Karl S. Day, a retired Reserve, writing in 1965, vividly recalls how it really happened. He wrote:

Nobody in the Regular establishment—or at least very few—ever heard of a Reserve at this time. There were 2 types of enlistment—4 years and "duration." To all intents and purposes, these duration people were Reserves. As an example—I went down to Headquarters about April 20th, 1917, to talk to "Major Thomas Holcomb" about getting a commission. Major Holcomb explained that there were only a very few vacancies in the Regular corps but that the Corps would need many many officers for the duration of the war and they were to be carried as "Temporaries" or "Reserves" or in some such category, they had not yet determined just how it would be handled. I took my physical at Chicago on May 21 along with some 30 or 40 other young men: 4 of us were designated "Regulars," the balance who passed were designated "Temporaries." All of us were commissioned into the Reserve that night as a device to hang on to us and subject us to orders until such time as the Senate got around to confirming us. It is my recollection that all those who were not designated to be Regulars were later commissioned as "Temporaries" this, of course, after the Senate had blessed us. On that same date, May 21, the same process was going on at a number of places—Mare Island, N.Y., New Orleans (I think)—I guess at each Marine Corps Recruiting Headquarters or the various areas.

As related by the World War I author, Regular Brigadier General A. W. Catlin:

> If we had had time and opportunity to pick men individually from the whole of the United States, I doubt whether we should have done much better. They were as fine a bunch of upstanding American athletes as you can meet, and they had brains as well as brawn. Sixty percent of the 6th Regiment—mark this—60 percent of them were college men. Two-thirds of one entire company came straight from the University of Minnesota.

One of these Minnesota Marines was Gerald Thomas whose career led him to the heights of a four-star general. Reminiscing late in 1964, General Thomas added the names of Carlton Wallace, Frank Strong, and Earl Martineau to those of Lagore, Moore, Murphy, Maynard, and Overton mentioned by Catlin as typifying the outstanding athletes who fought in France. Although World War I Reserves approximated only 10 percent of the Regular Establishment, the ratio of Reserves on the frontlines in France was considerably higher.

Besides the Regular Establishment's 2 basic types of enlistments, there was a third choice: enlistment in the Reserve. Since recruiting for both Reserve and Regular quotas was handled by the Regular Establishment, it was only natural that Regular Establishment needs were met first. In many cases, only when Regular quotas were filled did individual recruiting officers, scattered throughout the country, turn attention to Reserve recruitment. The Reserve *did* grow, however, attracting a high percentage of college students and technically qualified young men.

A Philadelphia Story

Reserve Brigadier General John J. Carter sent in a Philadelphia summary from retirement in 1965:

> Immediately following the Declaration of War in 1917, a Recruiting Office was established at 210 South 13th Street, Philadelphia, for the recruitment of U.S. Marine Corps Reservists. Many of the original enrollees were obtained from Major "Tony" Biddle's "Junior Marines" that he had established and drilled every weekend at Lansdowne, a suburb of Philadelphia. The "enrollments" were for a period of 4 years and consisted of 2 Classes—Class II, requiring an age minimum of 18 years and physical fitness that would allow for service beyond the continental limits of the United States. Class IV required a minimum age of 16 years *with* parents' consent, or 18 years *without* parents' consent, and was for duty within the continental limits of the United States. Later, on request, Class IV's, if 18 years, could transfer, after an additional physical examination, to Class II, and be eligible for duty beyond the continental limits. Many transfers of this nature were offered after reporting for duty at the Philadelphia Navy Yard.
>
> With few exceptions, the men were ordered immediately to the Marine Barracks, Navy Yard, Philadelphia, where they were assigned to duty with the 1st, 2d, and 3d Reserve Companies and billeted in No. 1 and No. 2 Barracks, facing the parade ground. While a regular Recruit Training Camp was established in an area beyond the barracks, the three Reserve companies had no connection with it but were trained separately under the command of one Captain Sumner, USMC, assisted by two outstanding D.I.'s, Sergeants Kramer and Parker. The rosters of these companies included many names of the old first families of the Philadelphia area and received much publicity.
>
> One such group known as "The Famous Five" were freshmen classmates at the Uni-

versity of Pennsylvania (Thomas Roberts
Reath, Sydney Thayer, Jr., Percival Glen-
denning, Henry S. Geyelin, Jr., Sydney
Guest). Sergeant Reath was killed in action
(Philadelphia's Marine Post of the American
Legion bears his name); Thayer and Glen-
denning were commissioned in the field and
completed their service as First Lieutenants.
After the 5th and 6th Marines had been
mounted out for duty in France, the balance
of the three companies that were Class II
were attached to the 7th Regiment and
shipped to Guantanamo Bay as the Expeditionary Force to Cuba 1917. The few Reserves that remained in Philadelphia were
assigned to various duties at the Depot of
Supplies, Fort Mifflin, et cetera. The
7th remained at Gitmo [Guantanamo,
Cuba] from August to November 1917,
when they were relieved by the 1st Regiment and moved the Headquarters to
San Juan Hill, just outside of Santiago.
Two companies were shipped to Camaguey
and one each to San Luis and Guantanamo
City. The remaining companies stayed at
San Juan Hill. Late 1918 saw quite a few
Reserves transferred back to the States to
become part of General Butler's 13th
Marines.

Growth of Reserve in World War I

On 6 April 1917, when Congress declared a state of war between the United
States and the Imperial German Government, the entire Marine Corps Reserve
was just 3 commissioned officers and 32
enlisted men. In addition, the Marine
Corps Branch of the National Naval Volunteers had 24 officers and 928 enlisted
men. After recruiting for the Marine
Corps Branch of the Naval Militia was
discontinued on 1 April 1917, the number
of enlisted personnel in that category decreased steadily. The Marine Corps Reserve was materially strengthened on 1
July 1918 when the Marine Corps Branch
of the National Naval Volunteers was
consolidated into the Reserve.

The extent to which individual Marine
Reserves were involved in World War I
is not clearly documented. Many writers
and correspondents considered the young
men who were actually Regulars in for
the duration as being "Volunteers" or, in
a sense, Reserves. As Colonel Julius S.
Turrill, an outstanding battalion commander in France, observed in 1930:

> Before Belleau Wood, in France, little
> was known of the Marine Corps even in our
> own country. In 1918 its renown and glory
> thrilled the World and brought consterna-
> tion to our enemies. This page of military
> glory was written by the fighting Marines
> overseas . . . they were volunteers and a
> few regulars dedicated by individual resolve
> to conquering the enemy.

However, there were many Reserves
among the 834 officers (not including observers) and 30,481 enlisted men who
served overseas with the American Expeditionary Force (AEF) and naval service during the Great War.

Most of these Marines served with the
4th Infantry Brigade, an all-Marine
Brigade which was a part of the Army's
2d Division of Regulars. The story of
these fighting organizations in World War
I has been so well told elsewhere that only
a few highlights need be mentioned. The
2d Division was a unique organization
with the command and staffing of its Headquarters shared between the Army and
Marine Corps. Its early wartime Army
Commanding Generals were Brigadier
General Charles A. Doyen; Major General Omar Bundy, who assumed command
during the operation at Verdun and
Chateau-Thierry; and Major General
James G. Harbord, at Aisne-Marne (Sois-
sons). Then, from 28 July 1918 until the
division was demobilized in August 1919
in the United States, Marine Major Gen-

eral John A. Lejeune commanded the historied "Second."

The division, whose motto was "Second-to-None," was composed of the 9th and 23d Infantry and the 5th Machinegun Battalion of the 3d Infantry Brigade; the 5th and 6th Marines and the Marine 6th Machinegun Battalion of the 4th Brigade of Marines; the 12th, 15th, and 17th Field Artillery and the 2d Trench Mortar Battery of the 2d Field Artillery Brigade; the 2d Engineers; 4th Machinegun Battalion; 5th Field Signal Battalion; 2d Headquarters Train and Military Police; 2d Ammunition Train; 2d Engineer Train; 2d Supply Train; and 2d Sanitary Train.

As a component of the 2d Division, the 4th Marine Brigade participated in 4 major operations, winning world renown in the Aisne defensive (31 May to 5 June 1918); the Aisne-Marne offensive (18 and 19 July 1918); the St. Mihiel offensive (12 to 16 September 1918); and the Meuse-Argonne offensive (1 to 10 October 1918 and 1 to 10 November 1918). The brigade was involved in a number of other operations: for example, the capture of Mont Blanc and St. Etienne were considered part of the Meuse-Argonne offensive. Similarly, the capture of Hill 142, Bouresches and the strategic Belleau Wood by the Marine Brigade assisted by artillery, engineers, and others of the 2d Division and the capture of Vaux by the 3d Brigade, Engineers, and Artillery of the 2d Division, were termed local engagements rather than major operations. These are, however, only technicalities. They do not dim the glory which inspired the Commanding General, French VI Army to decree:

> In view of the brilliant conduct of the 4th Brigade of the 2d U.S. Division, which in a spirited fight took Bouresches and the important strong point of Belleau Wood, stubbornly defended by a large enemy force, the General commanding the VI Army orders, that henceforth in all official papers, the Bois de Belleau shall be named "Bois de la Brigade de Marine."
>
> Division General DEGOUTTE,
> *Commanding VI Army.*
> (signed) "DEGOUTTE"

As always, the price of glory was not cheap. Marine casualties—including those of the 4th Marine Brigade and Marines who fought in the Champagne-Marne defensive, the Oise-Aisne offensive, and the Ypres-Lys offensive—totaled 356 officers and 11,612 enlisted, almost one-third of all Marines in France. The detailed casualty list read:

> Killed in Action: 55 officers, 1,459 enlisted; Died of Wounds: 25 officers, 753 enlisted; Missing in Action: 161 enlisted; Wounded in Action: 252 officers, 8,277 enlisted; Gassed: 24 officers, 962 enlisted.

Marines were awarded 1,668 personal decorations, including 5 Medals of Honor and 8 Distinguished Service Medals. The role of the Reserve in France is obscure, partly because official records often combined, without proper designation, Regulars, "For the Duration Regulars," and Reserves. In a letter to the Secretary of the Navy dated 1 February 1919, the Commandant made the following report on Marine Corps Reserves in World War I:

> Total number enrolled (includes Fleet Marine Corps Reserves, also Classes 2, 4, and 5): 8,248; total killed: 7 officers, 155 enlisted; died of other causes: 8 officers, 61 enlisted; number cited for gallantry in action: 3 officers, 18 enlisted. All the wounded have been carried on one list, men enlisted for 4 years, those enlisted for the duration of war, and reservists. The total number found to date is: wounded severely: 1,992; wounded slightly: 415; wounded, degree undetermined: 4,028; total: 6,435.

Lacking a detailed breakdown, the discrepancies between these statistics and those previously cited cannot be explained. How the Marine Corps Reserve grew during World War I is reflected in the following comparative official statistics:

1917:

	Men, Active Duty
Apr	35
May	424
Jun	885
Jul	1,096
Aug	1,167
Sept	1,186
Oct	1,210
Nov	1,341
Dec	1,341

1918:

	Men, Active Duty
Jan	1,531
Feb	2,514
Mar	4,106
Apr	4,745
May	4,780
Jun	4,950
Jul	5,211
Aug	6,378
Sep	6,453
Oct	6,402
Nov	6,467
Dec	6,440

The growth of the Reserve during World War I is particularly noteworthy, because from it came the small hard core of dedicated men who were to keep the Reserve program alive during the lean years of the twenties. However, General Day believes the above "legal correct" figures are "completely misleading, in that they don't include the 'duration' people."

Early Aviation Reserve

Penny for penny, deed for deed, and man for man, the U.S. Marine Air Reserve has long been considered one of the best investments in national security the country ever had. Created by the same Act of 29 August 1916 that brought the Marine Corps Reserve into legal being, this new air program was named the Marine Corps Reserve Flying Corps.

Wartime expansion of the Marine Corps, commencing shortly after the Act of 29 August 1916, naturally caused pressures and confusions which precluded complete recordkeeping. Consequently, there is no very clear picture of how the Reserve Flying Corps was then administered.

In Marine Headquarters, an inadequately staffed Aviation Section headed by First Lieutenant Alfred A. Cunningham was responsible for air activities, including the Reserve Flying Corps. Since Cunningham was involved primarily in the selection and development of air training facilities, routine administration of the Aviation Section was, at best, difficult to handle. Moreover, few Marines of that day were interested in flying or participating in the aviation program, so the Marine Corps turned to the Navy for trainees. Many Navy trainees were rejected or disqualified at various stages of the Marine training program. However, General Day estimated that half of his squadron's pilots originated with the Navy but transferred to the Marine Corps because "they could expect to get action sooner."

Technically, Marine Aviation got off the ground on 22 May 1912, when Lieutenant Cunningham joined the naval aviation contingent at Annapolis, Md. With Cunningham, were Second Lieutenant Bernard L. Smith and Sergeant James Maguire. They were soon followed by Lieutenants William M. McIlvain, Francis T. Evans, and Roy S. Geiger.

Aside from this initial venture into the realm of aviation, little was done by the Marine Corps toward expanding its air arm until the country was on the threshold of World War I.

Among sources of information on the role of Marine Aviation in World War I, one document deserves special mention: Quartermaster Sergeant Lee Austin's narration on *Marine Aviation World War I*, compiled in 1944–45 and first published in the 1st Marine Aviation Force Veterans' Association booklet of 1945.

The account does not differentiate between Regulars and Reserves, but tells one rounded story of the team and, according to General Day, "not the most hidebound [team] militarily in this world. Nobody gave a damn and few, if any, knew who were regulars, temporaries, duration reserves, or what have you." In his story, based on personal knowledge as a member of the Northern Bombing Group and on responses to a questionnaire he mailed to all members of the 1st Marine Aviation Force, Austin wrote:

> The father of Marine Aviation was Lieutenant Alfred Austel Cunningham. He was the first Marine officer to be assigned to the Naval Aviation School at Annapolis. He was followed in order by Lieutenants Smith, McIlvain, Evans, and Geiger. It is quite natural, therefore, that these men individually and collectively did play an important part in Marine Aviation as it grew and expanded in World War I, under the leadership of Alfred Austel Cunningham.
>
> The first move to organize and equip Marine Aviation Squadrons for combat in World War I began with the transfer of the small aeronautical detachment from Pensacola, Fla., to League Island, Philadelphia Navy Yard. With this nucleus, the first Marine Aeronautic Squadron was formed with 18 officers and 180 enlisted men under the general command of then Captain Cunningham and under the direct command of Captain McIlvain. Another unit had been organized in the Navy Yard at the same time and, under the command of Captain Evans, had been sent to Cape May for further training and from there to the Azores on overseas duty. The first squadron under Captain McIlvain was ordered to Mineola, Long Island for training with Army Aviation.
>
> Those of the original group who served at Mineola remember the tent city in which they lived at the far end of the Army flying field . . . they remember, too, the howling winds and rain which swept in from the ocean and seemed to be continually blowing these same tents over about as fast as the ever-present morning, noon, and night detail could "put 'em up again" . . . they will never forget, either, living in those tents during the bleak, cold, snowy winter of 1917 . . . the ever-present hot coffee in the cook tent . . . the day Lieutenant Chamberlain's oil stove gave both him and the inside of his tent a complete black soot bath . . . the homemade shower bath which was built and used . . . the epidemic of colds and pneumonia that swept Camp Mills nearby, where the Rainbow Division was quartered . . . but, most of all they remember the snow and cold of that severe winter . . . and they remember too when the order was passed to pack up and head South and leave that 17 below zero wind howling in from the Bay.
>
> The trip to the next training center, the Army Flying Field at Lake Charles, was rather uneventful until the train was backed into the field at Lake Charles, La. The Army had no quarters for, or orders covering the disposition of, the 1st Marine Squadron. As a result, the group was forced to live in the coaches for 3 days until, finally, sleeping and living quarters were established in one of the Army Cadet Schoolhouses. The Marines quickly took over and in no time were operating the field, and soon enlisted men (some of them fresh from Parris Island) were instructing the Army boys where and how to "oil and gas up" the Curtis Jennys in use there, and how to wait out on the field when the sudden sandstorms hit and get a good hold on the "Jenneys" wings to keep them from turning over.

He reported that the 1st Squadron was then ordered to Curtis Field, Miami, for training with the Marine Aeronautic Detachment, formed there previously under Captain Roy S. Geiger. Another squadron, under Captain D. B. Roben, was also

organized there. After a period of training together and of further individual instruction, the units were ordered to head
North with the ultimate destination
France. He continued:

> The 3 Marine Squadrons arrived in
> Brest safe and sound. After several days
> in the rest camp, the trip was continued
> North to Calais in the French "40 and 8"
> parlor cars . . . with the utimate destina-
> tion Oye, France, for Squadrons A and B.
> Squadron C was based at La Frense, where
> it was joined by Squadron D on 6 October
> 1918, the latter squadron having suffered in
> England the loss of First Lieutenant Donald
> Cowles. Captain R. A. Presley organized,
> trained, and took this squadron overseas.
>
> With the arrival of the 4 Marine Squad-
> rons, the Northern Bombing Group was com-
> plete; being made up of one Night Wing of
> 4 Naval Squadrons, and one Day Wing
> of 4 Marine Squadrons. The Marine Day
> Squadrons used the DH-4, equipped with
> Liberty motor, and DH-9a's. The first DH-4
> arrived from Pauillac 7 September 1918.
>
> Meanwhile, training for flight personnel
> for active work against the enemy contin-
> ued in aviation schools in England and
> France. . . . Final training for pilots was
> accomplished by placing them with active
> British Squadrons at the front, operating in
> the same area in which the Northern Bomb-
> ing Group contemplated operations. Pilots,
> observers, and ground personnel were placed
> through permission from British authorities
> with . . . active British Squadrons.

Austin wrote that in addition to carrying out day raids as the Northern Bombing
Group, Marine planes made raids with
217 and 218 Squadrons RAF. The first
Marine Day Wing Squadron raid was carried out by 7 ships, DH-4's and DH-
9a's, on 14 October against railway sidings
and yards at Thielt. Raids were then continued against railway junctions, yards,
canals, and canal docks at Thielt, Steen-
brugge, Eecloo, Ghent, Deynze, and Lok-
eren. During these raids, at least 4 enemy

aircraft were believed destroyed and one
shot down out of control. He recalled that
1 Marine plane was lost when shot down
near the Belgium lines. A second, struck
by antiaircraft fire, was able to land safely in Holland. Pilots of the Marine
Squadron operated with 218 RAF and
were reported to have shot down 2 enemy
aircraft.

His narration continued:

> It was also during this period of duty in
> France that Marine aviators first dropped
> food and ammunition to a marooned ally.
> When a French regiment had been cut off
> by the Germans near Stadenburg in Septem-
> ber 1918, Captains F. P. Mulcahy and R. S.
> Lytle, Lieutenant Frank Nelms, and Gunnery
> Sergeants Arnie Wieman, H. L. Tallman,
> and Archie Paschal flew the ships that
> dropped over a ton of supplies to the ma-
> rooned Frenchmen. This aid from the air,
> the first time it had ever been done by Ma-
> rine aviators, continued 2 days in the face
> of heavy artillery, machinegun, and rifle
> fire. During its service in France, the North-
> ern Bombing Group was credited with hav-
> ing dropped 155,998 pounds of bombs and
> flown on 57 bombing raids.

Azores

Austin reported that the 1st Marine
Aeronautic Company had been organized
in the summer of 1917 at the Philadelphia
Navy Yard under command of Captain
Francis T. Evans. The unit left Philadelphia 14 October 1917 for Cape May, N.J. to
establish the Coastal Air Station. On 9
January 1918, the company boarded the
U.S.S. *Hancock* for the Azores, accompanied by a guard company of Marines to
man the 7-inch shore defense guns installed
in the Azores. The detachment landed at
Horta on 19 January. Beginning 3 days
later at Ponta Del Gada, St. Michaels, sun-
rise and sunset patrols operated from this
base, looking for German submarines and

other enemy craft. During this period Captain Evans made the first night ocean patrol flight in Marine Corps history.

In July 1918, the company was reorganized and continued routine patrol duty until February 1919, when it returned to Miami to be mustered out.

Austin's story continues:

> Those who served in the Azores remember towing back to the base a few ships that were forced to land at sea because of gasoline shortage or mechanical trouble . . . the thrill of guessing whether the gasoline in the ship was sufficient to get back to the base . . . the many times a ship was landed with no more than a gallon of gas to spare . . . the crash that killed Lieutenant W. S. Pogue . . . the bull sessions and blackjack games in "Socco" Reagan's tent . . . the hulk of the 4-masted schooner sunk just off shore by German submarine. [A chubby corporal named Mel Maas was a mess cook in the Azores.]

> The dive-bombing technique of diving a plane at the target was unknown in World War I, but a member of the Azores Company, Sergeant Elmo Reagan, spent many hours propounding his theory that the proper way to bomb an objective was by the now well-known method of dive-bombing. Sergeant Reagan believed in it and later, at Quantico, spent considerable time giving practical demonstrations of his theory. Although the U.S. Navy is given credit for pioneering dive-bombing, one of the real pioneers was 1st Sergeant Reagan of the 1st Marine Aeronautic Company, who later became a pilot and was killed in a crash-dive at Pensacola, Fla.

He concluded his account:

> That is the story of the combat side of Marine Aviation in World War I. Those who served in France remember well the terrific toll of officers and men taken by the flu epidemic which cost the life, among others, of Major D. B. Roben who had just previously been promoted to that rank along with Geiger and McIlvain, Presley having attained the rank of Captain about the same time.

> Following the Armistice on 11 November 1918, the squadrons [in France] were assigned transportation space and left from Calais for another trip in the French "40 and 8" parlor cars to St. Nazaire. Another trip to an Army rest camp and then aboard the U.S.S. *Mercury* for home. After one of the roughest trips imaginable, the ship docked at Newport News, Va., on a bright and sunny morning, 16 days later on December 20; then to the Marine Barracks at Portsmouth; the parade through Newport News; then all hands were given 30-day furloughs which meant home for Christmas to most of them. At the expiration of the furloughs, most men reported back to Norfolk and the squadrons entrained again for Miami. Here discharges were the order of the day for many of the "duration-of-war-enlistees"; some shipped to Haiti, Santo Domingo, for further service in Marine Aviation, while others stayed on at Miami. To the credit of these pioneers of Marine Aviation, it can be said that many who stayed on in the Marine Corps and others who returned to the Corps with World War II, have just finished writing another glorious epoch of Marine Corps tradition in the Pacific, one of which Marine Aviation can well be proud.

Besides the Marines mentioned in Lee Austin's 1945 narration, several Marine pilots had been flying with the U.S. Army in France for at least a year before the creation of the Northern Bombing Group. The Marine pilots who were taught to fly by the Army wore Army wings because they were detached from Navy and assigned to Army. Such pilots were not qualified for Navy wings until they had 3 hours flying time in seaplanes. Marine Reserve Second Lieutenant Kenneth P. Culbert served with the Army and died while on a mission. He was posthumously awarded the Silver Star by the Army for gallantry in action in the Toul

Sector of France on 15 May 1918. Marine Reserve Second Lieutenant Marcus A. Jordan crashed and died while serving in Italy under command of Captain Fiorello La Guardia (Air Section; Army Signal Corps) who later became a U.S. Congressman and a distinguished mayor of New York City.

General Day, in recalling the origin (and disposition) of the 18 officers of the 1st Marine Aeronautic Company mentioned by Austin, makes the following colorful contribution:

> Beginning about July 4th [1917] at Quantico, the 1st Marine Officers Training School—or whatever its official name was— was convened. Approximately 300 fresh caught Second Lieutenants commissioned from civil life. Some time during the summer, Major Cunningham came down looking for pilot volunteers and got an almost unanimous response. Later 18 of us were picked—God knows how—and if Cunningham knew, he never divulged it. Upon graduation from the school at Quantico, these 18 reported to the 1st Aeronautic Detachment at League Island on 12 October. Six of them (including Petie Hill) were assigned to seaplanes, Cocky Evans, and the Azores: the remaining 12, long known to bawdy song and bawdier legend as the Dirty Dozen, were assigned to landplanes, which meant Jennies, Hazelhurst Field, and McIlvain. The point I am trying to make is that of the 18 officers mentioned, 12 were just graduated from Quantico and of the 12 at least 9 (and I think it was 10), were "temporaries"—in other words, in every true sense of the word, reservists. Pat Mulcahy and I were Regulars—and maybe Kipp— though I'm not sure, and the balance were Reserves. As a matter of fact, of the other 6 officers—Batts and Brock Davy—were Reserves (temporary or what have you).
>
> The Regulars were McIlvain, Presley, and Scrappy Williams (the Quartermaster). Gove Compton is the missing name from this 18—and I think he was temporary. And

> I think you've got to consider these temporaries as Reserves.

Besides being combat pilots and patrol pilots, some early Reserve fliers gained distinction as test pilots. Among these were Second Lieutenants Wallace D. Culbertson, Gwendall B. Newman, and Edwin C. Musick. First Lieutenants Basil G. Bradley and Harmon J. Norton, and Culbertson made several speed runs at 168 miles per hour in a Curtiss-Kirkham triplane fighter—a world record for 1918. Newman, an outstanding test pilot, died of injuries in January 1920 when the Loening that he was flying actually fell apart while he was coming in for a landing. Musick and Culbertson later became senior captains with Pan-American Airways. Musick was killed with all of his crew near Pago-Pago, Samoa—when their plane, a "clipper," blew apart while he was exploring a route for Pan-American to Australia.

Official records clearly show that Lieutenant Cunningham was the first *Marine Corps* pilot. Who was the first *Marine Corps Reserve* pilot is open to conjecture, however, because of administrative delays and errors involved in processing basic flying certificates and documents and integration of U.S. Naval Reserve Flying Corps (USNRF) personnel and National Naval Volunteers (NNV) into the Marine Air Program. One young pilot, Second Lieutenant Ralph Talbot, in October 1918 became the first known reservist in World War I to win the Medal of Honor, awarded posthumously for his many successful air strikes against German fighter planes.

The official *Precedence of Naval Aviators* (1–1000), prepared by the Aviation History Unit of the Navy Department on 3 September 1959, lists all of the Marine pilots as "USMC," none as "USMCR."

According to this document, the order of precedence of the first 37 Marine pilots is as follows:

1. Cunningham, A. A. NA#5 USMC
2. Smith Bernard L. NA#6 USMC
3. McIlvain, W. M. NA#12 USMC
4. Evans, F. T. NA#26 USMC
5. Geiger, Roy S. NA#49 USMC
6. Brewster, D. L. S. NA#55 USMC
7. Chamberlain, E. G. NA#96½ USMC
8. Presley, R. A. NA#100¾ USMC
9. Derbyshire, William H., Jr. NA#533 USMCR
10. Davy, Frederick B. NA #534 USMC
11. Roben, Douglas B. NA#535 USMC
12. Page, Robert H. NA#536 USMC
13. Compton, Gove NA#537 USMCR
14. Shearer, Thomas R. NA#559 USMCR
15. Rogers, Ford O. NA#560 USMC
16. Stovall, Harry E. NA#568 USMC
17. Brewer, Everett R. NA#589
18. Kipp, John G. E. NA#586 USMC
19. Kolb, Frederick L. NA#587 USMC
20. Kremm, George F. NA#588 USMCR
21. Nelson, Jesse A. NA #589 USMCR
22. Jesse, Berman J. NA#590 USMCR
23. Head, William W. NA#591 USMCR
24. Kaemerling, Gus G. NA#592 USMCR
25. Dunlap, Jesse F. NA#593 USMCR
26. Williams, Trevor G. NA#594 USMCR
27. Bates, Clyde N. NA#595 USMC
28. Sullivan, Melville E. NA#596 USMC
29. Mulcahy, Francis P. NA#597 USMC
30. Harper, B. B. NA#598 USMC
31. Batts, Hal W. NA#599 USMCR
32. Dunn, Henry T. NA#600 USMC
33. Day, Karl S. NA#601 USMCR
34. Robillard, Fred S. NA#602 USMCR
35. Trelfall, Melchoir B. NA#603 USMC
36. Major, Harold C. NA#604 USMCR
37. Lytle, Robert S. NA#605 USMC

(The Reserve status (R) has been added by the authors to those who are reservists according to the records of the late Major General William P. T. Hill, who died in 1966. General Hill, who was NA#853 and devoted years to research on Marine aviation in World War I, was undoubtedly one of the most authoritative sources on this question.)

The following footnote appears in Robert Sherrod's *History of Marine Corps Aviation:*

> The first USMCR aviator was Lieutenant Allen Boynton, 21 September 1917.

However, Boynton is listed as NA#856 preceded by 118 other Marine pilots in the official *Navy Precedence of Naval Aviators.* Actually, the word "student" was inadvertently left out of Sherrod's text and its omission was undiscovered throughout several rewrites. Other records confirm the fact that a great many of the early Marine pilots were Reserves.

Another footnote is the behind-the-scenes story from General Day, who said:

> The order of qualification for Naval Aviators is undoubtedly correct but misses most of the story. The Navy would only permit qualification tests for Naval Aviator on a seaplane or flying boat. Most of us were flying Jennies and Tommy Morse Scouts and DH's and those of us who were the busiest in instructing et cetera on land planes were the last to be able to take time off to go over to Dinner Key and solo those funny H and F boats.

The following Marines are listed by General Hill as being the first 20 Marine Reserve pilots. Further, General Hill commented that excepting Amor L. Smith, a civilian pilot, and H. A. Peterson and G. M. Laughlin, both National Naval Volunteers, all of these pilots were originally members of the U.S. Naval Reserve Flying Corps, including civilian pilot instructors from Mineola and Lake Charles who integrated into the Marine Corps Reserve Flying Corps:

1. Smith, Amor L. NA#2761 (28 September 1917)
2. Bradford, C. D. NA#111 ½
3. Webster, Clifford L. NA#112
4. Wright, Arthur H. NA#148
5. Shea, L. L. NA#153
6. Peterson, Harmon A. NA#163 ½

7. Laughlin, George M. NA#165
8. Ames, Charles B. NA#193
9. Weaver, John H. NA#251
10. Prichard, Alvin L. NA#279
11. Willman, George C. NA#299
12. Batts, Harold W. NA#599
13. Pratt, Hazen C. NA#426
14. Clark, Sidney NA#442
15. Schley, Frederick C. NA#443
16. Needham, Charles NA#444
17. Bates, J. B. NA#449
18. Talbot, Ralph NA#456
19. Clarkson, Francis C. NA#474
20. Williamson, G. M. NA#477

The following documentation is an example of USNRF personnel who subsequently appear as Marine Reserve Aviators on General Hill's list of Reserve pilots:

AS/YM/GB.   DECEMBER 31, 1917.

From: Commandant.
To: Bureau of Navigation.

Subject: Aviation Designation of Prichard, Alvin L., QM1c. USNRF.

1. I have this day appointed and detailed the above named man as Naval Aviator (Seaplane), for duty involving actual flying in aircraft, including dirigibles and airplanes, in accordance with Acts of Congress approved March 3, 1915, and August 29, 1916. Approval of this detail is requested.

2. This detail to be also effective, in case of commissioning, from date of such commissioning.

F. M. BENNETT.

JANUARY 14, 1918.

From: Bureau of Navigation.
To: Commandant, Naval Air Station, Pensacola, Fla.
Via: Naval Aviation.

1. Returned, approved.

2. In case of resignation, disenrollment or revocation of appointment, the Bureau must be immediately notified. Special report must be made to Bureau when officer is transferred.

ELLIS S. STONE.
By direction.

Regardless of their lineal precedence or their designation, all Marines in aviation during World War I have won a place in the military annals of the United States by their accomplishments as pioneers. While they cannot point to the glory of a Belleau Wood, they can point with pride to the fact that from their experimentation, actual bombing, and food dropping operations came the techniques of flight maneuver, which would be standard operating procedures in the "Banana Wars" of Central America during the 1920's and early 1930's, techniques which were later refined into the close air support operations of World War II and Korea.

Women, World War I

Enrollment of women in the Marine Corps Reserve was authorized by Secretary of the Navy Josephus Daniels on 12 August 1918 and Mrs. Orpha May Johnson, the world's first Lady Marine, enlisted in Washington, D.C., the following day. Opening ranks of the proud Corps to distaff Marines was based on a Government estimate that "40 percent of the work at the Headquarters Marine Corps can be performed as well by women as men."

Recruiting officers were instructed to enroll only women of excellent character, neat appearance, and with business and office experience. Greatest demand was for competent stenographers, bookkeepers, and typists, but women who possessed a working knowledge of correspondence or general clerical skills were also eligible. A strong sense of patriotism motivated the women as well as the men to join. Some of the female reservists who enlisted had husbands, brothers, or fathers already on the frontlines in France. In one family there was such regret on the part of the parents that they had no sons to send to the war, their twin daughters promptly answered a newspaper ad which announced the Marines were seeking women for the Corps and were enrolled. Less than a month after the initial recruiting call, 31 female reservists were on duty. And by mid-September 1918, the Major General Commandant was in a position to direct the transfer to active duty in the line of:

> . . . all men at Marine Corps Headquarters, in staff offices, and in recruiting offices, employed on clerical or other routine duty and who were classified under selective service regulations, provided, of course, their services could be spared without detriment to the government service and the women clerks available were competent to fill their places.

Age limit for the women Reserves was announced as being between 18 and 40. Leeway was granted, however, for an applicant "slightly under 18 years of age, who is in every respect desirable, may be enrolled with the consent of her parents." All women were advised that they would be subject to the same rules and regulations as enlisted male Marines. If either their services or behavior was unsatisfactory, they could expect to be "summarily disenrolled."

Typical Marine Corps insistence on precision not only governed the dispatch with which they performed their clerical duties, but also extended to their smart appearance as a marching unit. Women Marines in World War I, or "Marinettes" as they were called at the time [a term which has fallen into disuse] were instructed in the "simpler drill movements . . . before 9 o'clock on the ellipse in Potomac Park" under the watchful eye of a stern Marine noncommissioned officer. They also participated in victory parades and other ceremonies in the Nation's Capital. A month prior to disenrollment in 1919, the entire unit was included in the guard of honor, facing the Presidential Reviewing Stand at the White House, for a parade of troops just returned from the front. The showing was pronounced "creditable to the girls and to the Marine Corps."

A total of 277 women reservists had volunteered for duty by 11 November 1918. Records show, strangely enough, that some were enlisted following Armistice Day and the official ending of the war. Of an eventual total of 305 women, many who had proved "capable and industrious" were promoted to private first class, corporal, and sergeant, the highest grade obtainable. They received the same pay and allowances as enlisted men of corresponding rank.

Articles of uniform consisted of a specially-designed shirt and coat, overcoat, chambray shirt, regulation tie, and "overseas" cap and campaign hat—both of which bore the globe-and-anchor insignia. The overseas cap, both in winter field and summer khaki, was the preferred headgear. Khaki and low tan oxfords formed the uniform of the day for summertime; greens and high-laced dark tan shoes were issued for the winter. All uniforms were tailored of material similar to that worn by male Marines. Raincoats, gloves, and purses were not issued; and although photographs show some women wearing gloves, handbags were not permitted on any occasion. Chevrons of appropriate rank were worn and the Women Reserves were also eligible to earn—and wear—certain awards, such as the Good Conduct Medal, Victory Medal, and District Medal.

Military privileges for women included eligibility for Government insurance, a $60 bonus on discharge, World War compensation, free medical treatment and hospitalization for service disability, plus 5 percent added to earned rating in examinations for classified service under Civil Service regulations.

Although most of the reservists (F) were assigned to duties in Headquarters, such as the Paymaster, Quartermaster, Adjutant and Inspector, or the Commandant's office, a handful were stationed in recruiting offices outside of the Washington area, even as far away as San Francisco and Portland, Ore.

On 30 July 1919, orders were issued by Major General Commandant George Barnett for the immediate discharge of all "female reservists," and those still on active duty were transferred to inactive status in the Reserve. In reviewing the role of women in the Marine Corps, he stated on that same date:

> It is a pleasure, but not by any means an unexpected one, to be able to state that the service rendered by the reservists (female) has been uniformly excellent. It has, in fact, been exactly what the intelligence and goodness of our countrywomen would lead one to expect.

Of the 305 women reservists, 118 were discharged, 185 were transferred to an inactive status, and 2 died while in service. By October 1920, of the 185 female reservists still carried on inactive duty rolls, 22 were sergeants, 71 were corporals, and 92 held the rating of private. Discharged enrollment from the Marine Corps Reserve (inactive status, Class 4) took place at a steady—but gradual—rate, and eventually all women were discharged, in some cases as late as 1922.

A special Memorandum issued by the Major General Commandant left the door open for the women to continue to serve the Marine Corps. In discussing the transfer of reservists to inactive status, he decreed that: "The female members who so desire and whose conduct, services, and efficiency have demonstrated the desirability of their retention may be recommended for temporary civil appointment." With typical Marine esprit, some of the women reservists happily elected to do so. More than a dozen, after becoming civilians, remained on duty at Marine Headquarters, supply depots, and recruiting offices where they continued to work for the Marine Corps in a civil service status.

Some were to return to service in World War II, like Martrese Thek Ferguson and Lillian O'Malley Daly. Among those who stayed on at Marine Headquarters in a civilian capacity through World War II was Mrs. Jane Van Edsinga Blakeney, who eventually served as Head of the Decorations and Medals Branch, Marine Corps Headquarters during the tenure of 3 commandants.

CHAPTER TWO

The Intermediate Years

The period from 1919–39 may well be called the "Years of Indecision" for the Marine Corps Reserve. On 11 December 1918 the Marine Corps was just entering the throes of demobilization and numbered 74,901 persons including 483 Reserve officers and Reserve warrant officers, a total of 6,704 enlisted (male) reservists, and 269 enlisted (female) reservists. Although the "temporary" and "duration" Marines were technically Regulars, they were in every real sense of the word "reservists" so the raw statistical figures don't tell the whole story.

SECTION ONE

The enthusiasm for participating in the defense of the country continued to hold for a few months after war. However, postwar disillusionment set in, and most Americans, particularly young men, lost interest in the military. The Regular Establishment became sharply reduced in size. The greater part of the prewar noncommissioned officers who had contributed so much to wartime cohesion and esprit of the Corps left when their enlistments were up. The young men who left the campus to sign up for duration returned home to pick up the threads of civilian life.

The 31 March 1919 Reserve lineal list included 7 majors, 34 captains, 49 first lieutenants, and 100 second lieutenants [not included here] still on active duty:

MAJORS

John J. Dooley
Reginald R. Hogan

Pere Wilmer
Oliver C. Hine
Thomas G. Sterrett
William J. Crosson
Anthony J. D. Biddle

CAPTAINS

Sidney S. Simpson
Thomas R. Shearer
John N. Sadler
William N. Pearson
James H. Johnston
Louis J. Hughes
Samuel F. Birthright
John J. Darlington
Horace W. Mitchell
Rudolph C. Rasmussen
William L. Riley
Silas M. Bankert
Henry S. Hausmann
Frank Pilotte, Jr.
Bernard J. Doherty
Joseph I. Nettekoven
Frederick M. Howard
Charles A. Ketcham
James Maguire
Robert P. Harris
Eugene E. Brong
Harry H. Shepherd
Ralph G. Anderson
Frank J. Maloney
Edwin J. Mund
Melville E. Chapman
Harold E. Wood
William P. Peake
Douglas H. Booth
Frank S. Flack
William J. Livingston
Joseph J. Lackey
Howard M. Peter
Fred S. Parsons

FIRST LIEUTENANTS

Charles P. Cushing
Brownlo I. Byrd

Owen Arbogast
Albert B. Sage
John D. Lockburner
Harry B. Lamont
Gustaf A. Brodstrom
Richard Livingston
Fred B. Hoyt
Paul F. Howard
Claude T. Lytle
Fred O. Brown
James Duffy
Thomas L. Hewitt
Ralph F. Thompson
William S. Hilles
William F. McDonnell
George W. Shearer
Charles Gorkum
George S. Fynmore
Eli Savage
Chester A. Fachman
Harold E. Potter
Clinton A. Kephart
Grover C. Wright
George Kneller
Clinton K. Seymour
Frederick D. Harbaugh
George Occhionero
Charles C. Carroll
Hans G. Hornbostel
John F. Cassidy
Brady L. Vogt
Edward W. Franklin
Carl F. Merz
Norman Johnston
Alexander McL. Arnold
Jerry W. Blazek
Sydney J. Handsley
George W. Farnham
Donald M. Taft
John D. Brady
Casper M. Burgdahl
George A. Plambeck
Charles W. Henkle
Spencer N. Phillips
Berkley S. Blake
William P. Kelly
Adolph Stahlberger

In the words of Major General Commandant John A. Lejeune:

Nearly all of the splendid men who had enlisted for the period of the emergency have resumed their civil occupations; many wartime officers had separated themselves from the service; the number of enlisted men being only about 15,000, which was altogether insufficient to perform the important duties assigned to the Corps, there was much unrest among the officers owing to their uncertain status; and the lavish expenditures incident to war were to a great extent still prevalent.

General Lejeune considered that one of his major goals—which continued throughout his long tenure as Commandant (1920–29)—was "to recreate the Reserve as a constituent part of the wartime strength of the Marine Corps." Despite his declared interest, his Report to the Secretary of the Navy 14 October 1920 only mentioned the Reserve relative to a selection board to consider wartime Reserve officers for Regular commissions and a tabulation showing 1 Reserve officer and 24 reservists on active duty. Concern about the future status of the Reserve, however, was reflected in a staff memorandum to the Commandant, dated 6 March 1920, which was subsequently approved by the Commandant:

1. It is recommended that a definite policy be reached concerning the future activities of the Marine Corps Reserve, especially regarding the following:

(a) Whether or not it is to be maintained on an approximate strength of 5,000 officers and men.

(b) Whether or not the present unconfirmed officers and men now enrolled in it are to be confirmed.

(c) The calling out for training service of its personnel, commissioned and enlisted.

2. The present strength of the Reserve is:

Officers active	6
Enlisted men active	71
Officers inactive	540
Enlisted men inactive	5, 419
Total	6, 036

3. Approximately 1,000 of the enlisted men enrolled in the Reserve are former members of the National Naval Volunteers, Marine Corps Branch, transferred to Class 2 of the Reserve by the Naval Appropriation Act of July 1, 1918. Their enrollments are to expire within a period beginning now and extending over the next 90 days. In accordance with your orders all other members of the Reserve, both commissioned and enlisted, are being discharged for their own convenience upon their personal request. Thus, the strength of the Reserve is being constantly reduced. You had recently authorized the enrollment in Class 2 of the Reserve any former duration of war men. This will serve to counter-balance the reduction in strength by the discharges mentioned above.

4. Up until the Fall of 1918 confirmations of enlisted men in the Reserve had been authorized and made. Since that time, by direction of the Secretary of the Navy, no enlisted men have been confirmed. There have been no confirmations among the commissioned ranks of the Reserve in any class, except the Fleet Marine Corps Reserve, where the rank upon entrance is a confirmed one.

5. All enlisted men in an inactive status in the Reserve are holding either the confirmed or the provisional ranks in which they were serving upon date of transfer to an inactive status.

It was evident that the Corps believed the Reserves had rendered very efficient and useful service during the war. Among other things, existence of the Reserve made possible the recruitment of personnel in addition to the authorized strength of the Regular Establishment. This had kept recruiting offices open even after Regular quotas were filled. Size and composition of the Reserve were moot questions. Quality rather than quantity was stressed, with a commissioned and enlisted strength varying between 2,000 and 5,000. Headquarters wanted reservists who desired an affiliation with the Marine Corps and who desired annual training duty at posts within the continental limits and, perhaps, duty in the field.

Which Way the Reserve?

The paramount question in the early 1920's was whether or not the Reserve could be made sufficiently useful in time of peace and in time of emergency to justify expenditure of public funds, or whether it should be allowed to sink into a state of uselessness. Unfortunately, the problem of building a truly useful Reserve was only one of many problems. No mention of the Reserve was made in the annual report to the Navy Secretary 1 June 1921, which stated in part: ". . . the authorized strength of the Marine Corps was 27,400 but Congress appropriated for an average strength during the fiscal year of 1921 of 20,000." Recruiting for the Regular Establishment was hitting rock bottom when, on 15 June 1920, the Commandant requested authority from the Navy Secretary to recall 1,000 active enlisted Reserves. The request was disapproved.

The Reserve continued to dwindle and, by 21 September 1921, had 555 officers and 4,068 enlisted men, when a Headquarters memorandum noted that considerably more than:

> . . . one-half of the enlisted personnel of the Marine Corps Reserve will be discharged upon expiration of enrollments by April 1, 1922, unless new enrollments or reenrollments offset the losses, which is not expected unless a drive for new recruits is made. There have been 88 enrollments during the present calendar year.

One major problem was lack of communication between the Corps and its Reserves. No Marine Corps Headquarters office had full or significant responsibility for the Reserve program. Headquarters offices handled Reserve matters much in the same way as Regular matters, except that little importance was placed on the Reserve. In the field, former and active reservists were struggling to retain some sort of a tie with the Corps. William Rochford, a former Marine Corps reservist, approached by Army officers in 1921 with a proposition to join an Army Reserve unit, wrote the Commandant "Are you going to let us fellows who are loyal to the Corps . . . put on a doughboy's outfit, when there ought to be a chance to get out the red and blue . . . give us a chance to have a reserve corps here if there will be any at all."

The Reserve picture was further complicated by the continued existence of Marine Corps companies attached to the Naval Militia. Until 30 June 1923, the various States and Territories having a Naval Militia with Marine Corps companies could permit members to enroll both as members of the Naval Militia and the Marine Corps Reserve. However, enrollment of these Naval Militia Marines in the Corps required specific authorization by the Commandant. The strength of the Marine Corps Reserve continued to ebb. On 30 June 1922, there were only 446 officers and 110 enlisted, all inactive except 6 officers undergoing training. Since the Armistice, 87 percent of the officers and 90 percent of the enlisted had been demobilized by discharge. Total demobilization was to be effected by 11 November 1922. No officers or enlisted men of the Reserve were on active duty except for training during fiscal year 1922.

Retired Lieutenant General Edward A. Craig recalled his period of duty as General Lejeune's aide in 1927–28, saying that the Commandant many times mentioned the Reserve and had a habit of working directly with Members of Con-

gress and the Secretary of the Navy either by telephone or personal contact. He said that the eventual Congressional action in 1925 was in large measure due to his work at a time when the Regular Corps was having rough sledding for appropriations while engaged in operations in China and Nicaragua.

As another uneventful year passed, the Commandant's report again reflected further decline of the Reserve. The reported strength on 30 June 1923 was 136 officers and 443 enlisted. Only 6 officers and 21 enlisted had undergone active duty for training that year. The fiscal year ending 30 June 1924 showed a gain in Reserve strength for the first time since the war. The increase of 1 officer and 59 enlisted brought the total to 137 officers and 502 enlisted reservists. The tide was turning, however, and a whole new future was in sight. With passage, on 28 February 1925, of an "Act of Congress to provide for the creation, organization, administration, and maintenance of a Naval Reserve and a Marine Corps Reserve," there *was* a future for the Marine Reserve.

The Act of 1925

The Act became effective 1 July 1925 and contained the following provisions regarding the Marine Corps Reserve:

> Section 2. That the U.S. Marine Corps Reserve, established under the Act of August 29, 1916, is hereby abolished and in lieu thereof there is created and established, as a component part of the U.S. Marine Corps a Marine Corps Reserve, under the same provisions in all respects (except as may be necessary to adapt the said provisions to the Marine Corps) as those contained in this Act or which may hereafter be enacted providing for the Naval Reserve: Provided that the Marine Corps Reserve shall consist of 2 classes, namely: the Fleet Ma-

rine Corps Reserve and the Volunteer Marine Corps Reserve, corresponding as near as may be, to the Fleet Naval Reserve and the Volunteer Naval Reserve, respectively.

The new Act put the Marine Corps Reserve on a solid footing and provided many new features lacking under the 1916 Act including:

(a) The commissioning of officers during the pleasure of the President instead of for a period of 4 years;

(b) The authority to commission a limited number of officers in grades up to brigadier general;

(c) The appointment of 25 men to the Naval Academy each year from the Naval Reserve and the Marine Corps Reserve;

(d) The payment of drill pay for actual services rendered on a basis similar to that provided for the National Guard, in lieu of retainer pay;

(e) A liberal uniform allowance for the Fleet Reserve;

(f) Transfer to an honorary retired list without pay upon reaching the age of 64, after completing 25 years of service or if found physically unqualified;

(g) Reservation of the benefits of continuous service to men enlisting in the Reserve within 3 months of discharge from the Navy and the Marine Corps;

(h) Safeguarding of the interest of transferred members of the Fleet Naval Reserve and Fleet Marine Corps Reserve;

(i) Authorization of military leave for officers and employees of the United States during absence while performing military duty;

(j) Establishment of classes of Reserves including a Volunteer Marine Corps Reserve;

(k) Authorization of subsistence for weekend cruises; and

(l) Extension of the benefits of the Federal Employees' Compensation Act to members of the Naval and Marine Corps Reserve injured in line of duty.

The call of William Rochford and many others for a definite Reserve program and

organization was thus answered. The Reserve backbone now became the Fleet Marine Corps Reserve with the "company" as its basic unit with a strength of 2 commissioned officers and 45 enlisted. The FMCR offered reservists the opportunity to "troop and stomp" as uniformed Marines. It was to become the vehicle through which many enlisted men became officers and served with distinction during World War II. The FMCR corresponded to today's Class II or Organized Reserve. The VMCR didn't really resemble today's Class III or Volunteer Reserve as it was actually a paper Reserve, mainly a pool of manpower from which a limited number were assigned annually to the Fleet Marine Corps Reserve as vacancies occurred. Reorganization of the Reserve did stimulate nationwide interest and many World War I veterans returned. Among the first to apply were Captain William J. J. Elger of New Orleans, La.; Captain Richard R. Day of Dallas, Tex.; and First Lieutenant Frank M. Cross of Los Angeles, Calif. Also returning to the Reserve were such distinguished Marines as Edwin Denby, former Secretary of the Navy, and Samuel L. (Roxie) Rothafel, radio and theatrical figure.

The basic plan for administering the program called for 4 Reserve areas, corresponding in name and boundary to the existing Regular recruiting divisions, each under a Reserve area commander who was the area Regular officer in charge of recruiting. The 4 Reserve areas and their respective Volunteer Marine Corps units were as follows:

(a) In the Eastern Reserve Area, with headquarters at Philadelphia: the 7th Regiment, with headquarters at New York City; the 8th Regiment (less one battalion), with headquarters at Philadelphia; and an Observation Plane Squadron (V.O.) and a casual company, both with headquarters at Philadelphia.

(b) In the Southern Reserve Area, with headquarters at New Orleans: the 3d Battalion of the 8th Regiment, a Fighting Plane Squadron (V.F.), and a casual company, all with headquarters at New Orleans.

(c) In the Central Reserve Area, with headquarters at Chicago: the 9th Regiment, an Observation Plane Squadron (V.O.), and a casual company, all with headquarters at Chicago.

(d) In the Western Reserve Area, with headquarters at San Francisco: the 3d Regiment, an Observation Plane Squadron (V.O.), and a casual company, all with headquarters at San Francisco.

Within these areas, but not under the regimental jurisdiction, were the FMCR companies. The basic difference between the VMCR and the FMCR was that the Volunteer Reserves could be called out only in event of war or national emergency and ordered to training duty only upon their own request. The FMCR had to attend drills and summer camp or get out. The FMCR companies were given designations greater than 300, the VMCR companies greater than 400. The new Reserve gave the Commandant a pool of reservists available to report for duty at various Naval and Marine Corps depots, shipyards, et cetera, in event of national emergency, relieving Regulars who would be sent to mobilization centers. Specifically, 2 reservists were to be enrolled to take the place of each Regular on duty!

One Regular officer was assigned to each Reserve regiment as commanding officer, and another as a staff officer. Within 1 year, nearly a quarter of the authorized strength of each regiment of 100 officers and 2,671 enlisted men was enrolled. Yet, these regiments were not drill units. They

existed only on paper. Perhaps the most significant development under the 1925 Act was, however, the plan to create a Reserve Section as an independent entity in the Office of the Commandant. No longer would Reserve functions be distributed to appropriate staff agencies. For the first time, Reserve affairs were to be concentrated in a single staff agency, with functions including procurement, instruction, training, discipline, and distribution of Reserves and Reserve budget preparation. The officer in charge, as adviser to the Commandant on Reserve matters, would play a major role in determining Marine Corps policy for the Reserve. The idea was obviously a sound one, but like many plans, things really did not begin to click until 1928 when Brigadier General Ben H. Fuller, Assistant to the Major General Commandant, was designated as Officer in Charge, Marine Corps Reserve.

In the interim, the old system of distributed functions continued. A number of Regular officers deserve special mention because of their role in handling Reserve matters during this interim period. They include Lieutenant Colonel James J. Meade, Major Philip H. Torrey, Major Calvin B. Matthew, Major Joseph C. Fegan, and Captain Oliver P. Smith (who was destined to lead so many Reserves in Korea). Also to be included is the name of John A. Hanschmann whose active participation in a number of capacities in the Reserve was and still is most unique. Beginning on 15 April 1926 as a clerk in the Headquarters Personnel Section handling Reserve matters, his career spans almost 40 years. Discharged from the Marine Corps on 23 October 1928 as a sergeant, he accepted a civil service position and returned to his desk as a civilian. Except for 2 of the past 40 years, Hanschmann has served the Reserve at Headquarters as a Regular, VMCR, FMCR, and civilian.

Building Up the Reserve

The Commandant, pleased with the new structure and status accorded the Marine Corps Reserve, in his annual report of 30 September 1925 stated:

> Under this new Reserve bill, the Corps has the opportunity to build up a real Reserve so that in the event of an emergency we shall be able to get the necessary officers and men to put the Marine Corps on an emergency footing. With this in view, enrollment for the reserve commenced. At the present writing 3 Reserve rifle companies, Fleet Marine Corps Reserve, have been authorized, one each at Brooklyn, N.Y.; Saginaw, Mich.; and Los Angeles, Calif. Communications have been received from Reserve officers requesting authority to organize other companies, and headquarters has directed these officers to submit plans, and if they are satisfactory, the authority to organize other companies will be given. One particular feature of the new Reserve bill is the opportunity to enroll in the Reserve, men leaving the service at the end of an enlistment in good standing . . . the Corps should be able to have a Reserve of 10,000 men of this class in a few years.

By 16 August 1926, the new Reserve program was slowly getting underway. Its early fortunes rested largely on the shoulders of a few officers. The field grade officers of the entire Reserve could almost be counted on 2 hands. They included:

Name	Class	Date of rank
LIEUTENANT COLONELS		
Dooley, John J___	VMCR	1 Jan 1926
Fay, William G__	FMCR	18 Jan 1926

Name	Class	Date of rank
MAJORS		
Biddle, Anthony J. D.	VMCR	18 Aug 1924
Bigler, Epaminondas L.	FMCR	26 Mar 1917
Denby, Edwin___	VMCR	10 Mar 1924
McIlvain, William M.	FMCR	3 Mar 1926
Morrison, Victor I.	FMCR	22 Apr 1917
Nevin, John D___	FMCR	27 Apr 1920
Rorke, James F__	FMCR	8 Jan 1926
Rothafel, Samuel L.	VMCR	1 Apr 1925
Schiesswohl, Ralph L.	FMCR	1 Jan 1926
Sinclair, Charles G.	VMCR	15 Jan 1920
Timmerman, Louis F.	FMCR	8 Jan 1926
Waller, Littleton W. T.	FMCR	22 May 1917

In his report of 24 September 1926, the Commandant clearly defined the Reserve mission as:

> . . . a trained force of officers and men available to serve as reinforcements to the Regular Marine Corps in time of War or national emergency. To make it possible to carry out this mission, it is absolutely necessary that there be in the Marine Corps prior to the emergency an adequate and well trained Reserve.

MCROA Formed

A professional guild of Marine Reserve Officers was formed that year (1926) under the presidency of Congressman Melvin J. Maas, a Republican from St. Paul, Minn. Called the Marine Corps Reserve Officers Association (MCROA), its members were to engage in many battles both within and without the Corps in the next

40 years. The officers banded together in the beginning to obtain a training program for the Reserve, since none was provided at the time. It was successful in its first undertaking, and after long, hard, patient work, in the words of its own official summary, "induced the Marine Corps to prepare a program of Reserve training, and obtained from Congress, by their own direct contact, small appropriations for such training. This appropriation was increased slowly from year to year as a result of their continual pleas."

In 1932, MCROA took the lead in exposing an attempt by the Army to have the Marine Corps disbanded. In 1938, its members sponsored, initiated, and helped obtain a basic new Reserve law, the Naval Reserve Act of 1938, the greater part of which was written by its president, Congressman Maas of the House Naval Affairs Committee. But, that is another story and comes later.

Enrollment for the Reserve presented many problems during the early days. Captain John J. Flynn, first Company Commander of the 301st Company, FMCR, had this to say about the problems and how he solved them in 1926:

> Realizing that the most important factor in recruiting a company is publicity, we immediately got a notice ready for the press and I called on the City Editor of every daily newspaper in Boston. The papers were very generous to us and we kept them deluged with Reserve news. When we could think of nothing else to say, we would announce the number of vacancies in the Company for the Quantico trip (summer camp). We had Bulletins printed which were mailed to every club, fraternity house, school, college, in fact all places where men of the type we were endeavoring to secure might congregate, in many instances calling personally and talking to the men. We called on the personnel managers of all department

stores, factories, industrial concerns, public service corporations, and had notices containing full information posted on the bulletin boards in the men's recreation rooms and in many instances we succeeded in selling the Personnel Manager the idea to such an extent that he acted as agent for us, interviewing likely candidates in his employ and sending those best qualified to the Recruiting Office. On May 14th 1926, the first drill was held in civilian clothes on the Marine Barracks parade ground, Charlestown Navy Yard, with 33 men present. The men worked hard on all drill nights, being careful of their posture and executing their movements with precision, but the first drill in uniform was such an improvement that it emphasized the importance of getting the men into uniform as soon as possible. In uniform they felt more like Marines and in consequence "put out" even more than ever. Great pains were taken to see that the men received proper fittings.

The First Reserve Camp

Captain Flynn also wrote of the first summer camp at Quantico during which the Commandant and his staff plus a delegation from Congress reviewed the Reserve battalion commanded by Major Louis F. Timmerman, on 24 June 1926. A battalion attack problem was held with the following FMCR organizations participating: 301st Company of Boston, right assault company, commanded by Captain John J. Flynn; 302d Company of Rochester, N.Y., left assault company, commanded by First Lieutenant Edward F. Doyle. The companies in reserve were the 305th Company of Philadelphia, commanded by First Lieutenant John D. Marine; 306th Company of Detroit, commanded by First Lieutenant Clarence W. Videan; the 309th Company, commanded by First Lieutenant Windsor B. W. Stroup; the Howitzer Company, commanded by Captain Philip DeRonde; and the Machinegun Company, commanded by Captain Bertrand T. Fay.

Captain Fay wrote a pamphlet at the request of Headquarters and the following liberal quotations from it highlight not only the informality and mutual esteem which was to be a hallmark of future years, but the success of this 1926 first camp from both Reserve and Regular viewpoints:

> The training schedule was skillfully arranged to give the widest and most thorough instruction possible in the short time available. Instead of endeavoring to achieve perfection in a few subjects by concentrating on them during the 2-weeks' period, the student officers were taken rapidly, though thoroughly, through a wide course of instruction contemplated to serve as the groundwork for more detailed study through the new Correspondence Courses to be conducted by the Marine Corps School under the direction of Major Harold H. Utley, USMC. Practically all the Reserve officers attending the first camp registered for the Correspondence Courses which were to start in September 1926.
>
> The program of training consisted of a series of lectures and practical demonstrations in the field. Special attention was given to the infantry weapons, all officers being instructed in the use of the bayonet, rifle, pistol, hand grenade, machineguns, 37mm howitzers and the 3-inch Stokes Mortar battery. Running the bayonet course—which came first on the program every morning—seemed to be most popular. Reporting at the course at 7 a.m., after a brisk walk of some distance from quarters, then going through the strenuous task of running the course in an attempt to make record time, was found by the officers to be a splendid conditioner, especially for those whose civilian occupations require little physical exertion. The interest they took in this particular phase of the instruction is perhaps best reflected in the fact that of the 16 officers who ran the course for record, 11 qualified as expert bayonetmen, 1 officer running the course with 100 percent rating

> thus becoming 1 of the 3 who have made this perfect mark since the course was established at Quantico. A good percentage likewise qualified with the rifle and pistol. There was not sufficient time to work for record with the machineguns and howitzers, but the aptitude shown by the officers in the handling of these weapons brought forth commendation from their instructors.

Fay, now a retired Reserve lieutenant general, said that Major General Eli K. Cole, Commanding General at Quantico, exercised a keen personal interest and visited classes to observe first hand the progress of student officers. After the first week's training, the battalion and the Reserve officers' class were reviewed and inspected by Brigadier General Logan Feland. Leave was granted all officers from Friday evening to Monday morning. Many visited Washington and nearby Brown Field where permission was granted for Reserve officers to take flights. He continued:

> One of the most interesting events in the course of instruction was the visit during the second week of training of the Major General Commandant accompanied by a delegation of Congressmen in which were included representatives from the hometowns of the Reserve companies. The party was received at the entrance to the Post by Major General Cole and his staff and the class of Reserve officers. The Reserve Battalion, headed by the Post Band, was drawn up at attention in Transportation Avenue and rendered the appropriate honors. Each officer was personally presented to Major General Lejeune and the Congressional delegation. Later the Major General Commandant and his guests witnessed a demonstration by the Reserve Battalion of an attack upon an imaginary enemy with warlike conditions simulated and .live ammunition fired. Two rifle companies made up the assault echelon, with 3 companies in reserve, and [another] company equipped with machineguns and howitzers, and augmented by the Reserve officers' class, supported the

advance. The complete maneuver was handled exclusively by Reserve officers and elicited the hearty congratulations of the Major General Commandant. Following the demonstration the Congressmen representing the home districts of the Reserve companies had lunch in the mess of their respective organizations, while Major General Lejeune and the remainder of the Congressional party were the guests of the Reserve Officers' Mess.

A great deal of credit for the success of the training period is due Captain Victor F. Bleasdale, USMC, who was commanding officer of the Reserve Camp, and to the other officers of the Regular service who assisted him.

The Reserve officers were comfortably quartered in barracks buildings and conducted their own mess with First Lieutenant Ralph C. Alburger, USMC, as Mess Officer. The food and service met with unanimous approval. Captain J. J. Staley, USMC, assigned to the Reserve Section at Headquarters in Washington, made it a point to visit camp nearly every day and was very helpful to the Reserve officers in attending to many details incidental to their stay in Quantico. In addition to serving as a general information bureau, Captain Staley rendered valuable service of a personal nature to many officers who were obliged to keep in close touch with their civilian business interests.

The 2 weeks slipped by with incredible rapidity without a single hitch to mar the encampment and all officers were unanimous in declaring the training period a splendid success, not only from the standpoint of the increased professional knowledge gained, but from the physical benefits derived, the recreational features enjoyed, and the good fellowship which prevailed.

The enthusiasm and drive of the various FMCR companies and success of the first encampment resulted naturally enough in a continuing expansion of the Reserve. On 30 June 1927, the Reserve consisted of 6,100 officers and men: Fleet Reserve: officers 219, enlisted 3,315; Volunteer Reserve: officers, 196, enlisted 2,370. During this period, correspondence school courses at the Marine Corps Schools were made available, and a large number began participating. Additional FMCR members were also authorized to take courses at the Marine Corps Institute.

Growth of Reserve

A worthwhile insight into the growth of the Reserve was made by Major William C. Wise, Jr., USMC, who stated:

> When we consider what inducements the Corps has to offer a man (engaged in the struggle of earning his own living in civilian life, and in supporting his family) to join the Reserve, we find there are but 2; one, to offer a means of preparing him for an eventuality, which may never become a reality, that is, for defense of his country, and the other, which after all is but a minor one, to be assured, if war does come, and the draft effective, that he is in a service of his own choice. In the final analysis, our only real appeal is to a man's patriotism, to his belief in National Preparedness, and to his desire to be associated with an arm of the service possessing the record of the Marine Corps—their wartime value is not fully realized by those of the Regular service until they come into contact with them. It is really an inspiration to meet the ideal type of patriotic American citizens who are coming into the Reserve; men activated by no motive other than their desire to serve their country when needed; men who are keenly interested in the Corps, its past and its future, and who, in joining the Reserve, signify their willingness to sacrifice their time for both pleasure and business in order to prepare themselves for an eventuality which may never materialize; and men who will assist the Corps in every possible way.

The increase by 2,679 members is reflected in the Commandant's report of 1928 which showed the Reserve strength at 8,779: FMCR, officers 167, enlisted 3,495; and VMCR, officers 246, enlisted 4,871.

Problems and Progress

There were problems building up for the Reserve program—problems which were to become more acute, rather than less, with the passage of time. In recruiting for the Reserve, generally, only men who had completed basic individual training in a military service were permitted to enlist. Further, the 2,371 just-trained enlisted men assigned to the Reserve upon termination of a Regular enlistment were limited by the money appropriated in the Reserve budget for their pay. It was set at $25.00 per year per man! This lack of sufficient appropriations was also an important factor in Reserve training, since it limited the number of Reserves who could undergo summer camp training. Nevertheless, 88 officers and 207 enlisted men were trained during fiscal year 1929. In 1928–29 the training program was carried out for the first time on a progressive schedule, including basic advanced company officers courses and signal officers courses.

Also, during this period, 6 additional companies of the FMCR were authorized:

> 308th Company, Worcester, Mass.—Commanding Officer, Lieutenant Ivan E. Bigler, FMCR
>
> 312th Company, Portland, Maine—Commanding Officer, Captain Charles E. Fogg, FMCR
>
> 313th Company, Milwaukee, Wis.—Commanding Officer, Lieutenant LeRoy Hauser, VMCR
>
> 314th Company, St. Paul, Minn.—Commanding Officer, Lieutenant George R. Lewis, FMCR
>
> 315th Company, Chicago, Ill.—Commanding Officer, Lieutenant Donald T. Winder, FMCR
>
> 316th Company, Seattle, Wash.—Commanding Officer, Lieutenant William O. McKay, FMCR

During November and December 1928, a Marine Corps Reserve Board with Brigadier General Ben H. Fuller as president convened to consider policies and regulations to promote efficiency. General Fuller, Assistant to the Major General Commandant, was also designated as Officer in Charge, Marine Corps Reserve, and served with distinction from 14 September 1928 to 9 May 1929. For the first time, the Reserve program was being administered by a Reserve Section with one responsibility—*to make the Reserve into the kind of a Reserve that would enable it to fulfill its mission.*

By June 1929, the Reserve had 9,564 members: FMCR, officers 178, enlisted 4,236; VMCR, officers 267, enlisted 4,883. To conform with the Regular table of organization, FMCR company strength was increased to 3 officers and 93 enlisted. FMCR companies were increased from 10 to 16. Two of the new companies were designated as artillery. Insufficient funds continued to limit activities and, for the first time, Reserve units began issuing renovated serviceable clothing.

Training Camps

A 12-page article, "Training Camps," written by Captain J. J. Staley, FMCR, although brittle with the passage of 18 years, brings a flavor no rewrite could attempt and is included here as written, minus the several pages of names of officers making up the various companies. Staley wrote:

> Summer training for officers and enlisted men of the Marine Corps Reserve began on Sunday, July 7th, 1929, at the Marine Barracks, Quantico, Va., with the arrival of the 302d, 305th, 306th, 308th, 310th, and 312th Companies of the Fleet Marine Corps Reserve forming a provisional battalion with Major James F. Rorke, FMCR, commanding. This battalion, with a strength of 24 officers and 400 enlisted men, began to arrive at

Quantico on the R.F. & P. railroad at 10:15 a.m. The 302d of Rochester, N.Y., the 306th of Detroit, Mich., and the 308th of Worcester, Mass., came down on a special train. In addition, 100 officers reported for active training for instruction. These officers were divided into classes in accordance with rank and experience and were assigned to Advanced Company Officers, Infantry Basic, and Signal Courses.

The Camp, located on the ball diamond in the Ship Yard Area, is under the direction of Major D. M. Randall, director of training, and is one of the finest ever set up in Quantico. It is laid out in accordance with regulations; each company having its own street and every tent lighted individually with electric lights. Enlisted men are quartered in pyramidal tents, 6 to a tent. The Officers are quartered in 9' x 9' wall tents, 2 to a tent. Galleys have running water, are screened, and are well lighted by electricity.

The Officer's Camp is located on the high ground to the north of the battalion camp. Here again tents are electrically lighted and galleys and showers have been erected.

The Battalion

Major James F. Rorke, FMCR, in command of the provisional battalion, is assisted by Lieutenant Clarence L. Jordan as Adjutant. Major Rorke is an officer of years of experience in the National Guard of the State of New York and Marine Corps Reserve. During the war he served overseas as a first lieutenant in the 5th Regiment and participated in the various battles of that organization. He is in direct charge of the battalion camp, all company officers reporting direct to him. The 302d Company, commanded by First Lieutenant Edward F. Doyle of Rochester, is an organization that was in existence before the World War, the Company coming into service at that time. Lieutenant Doyle is a former Marine with wartime experience.

The 305th Company of Philadelphia was formed about 2 years ago and has a very fine record of efficiency during training camps. Last year the organization won the marksmanship trophy. This company is commanded by Lieutenant Howard S. Evans.

Lieutenant Evans is a former Marine and served in the Marine Corps during the World War, and was formerly an officer in the Officers Reserve Corps, U.S. Army.

The 306th Company of Detroit was organized originally as a Naval Militia unit of the State of Michigan, and has always been a successful company. It is commanded by First Lieutenant William V. Calhoun of Detroit, a former Marine who served overseas with the Marine Corps during the World War, and later, with the organization of the 306th, was commissioned in the Marine Corps Reserve. Lieutenant Calhoun is one of the few officers in the Reserve who graduated from a Marine Corps School, having attended the Basic School in Philadelphia.

The 308th Company of Worcester, Mass., is one of the newer organizations. This will be its first training camp. It has the unique distinction of being the first Marine Corps Reserve company to reach its full authorized strength. It has 3 officers and 93 enlisted men. The commanding officer, First Lieutenant Ivan E. Bigler, was an officer in the Marine Corps during the World War and is well qualified to handle the organization.

The 310th Company of New Orleans was organized about 2 years ago and at the first training camp in the summer of 1927, a few weeks after its organization, was awarded the Efficiency Guidon as the most efficient company of all organizations training at Quantico that year. First Lieutenant Alfred A. Watters is the commanding officer of this company.

The 312th Company of Portland, Maine, is another of the newer organizations coming to camp for the first time. This company is commanded by Captain C. Eugene Fogg of Portland, Maine, and he has had years of experience in the Naval Reserve and in the Naval Militia, of the state of Maine.

Second Camp of Instruction

The Second Camp of instruction will begin Sunday, July 28, 1929, with the 303rd Company of New York City, 309th of Milwaukee, Wis., the 315th of Chicago, 311th of St. Paul, 401st of Washington, and 402d of

Roanoke, Va. This battalion will be under the command of Major Ralph L. Schiesswohl FMCR, and in addition to the enlisted men, which will number approximately 450, there will be 80 student officers. Instruction at this camp will be the same as outlined for the period of July 7th to July 20th.

At this second camp of instruction there will be 2 new companies of the Reserve, officially designated as the 401st and 402d Companies, Volunteer Marine Corps Reserve. The organization of these companies is the same as for Fleet Companies, but they are only required to train annually and not report for weekly drill, and no drill pay of any kind is allowed. The men are issued for uniform, khaki and such other clothing as may be necessary for training purposes, but do not draw dress blues.

The first company of this type was authorized in Washington, D.C., with Captain Harvey L. (Heinie) Miller in command, and so far it has made a very favorable impression. The second company was authorized at Roanoke, Va., with First Lieutenant Carleton Penn in command. These companies have been received very favorably by men who do not care to obligate themselves to weekly drill, but at the same time are anxious to associate themselves with the Marine Corps and receive annual training. These 2 companies are the beginning of this new organization, which it is hoped funds will permit to spread rapidly.

The need for the Reserve and the inherent problem of inadequate funds for the Reserve were restated by the Commandant in 1930:

> Under plans of the Navy Department the mission to be assigned the Marine Corps in the event of a major international emergency involving the United States contemplates a high degree of initial preparedness, to which the peacetime strength of the Corps is inadequate. Therefore the maintenance of a thoroughly trained and sufficient Reserve is essential. With this objective in view, progress is being made notwithstanding the necessity of practicing the strictest economy in the expenditure of funds.

In the Reserve Section, 2 major personnel changes had a great impact upon the whole Reserve program. First, Colonel Julius S. Turrill, an outstanding battalion commander in France during World War I, became Officer in Charge on 9 May 1929, serving until 30 June 1932. Second, and perhaps more important, Captain Staley was assigned as Assistant to the Officer in Charge. Both were anxious to prepare the Reserve to meet its responsibilities and both believed a new approach was needed.

The Reserve still consisted of the 4 VMCR regiments, 4 VMCR casual companies, 4 VMCR aviation units, and 16 FMCR companies. The training and growth of the VMCR units was negligible. They continued as paper organizations. Nonetheless, they were a prime source of manpower. The FMCR companies were developing into efficient units and consisted of a high percentage of well-trained officers and men. However, Staley was dissatisfied with excessive transportation costs of sending reservists to camp at Quantico or San Diego and recommended that units receive summer training at Navy and National Guard facilities closest to their respective Headquarters.

The "New Reserve"

After a careful study of costs, the team of Turrill and Staley decided the new approach should combine the VMCR and the FMCR and form Reserve regiments composed of officers and men who would serve without drill pay; be willing to purchase their own dress uniforms, if dress uniforms were desired; and also bear a large part of Reserve expense from private funds. Most FMCR companies would be disbanded and personnel placed where needed within the new regiments. An intensive effort would have to be made to get VMCR members to become active participants.

Major General Commandant Wendell C. Neville approved the reorganization plan, dubbing it the "New Reserve." The first step and pilot project in the new program was the creation of 2 Volunteer companies: the 401st Company, Washington, D.C., organized by Captain Miller and composed almost entirely of policemen and firemen; and the 402d Company, Roanoke, Va., organized by Captain Penn. Both companies went to summer camp at Quantico in 1929 and made very creditable showings. During this summer camp, the contrast between the new "volunteer" program and the casual officer training program which had existed since 1926 came into sharp focus. The casual officers were known as members of the House of Lords and the Volunteer Company officers as members of the House of Commons. The House of Commons had Marines to drill and train. The House of Lords had none. The khaki uniforms of the House of Commons were most often sweaty and dirty. The House of Lords wore only white shirts and blouses and went to class. The House of Lords didn't have to play soldier, while the House of Commons had more than their share of drill, dirt, and dust.

Largely because of the active interest and support of the "New Reserve" by the Commandant, the overall plan got under way on 31 October 1929 when the Commandant authorized Lieutenant Colonel Rorke to organize the 19th Reserve Marines with Headquarters in Brooklyn, N.Y., with an authorized strength of 775 officers and men. Companies carried 2 designations, an appropriate letter plus a special Reserve numerical in the 400 series.

The Regiment was successfully organized as follows:

> *Headquarters 19th Reserve Marines*, Lieutenant Colonel James F. Rorke, Commanding; Captain George W. Bettex, Regimental Adjutant
> *First Battalion-Headquarters in New York City*, Major Melvin L. Krulewitch, Commanding
> Company B (414th) (Brooklyn), Captain Edwin C. Johnson, Commanding
> Company C (415th) (Brooklyn), Captain John J. Dolan, Commanding
> Company D (416th) (New Rochelle), Captain George A. Whiteley, Commanding
> *Second Battalion-Headquarters in East Orange, N.J.*, Captain Paul A. Sheeley, Commanding (acting)
> Company E (417th) (Elizabeth), Second Lieutenant Otto Lessing, Commanding
> Company F (418th) (Irvington), Captain Malcolm K. Beyer, Commanding
> Company G (419th) (East Orange), Captain Paul A. Sheeley, Commanding
> Company H (420th) (Elizabeth), Captain Edwin L. Gidley, Commanding
> *Third Battalion-Headquarters, Marine Barracks No. 2, Navy Yard, Philadelphia*, Major Howard N. Feist, Commanding
> Company K (422d) (Philadelphia), Captain James J. Gannon, Commanding
> Company L (423d) (Philadelphia), Captain Richard A. Taussig, Commanding
> Company M (424th) (Philadelphia), Second Lieutenant Charles H. Cox, Commanding

The 20th Reserve Marines, soon authorized, was formed in Washington, D.C. and, on 3 April 1930, the Commandant presented their colors, saying:

> Herewith I have the honor to present the colors of the Twentieth Marines. The Regiment is the result of a new departure in Marine Corps Reserve policy. This year you will be on your own, providing for your training, messing, and the quartering of your men without direct help from the regular service.

This was the first time a Reserve Regiment was presented colors.

At that time, the regiment was organized under the slogan: "Not how much do I get out of the 20th, but rather, how much can I put in?" More than 3 decades later, President John F. Kennedy was to put the question in a similar vein at his Inaugural.

Headquarters 20th Reserve Marines, Lieutenant Colonel J. J. Staley, Commanding; Captain Charles W. Tegge, Adjutant; Lieutenant Commander Donald S. Knowlton, Surgeon

First Battalion-Headquarters in Washington, D.C., Major Earl C. Lane, Commanding

Company A (401st) (Washington, D.C.), Captain Frank L. Ach, Commanding

Company B (403d) (Washington, D.C.), Captain Windsor B. W. Stroup, Commanding

Company C (404th) (Washington, D.C.), Captain Willard L. Hart, Commanding

Company D (405th) (Washington, D.C.), Captain Russell I. Whyte, Commanding

Second Battalion-Headquarters in Washington, D.C., Captain Harvey L. Miller, Commanding

Company E (406th) (Washington, D.C.), First Lieutenant Homer L. McCormick, Commanding

Company F (407th) (Washington, D.C.), Captain Francis R. Geraci, Commanding

Company G (408th) (Chevy Chase, Md.), Captain Robert H. Winn, Commanding

Company H (409th) (Washington, D.C.) Captain Sigsbee H. Yorkdale, Commanding

Third Battalion-Headquarters in Washington, D.C., Major Melvin J. Maas, Commanding

Company I (402d) (Roanoke, Va.), Captain Carleton Penn, Commanding

Company K (410th), (Capitol Heights, Md.) Captain Thomas J. Luckett, Commanding

Company M (412th) (Rockville, Md.) Captain Harold C. Smith, Commanding

Catholic University Company (Washington, D.C.), First Lieutenant Joseph O'Brien, Commanding

On 24 May 1930, the 1st Battalion, 22d Reserve Marines was authorized in New Orleans, formed on a nucleus of the former 310th Company FMCR:

First Battalion in New Orleans, Major Alfred A. Watters, Commanding

Company A (428th) (New Orleans), Second Lieutenant Walter J. Barnes, Commanding

Company B (429th) (New Orleans), Second Lieutenant Newton B. Barkley, Commanding

Company C (430th) (New Orleans), Gunner Frank R. Worthington, Commanding

Company D (431st) (New Orleans), Second Lieutenant Eugene B. Diboll, Commanding

On 24 August 1930, the 1st Battalion, 21st Reserve Marines (Artillery) was organized in Philadelphia. Up to this time, there had been no Reserve artillery.

First Battalion-Headquarters in Philadelphia, Major Robert C. Pitts, Commanding

Battery "A" (Philadelphia), Captain Daniel J. Littley, Commanding

Battery "B" (Delaware City), Captain Joseph R. Knowlan, Commanding

The 1st Battalion, 24th Reserve Marines, was formed on 20 October 1930 at Chicago, under the command of Major Donald T. Winder and was soon expanded to a regiment, 24th Reserve Marines, with companies in Decatur, Ill.; Milwaukee, Wis.; Toledo, Ohio; Detroit, Mich.; and two companies in Chicago (in 1933). Later, on 18 March and 25 April 1931, Los Angeles and San Francisco were each authorized one battalion of the 25th Reserve Marines.

This expansion was not without problems, and one retired Reserve general officer, commenting on the development of the Reserve with its early Fleet Companies and Battalions and the later development of major units, said that "the entire Marine Corps Reserve was riddled and diluted by local politics as well as by gross mismanagement of Commanding Officers and noncoms...."

Sacrifice, Time, Money, and Effort

The showing made in camp during the summer of 1930 proved that the new type of Reserve could provide for itself. Thus, a further expansion was authorized. On 18 March 1931, the 6th Marine Reserve Brigade, consisting of Brigade Special Troops, the 20th Reserve Marines, and the new 23d Reserve Marines, was formed with a strength of 88 officers and 1,458 enlisted men. Under the command of Lieutenant Colonel Staley, the new brigade faced many problems, including lack of funds. The 20th Reserve Regiment had, during its brief existence of approximately one year, incurred total expenses of approximately $50,000 of which $21,672 had been met by individual contributions or from other private sources.

Under the influence of the "New Reserve" program, the Reserve continued to grow. On 30 June 1930, for the first time it exceeded 10,000 members. The total of 10,753 reservists included: FMCR, 223 officers and 5,455 enlisted men; VMCR, 265 officers and 4,810 enlisted men. Training of both individuals and units continued to receive a high priority despite the limitations of funds, and nearly 1,000 officers and men attended summer camp at either Quantico or San Diego that year. The "New Reserve" was designed for those officers and men who were willing to sacrifice much of their time and effort, not to speak of money. The policy of the Commandant was to appoint only the most dedicated officers in the active units of the Marine Corps Reserve. Casual officers who took no special interest were not considered.

Officers and noncommissioned officers were appointed in appropriate grades. A company commander was usually a cap-tain, the battalion commander a major, et cetera. These officers, however, held their commissions only so long as they were active and interested. In the 18-month period ending in May 1932, for example, 25 officers were relieved and detached from the 6th Marine Reserve Brigade and discharged from the Reserve for a variety of reasons which had made it impossible for them to carry on Reserve activities. This policy of promotion and retention was not without its critics, and Staley's promotion over many competent senior majors created personal ill feelings that never completely vanished. There is considerable evidence, however, that nobody else wanted the brigade job.

The Commandant's Report of 12 September 1931, showed a decrease of 818 members in the Reserve but a substantial rise in FMCR. The combined total was 9,935 and included: FMCR, 247 officers and 6,677 enlisted; VMCR, 263 officers and 2,748 enlisted. Training was stressed and 184 officers and 2,850 enlisted went to camp in 1931, almost triple the previous year. On 1 May 1931, the 300 series FMCR companies not yet integrated into the Volunteer regiments were no longer required to drill weekly, but could drill voluntarily—without pay.

The high level of Reserve enthusiasm is all the more remarkable since these early Marine reservists voluntarily drilled and participated without pay while other military service Reserves and National Guardsmen were being paid for similar activities. A story (of the Philadelphia Reserves) supplied for this book by Brigadier General John Carter in 1965 is a refreshing sidelight:

> In 1930, when Headquarters Marine Corps authorized Units of Battalion strength, the 309th Company was used as the nucleus for

the 3d Battalion, 19th Marines. Later the 305th Company was also integrated with the battalion. Annual Field Training in 1930 as the 3d Battalion, 19th Marines, took place in Quantico. In 1931, the 19th Marines trained in the Connecticut National Guard Camp at Niantic, Conn. In 1932, the 3d Battalion received authority to use the National Guard Camp at Sea Girt, N.J., and trained as a separate battalion. In later years, all battalions from Boston, New York, New Jersey, and Philadelphia were formed into a Brigade organization and used Sea Girt as a training site until the establishment of the Reserve Training Camp beyond the old Artillery area of Quantico. The 3d Battalion was redesignated as the 6th Reserve Battalion, OMCR, and all Battalions operated separately instead of regimental units. Each year a number of battalions were integrated with the battalions of the regular establishment of the Fleet Marine Force and trained at Quantico. This was routine until 1939.

The transition period from Fleet Companies to Battalions was rough on all hands. While the Fleet Companies had been completely outfitted with uniform clothing, even to underwear, socks, et cetera, the new battalions were allowed only the bare necessities of the khaki uniform, were required to purchase shoes, and received no pay except for the period of annual training. This situation continued for several years until sufficient funds were appropriated to cover pay and basic clothing allowances although not including the dress blue uniform. It was during this period that the real character of these Marines shone the brightest. Attendance was excellent and morale high. Many without jobs and with no carfare would walk and hitch-hike for miles to the Navy Yard to report for drill, even during blizzards.

Much credit goes to Staley, however, for his continuous striving for economy and efficiency in administering the Reserve. Under his influence, the cost of training and maintaining the individual reservists per year declined substantially:

Fiscal Year:

1928–29	$459. 95
1929–30	193. 49
1930–31	62. 83

The number of reservists trained was correspondingly increased:

Fiscal Year:	Officers	Enlisted
1928–29	180	207
1929–30	215	891
1930–31	184	3, 120

This was done without any increase in the overall Reserve appropriation and reflects the decentralization of training to local facilities and the willingness of reservists to serve without drill pay and to purchase their own shoes and many other necessary clothing items. By 30 June 1932, with a strength of 651 officers and 8,437 men, the Reserve was composed largely of trained men. Almost 95 percent were adequately trained or in the process. The Fleet Marine Corps Reserve component continued to grow while the VMCR shrank as reflected in the 1931 fiscal year figures: FMCR: officers 322, enlisted men 7,932; VMCR: officers 239, enlisted men 505.

Staley's Summary

The period of 1925–34 was one in which reservists were, in effect, paying for the right to be reservists. Staley, writing in 1932, presented in detail the heavy financial burden assumed by the members of the 6th Marine Reserve Brigade:

> Since 1925, personnel of the Marine Corps Reserve have not received the 2 months pay of their grade each year. They have not received drill pay for weekly attendance at drill, having waived this in order that training in larger numbers could be had and the Marine Reserve appropriation is used now only to provide annual training and necessary overhead such as armory rental, and

other necessary miscellaneous. Membership in the 6th Marine Reserve Brigade is expensive and the total cost of this organization to date to its members, paid out of the private funds, would be startling.

Beginning with the band, instruments are the personal property of the men of the 6th Brigade. Music has nearly all been purchased from private funds. Music pouches (45 in number) are the property of the brigade.

Medical Units—the Field Hospital, 20th Reserve Marines, the Field Hospital, 23d Reserve Marines, and the field dispensaries are largely equipped by the personal funds of the medical detachment. Two ambulances, field type, are the property of the brigade.

Trophies and Awards—which include cups, medals, and trophies—are all the property of the brigade, purchased in the most part by officers from personal funds.

Guidons—all purchased from private funds.

Armory Decorations—pictures, et cetera, are for the most part private property.

Shoes are purchased by each man individually. One thousand men times $3.53 plus 10 percent gives the investment in shoes.

Uniforms for officers average $300 each—we have 70 officers—a total of $21,000 expended by our officers not including dues or other incidental expenses. The uniform gratuity allowance is $100—officers have khaki, white and blue dress, and overcoats.

Blue Dress uniforms—approximately 400 enlisted men have purchased their own dress uniforms at their personal expense.

Dues—officers pay $15 a year, enlisted men $3. This fund is used for armory maintenance, music, camp expense, and for miscellaneous expenses of maintenance during the year for which bills received are sometimes of startling proportions. Also, last year transportation to camp and return by road for the Motor Transport Company came out of this fund and was not paid for by the Government.

Costs extending over an indefinite period are most difficult to compute and only in a general way can costs be shown on the items listed above.

Since 1 May 1932, however, a record has been kept of personal expenses made by the personnel of the 6th Brigade, which to 12 July 1932 (a period of approximately 2 months) totaled $3,962.62.

Not included in Staley's report is the fact that the Washington, D.C., Armory which served as Headquarters of the 6th Marine Reserve Brigade was heated by the simple expediency of piping the steam heat into the Armory from the adjacent Headquarters of the Metropolitan Police Department whose officials conveniently chose to ignore the matter.

Commanding Officer, Both Recruiter and Leader

Even more significant among the accomplishments of these early reservists is the fact that they had to create their own organization. A company or unit commander did not receive his men and officers from a training station or through recruiting offices, but had to go out and recruit them. He had to interest his friends and acquaintances in the program and use every available tactic to get them to join his unit. The standards for membership were high—the financial expense kept out a certain class of possible recruits; selection and company pride were often key factors in determining the desirability of a potential member. Finally, the stringent physical examination often disqualified otherwise qualified recruits. Thus the problems of recruiting 60 men kept the company commander and his staff busy almost every night. The benefits of really knowing every man in his command enabled the company commander to forge a unit with a high sense of personal loyalty to the Corps and the unit. And, there were incentives available which contributed to recruiting drives. A good sergeant, given the opportunity of becoming the company's first sergeant, would most often be a key factor in recruiting the men needed to activate a Reserve company. In order to get a good recruit, a company commander would frequently buy shoes for him.

The interest and sacrifice of reservists themselves during this depression period kept the Reserve alive. No story of this period would be complete without tribute to Lieutenant Colonel Staley who, despite a full active duty workload in the Reserve Section at Marine Corps Headquarters, found time to command the 6th Marine Reserve Brigade and devote 6 to 7 nights per week, usually from 6:30 p.m. until past midnight, to administering his Reserve command. He was riding high, and hard, but he was due for a bad fall within a few short years.

Enlisted Were Key Men

Lieutenant General James P. Berkeley, Jr., tells the amusing story of his impressions of the "real" beginning of the Marine Corps Reserve. It seems that, at one time in the mid-1930's, a Reserve battalion arrived in Quantico and took a position in front of the Regular battalion. The order was given to fall out and then the order was given for both battalions to fall in as one unit, according to height! In General Berkeley's mind, "this was the beginning of your modern, well-trained Marine Corps Reserve."

John Hanschmann recalled that at the close of annual field training in 1931 the brigade hiked from Quantico to the home of District Commissioner Hazen where they bedded down, only to have their pup tents almost washed away by a torrential downpour. On another occasion, the brigade boated from Quantico to Stump Neck across the Potomac near Indianhead, Md., and then hiked back to their armory in the District of Columbia.

Reserve Brigadier General John E. Fondahl, speaking from retirement, gives great credit to senior noncommissioned officers and other enlisted personnel during the early days of 1931 and 1932. These key men voluntarily contributed time and effort in attending Reserve Training Courses, particularly the Basic Weapons Courses in Quantico in 1931 and 1932, he recalls. These men sacrificed their annual 2-weeks' vacation period with their families to attend summer training camp, and Reserve service often entailed prejudice to their employment. In spite of State and Federal laws, men were often refused employment or discharged because of Reserve membership or because of their necessary attendance at summer training camps. No history of the Marine Corps Reserve would be complete without paying tribute to the many enlisted men who served for long periods of time in the Fleet Marine Corps Reserve companies, particularly during the depression years when both jobs and money were scarce.

The Commandant's Report for fiscal year 1933 contained no statistics on the Reserve strength but dealt with the progress achieved in efficient management despite lack of funds and inadequate quarters and facilities. Special emphasis was placed on rifle training and qualifications.

Air-Ground Reserve Activity

The first air-ground problem ever undertaken by Marine Corps Reserve units was successfully accomplished on 20 August 1933 on the West Coast by the 1st Battalion 25th Reserve Marines and Fighting

Squadron 4 and Observation Squadron 10. The problem was executed amid the rolling country north of San Rafael, Calif. At this early date, the Marine Corps had not formulated its famous close air support concept and, in retrospect, it is interesting to note the comments set forth in 1933 on the advantages of this type of training:

> (a) It increases the interest and knowledge of officers and men of both infantry and aviation units as to the powers and limitation of each arm.
>
> (b) It gives an intermediate step in training between armory training and the annual training period.
>
> (c) It brings the infantry and aviation units into closer contact with mutual benefits to each.
>
> (d) It increases the interest of the civil population in military affairs.
>
> (e) It brings desirable publicity not only for the Reserve, but for the Regular Marine Corps as well.

On 24 September 1933, Navy Yard Guard Reserve Detachment (462d Company) and Marine Reserve Aviation Squadron (VO–6) staged the first air-ground exercise ever undertaken by East Coast reservists. A complete battalion problem over terrain closely approximating the famous Belleau Wood, and extending over several miles, was worked out with success and enemy forces were captured before the final objective was reached. Instrumental in the maneuver's success were commanding officers of the 2 Reserve units, Captain Stephen McClellan (VO–6) and Captain Bernard S. Barron (462d Company).

Back at Marine Corps Headquarters, Colonel James J. Meade, long associated with the Reserve program, replaced Turrill as Officer in Charge on 30 June 1932 and served until 1 September 1934. During this period, Major Percy Crosby,

FMCR, a World War I veteran and creator of the famous urchin "Skippy," published "Always Belittlin'," a record of his struggle to improve the military services. "Always Belittlin'" was built around "the inside story in word and picture of how beautifully our statesmen are taken to the cleaners when they go forth to European arms-stashing conferences." Among his accomplishments, Colonel Meade authorized the publication, on a quarterly basis, of the *Marine Corps Reserve Bulletin*. *The Bulletin* was designed to cover all types of information of interest to reservists. Down through the years, it has been the main pipeline between Headquarters and individual reservists. Typical of the news featured in early issues of *The Bulletin* were the following:

> During annual training of the 24th Reserve Marines, Chicago, Rear Admiral W. T. Cluverius, USN, presented the Purple Heart Decoration to First Lieutenant Raymond W. Hanson, FMCR, and the Nicaraguan Order of Merit to Master Technical Sergeant George J. Boyle, FMCR, following a sunset parade of that organization on the Avenue of Flags to the Hall of Science at the Century of Progress exposition in Chicago in 1933.
>
> The 3d Battalion, 25th Reserve Marines, from Seattle, Wash., and vicinity, Major William O. McKay, commanding, with 7 officers and 89 enlisted men reported to the Marine Barracks, Navy Yard, Puget Sound, Wash., on 11 June 1933, for 2 weeks training. Included in this was close and extended order drills, ceremony, rifle marksmanship, and battalion attack and defense of a beach line.
>
> VJ Squadron 7-MR, NAS Anacostia, D.C., is a comparatively new squadron having been organized in October 1932. At the present this squadron consists of 7 officers and 27 enlisted men. In the temporary absence of Captain W. F. Marshall, the squadron is now under the command of First Lieutenant James E. Webb.

In the summer of 1933 Captain Merwin H. Silverthorn was assigned as Inspector-Instructor to the 24th Reserve Marines, possibly the first Regular officer so assigned. Later, he would direct the entire Marine Corps Reserve. During summer camp training at Quantico that same year, the 6th Marine Reserve Brigade provided its own Medical Detachment. The enlisted personnel of the Medical Detachment were all Marine Corps reservists enlisted for 4 years in the Fleet Marine Corps Reserve. Their qualifications attest to the high level of training and proficiency that was typical of Reserve personnel. The Sergeant Major, Robert L. Jenkins, had former service in the Medical Detachment, U.S. Navy. First Sergeant James N. Shippee, who made 4 training camps with the 6th Brigade, was graduated from Georgetown Medical School in June 1933, and was an interne at the University Hospital. Sergeant Alfred M. Palmer was graduated from Georgetown Medical School in June 1932, interned at Cleveland City Hospital 1932–33, and planned to open his office to practice medicine after return from camp. Corporal Francis D. Dean had begun his fourth year in medicine at the Georgetown Medical School. Corporal Paul J. Kelley had completed his premedical work and would enter Georgetown Medical that fall. Private First Class Jack D. Pitts was a second year student at the College of Medicine, University of Georgia. Many others of the Medical Detachment personnel had a high level of formal and practical training and experience.

The strength of the Reserve on 30 June 1934 was 8,221. This was down from the 1932 high, but training continued to be of paramount interest and 73 percent of all reservists who attended summer camps qualified as marksman or better. Enrollment in correspondence courses reached an all-time high as 95 percent of FMCR officers enrolled. Retired Colonel Justice M. Chambers, reminiscing about these early days in which he also played a significant role in the Washington, D.C., Battalion, recalled that:

> In addition to pressure from Heinie Miller (commanding officer) ably abetted by W. W. Stickney, to keep the outfit up to strength (502 enlisted), was the parallel pressure for officers to take correspondence courses and better themselves professionally in every possible way. Heinie even had our band leader (Leon Brusiloff) so charged up that he not only completed the correspondence courses but took extra active duty for instruction in machineguns and special weapons on several occasions. In spite of his reputation as a musician, there were those who claimed that he got his instructions to the band confused at times.

In 1934 for the first time, the Marine Corps commissioned in the Reserve a small number of Naval ROTC graduates. The Marine Corps Reserve was to receive approximately 20 percent of the anticipated 300 Naval ROTC graduates each future year. During this period, a great deal of thinking and planning went into determining the role and scope of Reserve activities. Reservists and Regulars both expounded upon all aspects of the problem and many thoughtful articles appeared in the *Marine Corps Gazette*.

Although enrollments remained high, there had been a very heavy turnover in personnel in the previous 3 years because of heavy demands upon personal lives and time of all reservists. Work without pay and buying military supplies that legally should have been issued could be sustained for short periods of time. But, as months and years rolled by, the appeal to idealism wore thin in some.

A Matter of Principle—and Helmets

Lieutenant General Edward A. Craig (Retired), speaking of the days in 1934 when he was Instructor and Adviser to the 1st Battalion, 25th Reserve Marines during field training at Marine Corps Base, San Diego, recalled:

> As an example of the attitude of higher headquarters at this time towards supplying equipment for the Reserves, I well remember the Commanding Officer of the Reserve battalion coming to me and wanting to know whether I could arrange to have enough of the 2,000 steel helmets, then awaiting auction at the Base Quartermaster, issued to his battalion. These helmets had been in General Smedley Butler's brigade in China and had been surveyed because they had holes bored in the front to take the Marine Corps emblem. The Reserves wanted just 300 of them in order to compete in appearance with the U.S. Army Reserve and National Guard units when parading in Los Angeles, and for field exercises. My request forwarded to Headquarters Marine Corps was strong and definite but was turned down flatly. Later the personnel of the Reserve battalion bought the required number of helmets from the junk dealer after he had bought them at auction from the Marine Corps at 10 cents each. Cost to each Reserve in the battalion was $1 each.
>
> My report of training to the Commandant contained necessary recommendations covering the points noted and I was glad to see some little improvements in clothing allowances, including shoes, the following year.

Expansion of the Reserve into regiments, and then into brigades, created further major problems of administration and command. If the Marine Corps was to be the spearhead of U.S. Regular military and naval establishments, then its Reserve had to be the very first civilian military component to be called. There was no question that the Corps needed a Reserve to provide additional manpower for immediate active service. What was in doubt was the size of unit which could best enable the Reserve to provide the Marine Corps with the necessary well-trained, properly equipped, and efficiently organized manpower.

Structure "Cumbersome and Inert"

Reserve Quartermaster Clerk Monte M. Jacobs, dropped this bombshell in February 1934 when he wrote, after serving as an instructor at several of the Reserve Training Camps:

> The one indelible impression that I gained is the fact that the regimental and brigade organizations are top-heavy, cumbersome, and inert, and therefore unsuitable for our business. They therefore destroy the very reason for the existence of a Reserve. Without speed of movement and flexibility in organization, both ashore and afloat, neither the regular Corps nor its Reserve can live. . . . Apparently some of our larger Reserve outfits have fallen victims of too much society with a decided leaning toward political games. The introduction of these hazardous elements into any military organization is certainly courting disaster, especially if they are permitted to take on the proportions of cliques and attempts to influence promotion, duty assignments, and stations . . . I vote to urge the immediate adoption of the battalion organization system for the Reserve. . . .

The internal pressures continued to pile up in the Reserve as it struggled with the problem of deciding what was the best organizational unit for fulfilling its mission. The problem was somewhat alleviated when administrative, appropriate duty, and drill pay for officers and drill pay for enlisted men were approved on 14 June 1934 with definite limitations on the percentage of personnel to receive these benefits.

Miller Replaces Staley

Yet, the basic problem of organization continued to plague the Reserve. Finally, the proponents of the battalion concept won out. The immediate result was disbandment of the 6th Marine Reserve Brigade. Soon afterwards, the other regiments went out under the category of reducing the operating budget. In their place, 13 separate battalions were authorized. Lieutenant Colonel Staley was relieved from active duty and placed in an inactive status. On 1 September 1934, Brigadier General Richard P. Williams was designated as Officer in Charge of the Reserve Section, a post he held until 15 May 1937.

Staley's was the fate of many pioneers who got shunted aside in the rush of progress. *The Washington Star* headlined the story, "Colonel Staley Loses His Command As D.C. Marine Unit is Abolished." It reported that:

> Major Harvey L. Miller, secretary to the District Boxing Commission, is to be commanding officer of the new combat battalion (the 6th Brigade was abolished and a new 5th Battalion instituted) while Lieutenant Colonel J. J. Staley, who until a few days ago was commanding officer of the Reserve, has now been retired to inactive status . . . .

Significantly, Major Miller said in this connection:

> The Continental Guard, the semi-military organization which sponsored the 6th Brigade, in that all the officers and men of the brigade paid initiation and dues in the Continental Guard, will not function in connection with the 5th Battalion.

Many prominent Senators and Congressmen had been commissioned in this informal unit which sponsored dances, parties, and fund-raising annual printed programs.

Lieutenant Colonel Guy Richard's un-published Reserve History has a chapter in which he tells the last part of the Staley story thus:

> Staley was too heartbroken to fight back. For several years he remained a defeated man. His nerves were shot. His health was bad. He became a representative of the American Red Cross in which capacity he traveled all over the United States. Sometimes he received letters addressed to him. More often he didn't.

> The Corps kept dunning Staley in behalf of a few bills that arrived at Indiana Avenue bearing his name. Three years later, the former paymaster of the old brigade, shot himself in a New York motel after he was found to have absconded with more than $18,000 from Marine Corps Headquarters. Staley was in no way involved with this case and it might have been presumed that the now proven thief, had been the cause of some or all of the leakage in the accounts of Staley's old command. No effort has ever been made, however, to prove or disprove the paymaster was the cause of the brigade's financial troubles. In these days, when the Government furnishes pay, uniforms, equipment, and armory space, it is easy to forget the extremes to which the trail blazers had to resort when they were trying to build up something from nothing; and then, when they had something (in Staley's case, a whole brigade) found themselves subjected to the same kind of scrutiny turned on a regular officer in command of troops trained, fed, equipped, and paid for by the Government.

> He is the only man who ever moved out of the unhallowed soil of civilian life to take over a brigade of Marines and a bevy of Senators and Congressmen. There is much more than mere heartbreak in the Staley case. Volumes could be written on what Staley contributed to the Reserve and the lessons the Reserve learned from Staley.

> There is no doubt whatsoever that it required a man something like Staley to start the ball rolling for a Marine Reserve. There is also little doubt that if it hadn't been for men who made flamboyant mistakes, there would have been no policy, no drill pay, and no Reserve.

"I am not an admirer of Staley's," Mel Maas remarked recently. "I fought him bitterly. But in all honesty I am compelled to admit that his energy and imagination provided the fireworks that lit up the whole damned sky. Under that light we could at least see where we were going."

Congressman Maas readily admitted that he frequently changed his mind. His 1954 statement to Richards was to be vastly different from his remarks in the *Congressional Record* of 16 February 1931. He later said:

I think Congress and the public owes a debt of gratitude to the men who conceived and worked out this Reserve plan. Particularly is credit due Lieutenant Colonel Staley who has worked untiringly and with unbelievable energy to make this regimental plan a success and to do it with almost nothing. I believe he should be made a brigadier general and permitted to demonstrate this type of Reserve organization on a brigade basis.

It would appear from the foregoing, and from other sources of information, that the U.S. Marine Corps was not the only outfit which had its share of unforgettable characters. It wasn't only the Regulars who bred the unreconstructed rebels, the nonconformists, the devil-may-care improvisors. The Reserve had, and still has, its share of "characters." In fact, anyone who tunes in on any "sea story" session at Division Reunions or Birthday Balls will be convinced that Reserves can and do produce their share of "characters," equal in every way to the Regulars, whether enlisted or officers. But, back to the story.

General Lemuel C. Shepherd, Jr., credits General Williams with rejuvenating the Reserve organization and for obtaining its proper recognition by the Commandant. In 1937 General Williams, in command of the FMF, brigaded various Reserve Battalions with the FMF units during the battalions' summer training periods at Quantico. General Shepherd felt that Reserves thus received a thorough course of combat training, rather than being left to themselves, as in the past, for elementary parade ground instruction.

Retired Lieutenant General Craig, in his description of what he considered to be the first Reserve unit in the Marine Corps to engage in combined training with supporting arms, said:

When the 1st Battalion, 25th Reserve Marines, reported to San Diego in 1934, I considered them a rather weak unit as far as equipment and training were concerned. I was, however, surprised that the Marine Corps did not issue shoes to these Reservists, only the summer field uniform without blouse. Equipment consisted of the bare minimum—rifles, belts, and field packs. The shoes were all of civilian type. No automatic weapons, mortars, or communications equipment was available. They had never had combined training in the field. Despite these lacks, their morale and interest was high and their officers demonstrated competence. I decided to guide them toward field exercises that stressed combined training with supporting arms and some amphibious training, rather than garrison training which could be given in their armory. My suggestion was met with real enthusiasm from all hands and I believe that this unit was the first in the Marine Corps to engage in combined training as part of a Fleet Marine Force unit.

Retired General Oliver P. Smith was impressed with the eagerness of the groups of reservists from the Washington Battalion who came to Quantico on weekends for instruction in the 1930's. One weekend the reservists appeared in a drizzling rain and, with General Smith, slogged around through the mud on a tactical walk. His reaction was that if these men were so eager to learn, he was willing to sacrifice his weekend and slog through the mud with them.

Another "New Reserve"

Thus ended a colorful period in the history of the Reserve and the beginning of another "new Reserve" which was to help prepare the Marine Corps for its role in the Pacific Area during World War II. Of all its accomplishments, the Reserve of the period 1919–34 possibly can point with greatest pride to those reservists, most of whom entered as enlisted men, who stayed in the program through lean days and who eventually served with distinction as officers or as senior noncoms during World War II. Space permits the mention of only a few, but all who served during these early difficult years deserve the gratitude reserved for pioneers. The following list includes ground enlisted reservists who served during this period, who were commissioned and eventually attained general officer rank, including several promoted on retirement:

N. B. Barkley, 04373
M. K. Beyer, 04583

H. W. Card, 04317
J. J. Carter, 04611
W. A. Churchill, 04608
C. L. Cogswell, 05676
C. H. Cox, 04414
J. E. Fondahl, 04958
J. R. Knowlan, 04591
J. R. Moe, 05866
E. D. Partridge, 05914
J. A. Scott, 05935
C. C. Sheehan, 06281
M. M. Smith, 05249
R. W. Thomas, 05431

In addition, many Reserves who served in World War I integrated into the Regulars in 1921 and went on to general officer rank.

By 30 June 1935, the Reserve had 7,916 members, including 138 FMCR officers and 4,317 FMCR enlisted men. The VMCR had 407 officers and 3,054 enlisted men. Implementation of the program to mold 13 battalions out of the old regiments and units was well underway in accordance with the following plan. (The aviation plan is found in the second half of this chapter.)

Ground Reserve

Old organization	Location	New organization
19th Reserve Marines Headquarters, 1st Battalion.	New York_____	1st Battalion, USMCR— New York.
19th Reserve Marines_____	Boston, Mass., Portland, Maine.	2d Battalion, FMCR.
19th Reserve Marines, 1st Battalion__	New York_____	3d Battalion, FMCR.
19th Reserve Marines, 2d Battalion__	Newark and Elizabeth, N.J_____	4th Battalion, FMCR.
20th Reserve Marines_____	Washington, D.C_____	5th Battalion, FMCR.
19th Reserve Marines, 3d Battalion__	Philadelphia, Pa_____	6th Battalion, FMCR.
21st Reserve Marines, 1st Battalion (Artillery).	Philadelphia, Pa_____	7th Battalion, FMCR.
24th Reserve Marines, 2d Battalion__	Toledo, Ohio_____	8th Battalion, FMCR.
24th Reserve Marines, 1st Battalion__	Chicago, Ill_____	9th Battalion, FMCR.
22d Reserve Marines, 1st Battalion___	New Orleans, La_____	10th Battalion, FMCR.
25th Reserve Marines, 1st Battalion__	Los Angeles, Calif_____	11th Battalion, FMCR.
25th Reserve Marines, 2d Battalion__	San Francisco, Calif_____	12th Battalion, FMCR.
25th Reserve Marines, 3d Battalion__	Seattle, Wash_____	13th Battalion, FMCR.

Platoon Leaders Class Begun

The Reserve program was further strengthened in 1935 by a new system of training and instruction designed to supply junior officers qualified to act as platoon leaders in national emergencies. Candidates were chosen from students who had completed their sophomore year at certain accredited colleges and universities which had no Army or Navy ROTC units. They received intensive training during two consecutive summer periods of 6 weeks each at Quantico or San Diego. Selection was made by Regular field grade officers and candidates passed the same physical examination required for Regular commissions. Upon successful completion of the two training periods and graduation from college with a degree, they were appointed Second Lieutenants, Volunteer Marine Corps Reserve.

The first classes were assembled 8 July 1935. Within the PLC, 2 divisions were created: the "Senior Division"—those who had completed their junior year; and the "Junior Division"—those who had completed 2 years of college. The whole program was designed to provide qualified platoon leaders and the entire training program was built around attaining this end. Candidates were subjected to a stiff routine of drill, study and firing of weapons, combat principles, and instruction on subjects ranging from courtesy and customs of military service to hygiene and sanitation. The first PLC camp was an outstanding success and the new program was well on its way. It was to provide a highly qualified and motivated corps of junior officers who played a significant role in World War II.

During this period, reservists learned firsthand the problems of amphibious landings. Lieutenant Melvin V. Johnson, FMCR, who later developed the Johnson Rifle and Johnson Machinegun, commented in early 1936:

> What about landing force boats? If we were ordered to land under fire at any time this year with the available equipment, the fellow who once figured out "USMC" to mean "Useless Sons Made Comfortable" would quickly change to "Useless Sons' Mortal Catastrophe."

He wrote further:

> It is reported that a high ranking officer, after observing a landing demonstration, stated that men would land at a dock like gentlemen if the beach were not defended, but should never try to land if it were.

Of course, the Corps had been experimenting with various craft since 1924 at Culebra and had plenty of ideas but no money to carry them out.

On 30 June 1936, the Reserve consisted of 9,311 members: FMCR, 152 officers and 4,015 enlisted; VMCR, 387 officers and 4,757 enlisted. The Platoon Leaders Class program remained popular and 236 students reported for 6 weeks training. Of these, 85 completed the training that year and became eligible for Reserve commissions. In addition, 4 Naval ROTC students were commissioned in the Reserve: 2 from the Georgia School of Technology, and 2 from the University of Washington.

By the close of fiscal year 1936, 3 new FMCR battalions had been added: the 14th Battalion, Spokane, Wash.; the 15th Battalion, Galveston, Tex.; and the 16th Battalion, Indianapolis, Ind.

As the Reserve prepared to meet the demands of mobilization, it is interesting to review the lineal list as of 31 January 1937 of the field grade officers who had the responsibility for guiding the destiny of the Reserve.

Many were already famous like football coach Bernie Bierman and Alton Parker who was the first Marine to fly over Antarctica (1939). Others were to gain fame during World War II. The list follows:

COLONELS:

Mark Sullivan
William G. Fay

LIEUTENANT COLONELS:

James F. Rorke
Joseph J. Staley
William R. Coyle
Victor I. Morrison
Littleton W. T. Waller
Anthony J. D. Biddle
Melvin J. Maas
Clark W. Thompson
James Roosevelt

MAJORS:

Charles G. Sinclair
Ralph L. Schiesswohl
Louis F. Timmerman, Jr.
William M. McIlvain
John D. Macklin
Sydney D. Sugar
Melvin L. Krulewitch
Alfred A. Watters
Donald T. Winder
Vincent E. Stack
Iven C. Stickney
John J. Flynn
Frederick M. Bock, Jr.
Harry C. Grafton, Jr.
George W. Bettex
William O. McKay
Chauncey G. Parker
John J. Mulligan
Bernard W. Bierman
Woodbridge S. Van Dyke
Karl S. Day
Alton N. Parker
Edward P. Simmonds
Clarence H. Baldwin
Caleb J. Milne
Carlton Hill
James Wood
Chester L. Fordney
Earl C. Lane
Harvey L. Miller

Charles A. Ketcham
Frank A. Mallen
Charles L. Herterich
Louis S. Rosenthall
Charles C. Bradley
Robert E. Stone
William J. Platten
Bernard S. Barron
Stephen A. McClellan
Alford J. Williams, Jr.
Bertrand T. Fay
Francis E. Turin
Carleton Penn
Harold M. Keller
Otto Lessing
Joseph R. Knowlan
Wethered Woodworth
James McB. Sellers
Paul Sullivan

Of these men, their units, and others that followed, Reserve Brigadier General Edwin D. Partridge wrote in 1965:

> The memory is vivid of the early 1930's when, as others have remarked, members purchased their own abbreviated Summer Service uniforms and conducted drills in any building or area which could be used without cost. In the case of the 14th Battalion, such places included a high school gymnasium, a hardware warehouse, and an unused floor of a department store. Although it was accepted as a normal state at the time, engendering and maintaining morale and interest and esprit under those circumstances is a source of retrospective wonderment. Prior to recognition by Headquarters, 35 of our members paid our way from Spokane to Seattle and return in order to associate ourselves with the Seattle Battalion for 15 days of summer training at Bremerton.

The Reserve had a new strength on 30 June 1937 of 11,448 members. These were: FMCR, 189 officers and 4,924 enlisted; VMCR, 453 officers and 5,882 enlisted. During this period another 96 college students qualified for Reserve commissions under the PLC program and 1 Naval ROTC student joined the Reserve from the Georgia School of Technology. Reflecting the new status accorded the Reserve Program by Marine Corps Headquarters, Brigadier General William P. Upshur was appointed the General Officer in Charge of Reserves on 15 May 1937. He was very active in all phases of the Reserve and his leadership contributed much to the high level of preparedness attained by the FMCR battalions by the close of 1939.

A Coordinator Reports

As the Coordinator of Reserve Activities, New York Area, the then Major Melvin L. Krulewitch was issued orders on 20 May 1937, directing him to report to Quantico for active duty as Camp Commander of the 1st, 3d, 4th, and 6th Reserve Battalions, exactly 1 month later. The orders, signed personally by the Major General Commandant, were quite detailed and ran to 16 paragraphs. Following completion of the annual field training, Major Krulewitch on 27 July got off a 17½-page report to the Commandant which included information on personnel, rifle and pistol firing, and other matters such as the inadequacy of many of the facilities available to Reserves.

He asked for concrete on all tent decks; additional showers, wash rooms and heads; connection of officers' head to sanitary sewer; additional garbage can bins; commissary and quartermaster buildings in the Reserve area; 6 additional mess halls (many of the troops ate outside or in tents) ; live steam for washing mess gear; another galley with screened section; a recreation building (there was none) ; and "adequate water pressure in all heads so that they would flush properly." His recommendations, 8 in number, had a familiar ring for the times. They included: larger clothing allowances, an additional officer to act as executive or training officer for each battalion, authorization of a 4th Battalion band, annual mobilization of each battalion during its Armory training period, better instruction of battalion officers in machinegun and howitzer weapons, assignment of Naval Reserve enlisted to the medical detachments instead of the practice of drafting Marine Reserves for this duty, and an additional officer and enlisted, year-round, assigned to the Coordinator, in order to free battalion officers from this duty assignment.

His conclusion:

> Morale and efficiency of the 4 Reserve battalions trained at Quantico in June 1937 show a most decided improvement over their state of efficiency in 1936. The units are more seasoned and more self-sufficient than heretofore. They are gradually approaching that state of efficiency which, with a short intensive training in the field, would qualify them for duty with the regular units of the Corps.

On 1 September 1937, the organization of Reserve Areas, unchanged since 1925, was discontinued. In its place, Reserve Districts corresponding to the several Naval Districts were organized. Each Reserve District was commanded by a Regular officer, usually the Commanding Officer of the Marine Barracks most conveniently located to the nearby Naval District Headquarters.

Maas and 1938 Naval Reserve Act

Going into 1938, the Reserve was well led, highly motivated, and very active. Its strength as of 30 June 1938 had grown to 14,890 members, distributed as follows: FMCR, 385 officers and 5,948 enlisted; VMCR, 561 officers and 7,996 enlisted.

The big news of this period was again the oft-told story of a "new Reserve," this time reorganized under the Naval Reserve Act of 1938, passed by Congress on 25 June, which provided in part:

> SECTION 2. The U.S. Marine Corps Reserve established under the Act of February 28, 1925, is hereby abolished, and in lieu thereof there is hereby created and established as a component part of the U.S. Marine Corps, a Marine Corps Reserve under the same provisions in all respects (except as may be necessary to adapt said provisions to the Marine Corps) as those contained in this Act or which may hereafter be enacted providing for the Naval Reserve, and the Volunteer Marine Corps Reserve, corresponding as near as may be to similar classes of the Naval Reserve.

The Act provided that the Reserve should consist of:

> (a) Fleet Marine Corps Reserve
> (b) Organized Marine Corps Reserve
> (c) Volunteer Marine Corps Reserve

It further provided on 1 July 1938, all members of the FMCR as the result of 16 or more years of active Naval Service would be transferred to the FMCR created by the Act and would continue to receive the same pay, allowances, and benefits they were then receiving. All other members of the FMCR were to be transferred on 1 July 1938 to the Organized Marine Corps Reserve; all members of the Volunteer Marine Corps Reserve to the VMCR created by the Act. All these transfers were to be in the same grades and ranks held by the individuals concerned and with the same dates of precedence, for the unexpired period of current appointments or enlistments.

It also provided such requisites as increased pay, disability benefits, retirement with pay for continuous active duty reservists, and an honorary retired list. The

fight for its passage was led by Congressman Melvin J. Maas, who in his lifetime became a Marine Corps legend. He served in Marine aviation in both World War I and World War II, winning among other honors the Silver Star Medal and Legion of Merit. Moreover, he was the principal architect of the Naval Reserve Act of 1938 which provided the bridge between the "good old days" and the rapid mobilization for World War II.

This legislation gave the Marine Corps such a boost in effectiveness that it was the major element in the outstanding success achieved in World War II. Since the end of World War II, most of the Armed Force Reserve Acts and amendments have been largely based on the 1938 Act, for which General Maas received due credit to the day of his death.

Training continued to receive high priority. Approximately 2,000 reservists participated in summer training, and excellent progress was made in the development of training schedules and programs for individual Reserve battalions. Despite emphasis placed upon marksmanship training throughout the Reserve history, the Marine Corps Reserve first entered teams in the National Rifle Matches in 1938. The Number One Reserve Team (Class "A") placed fifth in team standing, considered an outstanding achievement for the first time out.

Under impetus of the 1938 Act, the Reserve continued its growth and development, although the actual numbers decreased slightly from 14,890 to 14,778 due to the basic category changes. On 30 June 1939, the distribution included: Organized Marine Corps Reserve, 237 officers and 5,776 enlisted; Volunteer Marine Corps Reserve, 593 officers and 8,172 enlisted. As provided under the 1938 Act, a Marine Corps Reserve Policy Board was convened in March 1939. As a result, Chapter 13 of the Marine Corps Manual, which pertained to the Marine Corps Reserve, was completely revised.

Carter Takes a Trip

Early in 1939, Captain John Carter of the Philadelphia 6th Battalion had the Chief Engraver of the Philadephia Mint design a sample of a medal for Organized Reserve Service. He then made a personal trip to Headquarters Marine Corps, Reserve Division, and presented the design, along with an official request that it be authorized for immediate issue to Organized Reserve upon completion of 4 years of almost perfect drill and annual training periods. Before the day was finished, it had the Commandant's approval and was on its way to the Fine Arts Commission and the Navy Secretary. After some discussion as to the ribbon colors and the actual requirements necessary to earn the award, it was actually authorized by the Secretary on 19 February 1939, as the Organized Marine Corps Reserve Medal.

For the first time, there were sufficient funds for drill participation by officers and enlisted. In fact, funds were provided for an anticipated 215 officers and 4,129 enlisted, but only 3,706 enlisted actually drilled. New heights were reached in individual and unit proficiency under the spur of the new recognition. The Reserve again entered 2 teams in the National Rifle Matches and Team Number One (Class "A") won the Rattlesnake Trophy and the Critchfield Trophy. The Fleet Marine Corps Reserve, provided for under the 1938 Act, was "activated" by the transfer into it of 1,600 discharged Regular Marines. As members of the FMCR, they received a retainer fee of $20.00 per year and were available for recall in the event of national emergency.

Colonel William C. James was appointed Director on 14 August 1939 and served until 15 May 1940. Thus, as 1939 closed, the Marine Corps Reserve found itself with a new Director and in a high state of readiness.

"Most Valuable Service"—Franklin D. Roosevelt

A letter from President Franklin D. Roosevelt in December of 1939 to Major Bertrand T. Fay, sent him in his capacity as President of MCROA, summed up the pride of the Chief Executive in his Marine Reserve, a Reserve which was to have the services of the President's son, James, in the Pacific during World War II. Fay is today a retired Reserve Lieutenant General. The President's letter wrapped up the Reserve period ending in December of 1939. He said:

> By their loyalty and devotion to duty, the members of the Marine Corps Reserve Officer's Association have rendered a most valuable service in supporting the national defense of our country during the past year. This service, often performed at personal sacrifice, is greatly appreciated and I extend to each of you sincere wishes for a Merry Christmas and a Happy New Year.

SECTION TWO

The Air Reserve

The demobilization of the Marine Corps after the Armistice resulted in the virtual elimination of its Reserve Flying Corps. Within the Regular Establishment, the responsibility for aviation rested upon Captain Cunningham, Officer in Charge, Aviation Section, until 12 December 1920.

However, very little attention was paid to the Reserve Flying Corps.

On Armistice Day there were 155 Marine Aviators, a majority of reservists. There were a limited number of openings for reservists to integrate into the Regulars, but most chose to resign at the end of their enrollment. Thus, following the Armistice, Reserve Flying Corps ranks were gradually depleted, as pilots ended their original enrollment periods. By 31 March 1919, only 11 first lieutenants and 63 second lieutenants remained on the rolls of the Marine Corps Reserve Flying Corps. These were:

FIRST LIEUTENANTS:
Clifford L. Webster
William H. Derbyshire, Jr.
Jesse A. Nelson
Gove Compton
Herman I. Jesse
William W. Head
Harold C. Major
John R. Bates
Basil G. Bradley
Gwendall B. Newman
Guy M. Williamson

SECOND LIEUTENANTS:
Alvin L. Prichard
John H. Weaver
Hazen C. Pratt
Herbert D. Elvidge
Charles A. Needham
William M. Barr
John E. Powell
William W. Torrey
Frank H. Fleer, Jr.
Thomas C. Comstock
Donald N. Whiting
Vincent C. Young
James K. Noble
Bunn G. Barnwell
Colgate W. Darden, Jr.
Chester J. Peters
Earl F. Ward
Edward T. Van Deusen
Edwin H. Witney
Roland K. Reed

Herbert E. Kragh
Edwin A. Bertolett
Edmund H. Ingalls
Henry E. Baker
Robert G. Moore
Maurice K. Heartfield
Samuel S. Richards
Dwight Spencer
Walter B. Pierce
Gerald F. Courtney
Lawrence L. Shea
Byron B. Freeland
Horace W. Leeper
Memory H. Cain
Ivan P. Wheaton
Wallace D. Culbertson
Paul S. Oakes
William W. Ferguson
Patrick L. Higgins
Chauncey V. Burnett
William K. Martin
Harmon J. Norton
Edwin Musick
Sheldon C. Grebe
Benjamin Reisweber
George C. Morgan
Manson C. Carpenter
Frank I. Lamb
Amos P. Booty
Clarence E. Lindstedt
Thomas J. Cushman
Clayton W. Stoner
Lucius E. Steere, Jr.
Paul Foxworthy
Lawrence H. Garrison
Elliot E. Underhill
Walter V. Brown
Lawson H. M. Sanderson
Henry A. Adams
Hugo Pagano
Harry L. Wilson
Cyril A. Gould
Henry H. F. DeFrise

Of this list, only 41 were to eventually reenroll in the Reserve. As such, they constituted the total membership of the Reserve Flying Corps until 1925. Some integrated into the Regulars in 1921. Others went into the Army or Navy Reserve or the National Guard. Many became air mail or airline pilots and some became air-line captains. General Order No. 8, dated 19 March 1921, which directed that avia-tors "be grouped, relieved, and returned to line duty upon the expiration of 7, 5, and 3 years of such service," caused Re-serves to hesitate and "practically killed aviation in the Marine Corps" in the opin-ion of one retired general.

On 25 September 1919, the Marine Fly-ing Field at Miami, Fla., which had been the main Marine Corps flight training base, was abandoned and the personnel and material transferred to Quantico, Va., and Parris Island, S.C. For the next 5 years while the Regular flying establishment struggled to maintain itself in face of the perennial battle against a Congressionally limited budget, the Air Reserve was vir-tually moribund. The Commandant made no mention of it in his Annual Reports from 1919 to 1925. At one point, there was so little money that the Commandant's Report (of 1 December 1921) could not even be printed and distributed. Lieu-tenant Colonel Thomas C. Turner was ap-pointed Officer in Charge of the Aviation Section in December 1920 and served until 2 March 1925. Because of budget limita-tions on both Regular and Reserve flying programs, he was frustrated in all major attempts to strengthen the Air Reserve.

General Butler's "March"

It was obvious that if the Marine Corps was to maintain itself as a force in readi-ness, something had to be done. That "something" was a highly publicized march of 4,000 Marines under the com-mand of Brigadier General Smedley Butler from Washington, D.C., to Gettys-burg, Pa., in 1922. The "march", actually a series of field exercises during which Marine pilots logged 500 hours of flight time, contributed much toward capturing the fancy of the corps of observers, which included President Warren G. Harding and many of the influential news media representatives. So great was the public interest in Marine aviation generated by the press that, in July 1922, the Chief of Naval Operations and the Commandant of the Marine Corps approved a new Table of Organization (T/O) for Marine Avia-tion effective 3 August 1922, which re-designated Marine Corps Aviation as the 1st Aviation Group, headquartered at Quantico.

By 1923, there were Marine Air units in Haiti, Santo Domingo, and Guam. Even so, only 46 officers, about half of them former reservists, and 756 enlisted men made up Marine Corps aviation. In June 1925, 3 years after Butler's "march," public support of Marine Corps aviation was still so favorable that the 2d Aviation Group was added with headquarters at the Naval Air Station, San Diego, Calif.

Night-Flying Reserves

With a group on each coast, Marine avia-tion rapidly became one of the leading factors in promoting recruiting activities for both the Reserve and Regular Estab-lishments. Reservists obtained such train-ing as could be sandwiched in without in-terfering with the Regular Establishment's activities. There was, as could be expected, some friction generated between Regulars and reservists over the problem of dual usage of the very limited numbers of air-craft and facilities. The Reserves also began logging night-flying hours while working on joint maneuvers with the searchlight battalions at Quantico, as well as preparing themselves to undertake the missions assigned to Marine Aviation. These missions included aerial bombing; aerial patrol; aerial reconnaissance; aerial photography and mapping; aerial scouting; spotting for artillery; transporting personnel and supplies; producing smoke screens; and offensive combat against marching columns and men in trenches.

A big boost was given to Reserve aviation under the 1925 Reserve Act which established aviation units within the newly organized Reserve areas. Aviation units were authorized as follows:

> Eastern Reserve Area-Observation Squadron 6–M, Division 2
>
> Central Reserve Area-Observation Squadron 6–M, Division 3
>
> Southern Reserve Area-Fighting Squadron 5–M, Division 2
>
> Western Reserve Area-Observation Squadron 8–M, Division 2

On 3 March 1925, Major Edward H. (Chief) Brainard took over the Aviation Section. He brought in Captain Thomas Shearer to head up the Reserve desk. During Brainard's tenure which lasted until 9 May 1929, he capitalized on the 1925 Reserve Act in spite of financial limitations throughout the period. Passage of this 1925 Reserve Act did not result in any immediate increase in the Air Reserve. Instead Reserve and Regular pilot interest was focused on barnstorming, air races, exhibition, cross-country flights, and special activities which drew crowds and stimulated interest in flying.

In 1927, Headquarters Marine Corps reorganized its Regular aviation units as components of the East Coast and West Coast Expeditionary Forces. Marine aviation was divided into Aircraft Squadrons, East Coast Expeditionary Forces, Marine Barracks, Quantico; and Aircraft Squadrons, West Coast Expeditionary Forces, San Diego.

With the creation of this new T/O for Regular squadrons, the way was paved for the entrance of Reserve personnel into Marine Aviation on a fairly permanent and significant basis.

In many ways, the Regular reorganization was the real foundation for the modern Marine Air Reserve. For each active squadron allowed by the T/O on each coast, there were one or more inactive squadrons. In theory, these inactive squadrons were ideally suited to serve as skeleton formations to be filled by reservists who could be quickly integrated into the Regular Establishment.

Lieutenant General Richard C. Mangrum, writing in 1966 as Assistant Commandant, explains the situation from his recollections of almost 40 years ago saying:

> Some aspects of my own experience in and with the Reserve may be useful. I entered the Marine Corps in 1928 through the flight training program described in the manuscript. For all its lowly beginnings, this was another in several far-sighted steps to create a broader Marine Corps base to meet the requirements of a war already perceived dimly on the horizon. These programs came at a time when the Marine Corps was quite small and its officer complement a close-knit 'stable group of somewhat less far-sighted all-Regular officers. Thus, the Reserve officer on active duty understandably was something of an enigma and outlander, vaguely mistrusted, and undoubtedly not here to stay! In a way, this was not a bad crucible for shaping good Reserve officers—they had to prove their worth. And did. It was uphill, however, for the first several years.
>
> It's fair to note that Marine Corps participation in the Reserve aviation program was built squarely on the Naval Reserve program conceived and commenced in, I believe, 1926. The Bureau of Aeronautics, under Admiral Moffett, must be credited for this farsightedness. As in all Naval Avia-

tion programs, however, the Marine Corps assisted and shared at the Washington level. The only point to my comment here is that any narrative of the Marine Corps Aviation Reserve needs some background of the broader Navy picture. . . . To a lesser extent, this applies also to our ground Reserve. This background is also important to placing in perspective the reactivation of our Reserve after World War II. Again, our Aviation Reserve, for obvious reasons, had to be restructured on the Navy foundation and that story is germane to the History. Again, too, close association at the Washington level during formulation of Navy programs provided the basis for Marine Corps programs to follow. Underlying all such programs, of course, were the matters of enabling legislation and establishment of policy at the executive and secretarial level, in all of which the Marine Corps exercised a vigorous influence.

In early 1928, there had been only 80 commissioned officers and 4 warrant officers on duty involving flying in the Regular Establishment. The Reserve Flying Corps at that time consisted, on paper, of 23 officers and 118 enlisted men. But, only 6 Reserve pilots had undergone training during the previous year and concern was expressed about the "age" of wartime flyers. General Lejeune helped fight Reserve battles and got the first drill pay for aviation at the end of the 1920's. Admiral Moffett had sent for the Director of Marine Corps Aviation and had advised him that the Congress, in the words of General Louis Woods, "was going to throw the Reserve out the window." General Lejeune went up to the Senate, as General Woods recalled it, and after some "horse trading" with a Senator who wanted a Reserve unit in his State, got drill pay for the Marine aviation reservists.

On 10 May 1929, Colonel Turner returned as head of the Air Section and served until 28 October 1931. During this period, efforts were concentrated on obtaining young pilots. The answer to the apathy and financial problems of the Air Reserve came in the Naval Appropriations Bill of 1929. It was designed to provide for the training of pilots who would be qualified and available to bring the Regular squadrons up to war strength in the event of mobilization.

Long-time personnel in Reserve Aviation at Headquarters were Sergeant Thomas Baisden and Adolph Beeg, a former Marine. "Limie" Baisden was the assistant to the early officers in charge of the Aviation desk and was succeeded by Beeg who did not retire as a civilian employee until after World War II.

Flight Training

Candidates for the new program were enlisted as privates, Class VI, Volunteer Marine Corps Reserve; promoted to privates first class; and assigned to inactive aviation duty until it was possible to give them primary flight training. At that time, they were ordered to the nearest Naval Reserve Aviation Station for primary flight training. This training consisted of 45 days of training duty. A primary flight syllabus provided 10 hours of instruction and 30 hours of regulated solo flight in a primary type plane.

Primary training was given at 4 Naval Reserve Aviation Stations: Squantum, Mass.; Rockaway Beach, Long Island, N.Y.; Great Lakes, Ill.; and Sand Point, Seattle, Wash. To assist in the training of students ordered to the various stations, 1 Marine officer and 3 enlisted reservists were detailed to permanent active duty at each Station. The officer, a Naval Aviator, instructed the students in flying. The enlisted men acted as plane mechanics. The Naval Reserve was reimbursed at the rate of $23.50 an hour for each hour that the plane was used by the student.

Upon completion of primary flight training, all students were sent to the Naval Air Station at Pensacola, Fla., for 60 days advanced flight training. It consisted of about 100 hours flying in advanced type seaplanes, ground and aerial machinegun work, bombing exercises, and navigational flights. On completion of advanced flight training, students were examined professionally for appointments as second lieutenants, Class V, VMCR. After appointment, each lieutenant was ordered to active duty with a Regular Marine Corps Aviation Squadron for a period of 1 or 2 years. Upon completion of duty, Reserve pilots were assigned to inactive duty and attached to a Reserve aviation unit.

The new program provided approxi-

mately 250 qualified young pilots over 5 years. The program was well received, and the necessary number of interested young men filled the training quotas each year. Training activities of the Reserve area squadrons were accelerated and, during 1931, some 184 officers and a large number of enlisted air reservists attended summer training for 15 days. Lieutenant Colonel Roy S. Geiger took over the Aviation Section on 12 November 1931 and served until 29 May 1935. Under his leadership, the Air Reserve commenced the planning and training which contributed so much to its effective mobilization. He perfected close air support and made his officers attend air and ground lectures and field demonstrations at Quantico. He required pilots to know the latest ground doctrines.

Although during 1931–32 the Reserve received practically no financial assistance from the Corps, there was an unprecedented growth in squadrons:

Unit	Location	Date organized
Service Company 7	Grosse Ile	11 Mar 1931
Service Company 4	Seattle	12 Mar 1931
Observation Squadron 7	Minneapolis	15 Mar 1931
Service Squadron 5	Squantum	23 Apr 1931
Fighting Squadron 6	Squantum	23 Apr 1931
Observation Squadron 8	Seattle	12 Jun 1931
Observation Squadron 6	Floyd Bennett Field, Brooklyn, N.Y.	13 Jun 1931
Fighting Squadron 5	Detroit	19 Jun 1931
Scouting Squadron 3	Miami (Opa Locka)	25 Jun 1931
Fighting Squadron 4	Long Beach, Calif	18 May 1932
Observation Squadron 10	Oakland, Calif	19 Jul 1932
Utility Squadron 7	Anacostia, D.C.	4 Oct 1932

One of the activated squadrons was commanded by the man to whom this book is a tribute, the then Major Melvin J. Maas. Since it is impossible to tell the story of all, perhaps a few vignettes—from a squadron history by the late Lieutenant Colonel

Marcus J. Maher—will give flavor to the official statistics. (While Marine Air Reserve Training Detachment Commanding Officer in 1956–58, Arthur H. Adams had requested Maher to prepare the history. Adams, whose first Reserve duty was an orderly to Mel Maas, is today a Brigadier General.   Director of Marine Corps Information while most of this book was being written he took over MARTCOM in early 1966.)   Maher's account indicated that Maas had 3 second lieutenants, Charles Schlapkohn, Avery R. Kier, and John V. Kipp, plus 12 enlisted men in the initial unit activated.   Kier integrated and today is a two-star general.   Maher reported that retired Brigadier General Warren Sweetser, then a Reserve second lieutenant, was the first Inspector-Instructor.   Maher wrote:

> Drills were held one night a week and one Saturday and Sunday of each month in Hangar "A" which was torn down during World War II. A concrete slab on the west side of the present Naval Air Station is all that remains of the 1 metal building which housed the Navy and Marine Air Arm in the Twin Cities. There was a large hot-air furnace in the middle. Two Consolidated trainers were tailed in on each end of the stove. The back part of the building consisted of stockrooms and offices. During evenings and weekend drills, members of the squadron assisted Naval Reserve personnel in adding two wings on the original building.
>
> In 1931, the Minnesota Air National Guard moved to Holman Field, St. Paul, and the Navy acquired 3 wooden hangars on the site of the present Naval Air Station. Six Fledgling trainers were alloted to the station in place of the Consolidated trainers. At this time, summer uniforms were issued. Few received the complete outfit, some a cap, others a shirt or trousers, but most everyone was issued a suit of blue overalls. Uniform shoes were paid for by the members themselves although they did not receive pay from the Marine Corps. Applicants for enlistment were required to attend drills for 6 months before being accepted in the squadron. When drill pay was authorized, everyone bought their own Marine dress blue uniforms.
>
> In 1932, the first maneuvers were held on the station. Some of the enlisted men were paid for 7 days and some for 10 days (although it was a 15-day maneuver). Not enough money had been appropriated to pay every member their full share. This was the first pay received by the squadron members. Prior to this training period, 8 Curtis Hell Divers were added to the 6 Fledglings assigned to the base. Lieutenants Kier, Hoidale, and Severson won fame as formation stunt fliers in the original Hell Divers.
>
> Shortly after the 1932 maneuver, a Loening amphibian and a T4M torpedo bomber became a part of the station assigned quota of aircraft. The T4M was a single-motored bomber with 3 open cockpits and room enough to walk around inside the fuselage. The then Lieutenant Colonel Maas used to say "it took off, cruised, and landed at 65 knots." In the spring of 1933, winter uniforms (except overcoats) were issued. Civilian overcoats were worn to and from drill and were of all colors and description. In the fall of 1933, a concentrated maneuver for 3 days was held at the Naval Training Station, Great Lakes, Ill., on a small field. Maas commanded the operation. Present were squadrons from Minnesota, St. Louis, and Detroit. The World's Fair was then in full swing in Chicago.
>
> In 1934, overcoats and gloves were issued and the first of 7 summer maneuvers was held in conjunction with the National Guard artillery and infantry units. The squadron put up and took down their tents, ran their own mess and PX. During this time N1N and N2N Navy Trainers replaced the Fledglings. Elimination flight training was conducted with these aircraft for applicants applying for Navy and Marine Corps Pilot training.

FMF and Aviation

The creation of the Fleet Marine Force on 8 December 1933, greatly affected both Regular and Reserve aviation.   The immediate effect was a reorganization of Marine aviation.   Aircraft One, Fleet Marine Force, was organized from Aircraft Squadrons, East Coast Expeditionary

Forces; and Aircraft Two, Fleet Marine Force, from Aircraft Squadrons, West Coast Expeditionary Forces. With the close of the Marine involvement in the "Banana Wars" in 1933, it is an interesting reflection that the Marine Corps, ground and air, not only had the invaluable opportunity to practice close air support prior to World War II, but it was the only American military service that actually saw combat between the World Wars!

Following the creation of the Fleet Marine Force, the Marine Air Reserve entered the final phase of its early evolution, a phase which brought it to a state of near-readiness for World War II. Since 1928 Marine Reserve squadrons had been designated Marine Reserve Service Companies. After 3 February 1934, they were known as Marine Reserve Service Squadrons. Under reorganization provisions, active duty pay was authorized for all enlisted Reserve personnel, appreciably increasing interest and drill attendance. Lieutenant General Field Harris, writing from retirement in October 1964, recalled an interesting occasion in early 1935 which he said "might illuminate." He wrote:

> It was then that General Geiger who was head of Marine Aviation, ordered Colonel Harold Major and myself to inspect the Reserve Squadron at Grosse Ile, Mich. It was rather an informal affair, but the Squadron put out a right creditable showing as to appearance in uniform, with one glaring deficiency: very few had on regulation shoes. For some unknown reason, the enlisted men of Marine Corps Aviation had never had an appropriation for shoes. During the next session of Congress, with the help of Congressman Mel Maas (Major General, deceased) and Jim Webb, now head of the Space Agency, and the secretary to Mr. Gardner in the Congress, they were able to get an appropriation for shoes. I might add

here that Mr. Webb was a very loyal Marine Reserve pilot. In inspecting the Machine Shop, I noted that a very large percentage of the men worked in the motor industry. They got $1.00 a day for their drill and spent $1.50 for transportation in and back from their homes. This is the eye opener— why would these people do this? That evening, we were entertained by the officers and their wives at a very fine dinner in a local hotel. I noted here that Harold Major and I were the only ones not in uniform. The reason for this was that these officers were very proud of their uniforms and being Marines. This was really my first experience with the Marine Reserve and right then I drew the conclusion that we in the Regular service could learn something from our Reserves.

General Harris, from 1935 to 1938, served as Assistant Director of Marine Aviation. During that period he recalled that the Corps:

> . . . tried mightily to bring our Regular pilot strength over 100 and I believe we did in 1938. During this same period, our Marine Reserve Pilot Program grew much faster due to the Navy Cadet System and we were building up a nucleus of fine young officers who were to be our mainstay in World War II. I believe that in 1938 our Reserve pilot strength must have been about 250. From this nucleus, we expanded to around 10,000 pilots during World War II, practically all of whom were Reserves. Since they had to go through the Regular Navy training, there was never any distinction that I could see during World War II between a Regular officer and a Reserve officer in aviation. Nobody knew or was interested in this particular category. I consider our pilots during World War II as magnificent, serving in every possible category from the jungles of the South Pacific, across this mighty ocean to Okinawa, as fighter pilots, dive bombers, torpedo bombers, B–25 bombers, transport pilots, et cetera. At one time, the Navy called on us to furnish Corsair Squadrons on their carriers. This was done without difficulty and with distinction. At

the end of World War II, we tried to preserve this talent for future emergencies and well we did.

Another retired general, this one Brigadier General Partridge, credits the Inspector-Instructor selection program both ground and air as being instrumental in making the Reserve the force that it proved to be in wartime. He wrote:

> The success of the Reserve program and its improvement in status during the late 1930's were based upon several circumstances, not the least of which was the attitude taken toward it by Headquarters. One especially important feature was the careful choice of Inspector-Instructor personnel and their resultant high caliber. These were specialized assignments and the selection of Officers and Noncommissioned Officers for such billets was obviously undertaken seriously. To guide and instruct without assuming command demanded patience and a delicate balance between personal desire and dedication to a program. G-1 and the Reserve Division should be credited with an exceptionally fine job in this respect.

Marine Corps Air Cadet Program

On 15 April 1935, the 74th Congress passed Public Law No. 37 which provided, among other things, for an aviation cadet program. On 1 May 1935, the Commandant sent all Marine Reserve Aviation units instructions regarding the selection and training of Marine Corps Aviation Cadets. This program provided much of the trained manpower which distinguished Marine aviation during the early days of World War II. The program was implemented under the leadership of Colonel Ross E. Rowell who served as Director of Marine Aviation from 30 May 1935 to 10 March 1939.

The early cadet candidates selected for elimination flight training under the law became a roster of Marine Corps heroes and included, among others: Gregory (Pappy) Boyington, Robert E. Galer, Kirk Armistead, William E. Gise, and James L. Mueller, whose individual exploits are recorded in the following chapter. With a firm foundation and a new cadet class each month, Marine Aviation expanded rapidly during the period of 1935 to 1941. For example, only 6 Marine pilots at Pensacola in 1935 had passed elimination flight training. In 1941, there were 3,104 Marine aviation cadets at Pensacola.

The problem of determining the precedence of Marine Corps Reserve pilots was a complicated one, as all Marine Corps aviators were listed as USMC until 1 October 1924.

The following 20 Marine Corps Naval Aviators were the first officially designated USMCR by the Bureau of Naval Personnel. Obviously, this list of the first USMCR's is inconsistent with earlier established listings, but it is of historical value because of the personnel involved:

Naval aviator number	Name and rank	Date designated
4301	Stedman, Livingston B., 2d lieutenant.	28 Feb 1925
4358	McClellan, Stephen A., 1st lieutenant.	15 May 1926
4367	Carroll, Thomas., captain.	12 Nov 1926
4386	Pickup, Christopher V., 2d lieutenant.	4 Mar 1927
4458	Gephart, Valentine, 2d lieutenant.	20 Apr 1929
4467	Maas, Melvin J., 1st lieutenant.	16 Jun 1929
4477	Mangrum, Richard C., 2d lieutenant.	20 Aug 1929
4482	Reynolds, Ferry, 2d lieutenant.	10 Sep 1929
4483	Bard, Elliot E., 2d lieutenant.	10 Sep 1929

Naval aviator number	Name and rank	Date designated
4484	Redfield, Ben Z., 2d lieutenant.	10 Sep 1929
4489	Mooney, Karl T., 2d lieutenant.	27 Sep 1929
4493	Omer, George D., 2d lieutenant.	1 Nov 1929
4494	Smith, Tracy S., 2d lieutenant.	1 Nov 1929
4495	Youngs, William P., 2d lieutenant.	4 Nov 1929
4498	Salmon, John T., 2d lieutenant.	11 Nov 1929
4499	Ostertag, William R., 2d lieutenant.	11 Nov 1929
4500	Norris, Benjamin W. 2d lieutenant.	15 Nov 1929
4501	Mazet, Horace S., 2d lieutenant.	15 Nov 1929
4502	Heaney, Mark S., 2d lieutenant.	15 Nov 1929
4503	Clifford, Nathaniel S. 2d lieutenant.	20 Nov 1929

It is noteworthy that #4477, a former Reserve pilot, became Assistant Commandant in 1965. Lieutenant General Mangrum also became the "Grey Eagle" of all Naval Aviation, having the earliest date of designation of all Naval Aviators on the active list of the Navy and Marine Corps. Included among the many distinguished Naval Aviators is a small select group of those Marine reservists who achieved the rank of General Officer:

> Lieutenant General Karl S. Day
> Major General Melvin J. Maas (Deceased)
> Brigadier General Harry Van Liew
>   (Deceased)
> Major General John L. Winston
> Brigadier General James E. Howarth
> Brigadier General William H. Henke, Jr.
> Major General Robert B. Bell
> Brigadier General Russell A. Bowen

These, and others, were among those who made their firm decisions for the Reserve during these years of indecision.

CHAPTER THREE

World War II

The World War II story of the Marine Corps Reserve and reservists—who were to comprise approximately 68 percent of total wartime Marine personnel—began in October 1940. At this time, 23 Organized Reserve battalions (combined strength: 239 officers and 6,192 enlisted) plus 13 Aviation Squadrons (92 officers, 670 enlisted) were called into active service under Presidential Order 8245, declaring the Nation in a Limited National Emergency. Approximately 85 percent reported for duty. Seven officers and 1,183 enlisted were disqualified physically or because of dependents whose reliance upon the breadwinner of the family made his going to war a hardship on the family. (Many of these men later entered the service voluntarily after Pearl Harbor when some of the original physical and dependency restrictions were removed.)

Therefore, at the time of the attack on Pearl Harbor there were 2 major groups of personnel within the Marine Corps, the Regulars and the Organized reservists. A dispatch from the Navy Department, dated 5 October 1940, put the battalions and squadrons on alert for callup:

From: Secretary of the Navy
Released by: Frank Knox
Date: 5 October 1940
051751
    Put all organized reserve divisions and aviation squadrons on short notice for call to active duty, call fleet reservists as necessary, call retired enlisted men who may be usefully employed and who volunteer. Active duty for other than fleet and organized reserves still on voluntary basis. No volunteer reserves will be sent to active duty for less than 1 year. Call as many Class V(3) reserves as may volunteer. Commandants authorized call local defense divisions when needed and quarters available. Fleet divisions and squadrons will be called on departments orders. Commandants recommend order in which these divisions and squadrons should be called.

General mobilization orders issued on 15 October in Circular Letter 396 directed the 23 Marine Reserve battalions to report to unit home stations no later than 9 November. From here, they were to proceed as soon as possible to initial duty stations, such as Quantico, San Diego, and the Navy Yards at Philadelphia, Mare Island, Norfolk, and Puget Sound. (A complete list of mobilized units will be found in Appendix C.)

Once underway, the mobilization machine of the Corps continued to roll. Callup of air reservists followed almost immediately. In November 1940, the Major General Commandant's order to the Commanding Officers, All Marine Corps Reserve Aviation Squadrons, was issued:

Subject: Mobilization Orders
    1. The officers and enlisted men of your squadron are assigned to active duty on 16 December 1940, at the Naval Reserve Aviation Base to which your squadron is attached, and will proceed as soon as transportation is available to . . . .

The greatest number of recalled reservists came from the States of California, New York, Virginia, Massachusetts, and

Pennsylvania, in that order. These events and others like them were the logical consequences of the Limited National Emergency, proclaimed on 8 September 1939 by President Franklin D. Roosevelt. War with the Axis powers was an apparent certainty. During the summer and fall of 1940, Congress had stepped up the procurement of aircraft, launched the 2-ocean navy building program, called Reserves to active duty, and passed the Selective Service Act.

Recruiting for the Marine Corps was accelerated to meet a new authorized strength of 36,000 men, almost double 1939 size. A 30 June 1939 report had listed the active duty strength of the Marine Corps at 19,432 (1,380 officers and 18,052 enlisted). Mobilization of Organized Reserves had brought approximately 5,000 more men to arms. Ten days after general mobilization orders were issued to Reserve battalions, the Fleet Marine Corps Reserve, composed of enlisted men honorably released from active duty after 16 or more years of service and transferred to the FMCR, was called back to the colors. The Volunteer Reserve, which included men not members of Organized units, was ordered up in 2 groups, the first on 14 December 1940, the second on 12 May 1941. These reservists, combined with Regulars, gave the Marine Corps a total strength of 66,319 on 7 December 1941.

Although toward the end of the war many units were composed largely of reservists, no Reserve unit was ever mobilized and put into service as such. Underlining this policy of the Marine Corps are the recollections of retired Reserve Brigadier General Charles Cogswell who commented in 1965:

> One of the events which has stood out in my mind was the trip of the 5th Battalion

and the 17th Battalion to Guantanamo Bay in January 1941. All hands believed they would join the FMF intact as a battalion. As we disembarked from the *Harry Lee*, all hands were immediately assigned to various units in the 1st Brigade, and the 5th Battalion and the 17th Battalion were no more. As you can imagine, confusion was rampant with Company Commanders separated from First Sergeants and First Sergeants separated from company clerks, and company clerks separated from muster rolls, payrolls, service record books, et cetera.

> After the administration detail had been accomplished, things worked out very well. During the period of shock which followed the disbandment, very few of us realized the wisdom of the Marine Corps in this move. However, it became readily apparent as we became integrated.

General Partridge has similarly recalled:

> Also mobilized in November of 1940 were the Western battalions, and these were integrated with FMF units at San Diego with commendable results. Commanding Officers and key personnel of those battalions also had to overcome their unique problems of recruiting and training, and shortages of facilities. Upon mobilization, they augmented every unit of the 2d Brigade, enabling it to acquire Division status. Readily remembered are: Indianapolis (Harold Keller), New Orleans (Adair Watters), Galveston-Houston (Clark Thompson-Victor Barraco), Los Angeles (John Flynn-Woody Van Dyke), San Francisco (Wallace Breakey), Portland (Albert Skelton), Seattle (Clarence Baldwin) and my unit from Spokane.

> The Reserve Battalions lost their identities when they merged with the brigade units. Individuals, also, quickly lost their their identities as Reserves, becoming indistinguishable from the career Marines with whom they trained side by side. It was at that point that the history of the Organized Marine Corps Reserve passed into a state of hibernation until the end of World War II.

The Integration

November 1940, which had witnessed the the beginning callup of reservists also, in effect, marked the end of the Organized Reserve for the years immediately ahead. On the Corps birthday, 10 November 1940, the Director of the Marine Corps Reserve issued a letter to his forces which launched the wartime integration of Reserve and Regular forces:

> It is quite a striking coincidence that on the 165th birthday of the Marine Corps we find its Reserve mobilizing.
>
> This act involves 3 steps: first, the changing of professional status; second, the closing of official homes; and third, the reporting for field service with the colors. Such service may take you beyond the seas; however, this call should be no news to you, as you have been trained for and are equal to such occasions. I will follow with pride your service!
>
> Such steps create both personal hardship and domestic anxiety. When our national entity is being challenged, then is the time when real Americans volunteer to serve in defense of homeland and families. You constitute this class of Americans!
>
> As you mobilize you leave my authority, the period of which has been far too limited, but a distinct pleasure to me. You carry with you my everlasting wishes for an opportunity to achieve glory which you so richly deserve.

This came from the late Major General Joseph C. Fegan (then a colonel), whose "Farewell Message" reflected the status of the Reserve and, in no small degree, the spirit that prevailed approximately 1 year prior to the Nation's actual entry into the war. That year there were some 15,000 Reserves, approximately a third in Organized units being mobilized. They were absorbed to become indistinguishable from all who bore the name Marine during World War II: a total of nearly 600,000 men. The Organized Reserve had fulfilled its mission as stated in the *Marine Corps Manual*, namely to ". . . provide a trained force of officers and enlisted men available to serve as reinforcements to the Regular Marine Corps in time of war or national emergency." The Marines then being mobilized would be fighting wherever there were Marines for the duration of the war.

Headquarters and Planning

Before considering the effect of mobilization and the actions which followed, it is necessary to have some background on the administrative machine that made it possible for the Corps to handle the gigantic manpower requirements of World War II.

After World War I and passage of Reserve legislation in 1925, a small complement of 3 officers and 6 clerks was set up at Headquarters, the beginning of a machine that was to proliferate and provide for thousands of men and women from the civilian population who would rally to the Corps during the 1941–45 war years.

Until late 1942 the organizational structure of Marine Corps Headquarters provided, through 4 major subdivisions, for all the administrative planning, paperwork, and processing to meet the demands of mobilization. These 4 units were the Adjutant and the Inspector's Department; the Division of Reserve, the Division of Personnel; and the Division of Recruiting. Apparently this organization of functions did not prove the most efficient way to accomplish the mammoth World War II manpower task. In January 1943, as result of a Navy Department survey, it was decided to abolish the A&I

as an independent department. In May a merger was completed under a Director of Personnel whose Department was to work in close cooperation with the Division of Plans and Policies to implement those policies which affected personnel.

A former Regular, Littleton W. T. Waller, Jr., had an important part in all these moves. Ordered to active duty as a Reserve Colonel in June of 1941, he headed up the Target Practice Section, was Director of Reserves for a short time, and then was shifted again to organize the Gunnery Section in Plans and Policies. When the A&I department was abolished, he was named by the Major General Commandant to organize the Personnel Division and made a Brigadier General, the first Reserve General on active duty in the history of the Marine Corps. As General Waller recalls from retirement:

> There was only 1 Reserve Brigadier General provided for and that was being held for Mel Maas. When my nomination went through, others followed—these from men with combat experience.

Thus the Division of Reserve, after the 1943 amalgamation, as the Procurement Branch of the Personnel Department, continued to administer the program of procuring officers from civilian sources and from the ranks of outstanding enlisted personnel. The Division of Reserve was responsible for developing officer candidate programs. It administered an extensive program that included separation and reclassification of Reserve officers; files of inactive, retired, or deceased officers; responsibility for Marine detachments in the Navy V–12 training programs; and selection of officer candidates for the new Women's Reserve.

As the Nation moved from the short-of-war phase into all-out war, Headquarters

continued to revise its personnel estimates upward as the need for Marines increased. The following statistics reflect the tremendous expansion planned. Reservists were to become the dominant personnel factor in Marine Corps planning.

Date of action	Period covered	Authorized enlisted strength
18 Apr 1941_____	Fiscal year 1942__	75, 000
16 Dec 1941_____	Fiscal year 1942__	102, 000
11 Feb 1942_____	By 30 June 1942__	130, 000
	By 30 June 1943__	160, 000
	By 31 Dec 1943__	180, 000
	By 30 June 1944__	200, 000
11 May 1942_____	By 30 June 1942__	135, 000
	By 30 June 1943__	220, 000
16 Jul 1942_____	By 31 Dec 1942__	223, 000
10 Sep 1942_____	By 30 June 1943__	285, 000
30 Sep 1942_____	By 31 Dec 1943__	334, 000
3 Aug 1943_____	By 31 Dec 1943__	358, 000
9 Nov 1943_____	Calendar year 1944	415, 000
Early Nov 1944__	Fiscal year 1946__	552, 000

Fantastic as these authorized statistics seemed for the prewar imagination, they were initially much less than the hordes of men who streamed to "join the Marines" following the attack upon Pearl Harbor and the initial successes of the Japanese throughout the Pacific. In January 1942 enlistments totaled 22,686 as against 1,978 for November 1941. Recruiting facilities were swamped and although there was a tapering off to 7,405 in April 1942, recruitments rose each month until December 1942.

On 5 December 1942, Executive Order No. 9279 was issued by the President, placing all services under provisions of the Selective Service Act. However, because of the backlog in enlistments, the Marine

Corps was permitted to continue its normal procurement procedures through January 1943. Thereafter, the Corps received tens of thousands of young men who, as selectees (USMCR–SS) and reservists, formed the bulk of the Marine Corps personnel strength.

The impact of the influx of reservists upon the growth of the Marine Corps is shown below:

Date	Enlisted Marines on active duty
1 November 1940	37, 604
1 December 1940	44, 072
1 January 1941	45, 340
1 January 1942	73, 669
1 January 1943	221, 171
1 January 1944	367, 832
1 January 1945	437, 112
1 August 1945	444, 270

Many Reserve officers were on duty at induction centers where the men were assigned to the Regular or Reserve Corps. If a particular applicant was desired by the Marine Corps, the officer on duty was contacted by Headquarters and a request was made that the individual be inducted into the Corps.

Although the tremendous expansion of the Marine Corps was accomplished at an accelerating rate and gained its greatest momentum through the induction of "selectees," 2 other categories were equally important. These were the volunteers who signed for a 4-year enlistment (Regulars) and volunteers who signed up for the duration of the war plus 6 months. Altogether, approximately 75,000 men were inducted into the Marine Corps during World War II (70,729 draftees, plus 5,241 Selective Service volunteers). The bulk of the Corps, however, was made up of personnel who had deliberately chosen the Marines—a factor which related favorably to their later morale and performance.

Six Classes of Reserves

To obtain the manpower needed, much had to be done. Six classes of Reserves were created. These Reserve classifications explain the makeup of Marines in World War II. They were:

Class I: *Fleet Marine Reserve.* This group was not large, but represented a highly experienced cadre, men retained in the Reserve after a tour in the Regular Establishment.

Class II: *The Organized Marine Corps Reserve.* Men in the 23 Reserve battalions and 13 air squadrons, first recalled to duty in late 1940.

Class III: *Volunteer Marine Reserve.* All reservists, trained and untrained, who were not in the Organized; or young men who were being trained, or who would be trained in the platoon leader, aviation cadet, candidate classes, and V–12 college program.

Class IV: *Limited Service Marine Corps Reserve* (irreverently dubbed the "Graybeards Reserve"). A newly created category for men 30 to 50 years of age, this class was designed to afford ex-servicemen not in the Reserve the opportunity to again serve their country. Authorized in January 1942, it set a goal of approximately 6,000 men (mostly Army and Marines) enlisted for guard duty at naval shore stations within the country to relieve younger men for combat duty.

Class V: *Specialist Volunteer Marine Corps Reserve.* Another small but highly important class formed to accommodate specialists such as linguists, radar, and transportation experts, and others whose specialized knowledge was vitally needed. Among these, the Nisei (Japanese-Americans) did major service in interrogation and interpretation throughout the war.

Class VI: *The Women's Reserve.* Eventually provided approximately the same number of Regular Marines (19,000) as were on duty just prior to entry into the war.

Collectively, from all these categories, emerged the response to an appeal for manpower to meet the needed wartime expansion program. The administrative machinery creaked and groaned under unceasing demands for more men and the momentum of fast, effective battle training. Nevertheless, this trickle of manpower rapidly became a torrent that was to ultimately rain havoc on the enemy in the far-off Pacific beachheads.

Officer Training—Ground

Among the many requirements facing Headquarters in the early 1940's was the need for young line officers. An expansion demanding a jump from a Corps the size of the New York City Police Department to one that put a 6-division, 4-wing Fleet Marine Force on the Pacific beat created an immense—and immediate—need for trained platoon leaders.

During the short-of-war period, the Corps had operated 2 separate officer training programs. The Basic School, located in Philadelphia, was attended by all newly commissioned Regular officers including U.S. Naval Academy graduates, meritorious enlisted men, honor graduates of Navy and Army ROTC, and selected members from the Platoon Leaders Class. The Basic Course was conducted once yearly for a 7-month period. Reserve officers, however, after the initial Reserve Basic School Class in 1940, were trained in Candidates Classes (an extension of the old Platoon Leaders Class) and Reserve Officers Classes (an advanced training course), given at Quantico, Va. These combined programs, conducted for a 30-week period, accounted for the bulk of the 560 Reserve officers graduated in fiscal year 1941. (The Candidates Class was later called the Officers Candidates Class.)

One of the first ROC's established a pattern for later classes: a heterogeneous mixture of Reserve officers from more than 25

States and twice as many colleges and universities. The men's backgrounds were as varied as their reasons for accepting active duty. Included were: the national emergency, an active interest in the Marine Corps and a desire for a Regular commission, desire for active military training, and (on the part of 3 officers) temporary lack of employment!

Following Pearl Harbor, the Commandant decreed that the CC–ROC program be expanded to meet the new officer training requirements. Eventually, it was estimated that 3,000 new officers would be needed for fiscal year 1943, nearly 6 times the number needed just 2 years earlier.

Length of classes was cut to 12 weeks and an overlap of classes (called the "block system") was established, so that 3 classes of students would be undergoing instruction at all times. Starting 1 May 1942 with the 6th OCC, a new class began every 4 weeks. The Basic School at Philadelphia was closed and its instructors were transferred to Quantico to help run the ROC under the block system.

Quantico became a boom town. Fifty thousand acres were purchased in fall 1942 in what become known as the Guadalcanal area, and new barracks and 3 classrooms (each with a seating capacity of 200) were hastily constructed. A greatly enlarged military reservation allowed for more realistic field training. In the town proper, new clothing stores and restaurants blossomed on both sides of Potomac Avenue, the formerly sleepy little main street. Such was the crush and population explosion at the Officers' Club that attendance by an ROC class was limited to 1 designated evening per week, from the hours of 1700 to 1900. Only weekend liberty was permitted and the hours were restricted to the period from late Saturday afternoon until Sunday midnight. This privilege was often rescinded for a company whose performance had fallen below par during the week. Attendance in study halls was mandatory every weekday evening and the whole atmosphere was one of dedication to the task at hand. It paid off. Training cycles were completed on schedule, with new officers pouring out to the FMF in increasing numbers.

Before Pearl Harbor, during the Limited Emergency period, the pace for classes in Quantico had been fast and arduous. But, there was still an aura of only near-war. Candidates held their own stage productions in the base theater, and some of the old traditional practices of preemergency days persisted. New officers were seen in their shiny boots and Sam Browne belts. That atmosphere changed drastically on that historic day in December when war arrived. The 4th Candidates Class and 6th Reserve Officers Class felt the impact that set the new pace—a pace that would not slacken until the manpower requirement ended.

By early spring 1942, the ambitious quota of 9,000 college students needed to fill the CC–ROC programs was short by 60 percent. It was decided to open the programs to qualified enlisted men, a practice not without precedent in the Corps. Field promotions were used to obtain necessary numbers of officers during the early part of the war. In 1942, of 4,210 new general duty officers, 1,236 received their commissions in the field. This new source of candidate input provided an excellent new quality of experienced potential officers.

Recipients of field promotions were not required to attend formal schools. Post, station, and organization commanders could conduct schools for newly commissioned members of their commands but were not required to do so. Only 1 such school—located at Camp Elliott—was set up in continental United States. Sometimes called "Green's Farm," this particular school was begun by the 2d Division while stationed at Elliott and was continued as an officer candidates class by the training center after the division's departure. Men were enrolled in the course before becoming officers, and only those who sucessfully completed it were commissioned. These men had the advantage of experience, but they were disadvantaged by briefer formal training than ROC graduates, since their course lasted only 4 weeks.

Although formal classes were stretched out or shortened to adjust to demands for troop officers, lack of basic recruit training for young officers plagued the entire officer training program throughout 1942. As Colonel Emmett W. Skinner noted after an inspection visit to Quantico in October 1942: "Better officers would be obtained if all candidates were required to take . . . recruit training. . . ." This recommendation was eventually adopted.

An Officer Indoctrination Course was also established at Camp Lejeune for men commissioned into the Reserve direct from civilian life. These were men who, because of prior ROTC training or their civilian specialties, were commissioned in ranks of warrant officer through major. As Lieutenant Colonel Lewis M. Nutting, a graduate of the 6th Class, recalls:

> In my class there were some officers who had no military training and some who had been in the military but had dropped out. I had been commissioned an Army 2d Lieutenant from Cornell ROTC in 1932 and had resigned my commission in 1937. I volunteered in the Marine Corps and was commissioned a 1st Lieutenant and sent to OIC from 25 March 1943 to 1 June 1943. There were about 80 officers in my class as I recall.

There were 2 or 3 other classes that followed the 6th class. I was the only officer to be assigned to Fleet Marine Force at Tent Camp, Camp Lejeune; however, as the war progressed, I met some of these Reserve Officers in the Pacific Area and some of them were assigned to the 4th Marine Division. I would imagine that the other divisions, also, got officers from the OIC. At least 500 officers must have come into the Reserves from OIC at Camp Lejeune.

Candidates Shift to Parris Island

As the war progressed, the expansion continued. From the initial training at Philadelphia and at Quantico, it became apparent in 1943 that additional Marine Corps facilities should be put to use for the important training mission. In the summer of 1943, it was decided to transfer all Officer Candidates and all V–12 candidates, on completion of college, to the Recruit Depot at Parris Island. This released a great deal of the badly needed space at Quantico for more specialized officer training.

A 40-week training program was inaugurated in May 1944. This new schedule called for the candidate to spend 8 weeks at a recruit depot, 8 weeks at a pre-OCC course, 12 weeks at OCC, and another 12 weeks in ROC. This looked like the ultimate for officer training, an evolution from the crash programs of a year or two before. The Corps felt that it now had a thoroughly comprehensive program.

But the exigencies of war made this a vain hope. Heavy casualties during the Marianas campaigns that began the following month required a change in such a leisurely training pace. The FMF needed replacements! To meet the increased demand, output of new officers from the schools had to be speeded up. This was done in 2 ways: first, by es-

tablishing a special OCC and ROC at Camp Lejeune; second, by shortening the training cycle in the regular OCC and ROC at Quantico. As a further speed-up in officer production, the pre-OCC requirement for candidates selected from the ranks was modified. Men selected from the ranks would no longer take the 8-week pre-OCC course at Lejeune, but were sent directly to Quantico.

The effect of such acceleration is always costly; necessity often limits the chance of achieving *the best* and forces one to do *the best possible*. This option was expensive. In the early days of the war (1941, 1942, and 1943), attrition in training had hovered around 25 percent. In the 50th OCC which was called up from Parris Island, bypassing Lejeune, attrition jumped to 60 percent. The price of expediency was attrition. But the expedient worked! Four hundred thirty candidates were commissioned on 30 December 1944 at Camp Lejeune, in a special OCC speedily set up to fill the gap. Although in terms of experience the replacements represented a group with the least training of any graduated from Marine Corp officer schools during the war, these men went on—even without further formal training—to distinguish themselves in the field at Iwo Jima and Okinawa. They graduated in the proud tradition, were flown to the Pacific from California embarkation points, and put their classroom training to test in the ultimate laboratory: the battlefield.

Early in 1945, the officer training program was again revamped. The OCC and ROC were abolished. The Platoon Leaders Class was reactivated. Under this program, a single course of 16 weeks, leading to a second lieutenant's commission, was developed. This proved a much more efficient means of training officer candidates and eliminated many of the problems encountered in the more unwieldy 40-week schedule. Trial and error—and the continuously changing conditions of near-war, war, and war's end—had resulted in innovations, modifications, and a myriad of altered standards.

Two Generals Sum Up

The officer training programs had many drawbacks; but, to the lasting credit of the Corps, these programs turned out the bulk of the officers who served so well in the Pacific. Two senior retired officers who have particularly cited the results produced by the training of this era are General Gerald C. Thomas and Brigadier General Wayne H. Adams. General Thomas recalled that the Platoon Leaders Class was a Reserve program that "really paid off." He said:

> We fought World War II with those boys, first as platoon commanders and then as company commanders . . . They helped expand our 2 divisions, making Iceland and Samoa possible.

For his part General Adams remembers both in OCC and ROC classes:

> . . . the individual's drive and keen desire to successfully complete the courses which impressed me . . . I believe that I can truthfully say I have never seen a group more motivated by competitive spirit than were the Officer Candidate Classes. . . .
>
> Statistically, the young Marine officer during 1941–45 was a Reserve, although no one thought to distinguish him from the relatively few Regular young officers. Furthermore, the war in the Pacific for the Marine Corps was a small unit war, whose success depended upon the competence of the company grade officers.

One of the most serious shortcomings of these officer programs stemmed from the policy which permitted a man in the ROC phase of training to resign his commission and return home. This action resulted in more than a few resignations for reasons of disinterest or failure to meet standards. The Marine Corps lost these men, fully trained Marines, who later were usually accepted through Selective Service for other branches. In many cases, these men were immediately commissioned in their new service without further training. Some of the resignees returned home to await draft; in too many instances, they awaited this call in mufti for unduly long periods. Not only was the Marine Corps losing trained men; it was contributing to inequities that could hardly be defended.

Ultimately this problem was corrected. The commissioning of OCC graduates ceased. Upon entry to ROC, the new policy provided that the classes be filled with lieutenants holding "temporary appointments." If, at any time, the attitude or performance of an officer so appointed was found unsatisfactory, he was reduced in rank (usually to that of corporal) and ordered immediately to a duty assignment in the Corps just as those who washed out of the OCC.

With all its shortcomings, the record of officer training for the period from the near-emergency of the early 1940's to V–J Day was highly commendable. The training program, as it actually developed, was a collection of improvisations, each taken in response to a specific problem and consisting, at its most complex, of 4 separate officer courses. Actual performance in the field, however, is the ultimate measure of success for any recruitment, selection, and military training program. For the 16,084 officers graduated from these wartime assembly lines, the record of military effectiveness burned in Pacific deeds spelled out clearly the measure of its worth.

The Navy V-12 Program

Discussion of the officer training program cannot be left without mention of another dynamic aspect of its curriculum. Part of the total mobilization effort is to be found in the V-12 activities under which selected college and high school students were enlisted in the Marine Corps Reserve for eventual assignment to officer training.

From the beginning of the war, the Navy had been devising programs to recruit and train college students for future service as line officers. When the V-12 program was recommended as the plan best suited for this purpose, President Roosevelt gave it his blessing. The President saw it particularly as a "grand chance to save some little colleges" whose existence was threatened by the drain on their student populations at a time of total mobilization of the Nation's youth. Sixteen hundred colleges applied for participation in the program and 131 contracts were awarded. The Navy provided spaces for 11,500 Marines to be included for training. The program was launched 1 July 1943. Maligned and ridiculed at first, it later proved an invaluable source of officer material.

Candidates were selected both on the basis of their standing in the Navy Advisory Educational Council Test and on recommendation of college authorities. The program, from its inception, appealed to the college student. Here was a chance to remain in college until called for active duty: it possibly afforded the opportunity to graduate from school before going into active service. Most officer training programs at that time were limited to college juniors and seniors. Here was one that accepted college freshmen, even high school graduates.

The first classes were formed of students from 800 colleges and 300 secondary schools. A student was normally retained at the college he was attending if that college had a V-12 unit. Others were sent to schools as close to their original alma mater as possible. They were sworn into service as privates in the Marine Corps Reserve and assigned to the Marine detachment at the college. (Enlisted personnel selected for college training followed the traditional policy of reduction in rank so that all candidates would be placed on the same footing.) In most cases, they were allowed to continue with their major studies, although most curricula also included required courses in physics, naval customs, and mechanical drawing. Marine noncommissioned officers, most of them newly returned from Pacific campaigns, handled indoctrination, drill, and physical training. A Marine officer, preferably one with college administrative experience, was assigned as the administrative officer at the college.

The program had its flaws and its successes. The attrition rate in the V-12 program was only 8 percent. Of this attrition, 42 percent was charged to insufficient intellectual ability to cope with the curricula, and 32 percent of the dropout total was attributed to lack of motivation. Critics claimed that V-12 stood for "victory in 12 years or we fight," a barbed reference to the length of time a candidate could spend in college before he even got to boot camp. The age of this group (plus or minus 18) would have precluded earlier commissioning. But, by 1 November 1943, 2,400 men were ready for boot camp! Some 2,000 Marine reservists were readied for action, so many men that the already overcrowded Parris Island could not accommodate them. Many were allowed to remain in school an extra semester to await admission to arms. Some were afforded the opportunity to transfer to the Naval Reserve, but few accepted this option. The Marine in the college atmosphere had been well indoctrinated. His morale was high and he *wanted to be a Marine*.

The V–12 program for the Marine Corps continued until 1 July 1946 and at its height had Marine detachments at 40 different colleges. The majority of junior officers who served at Iwo, Okinawa, and in the occupation of Japan and China after V–J Day were obtained through this program.

Air Cadets

The beginnings of the wartime Marine Corps aviation cadet program go back to April 1935 with passage of Public Law No. 37 by the 74th Congress. Marine aviation continued its own aviation cadet procurement program until July 1942, when it was combined with the Navy. Under this Navy program, the Marines had 3 sources of pilots: Regular Marine infantry officers assigned to flight training; naval aviation cadets who were commissioned second lieutenants in the Marine Corps after flight training; and naval aviation pilots (NAP's), enlisted Marines who had earned their wings.

Training of the Marine pilots paralleled that of the Navy's own airmen through completion of intermediate training. Three months before getting their wings, cadets asked for duty with either Navy or Marine aviation. After 14 to 18 months in advanced flight training at the Naval Air Stations at Pensacola, Fla., or Corpus Christi, Tex., aviators were designated pilots in either the Marine or Naval Reserve.

During operational training at East or West Coast Marine airbases, major emphasis was placed on mastery of the offensive plane type to which the pilot was assigned. After joining a squadron, the flier concentrated on formation flying, night operations, all phases of gunnery, air tactics, instrument training, and carrier landings. This aerial work was thoroughly complemented by previous weeks of rigorous classroom schooling in allied subjects.

The pilot factories were divided between the 2 coasts, with the largest located at Cherry Point. Tactical air training in maneuvers was carried on with infantry units, divebombing, high- and low-level bombing, strafing, intruder tactics, air combat with gun cameras, and antisubmarine patrols. A vital part of pilot indoctrination included night fighting, training of air warning squadrons in group control interception, and ground-to-air fighter direction. As the curricula and numbers of students increased, a network of 11 outlying airfields was established, the training command becoming known as Marine Corps Air Bases, Cherry Point.

Marines established the first operational training squadron at Cherry Point in February 1943. This school for PBJ (B–25) training—one of the few solely under Marine Corps direction—was transferred the following year to Edenton, N.C. During the 2-month course, pilots, aircrewmen, and ground crews received intensive ground and flight instruction before being sent to the combat zones.

Aviation Ground Specialists

To relieve pilots from ground duties and implement its squadrons with civilian specialists, the Corps began its Aviation Volunteer Specialist (AVS) program. Early in 1942, it was recommended that 1,100 nonpilot officers be assigned to air units. Because of the high age bracket of the first AVS class at Quantico—many of them retreads from World War I—the officers dubbed themselves the "Blind Tigers."

The AVS was a select group of highly educated officers, trained at Quantico in the OCS courses, who then took additional specialist schooling. They performed ground duties with aviation units in the fields of administration, communications, engineering, ordnance, intelligence, and similar categories. As Major General Ralph K. Rottet recently recalled:

> . . . almost every one of these Reserve AVS officers that I encountered was truly outstanding. They seemed to be able to do anything regardless of the technical complexity or operational conditions involved. I saw them operating in garrison at Cherry Point, in transit to the West Coast, at Samoa, further on to the Gilbert and Ellice Islands, and finally to the Marshalls. They moved the units, embarked and unloaded the ships, set up the camp, and put the base in operation. They were indispensable to all aviation units.

Sixty-four Reserves completed the 2-month training period in July 1942 and, as did succeeding classes, went directly to tactical units or to specialist schools throughout the country for Intelligence, Aerology, Photography, Photo-Interpretation, Fighter-Direction, Gunnery, Engineering, Radar Training, or Aeronautical Engineering.

By September 1945, there were 1,441 AVS officers on duty in the United States or in the Pacific in every conceivable ground capacity from camp commanders to mess officers. (From a total of 39 aviation ground officers in January 1939, there were 5,000, including the AVS, in aviation at the end of the war.)

Marine Air Infantry Training

Early in 1944, Marine Aviation undertook the first step in resuming its long-standing practice of infantry training for its airmen. Prior to the war, its fliers were invariably pilots who had months and even years of line training before assignment to flight school, on the premise that they were Marines first and pilots afterward. This was in keeping with the Marine air-ground team policy.

After a temporary lull due to wartime pressure, Camp Larkin was established at Cherry Point, where pilots reporting from naval flight schools were given a 2-week infantry indoctrination course. Living as enlisted men, the fliers were given a curriculum which included night patrol actions, 35-mile hikes, judo, demolition, and the use of basic infantry weapons. As its finale, the airmen participated in an amphibious landing under simulated combat conditions.

During the mock exercise, half the trainees set up beach defenses, complete with TNT charges, bangalore torpedoes, machinegun emplacements, and foxholes. The "invading" pilots landed in the surf from small boats and waded ashore behind a smoke screen laid down by other fliers who had completed the course. At Camp Larkin, the aviators learned the value of precision in close air support and, basically, how the other half of the Marine team lived and fought. Originally an interim measure due to a scarcity of training planes, the school was continued at the request of the pilots themselves.

A permanent step toward greater teamwork between aviation and the infantry was the Marine Air-Infantry School at Quantico, Va. Originally called the Aviation Ground Officers School, it was redesignated in February 1945. Its mission was to indoctrinate Marine aviators and ground officers in the conduct of air-amphibious operations and the functions of amphibious infantry, basically air-ground control techniques. Stress was placed on the integrated operation of battalion landing teams and air squadrons.

Many of the first airmen ordered to the school in October 1944 were combat veterans from the Solomons. Succeeding classes in the 16-week course had a high ratio of experienced combat officers. Making like "mud Marines" was not a popular pastime with the birdmen at first, but they found it much less objectionable as they worked to overcome the failings common to precision air-infantry support in the field. Scores of Reserve Marine fliers and ground officers completed the course before the end of the war, with early graduates going directly to combat units and air support operations in the Pacific.

The Backbone: The Enlisted Marine

Regardless of whether a man was USMCR or USMC, the initial "scalping" by Recruit Depot barbers and the taunting "You'll be sorry" cries of already organized recruit platoons soon reduced all newcomers to just plain "boots."

Marine recruits came from every State, from every territory—plus 379 Americans enlisted from foreign countries where they had been living and working.

It seemed that every platoon had a "Texan"; yet, statistically, 5 other States provided the Corps with more Marines than the Lone Star State's contribution

of 33,980. New York sent 63,488 men; Pennsylvania, 55,518; Illinois, 41,539; California, 40,870; and Ohio, 37,371.

The transition of these thousands of raw recruits into Marines is a story unto itself, told and retold in letters home, in newspapers and magazine accounts, and by Marine writers like Jim Lucas in *Combat Correspondent* and the late Gilbert P. Bailey in *Boot*. Words which were to become gospel were crammed down the recruits' throats by an all-powerful demagogue called a drill instructor (D.I.). The floor became a deck; walls became bulkheads; bathrooms were called heads; and the short men who stood at the left-hand end of all platoons and were always left far behind on the interminable marches were called feather merchants. Despite the modern interest in facts and figures, one statistic that will always remain obscure is the number of recruits who slept with their rifles because of the unpardonable sin of calling a rifle "a gun."

Gil Bailey, later to serve with distinction as a Combat Correspondent with the 4th Marine Division and at CINCPAC, wrote:

On a small sandy island just off the coast of South Carolina is a training ground for fighting men. Her streets are named for the valor of her sons who have fought and died in far-off places. Through the gates of this island and down these streets, by the untold thousands, flow men and boys of every class and trade. "Boots" they call them, or just plain "Joe." It is Marine Corps custom to send them all through a grim process called "boot camp." Each man loses most of his hair and much of his identity as he learns how to drill, how to shoot, and above all, how to subordinate himself to the overall purpose of winning the war.

Boot camp is no mere training ground where men are taught the fundamentals of combat. It is the price of membership in a proud fighting fraternity. It has a personality, a mood, and a momentum of its own which mark its graduates. For most of us it is also an indelible memory, driven like a wedge between the past and future.

Key man in the boot camp process is the Drill Instructor, the uncelebrated "D.I." Teacher, taskmaster, and living example; inspector, guardian, guide, and general manager of his platoon, these "noncommissioned colonels" see to it that their boys "get the word" and "the works." But most important of all, although he would never suspect it, is "Joe" himself. From him the U.S. Marines draw the strength to support their fighting tradition.

Basic training at either the East or West Coast recruit depot was rigorous, every-minute-accounted-for 7 weeks, with an initial 3 weeks at the depot, 3 weeks at the range, and a final week at the depot. A reservist was quickly acclimated to fundamentals of military life as well as a thorough physical conditioning to prepare him for the rigors of combat. He became intimately familiar with his rifle, mastering its mechanical functioning and firing it for record on the range. And he received basic instruction in infantry combat subjects, including the digging of foxholes, bayonet, grenades, chemical warfare, map reading, and squad combat principles. When the 7 weeks was over, the recruit wore "greens" or "khakis" for the first time and was probably never so happy to see a new suit of clothes.

Following graduation of his platoon, he, along with 50 to 60 other former farmhands, bank clerks, mechanics, salesmen, students, even ne'er-do-wells, became miraculously transformed into the proud standard bearers of the Marine Corps. The old salts told them that "once a Marine, always a Marine." This saying might just as accurately have been "once a Marine, most likely a reservist!"

Most of the enlisted personnel were Reserves, both those who volunteered and those brought in through Selective Service. Hence enlisted training, as described here, refers heavily (although not exclusively) to the Reserve Marine.

The following highlights, quoted or paraphrased from *U.S. Naval Administration in World War II*, summarize the story more effectively than any backward look might do:

Every recruit or inductee who came into the Marine Corps was given the same course of basic training, regardless of what plans existed for his future employment. In other words, every newcomer was trained first and foremost to be a combat trooper, and any idea of making a specialist of him at a later date was subordinate to that original purpose.

It cannot be too strongly emphasized that from the first days of combat, in the campaign for Guadalcanal, and throughout the rest of the war in the Pacific, the theory behind this practice proved valid. In the Guadalcanal campaign, for example, on 25–26 October 1942, a night attack by the enemy on the left flank of the Matanikau River defenses gained some ground. A counterattack, by a heterogeneous group of Headquarters troops and Weapons Company troops, regained the lost ground. This degree of success could not have been possible without the basic training which the men had undergone.

The 2 recruit depots (San Diego and Parris Island) offered essentially the same training course, although a slight difference in climate caused some difference in the length of time that could be devoted to subjects needing outdoor treatment. At each depot, the recruit lived a hard and secluded life for the period of his training; at each, he was given a thorough course in handling the basic infantry weapons—the rifle, the pistol, and the BAR.

The following statistics give some idea of the number of men trained at each of the 2 depots, as well as the size of the training staff at each:

The total number of Recruit Depot personnel, including Rifle Range officials (D.I.'s, Range Coaches, et cetera), increased at Parris Island from 385 in June 1941 to 1,370 by January 1944; during the corresponding period of time, San Diego showed an increase from 467 to 2,043.

The number of recruits undergoing training, including those on the Rifle Range, rose accordingly:

	1942	1943	1944
Parris Island:			
1 January_____	_____	11, 759	12, 875
1 June_____	8, 199	10, 670	12, 218
1 October_____	11, 966	11, 624	5, 268
San Diego:			
1 January_____	_____	14, 728	14, 086
1 June_____	7, 795	11, 973	17, 882
1 October_____	17, 677	14, 405	11, 083

These statistics give some indication of the tremendous activity involved in the training. A typical month's report reveals the turnover. In a few short weeks thousands had been transformed from civilians into Marines.

San Diego (activity for February 1943)

Number on board, 31 Jan 43_____	12, 595
Arrived_____	6, 191
Transferred_____	5, 983
Discharged_____	282
Deserted_____	3
Total departed_____	6, 268
Net change_____	−77
Number on board, 28 Feb 43_____	12, 518

On 6 February 1943, 1,891 men were transferred out. Of these, 407 went to FMF Training Center, Camp Elliott; 743 to Air Base Group No. 2; 650 to specialized schools and 91 to various posts to duty.

Basic training only was conducted at the Recruit Depots. Graduates were sent to the Fleet Marine Force, aviation, sea duty, and posts and stations. Those who went to the FMF generally were destined for combat service, as were many detailed to aviation.

Sea duty personnel, after further specialized training following release from Recruit Depot, went to various ship details with the Fleet. The size of Marine Detachments serving aboard ships varied in size with the class of the ship. Generally, they were as follows:

BB (Battleship): 78–101 enlisted; 1–3 officers

CV (Fleet Aircraft Carrier): 81 enlisted; 1–3 officers

CVL (Light Fleet Carrier): 43 enlisted; 1–3 officers

CB (Large Cruiser): 83 enlisted; 1–3 officers

CA (Heavy Cruiser): 43 enlisted 1–3 officers

CL (Light Cruiser): 43 enlisted; 1–3 officers

AP (Transport): 31 enlisted; 1–3 officers

Recruits sent to posts and stations were assigned to routine guard or administration duty at Marine Corps and Naval Stations.

Paul Douglas—Marine

Possibly one of the most distinguished "boots" who trained at Parris Island during the early years of the war was Paul H. Douglas, noted economics professor and University of Chicago "Round Table" commentator who was a recruit there in the summer of 1942. Douglas had not sought a commission, saying at the time he wanted to "get quickly into combat duty because losing the war would mean economic slavery or worse." The educator was to become a "victim of his own eloquence," as he put it, because Colonel Harry L. Smith, commandant of the recruit depot, turned the tables on Private Douglas and assigned him to lecturing recruits on the necessity for winning the war. While in boot camp, the 50-year-old Chicagoan won pistol and bayonet medals and was rated by his surprised D.I. as being the "best all-around man in the platoon."

Altogether from Pearl Harbor to V–J Day, the Parris Island and San Diego recruit depots trained approximately 450,-000 new Marines. The course of instruction, 7 weeks at the beginning of hostilities, increased to 8 weeks by the end of the war. In content, an increasingly greater emphasis was placed on weapons instruction, field subjects, and physical conditioning—all subjects which contributed directly to combat readiness. Instruction in garrison-type subjects underwent a comparable decrease. Instructional methods themselves were little changed. As in 1941, the hardworking enlisted drill instructors and rifle range coaches transformed raw and untried American youths into good basic Marines, ready to pass on to the FMF or replacement training centers for intensive combat training.

As Gil Bailey ended his book, he summed up the sweat and the certainty, the guts and the glory:

> Boot camp is a training ground where even the most stupid of clowns are somehow whipped into shape. It is also a clearing house of military talent where raw boots are tested for intelligence, skills, and aptitudes; classified according to military usefulness; then assigned to jobs which fit them. Skill, aptitude, and ambition must be found and developed in special schools. By the time we had reported back from the range we had been classified and assigned to one of the great branches of the Corps.

He went on to say that 36 men of his platoon had been assigned to the FMF and the rest to special training, including aviation 4, radar school 5, motor transport 4, sea school 3, quartermaster school 2, pay school 1, field music 2, photographic school 2, and cooks and bakers school 1. Here in this microcosm was what had happened to 1 platoon of men and boys. Here was the Marine Corps through a microscope, a Marine Corps that was constantly changing just as life does under the microscope. Many of these enlisted Marines would go on to officer rank; many, both those who were commissioned and those who were not, would not return. Many would. For that was the way it was, 24 hours a day, 7 days a week, as the war ground on and as the platoons were formed, broken up re-formed and broken again as the men and boys from Parris Island and San Diego went through the almost constant movement of a machine at war.

Recruitment of Negroes for the Marine Corps began in June 1942. Initially, however, the first volunteers were placed on the Marine Corps Reserve inactive list until such time as the new camp at Montford Point, N.C., was completed. This site, then known as "Mumford" Point, had been selected in April of that year, with special funds allotted for construction and enlargement of the barracks and training camp.

Pvt. Howard Perry, of Charlotte, N.C., was the first wartime Negro recruit. He arrived at Montford Point in August and was assigned to the first special duty platoon that handled operations of the new camp. Drill instructors at Montford were old-time Marines who had campaigned in all parts of the world.

Negro Marines were stationed overseas in the 51st and 52d Defense Battalions, the 1st through 48th Depot Companies, and the 1st through 12th Ammunition Companies.

During the war Negro Marines served in garrison, defense, and combat duties at Guadalcanal, Peleliu, Tinian, Iwo Jima, Saipan, Guam, and the Okinawa campaign. Several Negro companies were awarded the Navy Unit Commendation and one, the Presidential Unit Citation.

The 3d Ammunition Company, attached to the 4th Marine Division, that went ashore at Saipan on D–Day (15 June 1944) was among the Division units awarded the Presidential Unit Citation. Recipients of the Navy Unit Commendation for action in the Iwo Jima campaign were the 33d, 34th, and 36th Depot Companies and the 6th Ammunition Company.

Distinction of being the only Negro Marine unit to reach Japan was the 42d Depot Company, assigned to repair the naval base at Sasebo.

Platoon Sergeant Ezra Kelly, from Mississippi, the first member of the 52nd Defense Battalion to kill a Japanese on Guam, accounted for 6 enemy stragglers during his tour of duty on the island.

The first Negro Marine commissioned was Second Lieutenant Frederick C. Branch. A former member of the 51st Defense Battalion, he graduated from Camp Lejeune officer training in November 1945.

Bulwark of Aviation

The old military truism that an outfit is only as good as its corporals was very much to the point in aviation where the captains and colonels readily admitted that it was the enlisted men who contributed that special mixture of brains and brawn, guts and ingenuity which made Marine aviation possible—and a success. After tough recruit or boot camp training, selected volunteer enlisted men were transferred to air units, where their duties varied from police detail through several dozen categories to aircrew and pilots.

From a roster of 5,788 men in January 1941, the peak was reached 4 years later when 109,321 enlisted Marines were on duty. Approximately one-third of them were trained as aviation specialists in Navy or Marine schools. Another third were given apprenticeship schooling. The rest made their stripes on routine Marine duties.

Overseas, the enlisted men were among the first ashore and invariably the last out of the combat areas, sweating out one island-hopping campaign after another to keep up with the flight echelons from atoll to island or aboard carriers. As one officer recalled, "Their combat performance was nothing short of outstanding whether under fire, garrisoning the atolls, or gouging some semblance of civilization into an island that hardly deserved it."

Infantry Marines often griped that air duty was a "soft touch" until they had some of it. Then they knew why rear gunners and ground crewmen were an indispensable link of the unique Marine air-ground team.

Enlisted Specialist Schools

Traditionally the Marine Corps has been a fighting service and has deliberately sought to put the greatest possible number of men on the firing line and to hold supporting functions to a minimum. Wartime expansion of the Marine Corps demanded a sharp increase in the specialist—both in terms of personnel to man critical billets and the number of new military skills which had to be learned to successfully fight—*and win*—a modern war.

At the outbreak of the war, the Marine Corps continued to use, as it had before Pearl Harbor, both Army and Navy institutions, civilian schools, and its own training schools. Navy courses (primarily at advanced level) included ordnance, communications, parachute, and other aerological subjects. The Army enrolled Marines in courses (both basic and advanced) dealing with chemical warfare, engineer, motor transport, ordnance, communications, and tanks. The civilian schools (also basic and advanced) included training in engineer, motor transport, ordnance, photography, communications, and landing boat tactics.

Throughout the war, the Marine Corps employed an increasing number of Navy courses and also greatly expanded its own specialty training centers. The Quantico Training Center—organized in October 1940 to train reservists called to active duty—soon proved inadequate; and early in 1942, an additional training center was set up at Camp Lejeune. Originally conceived of as a replacement and unit training organization, this was soon expanded to include specialty schools such as the Parachute, Engineer, and Motor Transport (the latter two transferred from Quantico). Also transferred from Quantico to the New River Training Center in 1942, were the Signal School with its component radio, field telephone, and radar courses; the Cooks and Bakers School; Quartermaster; and Administration. On the West Coast, a new FMF Training Center was organized at Camp Elliott in April 1942 for specialist and infantry replacements, but was soon moved to the newly activated Camp Pendleton. By the spring of 1942, formal school facilities had been expanded to include courses in barrage balloon, parachute, chemical warfare,

landing boats, and the Japanese language.

The high proportion of men receiving specialist training can be seen, in part, from the following: of the 5,584 ROC graduates assigned during 1943 to ground duty, 2,478 (or 44 percent) were ordered directly to formal specialist schools before taking up their duty assignments. Many others attended one of the approximately 75 courses available after service in the field.

Similarly, some idea of the extent of the advanced training program may be drawn from the following table showing the number of Marines assigned from recruit training at Parris Island to specialty schools:

Assignment of Recruits Completing Training at Parris Island

	May 1942	May 1943	October 1943	November 1943
Total to ground duty	2,652	3,060	3,015	3,343
Number to formal schools	958	1,428	1,424	1,933
Percentage to formal schools	37	41	47	58

During the war the expansion of Marine Corps schools resulted in a sharp reduction of non-Marine training facilities. By 1945, 72 percent of all specialist training was given in Marine schools. (The remainder were: Navy, 11 percent; civilian, 10 percent; and Army, 7 percent.) In general, the Navy and Army schools were used more extensively for the advanced level training given to officers returning from service in the field.

Again drawing from *U.S. Naval Administration*, about specialist training: combat troops were assigned to infantry training, which was carried on at Camp Elliott, San Diego (organized 14 December 1934), and at Camp Lejeune (1 May 1941). Camp Pendleton (15 October 1942) gradually took over the functions originally performed by Camp Elliott; and the latter, except for the Base Depot and tank training activity, passed to Navy control and use on 30 June 1944. Within the limits of training for combat duty, various special types of training were conducted: Communications Schools, Intelligence Schools, and various courses of study for those who required training in special skills. Motor transport, cooks and bakers, and quartermaster personnel were given special instruction in courses lasting from 1 week to several months.

In some cases, notably in communications, the school was conducted by the Marine Corps and staffed by Marine Corps personnel. As the Marine Corps grew in size and complexity, and as the communications equipment used by the Corps became more highly specialized, it became essential to equip the personnel involved with special skills. In order to accomplish this within a minimum of time, the Marine Corps arranged to have its men trained at various schools or to have special classes conducted by the Army, the Navy, and outside agencies—regularly established schools and colleges as well as, in some cases, the companies engaged in the production of the equipment in question. As early as 12 April 1942, the Commandant (through Letter of Instruction 121) listed 50 schools offering 67 specialized courses of instruction available to Marine Corps personnel.

Men who were detailed to duty with a combat unit—an infantry regiment, for example—were transferred to that regiment upon completion of the recruit training. Immediately upon reporting, these men were assigned to a battalion and later to a company. Thereafter, the training they received was that given to all men of the unit to which they were attached, regardless of length of time in the Marine Corps. Movement thereafter depended entirely upon the needs of the Corps, although a constant effort was made to satisfy any reasonable request on the part of individual Marines for special types of duty.

Indeed, during World War II, the Marine Corps revised its previous infantry training system and began to replace combat losses on an individual basis, rather than by unit. Instruction of infantry replacements was by far the biggest operation confronting the Camp Lejeune and Camp Pendleton training centers. Realism in training was the keynote, and the program was constantly modified to fit new battle needs. By early 1944 curriculum changes reflected the shift in combat operations from the south to central Pacific area. Jungle warfare was dropped, to be replaced by a course in bunker problems, to emphasize the specialized tactics developed by Marines to successfully assault heavily fortified islands in the central Pacific.

Women Marines in World War II

After a lapse of nearly 25 years and because of increasing problems and pressures of manpower shortages, women were again called upon to serve their country as U.S. Marines.

Addition of the Women's Reserve to the Corps—in February 1943—produced 2 great waves of seismic shock: one to the men of this ruggedly masculine outfit; the other, to the women who joined it. With a dedication and thoroughness that con-founded many an old salt, however, they quickly learned their way around the Marine Corps. As Commandant Thomas Holcomb observed less than a year after the women had come aboard:

> . . . they're real *Marines*. They don't have a nickname, and they don't need one. They get their basic training in a Marine atmosphere, at a Marine post. They inherit the traditions of the Marines. They *are* Marines.

It was no secret that the general had originally been opposed to the idea of women in the Corps. Congress had given the necessary authority the previous July. The WAACS (later WACS) and WAVES had been formed months before; the SPARS were nearly under way. But progress of the war and a critical need for more men on the Pacific battle lines indicated that additional manpower—or, as it was decided, *woman*power—would have to be secured. Moreover, a preliminary survey of Marine posts and stations in the fall of 1942 showed that more than 4,000 women were needed *at once* so that male Marines could be transferred to combat duty. Approval by the Commandant of a Women's Reserve on 7 November 1942 was the first step toward what later was to become a force of approximately 1,000 officers and 18,000 women.

Success of the new Women's Reserve, the Commandant felt, would depend largely on the caliber and capabilities of the woman chosen to head it. Various outstanding women leaders were considered and interviewed personally by the Director of Reserve, Colonel Waller, and his assistant Major Carroll B. Rhoads. Ultimately, Mrs. Ruth Cheney Streeter of Morristown, New Jersey, was selected. She had been President of her class at Bryn Mawr Col-lege. She was the mother of 4 grown children, including 3 service sons (2 in the Navy, 1 in the Army) and for more than 20 years had been an active leader in New Jersey health and welfare work. A high-spirited woman who only a year or so earlier had taken out both her private and commercial pilot's licenses, Mrs. Streeter had just the right combination of personal characteristics and organizational abilities that would be required of a Woman Marine Director. General Holcomb, the former doubting Thomas, and his staff had complete confidence in her from the start.

Prior to public announcement of the new program, Mrs. Streeter was quietly commissioned a Major, USMCWR, on 29 January 1943. She went on duty in Washington immediately to help map out early decisions and get the new organization started. Seven other women whose abilities and civilian experience fitted them for priority Marine Corps billets which needed to be filled at once (recruiting, training, uniforming, classification, public relations, West Coast representative, and assistant to the Director) were also "direct-commissioned." They likewise went on duty without formal indoctrination, with their new rank and in civilian clothes.

Official announcement of the Marine Corps Women's Reserve was made 13 February 1943, and procurement offices throughout the country found themselves suddenly swamped with women who wanted to be Women Marines. In the Nation's Capital, more than 100 filed applications the first 2 days after enlistments opened. Prospective candidates ranged all the way from widows of 2 Marine majors recently killed in combat, to school-girls, officeworkers, grandmothers, and college students who wanted to do something more patriotic than go to school.

Women Train at Navy Facilities

From the beginning, the Navy was more than generous to its new sister service. In addition to helping with enlistments, the Navy offered use of its own training schools (Hunter College for recruits; Mount Holyoke College for officer candidates) during those early months. The first class of 75 officer candidates began its training on 13 March 1943 and was commissioned 4 May. On 26 March, the first class of enlisted Women Reserves—numbering 722—entered Hunter, and graduated the following month. The 2 groups continued to train with the WAVES until July. Then both the officer candidates and enlisted schools were transferred to a new training complex (just completed at Camp Lejeune, New River, N.C.) that also included Women's Reserve specialists' schools. Together they comprised the Marine Corps Women's Reserve Schools where distinguished visitors, such as Madame Chiang Kai-shek, on occasion "inspected the troops."

Basic Marine Corps indoctrination for officers and recruits was similar.

Both studied—with an intensity they wouldn't have believed possible—Marine Corps Administration, Regulations, Organization, and History; Naval Justice; Military Customs; Interior Guard; Map Reading; Defense Against Chemical Attack; Drill and Physical Conditioning. The entire training program was drawn up with the prime objective of converting civilians into responsible military personnel *in the shortest time possible*. Close-order drill proved to be the most effective single training factor. Through this, the

Women Marines—as had generations of male Marines before them—learned the value of teamwork, military precision, instantaneous response to command, discipline, and order. Moreover, they learned a pride in outfit, a new pride in self, and the intangibles of the famed Marine *esprit*.

Highlight of all women reservists' training, were the field demonstrations—tactical use of all kinds of weapons, landing craft, even the war dogs. "By showing the women what the men faced when they were released for combat, their pride in the Corps was increased and they saw clearly their own part in it," Director Streeter observed. No other women's military service had such real-life battle demonstrations. Understandably, their members were somewhat envious of this aspect of the Women Reserves' training!

Although the Women's Reserve had received the "official frown" from high Marine Corps brass in the beginning, once the decision was made both men and women worked to make sure all turned out well. Two things were in the ladies' favor from the start. First, that the Marines freely shared their own name, a proud name that had witnessed 168 years of tradition, service, and fierce loyalty. Thus, they became the only women's branch of service that didn't have an alphabetical designation or quasi-official nickname. The Women's Reserve was accepted as a full-fledged part of the Marine Corps and was not an "auxiliary" service. Second, that the men's distinctive uniform was followed so closely, with requisite feminine modifications, for the Women Marines. As Colonel Waller, Director of Reserve, expressed it at the time, the men wanted the women to be attired in the traditional forest green of

the Marine Corps, the design being
"sufficiently like the Marine Corps uniform to permit no possibility of doubt as
to the branch of service to which the
Women Reservists are attached."

The winter service uniform consisted of
forest green skirt and blouse, with khaki
shirt and tie, visored cap, and identical
insignia and buttons, even down to the
pointed overlay cuff detail of the male
Marines' uniform. Summer service was
a 2-piece seersucker suit and buttoned
over-blouse designed for comfort and
efficiency; and the summer dress uniform,
a 2-piece sparkling white cotton with
gold insignia, white pumps and gloves,
and spruce green visored cap and pocket-
book easily won hands-down honors from
both Marines and non-Marines as the most
attractive and feminine uniform of *any*
women's service!

Free a Marine to Fight

Recruiting slogan for this last-orga-
nized of the wartime women's services was
"Free a Marine to Fight." How well the
women reservists lived up to this motto
was expressed by the late President
Roosevelt on the first anniversary of the
Marine Corps Women's Reserve, 13 February 1944:

> The Nation is as proud of you as of your
> fellow Marines . . . you have quickly and
> efficiently taken over scores of different
> kinds of duties that not long ago were con-
> sidered strictly masculine assignments; and
> in doing so, you have freed a large number
> of well-trained, battle-ready men of the
> Corps for action . . .

Exactly how many men were so freed
was always a subject for speculation.
The peak strength of the Women's Reserve, slightly less than 19,000, approximated the strength of a Marine Corps

division. The women always treasured
the statement made by General Alexander
A. Vandegrift, the second wartime Commandant, who once remarked they could

> . . . feel responsible for putting the 6th
> Marine Division in the field; for without the
> women filling jobs throughout the Marine
> Corps there would not have been sufficient
> men available to form that division.

In February 1944—just 1 short year
after formation—Women Reserves were
found on every Marine post and station in
the continental United States, plus all recruiting districts. The original prediction of "more than 30 kinds of jobs" had
grown into over 200 assignments. In
addition to the clerical jobs which released
male Marines for battle, the Women Reserves had been trained in specialist fields
such as communications, quartermaster,
post exchange, motor transport, food services, and aviation skills ranging from parachute rigger to control tower operator.

By 1 June 1944, the Women's Reserve
had scored another "mission accomplished." It had reached its recruiting
goal and had enrolled its full strength of
18,000 enlisted women and 1,000 officers.
And 18 months after formation of the Reserve, Women Reserves constituted 85 percent of the enlisted personnel at Headquarters Marine Corps and from one-half
to two-thirds of the permanent personnel
at all large Marine Corps posts and stations in the continental United States.

In September 1944, modification of Department of Navy regulations for the first
time permitted female Naval personnel
(Marines, WAVES, SPARS) to "serve
on a volunteer basis anywhere within the
Western Hemisphere, including Alaska
and Hawaii."

A factfinding trip to the Islands was
made by Colonel Streeter the next month.

It was decided to authorize 2 detachments of Women Marines, one at Pearl Harbor attached to the Marine Garrison Forces, and a smaller unit at the Marine Air Station at Ewa. In December, an advance party of 4 officers flew to Hawaii to make preliminary arrangements; a second advance party, for the aviation units, followed shortly thereafter. In January the first volunteers for the 2-year overseas duty were transferred to a staging area at San Diego, Calif., to undergo intensive physical conditioning and orientation. On 25 January the first contingent of 160 enlisted and 5 Women Reserve officers sailed from San Francisco aboard the S.S. *Matsonia*. Dressed in winter greens and trench coats and carrying blanket rolls, the women marched up the gangplank and aboard ship in column formation and proceeded to assigned quarters.

Upon their arrival in Hawaii 3 days later, there as in the States, the Women Marines replaced men not only in office jobs but in specialized fields as well. Approximately 1,000 women saw duty in Hawaii and nearly all agreed that overseas duty made them feel they were taking a more active part in winning the war. Surrender of the Japanese on 14 August 1945 brought their expected 2-year duty stint to an abrupt halt. The first group of women left Hawaii early in December 1945, in time to make words of the then-popular lyric "I'll Be Home for Christmas" really ring true, and the rest returned Stateside the following month.

With the ending of hostilities, demobilization plans moved ahead rapidly and efficiently under an "Adjusted Service Rating System" of points similar to that for the men. Credits for demobilization of the women were based on their length of service. At the end of the war, there were approximately 17,640 women and 820 officers on duty, or a total strength of 18,460. There were 28 units headed by women commanding officers, plus 17 smaller units; and additional women were assigned to specialist duties, such as recruiting.

The Women's Reserve was reduced to two-thirds of its peak strength by 7 December 1945. On that date its original Director, Colonel Streeter (twice promoted: to lieutenant colonel in November 1943, and to colonel in February 1944) resigned to be home for her 3 sons, all returning from overseas duty. She was succeeded by Colonel Katherine A. Towle, who assumed the Directorship on the fourth anniversary of Pearl Harbor. Terminal date for the demobilization of all women and Women's Reserve units was originally set at 1 September 1946, allowing for an equitable release of the women and an orderly administrative process for the service.

In the early months of 1946, when total demobilization was imminent, the Marine Corps realized the desirability of planning for a small nucleus of trained personnel in a postwar Women's Reserve, so that in event of a future emergency it would never again be necessary to "start from scratch." Following recommendations made by a special policy board convened by the Commandant, a handful of Women Reserves remained on duty at Marine Corps Headquarters to work out plans for such a postwar Reserve.

Thus, in 3 short years a new chapter was added to the Corps' history by the Women's Reserve. It had been amply proved that Marine Corps pride and loyalty—not to mention sheer dedication to the job at hand—could be as well-upheld by the gentler sex as by the heroes of Belleau Wood, Guadalcanal, and Tarawa.

Fleet Marine Force

During the early phases of World War II, the Fleet Marine Force, despite its imposing name, was little more than a vague entity consisting of Marine Corps ground units in combat areas or those in the United States scheduled for movement overseas to the combat zone. This paradoxical situation was understandable during the early war period when the Fleet Marine Force, beyond the continental limits of the United States, included 1 brigade in Iceland, another in Samoa, scattered defense battalions, and certain service troops in the Hawaiian area. Administration could best be handled under these circumstances by Headquarters Marine Corps in Washington.

By 1944, Fleet Marine Force units consisted of 4 divisions, a brigade which lacked only a regimental combat team of being another division, corps troops, and a constantly growing supply service. In the United States, the 5th Marine Division was under training and being equipped for overseas operations. The stage was thus set for the establishment of Headquarters, Fleet Marine Forces, Pacific Ocean Areas, under command of Lieutenant General Holland M. Smith. Fleet Marine Force, Pacific, would include the Administrative Command, Fleet Marine Forces, Pacific; the III Amphibious Corps; and the V Amphibious Corps. The final step came on 17 September 1944 with removal of the word "provisional" from the previously official title, Provisional Headquarters, Fleet Marine Force, Pacific.

Nimitz Salutes Marines

The 169th Marine Anniversary on 10 November 1944 brought these words from the late Fleet Admiral Chester W. Nimitz, USN, Commander in Chief of the U.S. Pacific Fleet and Pacific Ocean Areas, as he traced the Corps' buildup and battle prowess during the previous 3 years:

> The 1st Marine Division started the offensive, and it is still at it. After Guadalcanal came Cape Gloucester and most recently, Peleliu. The 2d Marine Division was at Guadalcanal, won lasting fame at Tarawa . . . and at Saipan and Tinian. The 3d Division won the beachhead and air field on Bougainville, and later it seized the Guam beachhead. The 4th Division scored a one-two punch on Roi and Namur in the Marshalls to win a 26-hour battle. It then smashed and bulled its way across Saipan and Tinian. I am happy that the President this week honored this division with the coveted Unit Citation for its action at Saipan and Tinian. The 6th Division, made up of veteran Raiders and the Eniwetok invaders, fought through Guam with the 3d Division.
>
> With these Marine Divisions go the veteran 1st, 2d, and 4th Air Wings. We know them well, the 1st Wing in the Solomons, the 2d Wing in the Solomons and at Palau, and the 4th in the Marshalls and Marianas.
>
> Under the Commandant, Lieutenant General A. A. Vandegrift and under Lieutenant General Holland M. Smith, commanding the Fleet Marine Force, the Marines in the Pacific have reached the ultimate in amphibious warfare. . . .

And, at war's end, the Corps stood at its maximum strength of 485,000, with 6 divisions and 5 wings. Reservists had constituted between 68–70 percent of its total numbers.

Perhaps the Citation presented by the President of the United States to the assault troops of the V Amphibious Corps,

Reinforced, Fleet Marine Force, which took Iwo Jima, can be considered as reflecting the tactical efficiency of the Fleet Marine Force, as well as the extraordinary heroism of the individual Marines who formed the Fleet Marine Force, Pacific.

Citation:

For extraordinary heroism in action during the seizure of enemy Japanese-held Iwo Jima, Volcano Islands, 18–28 February 1945. Landing against resistance which rapidly increased in fury as the Japanese pounded the beaches with artillery, rocket, and mortar fire, the Assault Troops of the 5th Amphibious Corps inched ahead through shifting black volcanic sands, over heavily mined terrain, toward a garrison of jagged cliffs barricaded by an interlocking system of caves, pillboxes, and blockhouses commanding all approaches. Often driven back with terrific losses in fierce hand-to-hand combat, the Assault Troops repeatedly hurled back the enemy's counterattacks to regain and hold lost positions, and continued the unrelenting drive to high ground and Motoyama Airfield No. 1, captured by the end of the second day. By their individual acts of heroism and their unfailing teamwork, these gallant officers and men fought against their own battle fatigue and shock to advance in the face of the enemy's fanatical resistance; they charged each strongpoint, one by one, blasting out the hidden Japanese troops or sealing them in; within 4 days they had occupied the southern part of Motoyama Airfield No. 2; simultaneously they stormed the steep slopes of Mount Suribachi to raise the U.S. Flag; and they seized the strongly defended hills to silence guns commanding the beaches and insure the conquest of Iwo Jima, a vital inner defense of the Japanese Empire.

Campaigns

The story of the various battles of the Marine Corps has been told and retold, and since operational narratives of Marine exploits in World War II have been fully documented in many other books, a duplication will not be attempted in this history. A total of 15 units, beginning with the Wake Island garrison, received the Presidential Unit Citation and 78 air squadrons were similarly cited during the 5 years of the war. It is upon the supreme sacrifice paid by Marines since 1775, however, that the true glory of the Corps rests. Listed below are the major campaigns of World War II in which 19,733 Marines made this supreme sacrifice:

MARINE CAMPAIGNS OF WORLD WAR II

Pearl Harbor–Midway	7Dec41
Guam	8–10Dec41
Wake Island	8–23Dec41
Bataan and Corregidor (Philippines)	8Dec41–6May42
Battle of Badoeng Strait (East Indies)	19Feb42
Battle of the Coral Sea	4–8May42
Battle of Midway	3–6Jun42
Guadalcanal-Tulagi Landings	7–9Aug42
First Savo Battle (Naval-air)	9Aug42
Capture and Defense of Guadalcanal	10Aug42–8Feb43
Makin Island Raid (Gilberts)	17–18Aug42
Battle of the Eastern Solomons	23–25Aug42
Battle of Cape Esperance (Naval)	11–12Oct42
Battle of Santa Cruz Island (Air)	26Oct42
Battle of Guadalcanal (Naval-air)	11–15Nov42

MARINE CAMPAIGNS OF WORLD WAR II—Continued

Battle of Tassafaronga (Naval)	30Nov–1Dec42
Battle of Komandorski Island (Aleutians)	26Mar43
New Georgia-Rendova-Vandunu Occupation	20Jun–31Aug43
Vella Lavella Occupation	15Aug–16Oct43
Cape Gloucester (New Britain) Operation	26Dec43–1Mar44
Green Islands Landing	15–19Feb44
Treasury Island Landing	27Oct–6Nov43
Choiseul Island Diversion	28Oct–4Nov43
Occupation and Defense of Cape Torokina	1Nov–15Dec43
Tarawa Operations (Gilbert Islands)	20Nov–8Dec43
Occupation of Kwajalein and Majuro Atolls (Marshall Islands)	31Jan–8Feb44
Occupation of Eniwetok Atoll (Marshall Islands)	17Feb–2Mar44
Capture and Occupation of Saipan	15Jun–10Aug44
Capture and Occupation of Guam	21Jul–15Aug44
Capture and Occupation of Tinian	24Jul–10Aug44
Capture and Occupation of Peleliu	15Sep–14Oct44
Leyte Landings (Philippines)	20Oct44
Iwo Jima Operation	19Feb–16Mar45
Assault and Occupation of Okinawa Gunto	1Apr–21Jun45

These figures of the Asiatic-Pacific Area do not include all the engagements which are considered official operations or those of the other areas. In addition to those killed in action, there were also 67,207 Marines wounded in action, or approximately 16 percent of the total 426,801 Marines who served overseas during World War II. To these battle casualties must be added the 3,829 Marines who died of disease or other causes, often directly or indirectly attributable to the battlefield. Marine Corps casualties thus totaled more than 20 percent of its entire forces which served overseas during World War II.

Medal of Honor Winners

The Citation usually begins: "For conspicuous gallantry and intrepidity at the risk of his life above and beyond the call of duty. . . ." The recipient of the Citation becomes a member of one of the most exclusive and honored groups in the World—a holder of the Medal of Honor.

During World War II, 79 Marines were awarded the Medal of Honor; of these, 44 were Marine Corps reservists. (Eleven of the 79 were from Marine Air. Of these 11, 6 were Reserves.)

In the following listing of these 44 reservists, asterisks mark the names of 25 who paid the supreme sacrifice. Their citations conclude with the simple and poignant line: "He gallantly gave his life in the service of his country."

Bonnyman, Alexander, Jr., 1st Lieutenant*

Boyington, Gregory, Major (Air)

Caddy, William Robert, Private First Class*

Chambers, Justice Marion, Colonel

Cole, Darrell Samuel, Sergeant*

Courtney, Henry Alexius, Jr., Major*

DeBlanc, Jefferson Joseph, Captain (Air)

Dunlap, Robert Hugo, Captain

Dyess, Aquilla James, Lieutenant Colonel*

Epperson, Harold Glenn, Private First Class*

Fleming, Richard E., Captain (Air)*

Foss, Joseph Jacob, Captain (Air)

Foster, William Adelbert, Private First Class*

Gonsalves, Harold, Private First Class*

Gray, Ross Franklin, Sergeant

Hanson, Robert Murry, 1st Lieutenant (Air)

Hauge, Louis James, Jr., Corporal*

Jacobson, Douglas Thomas, Private First Class

Julian, Joseph Rudolph, Platoon Sergeant*

Kinser, Elbert Luther, Sergeant*

Kraus, Richard Edward, Private First Class*

LeBelle, James Dennis, Private First Class*

Leims, John Harold, 2d Lieutenant

Lucas, Jacklyn Harrell, Private First Class

Lummus, Jack, 1st Lieutenant*

Martin, Harry Linn, 1st Lieutenant*

McCarthy, Joseph Jeremiah, Captain

Phelps, Wesley, Private*

Phillips, George, Private*

Power, John Vincent, 1st Lieutenant*

Roan, Charles Howard, Private First Class*

Rouh, Carlton Robert, 1st Lieutenant

Ruhl, Donald Jack, Private First Class*

Schwab, Albert Earnest, Private First Class

Sigler, Franklin Earl, Private

Sorenson, Richard Keith, Private

Stein, Tony, Corporal

Swett, James Elms, 1st Lieutenant (Air)

Thomas, Herbert Joseph, Sergeant*

Thomason, Clyde, Sergeant*

Walsh, William Gary, Gunnery Sergeant*

Watson, Wilson Douglas, Private

Williams, Hershel Woodrow, Corporal

Witek, Frank Peter, Private First Class*

First Marine reservist to be awarded the Medal of Honor in World War II was an aviator, Captain Richard E. Fleming, of St. Paul, Minn., who had enlisted in the Reserve in 1939. Fleming also had a bent for journalism, as evidenced by a continuous outpouring of articles about aviation that appeared under his byline in the *Marine Corps Gazette* during the early 1940's. He distinguished himself for many flights made from Hawaii to Midway during the first days of the war. Ten days after outbreak of hostilities, for example, he participated in a flight from Oahu, Hawaii, to Midway, a distance of 1,137 nautical miles overwater with no surface vessels assigned as plane guards. Captain Fleming was officially listed as missing in action on 5 June 1942 when he and his radio gunner failed to return to base from an attack mission against 2 enemy battleships some 140 miles off Midway. Officially declared dead the following day, he was posthumously awarded the Medal of Honor. His citation reads in part:

> . . . as Flight Officer, Marine Scout-Bombing Squadron 241, during action against enemy Japanese forces in the battle of Midway on 4 and 5 June 1942. When his Squadron Commander was shot down . . . Captain Fleming led the remainder of the division with such fearless determination that he dived his own plane to the perilously low altitude of 400 feet before releasing his bomb. . . .

The first Marine reservist in ground warfare to receive the Medal of Honor was Sergeant Clyde Thomason, 28, of Atlanta, Ga., who was killed in action during the raids at Makin Island in the Gilberts. His commendation for action during the Marine Raider Expedition on 17–18 August 1942 reads:

Leading the advance element of the assault echelon, Sergeant Thomason disposed his men with keen judgment and discrimination . . . On one occasion, he dauntlessly walked up to a house which concealed an enemy Japanese sniper, forced in the door, and shot the man before he could resist. Later in the action, while leading an assault on an enemy position, he gallantly gave his life in the service of his country.

The deeds and citations of other reservists who received the Nation's highest award include the following:

At Tarawa (20–22 Nov 43): 1st Lieutenant Alexander Bonnyman, Jr., USMCR

As Executive Officer of the 2d Battalion Shore Party, 8th Marines, 2d Marine Division during the assault against the Jap-held Tarawa, Lieutenant Bonnyman repeatedly defied the blasting fury of enemy shore batteries, organized his pioneer shore party, then directed the blowing up of several hostile installations. The following day he stormed against a large, heavily-garrisoned, bombproof Japanese emplacement, flushing out more than 100 of the enemy. Assailed by more enemy soldiers after he had gained his objective, he defended his strategic position, until he fell.

> . . . By his dauntless fighting spirit, unrelenting aggressiveness and forceful leadership throughout three days of unremitting, violent battle. First Lieutenant Bonnyman had inspired his men to heroic effort, enabling them to beat off the counterattack and break . . . the hostile resistance. . . .

At Bougainville (7 Nov 43): Sergeant Herbert J. Thomas, USMCR

This Marine was leading his squad through dense jungle undergrowth in face of severe hostile machinegun fire. Sergeant Thomas and his group pressed forward to the center of the Japanese position and destroyed the crews of 2 machine-guns by accurate rifle fire and grenades. Discovering a third gun more difficult to approach, Thomas

> . . . carefully placed his men closely around him in strategic positions from which they were to charge after he had thrown a grenade into the emplacement. When the grenade struck vines and fell back into the midst of the group, Sergeant Thomas deliberately flung himself upon it to smother the explosion. . . .

At Guam (3 Aug 44): Private First Class Frank P. Witek, USMCR

> . . . During his platoon's withdrawal for consolidation of lines, he remained to safeguard a severely wounded comrade, courageously returning the enemy's fire until arrival of stretcher bearers, and then covering the evacuation by sustained fire as he moved backward toward his own lines. With his platoon again pinned down by a hostile machinegun, Private First Class Witek, on his own initiative, moved forward . . . to the reinforcing tanks and infantry, alternately throwing hand grenades and firing as he advanced . . . destroying the hostile machine-gun emplacement and an additional eight Japanese before he himself was struck down by an enemy rifleman.

At Iwo Jima (24 Feb–6 Mar 45): Corporal Hershel W. Williams, USMCR

> [was] quick to volunteer his services when our tanks were maneuvering vainly to open a lane for the infantry through the network of reinforced concrete pillboxes and buried mines. . . . [he] daringly went forward alone to attempt the reduction of devastating machinegun fire . . . fought desperately for 4 hours under terrific enemy small-arms fire and repeatedly returned to his own lines to prepare demolition charges . . . to wipe out one position after another. On one occasion, he daringly mounted a pillbox to insert the nozzle of his flame-thrower through the air vent, killing the occupants and silencing the gun . . . on another he grimly charged enemy riflemen who attempted to stop him with bayonets and destroyed them with a burst of flame from his weapon.

At Iwo Jima (9 Mar 45): Platoon Sergeant Joseph R. Julian, USMCR

> . . . acting upon his own initiative, fearlessly moved forward to execute a one-man assault on the nearest pillbox . . . killing two of the enemy and driving the remaining five out into the adjoining trench system . . . jumped into the trench and dispatched the five . . . obtained more explosives . . . again charged the hostile fortifications and knocked out two more cave positions. Immediately thereafter . . . launched a bazooka attack unassisted, firing four rounds into the one remaining pillbox . . . completely destroying it before he fell, mortally wounded. . . .

At Okinawa (14 Mar 45): Corporal Louis J. Hauge, Jr., USMCR

> . . . boldly took the initiative when his company's left flank was pinned down under heavy machinegun and mortar barrage with resultant severe casualties . . . quickly locating the two machineguns . . . ordered his squad to maintain a covering barrage as he rushed across an exposed area toward the furiously blazing enemy weapons. Although painfully wounded as he charged the first machinegun, he launched a vigorous single-handed grenade attack, destroyed the entire hostile gun position and moved relentlessly forward toward the other emplacement . . . again hurled his deadly grenades with unerring aim and succeeded in demolishing the second enemy gun before he fell under Japanese sniper fire. . . .

The battle for Iwo Jima, where AP photographer Joe Rosenthal took what is considered the most inspiring picture of the war (later used to keynote the Treasury Department's 7th War Loan), raged nearly a month from D-Day 19 February to 16 March 1945. One of the most savage engagements of the war, it resulted in a total of 5,563 Marines dead and 17,343 wounded. It produced, incidentally, more Medal of Honor awards to Marine reservists than any other single action of the war: a total of 20.

One of these men so honored was Colonel Justice M. Chambers who, as a major, had been attending summer camp when Washington's 5th Battalion had been called up in late 1940. Chambers received the Silver Star Medal at Tulagi for evacuating the wounded and directing night defenses of a battalion aid station where he was himself a patient, already seriously wounded. He later commanded the 3rd Battalion, 25th Marines, in the Roi-Namur campaign. Once again he was wounded at Saipan when he suffered blast concussion, but returned to lead his command there as well as on Tinian. At Iwo Jima, on D-Day, Lieutenant Colonel Chambers commanded the 3d Battalion, 25th Marine Regiment. His battalion secured a strategic high ground emplacement from which heavy enemy fire was razing the entire landing beach operation. The 3d Battalion lost more than half its officers and nearly one-half its enlisted strength in the encounter.

His citation reads in part:

> Constantly in the frontline encouraging his men to push forward against the enemy's savage resistance, Colonel Chambers led the 8-hour battle to carry the flanking ridge top and reduce the enemy's fields of aimed fire, thus protecting the vital foothold gained . . . His zealous fighting spirit undiminished despite terrific casualties and the loss of most of his key officers, he again reorganized his troops for renewed attack against the enemy's main line of resistance and was directing the fire of the rocket platoon when he fell, critically wounded. . . .

Actual presentation of a Medal of Honor—even if not posthumously to the next of kin—is usually an occasion marked by considerable formality. An exception to the rule occurred in 1950 when the colonel was so honored. (He had been cited for a Medal of Honor, received a Navy

Cross instead, and later, on review, was authorized the award originally recommended.) This particular ceremony brought smiles of amusement to the faces of President Harry S. Truman and Marine Commandant Clifton B. Cates, as well as others gathered at the White House West Wing.

On hand for the presentation was the officer's family, including his wife, 3 older children, and 2 very young and lively twin sons, whom Chambers was holding, 1 in each arm. For a while, it was almost a tossup to see whether one of the pair would succeed in snatching President Truman's handkerchief out of his breast pocket as he read the citation and looped the ribboned Medal of Honor around the officer's neck. Decorum was maintained, but it was hardly the usual staid military occasion!

Nearly 40 Marine reservists also had ships named in their honor. This group included, incidentally, 1 father-and-Marine Reserve-son team (the U.S.S. *Pratt*) and 1 Marine Regular-and-Reserve brother team (the U.S.S. *Cook*). A complete listing of these Marines and the ships christened for them appears in Appendix D.

In recalling the contribution and courage of wartime reservists, Brigadier General Lewis C. Hudson recently declared:

> . . . Our doctors and dentists were Reserves and we had no braver men. Our Chaplains were Reserves and they were with us everywhere. . . .

Similar sentiments have been expressed by General Vandegrift, who paid high tribute in particular to those men of the cloth who served with him on Guadalcanal. These included Chaplains Frederic P. Gehring, Matthew F. Keough, William Richard (Big Joe) O'Neill,

Thomas Reardon, and Warren W. Willard. Chaplain Gehring won the Legion of Merit and the Navy and Marine Corps Medal for his action on the 'Canal. Aided by native scouts, he made 3 hazardous trips into enemy territory to rescue trapped missionaries and, as the General described it, ". . . lifted the morale of our men to an exceptional degree."

The Combat Correspondent

Another morale lifter was the fighter-writer known as the Combat Correspondent (CC). Both the Germans and the Japanese had used soldiers as reporters in the 20th century, but it was left to the Marines to develop it to a high art, helpful both to the Corps and to the men whose deeds were reported back home. Basically, the CC, as he was known, was a Marine noncommissioned officer who had gone through boot camp but who was either a reporter or a still or motion picture cameraman. A few were combat artists, like John Fabion, Elmer Wexler, and Harry Jackson. Most were former newspapermen who were assigned to the FMF, both ground and air, and who worked, wrote, and snapped pictures under the rather loose supervision of a Division or Wing Public Relations Officer (PRO) and an assistant.

Speaking in 1965 of the men he commanded as Director, Marine Corps Public Relations throughout World War II, retired Brigadier General Robert L. Denig, said pridefully:

> The Marine Corps Public Relations was actually built to the fine standard it attained in World War II by young men whose prior military experience was slight or none at all. From the small beginning of 2 officers and a first sergeant on duty in Washington (Denig, Major George T. Van Der

Hoef and Sergeant Major Walter Shipman), it grew by the war's end to a service of over 200 writers, photographers, and radio technicians. Out of this number of dedicated men of all ranks, my memory can recall to mind only 3 who failed, or only 1½ percent. The casualties of killed, wounded, and service-connected sickness ran over 15 percent. In covering actual battle scenes, they made use of radios, recordings, moving pictures, and public address systems.

Due to the high standard of their accomplishments in the above and other fields, the popularity of the Marine Corps among the people of the United States was enhanced and put on a firm basis. This was accomplished by a group of men nearly 100 percent Reserve, which of course redounds to their credit. To have commanded such a group was indeed an honor.

Actually, during the 5 years of World War II the total who served was higher than Denig's figures, but death, wounds, and poor health took their toll.

The postwar Marine Corps Combat Correspondents Association listed slightly less than 500 personnel who held public relations warrants as noncommissioned officers or as public relations officers, about one-tenth of 1 percent of the peak strength of the Corps! This is a far cry from the gibe from other servicemen who would say that a Marine squad included 8 men and a combat correspondent, or that every foxhole held a combat correspondent. In one division, the 4th, which fought from the Marshalls to the Marianas and across Iwo—all in some 14 months—there were 2 sergeants with each of the 5 regiments, 2 covering the separate units, 2 at division headquarters and 1 photographer and 1 artist. Of these 14 men and 2 officers, more than half received decorations and half were wounded. The CC's covered the men with whom they lived and died. Their PRO's handled the war correspondents and saw that copy, pictures, art, and wire recordings were expedited stateside. Together they made a fighting-writing team.

The first of these sergeants to see combat as a CC on Guadalcanal was James Hurlbut. Later in World War II, during the battle for Iwo, as a junior officer in CINCPAC Guam, he monitored the first wire-recording battle broadcasts prior to their dispatch stateside. The results were both noisy and nerve-wracking to the rest of the Marine staff trying to edit copy, check photos, et cetera. So an unused head (latrine) complete with swinging doors, was found for Hurlbut. This head-office was rigged up with a lamp, a fan, and a cot for the waiting hours as he sweated out the arrival of planes from Iwo.

In the late fall of 1965, after distinguished service as a prominent television commentator for NBC in Chicago, he was to accept orders to Headquarters on the personal request of the Commandant to prepare a series of documentaries for television and other use. Early in December, as a lieutenant colonel, he flew to Vietnam to supervise motion picture shooting of the Marine side of that war. In February 1966 he made colonel.

A team of still and motion picture combat correspondents, Master Sergeant Lou Lowery and Staff Sergeant Bill Genaust, accompanied the 2 patrols up the slopes of Surabachi and took pictures of the first and second flag raisings. Lowery's pictures of the original flag raising did not achieve the fame of Joe Rosenthal's later shot that made history, but for many years almost a generation of Americans at midnight turned off their television sets to Bill Genaust's motion picture footage of the second flag raising on Iwo which Rosenthal immortalized. Genaust was killed later in the battle for bloody Iwo, but today Lowery, a retired Reserve Captain, is *Leatherneck's* Photographic Director, under retired Reserve Colonel Donald L. Dickson, the World War II dean of Marine PRO's in the Central Pacific. In early service with the 1st Division, as a regimental adjutant on the 'Canal, Dickson's combat art blended with Dick Tregaskis' text for *Guadalcanal Diary*.

Writing in *American Heritage*, June 1964, Richard Wheeler tells how his 3d Platoon, Company E, 28th Marines climbed Surabachi and raised the flag and how their commanding officer had decided a larger flag was needed as a morale factor to troops far down on the island who could barely see the original 54 by 28 inch flag. He also told simply the danger which CC's like Lowery went through to get their pictures:

> The flag was barely up before it was challenged. A Japanese rifleman stepped out of a cave and fired at photographer Louis Lowery and BAR-man Robeson (PFC James A. Robeson). He missed, but Robeson didn't. He swung his BAR up for a long burst, and the man dropped heavily. . . . Several additional caves now came to life, and enemy grenades once more started to fly. Lowery had another narrow escape. A grenade landed near him and he was forced to leap down the side of the volcano, tumbling 50 feet before he was able to catch hold of a bush, and breaking his camera.

Air Reserves

Supplemented by increasing numbers of aviation cadets, the Marine Corps Air Reserve in 1940 consisted of 11 tactical squadrons and 2 service squadrons located at 10 Reserve bases. The last of these Reserve squadrons to be organized was VMS–11R, of Brooklyn, N.Y., which was to provide the Marine Corps with 2 of its greatest pilots: Joseph (Skipper Joe) Sailor and Karl S. Day.

Captain Joseph Sailor was to become perhaps the greatest of all dive bomber pilots, this claim being established by his incredible record of dive bombing attacks against Japanese ships during the Guadalcanal Campaign. Until killed while leading an attack against a destroyer, Sailor had scored direct hits on a battleship, a heavy cruiser, a light cruiser, and several armed transports. Karl Day had won the Navy Cross in World War I and, when recalled, was responsible for setting up the complete instrument school facilities in Atlanta, where Marine Corps and Navy pilots received their first instrument work. He also authored the book, *Blind Flying*, which became the handbook of air services, worldwide. The then-Colonel Day also organized OTS–8, the Corps's only multi-engine school, and went on to win the Bronze Star with Combat "V" at Peleliu during World War II. Currently (March 1966) he is a retired lieutenant general, the senior officer in the Marine Corps Reserve. Of the 7 Air Reserve general officers mentioned in Chapter II, all but 3 (Maas, Howarth, and Bowen) came from Day's New York Reserve squadron.

Writing of his squadron in 1965, Day said:

> Prior to World War II, there was no thought of retirement benefits. We didn't get drill pay for a long time, nor flight pay for a longer time—and in my outfit, each officer contributed one-half of his pay to a squadron fund to finance the purchase of blues for the men. No one was in that outfit for money. They loved it and we always had a waiting list both for officers and men . . . What I'm getting at is, that the spirit of the outfit attracted officers and men of the highest quality. They were not as well-trained professionals as the present crop, but they had the primary Reserve quality—get the job done using common sense and such professional knowledge as you had—and worry about the regulations afterwards. There is a tendency among some Regulars to say "no" to any proposal

Marine Reserves, Brooklyn, 1916. Below, Quantico trench warfare training, 1918.

World War I—Resting en route to front in France, 1918. Below, shell craters and dead branches provide protection for Marine machine gun crew in the Meuse-Argonne, 1918.

Above—DH-4 "Flaming Coffin" used in World War I bombing missions. Below, left—Woman Marine and Marine drummers, Quantico, 1918. Right, "Message delivered." Marine Reservist ("F") orderly reports to Navy CO aboard USS Arizona in North River, N.Y., 1918.

Seven Women Marines sworn in at New York City Recruiting Office, 1918. Below, with two unexplained exceptions, World War I Women Reservists serving at Head-quarters Marine Corps.

Summer Training—aboard boats in Potomac, Quantico, 1920's.   Below, boarding R. F. & P. at Quantico for trip home, 1920's.

In the butts—Reservists pull targets for rifle qualification during summer training. Below, Reserve band at Quantico during the 1919–1939 era.

*Inspection time at Reserve Tent Camp, Quantico.   Below, taking a road break at
Quantico.   Both, from the 1920's.*

Photo courtesy Col D.L. Dickson

*Fresh water for hot summer field maneuvers at Quantico during the 1920's.   Below,
Reserve cannon cockers from 301st Artillery Company of Boston fire "French 75's"
at Ft. Meade, Md., after two-day march from Quantico, 1929.*

Photo courtesy Col D. L. Dickson

USMC Photo 526895

Reserves parade in Philadelphia, Decoration Day, 1927.   Below, Reserve Rifle Team at Camp Perry wins Roumanian Cup, 1939.

USMC Photo 529632

USMC Photo 58874

World War II—Guadalcanal rest area, with protection, 1942.

Marines use Guadalcanal barracks for hospital, 1942.   Below, stretcher detail on the 'Canal, February 1943.

Marching Marines, Camp Lejeune, 1943.

"Over the top," a world away, at Tarawa, November 1943.   Below, breathing spell in shelter of friendly amtrac, Tarawa, 1943.

It could have been almost anywhere, Pacific Ocean Areas, but it was Cape Gloucester, 1943.

At Women Marines first anniversary ceremony (from left) Col Ruth Cheney Streeter, MCWR Director; BGen L. W. T. Waller, Jr., Director of Reserve; and Mrs. Eleanor Roosevelt. Below, women replace combat Marines who have trained them to run the Camp Lejeune water transportation system.

Black night, Jap bogey, white tracers in New Britain, 1943.   Below, Marine in Gloucester mud gives 6 x 6 a hand, 1944.

unless he can find some place in the book where it says "yes"; and if the book doesn't mention it, the answer is still "no." A reservist never knew the things he couldn't do. And, as long as you had high quality, it turned out very well. That is one of the reasons the Reserve did so well in World War II.

Further strengthening of the Marine Air Reserve occurred on the eve of the war with passage of the Naval Aviation Personnel Act of 1940, which authorized the President to appoint to the line of Regular Navy and Marine Corps "as many naval aviators of the Navy and Marine Corps Reserve as he may deem necessary."

The acid test for the Marine Air Reserve came in late 1940. Personnel of its 13 Reserve squadrons were mobilized and, as noted previously, integrated into the Regular Establishment for service during the Limited National Emergency that shortly developed into a full-scale war.

As expected, the war years from 1941–45 witnessed a tremendous growth in both planes and personnel. Despite its firm foundation for cadet training, Marine aviation was still pitifully small in the "hardware" or equipment department just prior to the war. On 31 December 1940 Marine Corps Aviation had consisted of 10 squadrons and 2 aircraft groups; on 31 December 1941, it numbered 13 squadrons, 2 aircraft groups, and 2 wings with Marine planes operating from Ewa and Wake Island; by 31 January 1945, it had soared to 135 squadrons, 32 aircraft groups, and 5 wings. At this time, Marine Aviation boasted a combined strength of 125,162 officers and enlisted men, the overwhelming majority being Marine reservists. Marine planes were based at nearly 20 different locations, including Ewa, Midway, Kwajalein, Guadalcanal, Bougainville, Admiralty Islands, Guam, Saipan,

Peleliu, Leyte, and with various aircraft carriers.

Much of the growth during these years must be attributed to President Roosevelt's pre-war announcement in May 1940 that the United States would initiate a 25,000-plane program, a goal later raised to 50,000 planes. This "Two-Ocean Navy" bill authorized a naval air fleet of 15,000 planes and allotted to Marine Aviation 2 air wings with 32 operating squadrons.

Marine Aviation plans also changed and expanded in line with recommendations of a number of Naval and Marine Boards, notably the Horne Board and the Navy General Board. Of these plans, those of the Horne Board were perhaps the most significant as they laid the foundation for expansion of Marine Aviation during the first 2 years of World War II. The Navy General Board of May 1941 modified the expansion program, proposing 3 wings for 3 divisions and 4 defense air groups for 4 defense battalions. A wing was to be composed of 959 pilots and 5,302 enlisted men. Following landing exercises in 1941, it was estimated that a single division making an amphibious landing would require 12 fighter, 8 dive-bomber, 2 observation, and 4 utility squadrons. But so great a number of squadrons was a long time in materializing. It must be remembered that at this period it was impossible to forecast the end of the war, much less to anticipate the extent of military requirements of the Nation. Military planning thus became more and more complicated, the only consistent factor being that *more of everything* was needed.

Fortunately, although aviation equipment was in woefully limited supply at the beginning of the war, what the Corps lacked in quantity it made up for in the quality of its small, highly experienced cadre of pilots and men.

Among its flying "pros" were: Gregory (Pappy) Boyington who, as a Flying Tiger in China, shot down 6 Japanese fighters and flew 300 combat hours before the disbanding of Claire L. Chennault's famous American Volunteer Group. Later, as a Marine Corps Reserve pilot, he won the Medal of Honor and Navy Cross for leading his famed Black Sheep Squadron against the Japanese. He became the Marine Corps ace of aces in World War II, with 28 enemy planes shot down, and after being himself shot down, survived 20 months in Japanese prison camps.

Robert E. Galer became a 13-plane ace and winner of the Medal of Honor, as well as a Distinguished Flying Cross from the King of England, for his brilliant leadership of VMF–224 at Guadalcanal from August to December 1942, during the most crucial period of the Solomons Campaign.

Kirk Armistead, who began his Marine Corps career as a reservist, won the Navy Cross for his extraordinary heroism as leader of VMF–221 during the defense of Midway on 4 June 1942.

William E. Gise commanded VMF–124, the first Corsair squadron on Guadalcanal. Before he was killed in action, he had gallantly led his squadron many times against the Japanese and played a major part in helping the Corsair earn the nickname of the "whistling death."

James L. Mueller became a member of Marine Reserve Scouting Squadron 9, and later served at Pearl Harbor, Iwo Jima, and Okinawa, earning the Bronze Star on Iwo.

Joseph J. Foss was appointed an aviation cadet in the Reserve in August 1940. He became a Marine Corps flight ace in the fall of 1942. Flying almost daily from 9 October to 19 November that year, he won his Medal of Honor by shooting down 23 enemy planes. Early the following year, he added 3 more enemy planes to his record. With a total of 26, Major Foss ranked as the number 2 flying ace at the end of the war.

Robert M. Hanson was famous for one killing spree in which he downed 20 enemy planes in 6 consecutive flying days. Reserve First Lieutenant Hanson was commended in his Medal of Honor citation for his bold attack against 6 enemy torpedo bombers over Bougainville in November 1943, and for bringing down 4 Zeroes single-handed over New Britain in January 1944. Hanson became well known for his daring tactics, total disregard for death, and mastery of individual air combat. He was listed as Missing in Action the following month when his plane crashed into the sea over Rabaul. With 25 enemy planes downed, he zeroed in as number 3 flying ace.

James E. Swett was another Reserve Medal of Honor aviator cited particularly for his daring flight to intercept a wave of 150 Jap planes over the Solomons in April 1943. He hurled his 4-plane division into action against a formation of 15 enemy bombers and personally exploded 3 hostile planes. Although separated from his division, he attacked 6 more bombers and brought his partially disabled plane down safely.

At the beginning of World War II, a number of Reserve officers had been associated with civilian airlines. Major General Frederick E. Leek gave a great deal of credit to such Reserves as Lieutenant General Day, Brigadier General Harry Van Liew (deceased), and Major General Robert Bell who helped to organize the

Marine Corps transport capabilities. "In fact," said General Leek, "the then Colonel Day was the guiding light in our twin-engine bomber program." Brigadier General Hugh M. Elwood also recalled that MAG–15 and MAG–25, the transport groups, were particularly filled with Reserve pilots, many being "million milers" from the airlines. These transport groups checked out the first Marines in their first B–24's and pioneered the first combat support air line, SCAT, in the South Pacific.

Reserves were also in the front rank in helping to develop techniques for night fighters. The development of radar and its association with the directional control of aircraft came relatively late, according to retired Lieutenant General Louis E. Woods, a former Director of Marine Corps Aviation (October 1943–July 1944). He recalled the specialist officers commissioned for work in this field were generally of a higher age level than those first called. "This fitted remarkably well into the overall system as these older officers were more mature and in general well-fitted to make sound and logical decisions under stress." Of these specialists, he particularly recalled reservists like Tom Baker, Henry Bransom, and Owen Hines (who recently served as Director of Reserve). Lieutenant Colonel Marion Magruder and his outfit, was "by far the best night fighter squadron . . . the first Marine night fighter ace was Captain Robert Baird of that unit who shot down 5 planes in the Okinawa campaign."

Remembrances

Another major contribution made by reservists, according to General Woods, was in developing aerial navigation. He tells how early attempts to get such training and the necessary sextants were unsuccessful, but that by an informal agreement with a Naval officer buddy, arrangements were made for 6 Marines (Captains Warren E. Sweetser, Jr., Henry C. Lane, Wilfred H. Stiles and Elmore W. Seeds, Lieutenant Russell L. Young, and Sergeant M. Gardner—3 of them Reserves) to train in Annapolis. General Woods recalls that:

> The first that Headquarters Aviation, Washington, knew about the whole affair was when the officers concerned appeared there to get money to pay for the sextants. . . . And from that humble beginning, all the aerial navigators that did such a marvelous job in helping Marine pilots to fly over water were trained. Their contribution to Marine aviation transport squadrons in helping them to carry out their missions over large bodies of water defies description.

General Woods, who 20 years after the war astounds fellow Marines with his impeccable memory for names and incidents, tells 2 stories in a humorous vein for this history:

> It was almost impossible to get cement on Guadalcanal during the early days and if you did get it, someone was sure to steal it. I had a friend ship me 1,000 bags, invoiced to me personally. I called in our Quartermaster officer of MAG–14 and told him that 1,000 bags were coming in, and that I'd give him 900 of the lot for unloading and taking care of my 100. I thought nothing further about it until he appeared at my Headquarters one morning and said the Army had taken it all. I asked "Why did you let them have it?" and he replied "He was a Colonel and said his orders were to put all cement into the Army dump.'
>
> So we went to Army Headquarters at once where I told the sad story. The Commanding General listened attentively, then rang for the Colonel concerned and ordered him to haul all the Marine cement to MAG–14's dump. I thanked the General and took my

Quartermaster officer back to camp. Some 2 hours later, I saw this same Captain in camp and asked him, in a rather crisp tone, what he was doing there and not tending to the unloading of the cement. Imagine my surprise when he said: "Did you hear what the General said: 'Haul all the cement to the Marine dump.' If I stay here long enough it will be all handled for me by the Army." You can see now why we won the war with smart officers like that—and most of them reservists!

Another incident that happened in the General's 2d Wing Headquarters occurred the night the Japanese lay down their arms. A lot of small arms firing broke out immediately after the news was received, and the general's area was no exception. Woods called for his driver but couldn't get him, so he commandeered the first Marine he could find to drive him to his office. He didn't think of the incident for several days but then remembered to ask his driver where he was when he called.

The latter's reply:

When I first came to Okinawa, I was standing in the chow line one evening. Without any warning, all my buddies disappeared and then I saw these little dust clouds appearing near me. I looked and saw a plane with a big red sun on it firing right at me. Ever since that time when I hear promiscuous firing I seek shelter and stay there until I know what it is all about—I hadn't found out when you called, so I stayed in my dugout.

Marine Air reservists played a leading role in the Pacific campaigns. And at the end, the Marine Air Reserve comprised about 90 percent of the Marine Corps' total aviation strength and produced a high percentage of the Marine Corps' 121 flying aces.

The memoirs of General Woods include many references to reservists who rendered distinguished service in the field with Ma-

rine aviation units. These included Lieutenants Edgar M. Culp and Alfred E. Zaniboni, "who handled communications and ordnance activities, respectively, at Guadalcanal during the early days," and Staff Sergeant McDonald, "who was a wizard at reading the scope of the radar during the critical days on the 'Canal. He could read the numbers and kinds of planes in an uncanny manner."

He also has praise for Colonel Bill Fox, "who did so much to construct Henderson and the other fields at Guadalcanal," and for Colonel Fiske Marshall "who flew General Geiger and me and other members of the staff from San Diego to the War Area and later was so successful in carrying out his duties as Executive Officer of MAG–25. I believe he has the distinction of taking out the first load of wounded from the battle area."

General Woods also remembered Captain Richardson Dilworth at Guadalcanal, "who acted as Intelligence Officer for the 'Cactus' (code name for Guadalcanal) Air Force and later became mayor of Philadelphia" and Captain Richard Hubler, "who was the first officer (with Captain John A. DeChant) to publish a book about Marine Corps aviation in the war, entitled *Flying Leathernecks*."

The General tells an interesting anecdote about Captain Ben Finney, "who could get anything needed like a microphone for the band and Christmas decorations for us at Guadalcanal the first Christmas." General Woods recalled his predicament at being promoted to brigadier general in the war area where there were no stars:

Ben finally got disgusted with the delay and got an Army ordnance man to fasten 2 dimes together and cut them down to make stars. He had the little posts on some

Marine Corps emblems cut off and welded in the stars. The set of stars, plus one for my cap, are my most prized possessions of World War II.

He also praised Reserve officers for the work done in developing napalm bombing techniques in the 4th Air Wing in the Marshalls and the development of the fighter as a fighter bomber.

Of course, there were many Reserves on the ground who did outstanding jobs during World War II, many of them improvising from their civilian experiences to bring to the Corps the blend of technology necessary to make possible the accomplishment of tasks and missions for which the necessary skills were either in short supply or almost totally lacking in the Regular Establishment.

Many of the hard core skills, such as engineering, electronics, and photography, and some of the specialties, such as postal and mess billets, were handled with great skill and daring by reservists who had no "book" to go by and who sometimes had to write their own book as did Major General George Tomlinson, who as a field officer wrote a standard text on mess in the field. Tomlinson, together with Brigadier General Albert G. Skelton, organized and developed the engineering section at Marine Corps Headquarters as a part of M-4 in early 1942, at which time both were majors. At the time of the Pearl Harbor attack, Skelton was building Camp Catlin as commanding officer of an engineering building company.

The service command of FMF Pac was manned almost exclusively by reservists who, now in 1966, are retired general officers such as Tomlinson, Walter Churchill, the late Skelton, and Colonel Philip L. Mossburg of Philadelphia.

Analysis in Retrospect

The mobilization of the Marine Corps for World War II was fraught with many faults and inadequacies, despite the fact that the machinery had been geared for the eventuality of war. Can men ever anticipate the future with accuracy? Monday morning quarterbacking is an American characteristic. Marines have their Monday quarterbacks too. Looking back, the Corps recognized that many things might have been done in other and better ways; perhaps an analysis in retrospect will be helpful for new tomorrows and new eventualities. (Indeed, such analysis made for a more effective mobilization in the Korean War.)

A critique of the times—found in records of the Historical Branch at Headquarters Marine Corps—yields interesting commentary for those who would profit from the lessons of history. Major Phillips D. Carleton, who spent a year in the Officer Procurement Program of that period, writes:

Between 1940 and 1943, the Corps had apparently filled its extra needs from members of its Reserve. It had called up older officers from its recruiting stations, for example, in somewhat leisurely fashion and had not recruited directly from civilian life. The expansion of the Corps demanded an enormous increase in trained specialists—for jobs ordinarily done by Regular officers, as well as such new specialties as radar. The process of procurement appointed officers to grades according to age: anybody over 40 was automatically a captain. Very few majors were appointed. What few lieutenant colonels there were had been spotted up. At this time the Corps had no Classification Section. One of the first tasks was to set up such a section. The Corps was very much in a position of repairing the bicycle while it was under way.

This report calls attention to the unanticipated. Without a classification system, the machinery was not too well streamlined. Units needing specialists wrote up the specifications. The job of getting the right man for the right job had to be done "manually" rather than by the more automated methods that were to become routine in the sixties. Some units tended to be excessive in their requests, while others "hoarded" personnel in order to protect their interests. As Major Carleton has stated in his critique:

> . . . getting the right man for the right job was (difficult). In new fields such as radar, the specifications for the man were vague; it was likely that men suddenly brought in might not have the necessary basis in mathematics to take instruction.

Or, as he noted:

> If a division wanted an automotive vehicle maintenance man, the man selected might turn out to be an administrator, the president of a busline, and useless for the purpose. At first there was no provision for retention of "mistakes"; men were returned arbitrarily to civilian life, very bitter against the Corps and out of pocket and pride.

Many pressures obviously developed in times of crisis. Mobilization was indeed a time of crisis. Political pressures, manpower pressures, facility pressures, all other types of conceivable pressures acted upon the machinery of World War II. It is to the credit of both the service and individual Marines that the achievement record shows we persevered in spite of the road blocks. Early instruction for those mobilized was haphazard. At first there were very few definitive plans for preparing civilians for their military duties. They were assembled in Quantico and permitted to be observers at the schools. This quickly proved an unsatisfactory system and indeed some of those early trained ex-

civilians were so lacking in formal military schooling as to be painfully ignorant of the fundamentals of wearing their uniforms, their expected conduct, or general military affairs. Similarly, at Lejeune, delays occurred in starting new courses because of dearth of qualified instructors. It was even necessary to make an instructor out of one officer who was himself being indoctrinated! Eventually the situation was rectified, of course. But the new enlistee was a Marine in spirit and determination and, as stated in the report ". . . the situation was remedied by the men themselves who were eager to learn and proud of their uniforms." With the spirit of cooperation of the newly mobilized and the developing war machinery of the Marine Corps system, these problems were faced and in due time resolved. As Major Carleton observed: "We managed to increase the Corps from 15,000 to nearly 500,000 and still preserved an esprit de corps . . ."

Motive in Mobilization

There is no single explanation to describe why men of the Reserve brought their muscle, spirit, and intellect to the great mobilization. It was WAR, and all Americans were anxious to serve their country. Organized and Volunteer reservists had already demonstrated that they were ready. Men and women who entered the service after Pearl Harbor and became Reserves were of the same ilk. Choice of the Corps as their preferred service was tacit evidence of their determination to be "good Marines," a concept which those drafted to serve came to share alike with the self-drafted. Reservists joined a service proud with tradition and record. They knew the type of organization the Marine Corps was reputed to be. That image in the eyes of the public, and even in the eyes of the enemy, made for strong, heady motive. The reservist quickly captured that spirit. As General Robert E. Hogaboom and others of the general officers who have commented to this history freely point out, the reservist was so indistinguishable from the Regular that to attempt a distinction is irrelevant. The Reserves of any particular day are pretty much a reflection of the Corps of that day. The reservist was there to be a Marine, to fight, to serve his country with pride. His reasons were multiple.

Discussing the readiness of the Marine Reserve at the outbreak of World War II, retired Lieutenant General Edward A. Craig reported "we would have been lost without this reservoir of trained officers and men to man our expanding Corps in World War II. The Reserve, although small in numbers and not always well trained, was a shot in the arm when war came." With the mobilization of large numbers of reservists, General Craig felt that the average reservist had not had the opportunity to receive the constant and intense training given to the Regular Marines. Once on active duty, however, this difference in military knowledge and skill rapidly disappeared.

Reserve Brigadier General Melvin M. Smith cited the performance of the 4th Marines, composed of a large percentage of reservists, which was evacuated from China to the Philippines just prior to Pearl Harbor. Activated on Pearl Harbor day was the 1st Samoan Battalion, a Marine Corps Reserve unit, composed of native Samoans and known as the Fita-Fitas. It was attached to the 7th Defense Battalion and in existence for approximately 3 years. Drill pay for unit members was 70 cents per drill for the first 4 months of service and scaled up to one dollar per drill thereafter. The original uniform consisted of white undershirts and plain khaki lavalavas. Soon afterwards, the uniforms were brilliantly enhanced with the addition of red piping around the borders of the lavalava and a red sash. Footwear remained nonregulation; these reservists always went barefoot! When the war started, the battalion went on active duty and found itself in the peculiar status of drawing overseas pay while defending the homefront. With the deactivation of the battalion in April 1947, the books were closed on one group of reservists who had enjoyed being, by choice, "shoeless Marines."

The participation of recently recalled Reserve officers in the 1st Marine Brigade operation, under command of Major General John Marston, was also recalled by General Smith. The brigade was stationed in Iceland from 7 July 1941 until late March 1942 and enabled the Marine Corps to garrison the island and thus relieve some British troops. Although proportionately there were not too many enlisted reservists in this 10 months' operation, there was a sizable number of officers. "With one exception, all of our 1st and 2d lieutenants in the 1st Battalion were Reserve officers," commented General Smith, then Commanding Officer of Company B, 1st Battalion, "and the same percentage applied to both the 2d and 3d Battalions, with the addition of a good many more captains than we had in the 1st." In other operations, members of Northwest Reserve units served with distinction, he recalled, as members of the famous 4th Marines on Bataan and Corregidor.

Commenting on the early war years, Lieutenant General Alpha L. Bowser,

Commanding General Fleet Marine Force, Atlantic, recalled that:

> . . . my entire operation in those days ran on Reserve officers, not Regulars. In World War II, I ended up commanding a battalion of 105mm howitzers with an officer strength of 35 to 40 men. Of this entire group, during a 15-month period, only my executive officer, 1 warrant officer, and myself were Regular officers.

That the Reserve Marine was, by and large, indistinguishable from the Regular is testimony to both his training and basic esprit. As Brigadier General Hudson has noted:

> Without the Reserves, we simply would not have had the 2d battalion, 25th Marines, 4th Marine Division, FMF. Thirty-six of the 38 officers of this battalion were Reserves and upon them fell the burdens of combat duties.
>
> As the war progressed, increasingly large numbers of the combat NCO's were Reserves. These officers and men were leaders—willing, confident; and, as soon as they gained a little experience, were more than a match for any opposition we encountered in combat at Kwajalein, Saipan, Tinian, and Iwo Jima. . . . On most of the Navy transports or LST's we found a vast majority of Reserves. Speaking from the level of the Marine infantry battalion, it was largely a war of Reserves during the latter period of World War II.

Several retired Marine Corps generals clearly recalled specific units, made up largely of Reserves, as early as Guadalcanal. The Philadelphia Reserve Artillery Battalion remained first in the memories of both Lieutenant General Robert H. Pepper and Lieutenant General Pedro A. del Valle. General Pepper cited this unit as being a splendid one and recalled that he never really thought of it as a Reserve unit. General del Valle reported, "I noted an artillery battalion on Guadalcanal, largely Reserves from Philadelphia,

who did a superb job—outstanding." And General Partridge looked to the 7th Service Regiment (formerly the 7th Field Depot) commended several times for rendering outstanding combat support during three Pacific operations and in the support of Occupation Forces in North China. During a regrouping phase on Okinawa it was accidentally discovered that of its 135 officers, only 2 were Regulars.

Brigadier General Joseph L. Stewart summarized the place of the Reserve in World War II when he said:

> By the time we got into battle in World War II, the Regular was a rare creature and the Reserve became the Marine that you saw everywhere you went. Never has a fighting organization been more successful than the Marine Corps in World War II; therefore, the only conclusion you can reach is that the reservist in World War II was of the highest quality attainable.

On the whole, the Marine Corps generals felt that once a Marine was in uniform, he was thought of only as a Marine; and had the general been asked during wartime if a member of his outfit was a Regular or a reservist, he would not have been able to answer the question—furthermore, he probably would have been puzzled as to why anyone should ask.

Any resentment that may have developed (and there was some) between reservists and Regulars was traced by Lieutenant General Frederick L. Wieseman to the fact that Reserve units, prior to World War II, had the authority to recommend promotion of officers within their organizations to fill vacancies; and that last-minute promotions to higher grades made Reserves into field grade officers who outranked their Regular counterparts. He recognized the fact that, human nature being what it is, the resentment that followed in some of these instances resulted in bad reservists being identified as reservists and good ones having their identities obscured. When General Vandergrift gave the order that all Marines would be designated as "USMC" in all administrative matters, except those cases where specific identification was essential, General Wieseman felt that "by this one action he did more to remove whatever distinctions still persisted at that time. By the end of World War II, service status as a factor in determining relative capabilities had entirely disappeared."

Brigadier General Ronald R. Van Stockum admits candidly that, as a young Regular officer himself, he was somewhat skeptical of the reservists. As he phrased it:

> I believe it was early 1940, while I was with the 6th Marines in San Diego, that the first group of Reserve officers came to active duty. I must admit that, along with a number of my contemporaries, I considered these officers to be a somewhat inferior breed. However, these illusions were rather quickly shattered when I discovered that reservists like Bill Jones not only had a better understanding of machinegun functioning, but also quickly established a rapport with the local Navy juniors. . . . During World War II, of course, the reservists of all the military services distinguished themselves, and the line between the Reserve and Regular disappeared.

Time and time again Marine generals have conveyed the thought that they never really bothered to inquire whether an officer or an enlisted man was a reservist or a Regular and that replacements in their commands were assigned according to the Marine's rank and military specialty. Lest the Regular officers and men were forgotten in discussing this question, several Marine generals purposely drew attention to an often overlooked fact: that is, it was the attitude of the Regular toward the reservist and the part of the Regular officers and men in the training of reservists in the limited time available for training that formed the basis for the good will so apparent between these 2 groups by the end of World War II. Indeed, Lieutenant General J. P. Riseley felt that "the attitude of the Regular toward the reservist—the Reserve toward the Regular—is our greatest blessing, our greatest strength; and when fighting side by side, the labels Reserve and Regular melt away." Lieutenant General Lewis W. Walt (in March 1966, Commanding General of the III Marine Amphibious Force combat troops in Vietnam) agreed with this concept when he wrote, "I think it is the responsibility of every Regular officer and enlisted man to do all he can to help our Reserves maintain their combat readiness and professional competence."

And, in testifying to the loyalty and love of country so often mentioned in connection with Marines, veteran airman and raconteur General Woods had one final thought about the men he had observed. In his own words:

> The Marines who had been prisoners of war, or repatriates as they were sometimes called, came to Okinawa first before being sent home. Inasmuch as the Army authorities were handling all arrangements, I did not bother them unless they especially asked to see me. I did have a goodly number of officers and men detailed to be with them and help in any way possible. The only requests I ever had were for Marine Corps ornaments for all and some small American flags. My hat's off to you and the organization that can instill such loyalty and love of country in our men who had been so long confined and brutally treated.

Requiem for Heroes

Typical of the spirit that motivated the Reserves—and Regulars too, for battle makes no difference—was the letter a young captain wrote from shipboard just before Iwo made him one of the thousands of Marine dead from that bitter battle:

Our ship's chaplain is a priest so we have been attending Mass and Communion daily. We are fortunate in this as it makes a great difference for many of these boys. You understand, we all know that many of our friends will be killed or wounded in this coming landing. However, the individual feeling is "It won't happen to me!"

Then to go a little further, besides taking advantage of the spiritual aid offered and its comforts, thoughts run like this—at least, my thoughts say "My responsibility to my loved ones has to be forgotten, to a great extent, because I feel that if I draw an unlucky number I'll stand a good chance of joining those many Marines guarding Heaven's streets."

One cannot afford to be worried by thoughts of everyone back home. By this I don't mean that all caution and common sense are tossed to the winds. No, rather, that the greater responsibility is making the correct decision and acting courageously so that the lives of many men depending upon my decision will be safeguarded. This is something new for me. Even though we are to be given every possible support, I can't help but feel that this one is really going to be Super-Duper. Going to close for now. When you receive this letter, we will have proved ourselves.

Writing to the parents of the young captain, his Marine brother summed up the war and the death in one paragraph shortly after the Iwo fight:

The Marine Corps and the country is the richer for his service. It is because of you folks and our country and our church that we go off to war fully aware of the choice we make, fully certain that ours will not be an easy life. Yet we are aware that without our efforts, all that we knew and loved would perish . . . I cannot tell you to dry your eyes because only time will do that. I cannot do anything to ease the long lonesome hours that will be yours in the days to come. There is nothing more I can say at this time, only know that I am with you in all things, in all ways in my thoughts and prayers.

CHAPTER FOUR

The Transition

The war was over and folks back home wanted their fathers, sons and brothers, husbands, uncles, and nephews returned. Families and friends also wanted their women Marines back. The pressure was on, and the Marine Corps point system, similar to the rules for Army and Army Air Force personnel, gave great credit for overseas duty and length of service. Thus, the Marine Corps had a great many eligibles in its far-flung, battle-scarred units. For the first time, there began to be a difference between being a Regular with a fixed period of enlistment and a Reserve, signed up for the duration or duration and six.

In the general rush to bring the boys home, the Marine Corps and the Navy did a heroic job in manning the ramparts in Japan and in China, as well as in other areas. However, the American people did not permit the Marines to stay longer and in greater numbers in China or our present world might have been far different. But, that's another story. In any event, the Marines came home, sometimes whole regiments and air groups together. The 4th Marine Division, not marked for occupation duty, was disengaged from its Maui base in Hawaii and came home in any kind of available ship bottom. It was disbanded 28 November at Camp Pendleton, Calif. The 3d Marine Division was disbanded at Guam, exactly 1 month later.

The Navy Subsidiary Post-War Plan, Marine Corps, dated 1 November 1945, had many items pertaining to the Reserve.

At that time, no publicity had been given to the Corps' intentions for its reservists, although other branches of the Armed Services had given out general information. The Corps was making sure it plans were in order, and had no intention of jumping the gun.

Major General Thomas E. Watson, as Director of Personnel, recommended issuance of Reserve information to the public in early December, saying, among other things:

> The interest of the people of this Nation, of the Government and its Armed Forces in the peacetime military and naval Reserve Establishments is evidenced by the press and the amount of current legislative proposals and enactments relating thereto. Some additional benefits to the Reserve may result from the latter. Benefits already existing include the opportunities for increasing personal knowledge in military and naval science; appointment to enlisted rank held on release from active duty; advancement in rank; the accumulation of service, which counts toward pay when on active duty; exemption from Selective Service under present law; and the assurance of serving during war or national emergency with the branch of service already chosen. Membership in the Reserve or inactive status in no way affects the rights and benefits to which an individual is entitled as a veteran.

Although this didn't exactly sum up "all the Law and the Prophets," it was a substantial mouthful wrapped up in one paragraph. It showed that the Corps was paying attention to its wartime members who had either gone into mufti or were moving in that direction.

Thompson, Maas, and Mangrum

As the Reserves came home with chests full of "fruit salad" ribbons, they were discharged or went on terminal leave picking up the threads of pre-war life. They married, returned to school, went into new jobs, or returned to old ones. They traveled, bought homes, got acquainted with their children, or shopped around to see what future looked best for them. Many stayed in the Corps. Many didn't, but maintained Reserve connections as a caretaker Division of Reserve shifted into high gear under the guidance of a couple of "old pro" reservists, Colonels Clark W. Thompson and Melvin J. Maas. Thompson was Officer in Charge, Division of Reserve, from May 1943 to September 1945. He has now been a Congressman from Texas for many years. Maas, a former Congressman (1926–44) had been ordered home from Okinawa. Together, they pushed papers, banged desks, and fought the memo battles of Marine Corps Headquarters in providing for the necessary transition from a wartime to a first-class peacetime Corps in which reservists would be trained, equipped, and provided with the necessary opportunities to serve their country.

At the same time, plans were drawn up to get aviation off to a flying start. In 1965, the Assistant Commandant, General Mangrum, recalled some 20 years later the postwar 1945 era. He wrote:

> One of the greatest satisfactions of my career is to have had a hand in the post-World War II reactivation of Reserve programs. Although long since a Regular officer it was because of my early experience with the Reserve that I was yanked out of West-Pac shortly after V–J Day to proceed to Washington. There, Major General Field Harris, the Director of Aviation, assigned me

to reactivate the Reserve Section of that Division and devise a new Aviation Reserve program. He thought we ought to make all haste with this, thus was sure I wouldn't mind deferring my customary homecoming leave for a little! In any event, it was 5 weeks in that fall of 1945 before I could go get my family and move to Washington. In that 5 weeks, we established the program substantially as it exists today and the show was on the road.

> A signal feature of the concept was that MARTCOM [Marine Air Reserve Training Command] would be the nucleus of a momobilizable 4th Wing. Also that each Organized Reserve Squadron would be so established in both the Marine Corps and in the Naval aeronautic organization that only a simple executing message could place it on active duty as a completely viable administrative concern.

"Mutual Appreciation"

The postwar mission was still short and to the point: to provide a trained force of qualified commissioned, warrant, and enlisted personnel to meet requirements for the initial expansion of the Regular Marine Corps in time of war or national emergency.

The Commandant, General Vandegrift, summed up his own pride and the country's debt to the wartime Reserve when he said:

> During World War II, Marine Reserves constituting the bulk of the Marine Corps had a major share in its wartime achievements. Unfailingly they demonstrated that espirit de corps which is the heritage of all Marines. All activities and personnel of the Marine Corps will share in the development and support of the Marine Corps Reserve. The objective for all, both Regular and Reserve, is the attainment of a mutual and cooperative appreciation to accompany a continuous program of military efficiency.

The Reserves who had fought, bled, and died side by side with the Regulars during the long war—and who almost to a man had scorned the "I want out" demands of so many military personnel in the other services during the demobilization binge which the country went through—this Marine Reserve was to continue at local armories and air stations and at summer camp to backstop the Regular service in a no-nonsense program of military efficiency. There were plenty of bugs in the program, even after the Congress held lengthy hearings and came up, eventually, with the 1952 Armed Forces Reserve Act. However, there were many skirmishes, marches, and countermarches up and around Capitol Hill as the country moved toward a unified Defense Department and slid toward the Korean War. In 1964, the updated *The Marine Officer's Guide* reported that:

> The post-war buildup of its Reserve was one of the greatest achievements of the Corps. Through good leadership (Regular and Reserve), through willingness to invest capable personnel in the Reserve program, and because of the unflagging loyalty of Marine alumni—the Reserve was in unmatched readiness to back up the attenuated Regular Corps when the Korean War flamed up.

The 1946 Organized Reserves (2,630 officers and 29,829 enlisted) were to back up the peacetime Regulars (7,000 officers and 100,000 enlisted) authorized on 18 April by Congress. *Marine Corps Reserve Bulletin No. 1*, dated 1 May 1946, soon advised all personnel released from active duty that they had the opportunity to retain connection with the Corps through membership in the Reserve. They had to be qualified for assignment to one of the 3 postwar categories: the Fleet Reserve, the Organized, or the Volunteer. As before, the Organized units constituted the Ready Reserve. The former Regulars of the Fleet Reserve and the Volunteer reservists made up the Standby. The Women's Reserve component was also under study.

The 1946 mimeographed *Bulletin* had the identical mission as today's *Reserve Marine:* to provide a communications channel for passing the word from Marine Corps Headquarters at the Navy Annex in Arlington to a Ready Reserve that is loaded and locked and ready to go and to a Standby which is less Ready but nonetheless talented and trained.

Armories and Air Stations

A survey of available armory facilities was conducted early in 1946 while aviation units were being established at various naval air stations already available. Aviators, being formed into units at 21 naval air stations in expectation of funds for drill pay and training pay under 1947's Appropriations Act, were cautioned not to be discouraged "if you find the availability of planes low at present."

A chatty Part II of the initial *Bulletin* challenged aviators:

> Can you spare the time from your new job to put in as much as 100 flying hours per year? Can you spend a weekend per month at your air station working with a squadron of the Reserve? Can you spend 2 or more evenings per month at your station maintaining and bettering your proficiency as an aviation officer? Can you go on active duty for 2 weeks each year with your squadron?

The answer was loud and clear. In June 1946 Reserves flew 2,616 hours in 1,733 flights. They were off and flying! Aviators were admonished not to "flat-hat" while on Reserve training. Pilots had already been killed at Reserve air stations "doing just that." The squadrons being organized were to have 45 naval aviators, 15 non-flying officers, and 190 enlisted.

They were to be commanded and manned by reservists themselves, assisted by training detachment Regular personnel. All were to be fighter-bomber squadrons, geared to Regular organization and employment. In addition, there were to be 4 air warning squadrons.

At Headquarters, the Director of Aviation was charged with the training of both Regular and Reserve aviation. The Air Section within the Division of Reserve provided the necessary coordination. The first *Bulletin* explained that the Marine Air Reserve Training Command (MARTCOM), an organization similar to a wing, at Glenview Naval Air Station would administer, coordinate, and supervise all Marine Air Reserve activities. Its first general officer, Brigadier General Christian Frank Schilt, had authority over and responsibility for Volunteer Reserve personnel only while they were performing training. This meant that aviation Volunteer Reserves would be carried on Marine Corps Reserve District rolls, a decision which made the best of a potentially bad system of divided command, bowing to the inevitable necessity of keeping planes and flying under aviators, while maintaining necessary command and liaison channels with Navy.

MARTCOM had been activated by Colonel Ferry Reynolds, on 26 February 1946, with a headquarters complement of 13 Regular officers and enlisted men and 8 enlisted reservists. Three Marine Air Detachments (MAD's) at air stations in Atlanta, Dallas, and Glenview were its original cadre. However, within a year the Organized Aviation Reserve had reached its authorized strength of 21 Marine Air Detachments, 24 Marine Fighting Squadrons (VMF), and 8 Ground Control Intercept Squadrons (GCIS), with approxi-

mately 94 percent of authorized strength. General Schilt, a 1928 Medal of Honor winner in Nicaragua, had served in several Pacific campaigns and, although under direct military command of the Commandant, was responsible to the Chief of Naval Air Reserve training for coordination, management control, and logistic support.

In a masterpiece of understatement, the Corps told its aviation Reserves:

> We know that the many facets of service in the Reserve are new to practically all officers. There is no way to explain them briefly. The organization is proceeding rapidly. Contact your nearest Marine Air Detachment commander for details.

The new fighter-bomber outfits bore the designations of World War II squadrons decommissioned on V–J Day or thereafter. By September 1946, 19 of the 24 squadron commanders had been picked.

1946 Squadron Commanders

The first wave of postwar squadron commanders included Major Harlin Morrison, Jr., of VMF–112 at Dallas; Major Robert S. Ingram of VMF–121 at Glenview; Major Thaddeus P. Wojick of VMF–213 at Minneapolis; Lieutenant Colonel Everette H. Vaughn of VMF–215 at Olathe, Kans.; Captain James O. Holton, Jr., of VMF–221 at St. Louis, Mo.; Major Frank S. Hoffecker, Jr., of VMF–244 at Columbus, Ohio; and Major Ralph G. McCormick of VMF–251 at Grosse Ile, Mich. California claimed Major William P. Boland, Jr., of VMF–123 at Los Alamitos; Major Grant W. Metzger of VMF–141 at Livermore; and Captain Frank H. Presley of VMF–234 at San Diego. In the South and Southeast, Lieutenant Colonel Horace A. Pehl commanded VMF–124 at Memphis; Major David Drucker commanded VMF–142 at Miami; Major Frank C. Drury was skipper of VMF–143 at New

Orleans; Major Herbert C. Langenfeld led VMF–144 at Jacksonville, Fla.; and Major Warren C. Mollenkamp commanded VMF–135 at Atlanta. In the East, the CO's and their squadrons were Major George S. Buck, VMF–217, at Squantum, Mass.; Captain Halbert J. Keller, VMF–321, Anacostia NAS in Washington, D.C.; Major Henry S. Miller, VMF–451, Willow Grove, Pa.; and Major Gerard M. Bruder, VMF–132, New York, N.Y.

Remaining squadrons VMF–216 at Seattle; VMF–233, at Norfolk; VMF–235, at New York; VMF–236, at Glenview; and VMF–241 at Los Alamitos, Calif., were to get their skippers later.

On the Ground

Meanwhile, down on the ground, the Corps was laying plans to activate 18 infantry battalions; 7 artillery, 1 tank, 1 amphibian tractor, and 1 antiaircraft battalions; 5 signal, 3 engineer, and 2 weapons companies. It was an ambitious program and was fully justified as international events were to prove. But, in 1946 the Corps was checking on available armory facilities, reviewing male population of military age in 26 communities, and considering the geographic distribution of units in relation to planned mobilization points and field training facilities. Little was left to chance. There was even a check-list on locally available technically trained individuals in the case of specialist units planned for a certain area. Whenever possible, joint armory facilities were to be shared with the Navy. This is still true today, although the Marines have moved from basements and top floors into their own buildings or coequal status with the Naval Reserve in many areas in the 20 years since the 1946 crash program.

Atlanta, Augusta, Birmingham, Boston, Buffalo, Chicago, Cleveland, Dallas, Detroit, Galveston-Houston, Indianapolis, Los Angeles, Newark, New York City, Norfolk, Philadelphia, Richmond, San Diego, San Francisco, Seattle, St. Louis, St. Paul, Toledo, Tulsa, and Washington, D.C., were the original locations for the postwar ground Reserve. The list read like the roster of the hometowns from which the Organized Reserve marched off to war prior to Pearl Harbor.

The ground rules were much the same as before. There would be Inspector-Instructors, Regular officers to supervise training and facilities. Opportunities for commissions were available for qualified Reserve noncoms. Chances for promotion of those already commissioned depended upon training duty attendance or completion of correspondence courses from the Marine Corps Schools. Enlisted personnel in Organized units could take correspondence courses. They could also qualify for selection and assignment to service schools, to platoon leader training, and to temporary active duty with the FMF. There was no favoritism, either way. Grades and ranks were identical to the Regular Marine Corps. Promotions were based on requirements similar to those of the Regular Service.

As with the aviators, the Organized ground would drill weekly and attend camp 2 weeks yearly. The latest techniques and types of arms were to be employed in training and "up to date methods of instruction" were to "insure interesting presentations." The Class III or "disorganized Reserve," as it was called by some of its more jocular members, could also train for 2 weeks annually, subject to the usual problems of budget and available facilities. Reserves were called to training duty in ranks held during the war and paid on the basis of total service.

An unusual editorializing paragraph completed the section of the first *Bulletin* directed to ground Marines. It read:

> The accomplishments of the Marine Corps Reserve during World War II have won the admiration of the Nation. It is no wonder the comrades-in-arms who remain in the Regular establishment are eager to further the development of the Reserve so that any emergency can be met quickly and with the combined might of a welded and rugged Corps.

It took the Corps a while to become molded to its Reserve after the Division of Reserve took up its postwar mission, and spot welding was needed from time to time in the years that followed. But there was never any doubt at Headquarters concerning the rugged capabilities of Reserves who had slogged ashore from Guadalcanal to Okinawa.

Special Staff Section

On 27 June 1946, the Division of Reserve was separated from the Personnel Department and became a special staff section reporting to the Commandant. The Director of Reserve acted for the Commandant of the Marine Corps in coordinating all Reserve matters with other Marine activities, with Reserve agencies of the other services, with the National Guard and States militia, with veterans' organizations and associations of military and Naval Reserve officers. These included the Marine Corps Reserve Officers Association which, in December 1945 under Colonel Mel Maas, got itself out of its wartime caretaker status and began to gird for the Congressional infighting that loomed ahead.

The first postwar Director of Reserve was Brigadier General Franklin A. Hart (September 1945–January 1946). He was succeeded for the next 14 months by Colonel Randolph McC. Pate, destined to serve as Director again while a general officer and later to become the 21st Commandant of the Marine Corps. The executive officer during this trying period was Colonel James J. Keating, a distinguished reservist who integrated.

The Reserve was off to a good start with words of praise for the wartime Corps from a very welcome source, the House Appropriations Committee, which, on 21 May 1946, in its report on the Marine Corps budget for 1947, said:

> The immortal deeds of the Marine Corps during the past war have served to implant further in the minds of the American people an abiding respect and admiration for this comparatively small, but exceedingly progressive, virile, and effective armed unit. The Marine Corps, possessed of men of vision in policymaking positions, has always pointed the way in methods and procedures of amphibious warfare. The discipline of the Corps has been exemplary. It is significant to note that complaints of a "caste" system have been notoriously lacking as regards the operation of the Marine Corps. Morale has been exemplary. . . . This committee is convinced that the American citizenry would never look with favor upon any move designed to bring about any loss or impairment of identity of this highly proficient and expertly trained arm of our national security.

The warning was clear enough. But some in policymaking places at the Pentagon and White House did not heed the rather broad hint that the Congress would take a dim view of any efforts to cut down the Corps. The Corps got the message loud and clear, however; and its Commandant, General Vandegrift, soon was calling on former Marines "to wrest a beachhead from the forces of indifference" by volunteering for the Reserve. He said:

> The formation of the Organized Marine Corps Reserve marks another key installation in the defense that the Nation must erect to insure the peace won with the lives of our comrades in arms. We are calling upon the men whose courage helped smash the enemy at Guadalcanal, at Tarawa, at Iwo Jima, and at Okinawa, to provide an attack force to seize one more beachhead. . . . If war should come, the men of the Organized Reserve, trained in the latest tactics and techniques, and armed with the latest weapons, will be ready to join with their comrades of the Fleet Marine Force in manning the Nation's first line of defense.

General Vandegrift also said Volunteer Reserves could maintain their skills by correspondence courses or optional tours of duty, so that they, too, could rally to immediate defense of their Nation's shores.

Bands and Boxing Gloves

It was obvious that the Commandant did not want, nor did the Congress expect, any "pogey bait" (a term for candy or sweets) Marines, but rather those who were less interested in what they got than in what they gave. However, every effort was directed to making sure that they got everything they needed to be good Marines, including a small band for each of the Organized battalions! In mid-1946, some $325,000 in recreation funds from post exchange profits on sales to military personnel were made available for the Organized Reserve for recreational and athletic equipment and facilities and for musical instruments. All reservists, including those on the Honorary Retired and Retired lists, were issued identification cards. Reserve officers were granted open mess privileges at Barstow and San Diego in

California, and at Parris Island, S.C. Public Law 305, approved 21 February 1946, made it possible for Reserve officers with a total of 20 years of active duty service—including active duty for training—to retire at half pay along with their Regular counterparts of the Navy, Marine Corps, and Coast Guard, and at the highest rank held. This helped make the Reserve more attractive, but it was not sufficient. Eventually, a broader law was passed. Headquarters was busy processing "permanent type commissions" for officers returned to inactive status and forwarding them as fast as they could be signed by the Secretary of the Navy. The Corps tried hard to catch up with and deliver medals and decorations to its discharged troops, including reservists on inactive status. While taking care of the past, the Marine Corps (no less than the Navy) was also looking ahead.

NROTC units were planned in 52 colleges and universities. Marine officers and enlisted were detailed to the units as staff instructors. One out of 6 graduates was to be eligible for a Regular or Reserve commission in the Corps. Plans were laid to reactivate the Platoon Leaders Classes for the coming summer to accommodate interested college students not attending NROTC colleges. The system was the same as before; selected students would attend summer training at Quantico during 2 summer vacation periods. Those who made the grade would be commissioned on graduation from college.

The Division of Reserve also had problems on matters of required items of uniforms; when reservists or discharged personnel could wear the uniform; and what to do about promoting Reserve officers with at least 18 months of continuous honorable war service who had received no promotion. This latter problem was solved by promoting all such eligible officers below the rank of lieutenant colonel. The Reserve Districts, later to become Reserve and Recruitment Districts and today known as Marine Corps Districts, were set up as independent offices with the major responsibility for administering the Reserve program in the various geographic areas. One of the Director's biggest headaches was finding available armory and training facilities for the ground Organized Reserve. The September 1946 *Reserve Bulletin* somewhat plaintively announced:

> Should any reservist know of a facility available and satisfactory for a Reserve armory and located in a city which could support a Reserve unit, it is requested that such information be forwarded to the Director, Division of Reserve.

The Director was already deluged with queries as to just what was expected of the Volunteer Reserve in a program where the obvious and urgent priority called for the establishment of a ready force of Reserve ground and air units. Complicating this situation was the initial decision, subsequently reversed, of separating temporary Reserve officers with permanent enlisted status at their highest enlisted rank. In September, all hands were advised of a policy change and Headquarters Marine Corps commenced tendering temporary officer and temporary warrant officer appointments to those officers and warrants previously discharged in an enlisted status.

Answer Your Mail—Please

If they qualified for membership and their location and civilian pursuits permitted, all inactive reservists were expected to apply for membership in an Organized Reserve unit. Otherwise: "All that is expected of them for the time being is that they keep their Reserve District Commander informed of their address and *answer official mail promptly.*"

This last was underlined in the *Reserve Bulletin*. One of the most frustrating jobs in the early postwar Reserve was knowing where the personnel actually were. Both the veteran population and Reserve District headquarters were quite fluid. Some wives, either anxious to keep their husbands home after a long absence or unfamiliar with military correspondence as new wives, simply destroyed anything arriving in a brown Marine envelope and told their husbands nothing. Amusingly enough, some checks and commissions, medals and decorations just disappeared. Reservist husbands laid the blame on a guiltless and overworked Reserve Division when the blame often was much closer home.

However, most reservists were getting their mail and answering promptly and enthusiastically. Responses to the initial *Bulletin* soliciting periods of availability and kinds of active duty training required gave the Corps valuable information for planning purposes in preparing budget estimates for the already pending 1948 budget. Reservists also made numerous excellent suggestions, many of which were adopted. And, they asked a variety of questions which Headquarters Marine Corps either answered in the *Bulletin* or promised to answer later after further study. Already one big problem was how to advise employers that summer training was in the Nation's best interests and not just an exercise at playing Marine.

Postwar Battalion Commanding Officers

Of the 9 battalion commanding officers selected to head the first postwar Organized (ground) Reserve, Lieutenant Colonels Charles H. Cox (Philadelphia) and Walter A. Churchill (Toledo) were eventually selected for flag rank in the Reserve and today are on the Reserve retired list as one- and two-star generals, respectively, and Lieutenant Colonel Robert N. Fricke (Richmond) was advanced to brigadier general on retirement. Others were Lieutenant Colonel Lewis N. Samuelson (New York); Lieutenant Colonel Alfred V. Jorgensen (Los Angeles); Major Arthur "J" Berk (St. Louis); Major Robert L. Holderness (Seattle); Major Nick E. Presecan (Indianapolis); and Major Henry G. Totzke (Detroit).

These officers command 7 infantry battalions and 2 105mm howitzer battalions (Richmond and Los Angeles). These were part of the revised formula for backstopping the Fleet Marine Force. The total organized ground units on the drawing board in mid-1946 included 16 infantry battalions; 5 105mm and 2 155mm howitzer battalions; 2 tanks and 2 amphibious tractor battalions; 10 engineer and 4 signal companies; 1 40mm battery; and 2 heavy antiaircraft artillery groups. These units were to fit into the M-Day (Mobilization Day) plans for an expanded Marine Corps in a Presidentially proclaimed national emergency.

In the summer of 1946 the Corps authorized issuance of a Reserve Special Commendation Ribbon award and the Secretary of the Navy approved awards to 15 senior reservists who had commanded Organized ground units "in a meritorious manner for a period of 4 years between 1 January 1930 and 7 December 1941."

Those who received this ribbon and medal have the distinction of being members of a most exclusive group since this is probably the decoration least known to the public and worn, even today, by a relative handful of hard-core reservists. Ground officers receiving the medals included the following who were either selected for flag rank or promoted to general officer rank on retirement because of decorations received in combat: Colonel Joseph R. Knowlan, Lieutenant Colonel Otto Lessing, and Colonel Melvin L. Krulewitch.

Others in this rare breed included Colonel Harold M. Keller, Colonel Bernard S. Barron, former Major George W. Bettex, Colonel Harvey L. Miller, Colonel Edward P. Simmonds, Colonel Iven C. Stickney, Colonel Alfred A. Watters, Colonel Clarence H. Baldwin, Colonel John J. Flynn, Colonel Clark W. Thompson, Lieutenant Colonel William C. Smith, and Colonel James F. Rorke.

Ten aviators who had commanded Reserve squadrons for at least 4 years were also honored by Navy Secretary James Forrestal. In addition to the command years, both aviators and ground officers had to have a total of 10 years in the Reserve to be eligible for the award. The aviators who received a special letter from Secretary Forrestal included Lieutenant Colonel Charles E. Adams, Colonel Joseph P. Adams, Major Theodore O. Brewster, Lieutenant Colonel Nathaniel S. Clifford, Lieutenant Colonel Raymond W. Conroy, Colonel William J. Fox, Colonel Valentine Gephart, Colonel Melvin J. Maas, former Lieutenant Colonel Stephen A. McClellan, and Major Alton N. Parker. Maas received his letter and ribbon from the Commandant at Headquarters 5 November 1946.

During this period of readjustment,

many Regulars were also getting out of the Corps and accepting commissions in the Reserve. However, there was more traffic in the other direction. No fewer than 7,880 Reserve officers and warrant officers applied for transfer to the Regular Establishment. More than half—3,640—had been approved for Regular commissions and were receiving their parchments by the time schools and colleges opened with a bumper crop of veterans in September 1946. Paper went up and down the chain of command. Officers firmed up their commissioned status. Both officers and enlisted men received their delayed decorations, medals, and promotions. Organized ground units got blue uniforms for their 20-man bands and .22 caliber rifles and pistols for training, recreation firing, and small-bore rifle and pistol matches. Reserve officers also were advised how to claim uniform gratuities.

Recruiting Stressed

Although the Corps was naturally preoccupied with retaining its officer Reserve, strong efforts were made to sign up qualified enlisted personnel, both in Organized ground and air units and in the Volunteer Reserve. All commanding officers and recruiters, both Regular and Reserve, were authorized to supplement the work of Reserve recruiting officers locally in effecting enlistments and reenlistments. Major requirement for the Volunteer Reserve was a Marine Corps honorable discharge. However, veterans of all services were eligible for the enlisted Organized Reserve, with approval of the commanding officer of the organized unit they desired to join. The minimum age was 17. There was no age maximum for either Class II or Class III. There was a height maximum of 74 inches

and a minimum of 66. Those under 19 years of age could be as short as 63 inches if recommended by a medical officer.

Volunteer Reserve Marines called "stationkeepers" were assigned to active duty with the Marine Air Detachments established to support Organized Reserve squadrons. These aviation stationkeeper specialists were not subject to transfer, could enlist at a station of their choice, and could return to inactive duty at their own request. The Organized Reserve was authorized 2,600 officers and 30,000 enlisted personnel for fiscal year 1947. Volunteer Reserve plans provided for 21,000 officers and 70,000 enlisted. Plans for the Women Marines, including Volunteer and Organized, totaled 500 officers and 4,500 enlisted.

A Marine Corps Letter of Instruction issued late in the winter of 1946 showed Marine Corps Reserve Districts consolidated in 10 cities: Boston; New York City; Philadelphia; Washington, D.C.; Charleston, S.C.; New Orleans; Chicago; Los Angeles; San Francisco; and Bremerton, Wash. They supervised the Organized ground units and the Volunteer Reserve. Glenview rode herd on Organized air squadrons at naval air stations.

It was a period of considerable activity as excerpts from *Marine! The Life of Lieutenant General Lewis B. (Chesty) Puller, USMC (Retired)*, by Burke Davis (Little, Brown & Co., Boston, 1962) indicated. Puller, who had wanted a postwar regiment, was assigned the New Orleans Reserve District, much to his initial annoyance. He reported down South in July 1946 and, as Davis writes:

Vandegrift was soon smiling over reports from New Orleans. Puller built his district until he had doubled the number of reservists, wangled barracks and training areas for them—and in his 2-year tour reached a peak of 6 battalions and in addition some 8,000 unattached men, a record for the country. He soon commanded a quarter of the Organized Marine Reserves in the Nation.

Soon after his arrival, the *Times-Picayune* featured Puller in color on its Sunday magazine cover with this quote:

> These days it looks like time for America to get realistic instead of starry-eyed. Whoever they are, whether they have atomic bombs or rockets or not, we can lick 'em if America gets hard, and American fighting men are trained to march 30 miles a day with a pack, and hit whatever they shoot at with any weapon they are trained to use. Just as long as Americans have the will to fight, we'll be all right.

Davis summed it up by saying, "That helped to draw a tide of recruits which never dwindled so long as Puller was in command." Although other District Directors were not racking up the same score, things looked good all around. Even though the actual on-site training frequently consisted of uninspired lectures and old movies, the continuity was kept and the camaraderie and esprit maintained.

Busy, Busy 1946

By the time the Commandant and the Director of Reserve issued 1946 Christmas greetings, a program had been adopted for Volunteer Training Units (VTU's or Class III); the Marine Corps Reserve Policy Board had met for 2 weeks, with Brigadier General William T. Clement as President; annual maneuvers had been scheduled for all Organized East Coast Reserve aviation squadrons at Cherry Point and for West Coast squadrons at El Toro in the summer of 1947; and the Corps was awaiting Congressional approval for an Organized and Volunteer Women's Reserve.

The formation of the VTU's had the most far-reaching effect, even today, for it provided Reserve Officers and noncoms a chance to maintain training and promotion status, even though not members of Organized units in a pay status. The Policy Board, by its composition and relative freedom of expression as representative of ground and air, Organized and Volunteer, and major Headquarters staff sections, played a most significant role in the postwar Corps. Originally, the Board met for 2 weeks and changed personnel each year. Slightly modified today as a year-round board with personnel rotated so that members serve for 2 years with an active duty period of 2 weeks each year and with an overlap of personnel to provide continuity, it retains most of its original elements. Perhaps it has a lesser sense of urgency today than during those years when the issue—not only of Marine Corps Reserve, but of a Marine Corps itself—was in doubt.

Colonels Maas, Krulewitch, Keating, and Cox were among the members who served on that first postwar board. Other high-caliber Reserves included Major William P. Boland, Jr., Major Julia Hamblet, Major Frank M. Chapman, Jr., and Lieutenant Colonel Edward J. Winters. The beloved Major Albert N. Bailey, who came closest to being the irreplaceable element in the postwar Division of Reserve and who served for many years as "father confessor" to both Reserves and newly assigned Regular directors and staff officers, was recorder.

Bailey had come to HQMC as a PFC in 1934 as a clerk in the Personnel Section of the Division of Reserve, giving up a sergeant's job at the Marine Corps Institute, but later taking a Special Order Discharge so he could work in Civil Service at the same desk. He was the only stenotypist at HQMC and sometimes bought his own paper. In 1939 he made Warrant Officer and became a Quartermaster Clerk. On 20 December 1941 he was mobilized, along with John Hanschmann who was QMC No. 1 in the Reserve. Bailey became administrative assistant to the head of the administrative branch in Reserve and served throughout the war and well into the 50's before retiring as a Major. His postwar job was research and he was involved in all legal matters having to do with the Reserve. A young lieutenant named Burton Daugherty was his understudy and took over when Bailey retired. Daugherty is now a Reserve lieutenant colonel and National Commandant of the Marine Corps League.

The VTU program was organized to develop progressively a pool of efficient general duty, staff, and specialist personnel. On call, it was to fill the needs for individuals or groups in an emergency. To the credit of the Corps and the reservists themselves, this was exactly its role in the 20 years that followed the initial announcement. Although the program took numerous turns and twists, was modified and revised, basically it does today what its Regular and Reserve planning parents hoped it would. It gives the Corps a place for qualified officers before and after service in Organized units and also provides for training and use of specialists, such as the unit which drew up this history.

There was no restriction placed initially on the number of VTU's in any one locality, so long as each had a minimum of 10 qualified members. Meetings were generally weekly. VTU 5–22 in the Washington, D.C., area broke its division staff into sections and, counting sectional meetings, reported as many as 70 to 82 meetings annually for several years. The senior officer generally commanded, although this was originally left fluid. Today, the senior must command or step out. Special staff sections were provided for, but this was not essential or desirable in specialist units such as communications, legal, public information, marksmanship, and civil affairs.

The main point established at the end of the first full calendar year after the war was, that the Corps was going out of its way to attract and retain a sizable body of qualified Reserve officers and enlisted personnel. The Corps wanted its Reserves as full partners and the Reserves responded in a manner unmatched by any of the other services. The Reserves knew they were wanted and needed. Although there were the normal gripes and problems, they were few by comparison. The family had weathered the initial postwar dislocation and, together, faced the pre-Korean years united and determined to be ready.

CHAPTER FIVE

Rebuilding

The year 1947 featured recruiting drives, publicity campaigns, and a command change in the Division of Reserve when Brigadier General Clement relieved Colonel Pate as Director on 1 April. During the previous 6 months, General Clement had closely observed plans unfold and gain momentum, and he spoke for the Regular Corps when he expressed gratitude at the progress made under Colonel Pate. As he began his 2-year tour with the Reserves, General Clement said: "There remains much ground to be covered, but with coordinated efforts and determination, we can develop and prepare our Reserve to promptly assume its role in case of an emergency."

Colonel Pate moved to the Navy General Board, praising all who had helped bring the Marine Corps Reserve closer to its final objective, "the achievement of a potent Reserve thoroughly capable of fulfilling its mission in the event of emergency." Thus, both incoming and outgoing Directors stressed the emergency role of the not-so-secret weapon, the Reserve.

During 1947, the *Reserve Bulletin* continually stressed the need for increased enlistments. All reservists were called upon to act as recruiters. Many Reserve officers became volunteer recruiters, visiting potential recruits at their homes. Others signed up reservists at their own offices or homes in the evening. A list of volunteer recruiters ran to 3 pages in the May *Reserve Bulletin*. Officers enlisted 1,500 in just a few months. By October 1947 more than 2,500 Reserve officers were helping to recruit for the postwar Reserve. Major Andrew R. Davis of the 8th District and Captain Byford H. Stout of the 5th each added more than 100 recruits.

During this period of feverish recruiting activity, the Marine Corps Reserve Officers Association was also building its postwar chapters into professional and social units linked to the Corps. Organized and Volunteer Reserve officers had a common meeting ground at MCROA Chapter meetings in 1947. Many chapters formed VTU's and served a double purpose. They had an official tie to Headquarters through the VTU, a professional and social tie to MCROA at the community level. The MCROA chapter president also served as commanding officer of the VTU since seniority was not a command necessity then.

The Marine Corps League (MCL), also active during 1947, provided an additional Marine outlet for social and community activity. Its 25th annual national convention in October attracted many Reserve, Retired, and Regular Marines. The beloved retired General Holland M. Smith was honorary chairman of the Miami "Victory Assembly" that year. One of the League's principal postwar aims, proclaimed at the convention, was support of a strong Marine Corps Reserve.

The Marine Corps Birthday parties across the country that year gave considerable impetus to the recruiting drive which the advertising and public relations firm of J. Walter Thompson and the Division of Reserve had organized. Civilian leaders played a large part in the organization and completion of the "Program of Community Action." Chairman of the Los Angeles Citizens Marine Corps Committee was Charles S. Thomas, later to be Secretary of the Navy under President Dwight D. Eisenhower.

In Seattle, the 11th Infantry Battalion featured a battalion drill team for their 2,000 Birthday Ball guests. In Chicago, several area units sponsored a party for 2,500 at the Medinah Temple. At Fort Omaha, the 18th Infantry Battalion cut a 7-tiered cake, reputedly the largest military pastry ever baked. In Los Angeles, more than a thousand guests gathered at the Ambassador Hotel in a combined party given by the 2d 105mm Howitzer Battalion, the 13th Infantry Battalion, the Woman Reserve VTU, and the local MCROA chapter. The Tun Tavern Detachment of the Marine Corps League teamed up with Philadelphia's 1st 155mm Howitzer Battalion at the Bellevue Stratford to raise funds for a $1,000 scholarship fund for the child, brother, or sister of a deceased World War II Marine.

As an aid to both morale and recruiting, the 11th Engineer Battalion of Baltimore fielded a football team in the Eastern Interstate League against several semiprofessional clubs. Bob Lamb was the coach for Lieutenant Colonel Theodore Drummond's Reserve battalion team. Late in April, Marine Corps Reserve Week was observed in Washington, D.C. Highlights were a big party at the Capitol Theater, a buffet for the Director of the Reserve hosted by the 5th Battalion, and a wreath-laying at the Tomb of the Unknown Soldier by U.S. Senator C. Wayland Brooks, a highly decorated World War I Marine. Reserve of VMF–321 flew overhead in salute during the ceremony at Arlington Cemetery, and 20th Century Fox showed the ceremonies to the world.

Although never published, a history of the Reserve was begun during this period by the then Reserve Major Guy Richards of the New York *Journal American*. It served as a useful reference source during preparation of this volume and remains in Marine Archives as an important collection of information about Reserve units in the pre-World War II period.

Reserves and Community Emergencies

Reserves of the 10th Infantry Battalion at New Orleans worked for hours, waist-deep in water, to repair the flood-ravaged levees following a fall hurricane which damaged the city and surrounding area in 1947. They were cited by Mayor deLesseps S. Morrison for their valuable assistance in rescue and rehabilitation work and for assisting the Red Cross volunteers in caring for homeless refugees.

Two Organized units and Inspector-Instructor staffs were commended for fire-fighting services in New England. The 18th Engineer Company of Portland, Maine and Company D, 2d Infantry Battalion, of Springfield, Mass., performed in below-freezing weather, helping to bring fires under control. Such favorable attention helped establish the Reserve as a valuable community asset. It also attracted recruits.

At Memphis, Tenn., VMF–124, commanded by Lieutenant Colonel Horace A. Pehl, was the first Organized unit to reach full strength. The 16th Engineer Company of Roanoke, Va., commanded by Captain William T. Watkins, was the first 100 percent ground unit, thanks to a combination of a Labor Day parade float, a downtown recruiting booth, roving recruiter patrols, and strong radio and newspaper publicity.

During the early recruiting drive in 1947, the 10th Infantry Battalion of New Orleans, the 17th in Detroit, and the 2d at Boston had jockeyed for the lead. The Boston unit, commanded by Lieutenant Colonel James J. Dugan with Lieutenant Colonel Ira J. (Jake) Irwin as executive officer, was typical of the Organized Ground Reserve. It had started as a company in 1926, moved to battalion size prior to World War II, was called to duty and deactivated as its officers and men served throughout the war, and was reactivated in 1946 with many of the same leaders.

The Bostonians referred to their postwar quarters, 3 decks of the Navy building in South Boston, as "the kind of setup which seemed only a dream to the prewar reservists." Bowling alleys, ping pong and pool tables, hobbycraft shops, and a band room were only some of the fringe benefits provided by a grateful city, State, and Nation for its Reserves—at least in Boston.

The 16th Infantry Battalion in Indianapolis had one of the finest basketball floors in the State. It also had a canteen at the joint Navy-Marine armory which provided refreshments and a place to relax, read, and enjoy music. Old timers inspecting newly issued equipment, couldn't say anything but "it was never like this before the war," an amended version of the ever-popular refrain that it was never like this in the "Old Corps."

The Director of Public Information had been given the initial responsibility of directing and controlling Reserve publicity, and several qualified Reserve information officers were assigned to active duty billets, including Major Robert H. Rankin who headed a Reserve section in the Division of Information. Another well-known reservist brought back to active duty in 1947 was Lieutenant Colonel Walter R. Walsh who took over the Target Practice Section in the Division of Reserve. Many enlisted reservists were assigned to continuous active duty (CAD) billets in the Reserve program at the Marine Corps Schools and elsewhere.

VTU's Are Formed

The honor of forming the first VTU went to Major Milton V. O'Connell of Chicago who was issued orders on 3 February 1947 authorizing him to form a public information unit at his Merchandise Mart office. Its curricular included instructions, lectures, and actual work in the media field. It wasn't that the Corps placed publicity first, rather that O'Connell just moved fast! The first Woman Reserve VTU was organized in Seattle, Wash., by Captain Nancy M. Roberts in January that year.

In addition to forming into VTU's, Volunteer reservists went on 2-week training during 1947, either before or after the July and August peak periods for the Organized Reserve units at Quantico, Lejeune, and Pendleton. Volunteer sessions in May featured classroom work, field demonstrations by post troops, and field problems by student officers. Training included general reviews and up-to-date looks at new military methods. Refresher courses were held for specialist officers in the fields of infantry, artillery, motor transport, quartermaster, communications, tanks, and amphibious tractors. Reservists fitted well into post and station routine. Constructive suggestions included many requests that more time be devoted to field problems.

By midyear, Woman Reserve VTU's had been added in New York; Boston; Kansas City, Mo.; Baltimore, and Washington, D.C. These units provided considerable administrative support to the rapidly expanding Organized battalions in their cities and formed the cadres from which the Organized Woman Reserve companies and platoons eventually were formed.

Aviators Train

In the air, the training during 1947 was so well handled that the Commandant sent a "well done" to MARTCOM personnel and those who participated in the Organized Reserve training at Cherry Point and El Toro. He praised the "high quality of leadership and efficient operation of your command and the loyal spirit of all Reserve officers and men." Many Volunteer aviation officers also put in for summer training, even though few actually could be ordered to duty. Such enthusiasm helped secure Congressional support for continuing and expanding Reserve training.

Many Volunteer Reserve aviation ground officers and pilots, however, did receive 15 days of training during four 2-week periods in October and November at Cherry Point and El Toro.

During the summer training of the Organized Reserve squadrons at Cherry Point, 176 Corsairs were flown from home stations by pilots from the 12 squadrons and were kept operational 87½ percent of the time at camp, an enviable record even for Regular ground crews. Pilots flew more than 5,000 hours of gunnery, bombing, rocket-firing, and tactical exercises.

The highlight of the 2-week period was the use of live ammunition and rockets in an exercise furnishing air support to the 2d Marine Division. Four ground control intercept squadrons set up a field control center for radar equipment to control night-fighter problems of VMF(N)–531.

Late in 1947, it was announced that 11 new Organized Ground units would be activated prior to 1948 summer training. This both increased and maintained the pressure on recruiting for the Reserve. New units were scheduled for organization before year's end at Tucson, Ariz.; Evansville, Ind.; Petersburg, Va.; Columbus, Ohio; Venice and Peoria, Ill.; and San Pedro and Fresno, Calif. Those at Corpus Christi, Tex.; Battle Creek, Mich.; Fort Wayne, Ind.; and Milwaukee, Wis., were scheduled for later activation.

To spur recruiting and help build up summer training quotas, Certificates of Appreciation were given that year to employers who permitted Reserves to attend summer training without loss of pay or vacation. This was another aid in getting the Reserve rolling.

National Security Act

The year was a busy one, with problems besides recruiting and publicity. The National Security Act of 1947 was passed in the summer. Although it was changed in many ways from its original form, both Regular and Reserve Marines were skeptical as to how it would work out. Many Reserves had opposed the Act, either as private citizens or acting together with MCROA or the Marine Corps League, because they felt the original Administration proposal offered few, or no, safeguards for the Corps.

As finally passed, the law provided for

a Marine Corps to include land combat and service forces plus their organic aviation units. A Fleet Marine Force of combined arms and supporting air was to be organized, trained, and equipped for service with the Fleet in the seizure or defense of advanced naval bases and for the conduct of land operations essential to prosecuting naval campaigns. The law reinstated the historic role of the Corps in developing techniques and amphibious operations and perfecting tactics, techniques, and equipment employed by landing forces. This development was to be done in coordination with the Army and the Air Force. All-important to this story was the provision for the expansion of peacetime components of the Marine Corps to meet the needs of war.

On 6 August, the Commandant issued a statement on the Act which pointed out:

> Although the role of the Marine Corps in the development of the tactics of amphibious warfare and the immediate readiness of the Corps to apply those tactics have for many years been a part of U.S. naval policy, the fact has never, until now, been formalized in law. Now, in unmistakable terms, the Congress has recognized the Marine Corps as an important and essential element of the national security structure.

Writing in the MCROA *Word* in November, Colonel Maas said some things that needed saying, and remembering:

> MCROA never wavered in its battle to assure the integrity of the Marine Corps and to preserve its vital functions by law. Even while others in high places yielded to the pressure from the Administration and Army supporters, MCROA stood fast and held the line. Mandated by the membership, national officers set as the minimum requirements provisions in the legislation that would define our missions and tasks in the scheme of national security. We insisted that the Marine Corps must by law have the mission

of amphibious tactics, that it must retain its own support Marine Corps aviation. This was in addition to serving aboard vessels of the Navy and guarding Navy property.

> The battle seemed almost hopeless when the Senate yielded to Army pressure and incorporated the weasel-worded provisions of the effect that the Marine Corps was not to be disturbed in its relative position— whatever that meant! The national officers of MCROA vigorously carried the fight to the House of Representatives where they were successful in getting their proposals written into law and then accepted in conference with the Senate.

> The 12 Marine members of the House and Senate who helped in this program deserve our gratitude and deepest appreciation for their valiant campaign in Congress on this matter. The "whip" of the tightly organized Marines in Congress was Major Donald Jackson. Every Marine Member of Congress is a member of MCROA. Marines can all go forward now with confidence that the Marine Corps is not going to be abolished or whittled down by insidious campaigns from inside or outside the other military services.

The Marines who had fought the good fight in the Halls of Congress during 1947 included Senators Brooks and Joseph R. McCarthy and Representatives Jackson, Francis Case, Andrew Somers, Walter K. Granger, Paul B. Dague, James C. Davis, Mike Mansfield, James T. Patterson, George A. Smathers, and George W. Sarbacher, Jr. They were joined on 23 August by Colonel Clark Thompson who was elected to replace Congressman J. J. Mansfield from the 9th Texas District who had died in office. Thompson had previously served one term in 1933. Of the 12 stalwarts of 1947, Case, Smathers, and Mike Mansfield later were elected to the Senate.

The Year 1948

On Army Day 1948, Colonel Maas wrote General Omar N. Bradley, new Army Chief of Staff:

In an age when there has been too much talk about competing roles of the Marine Corps and the Army, we wish to extend to you our cordial hand of friendship, confident that your demonstrated vision will be utilized in maintenance of friendly rivalry and mutual respect between our services.

General Bradley replied that he was sincerely grateful for the gracious message, expressed the deep thanks of the men and women of the U.S. Army and said he hoped "the friendship and esteem between the Army and the Marine Corps may increase and flourish in the years to come."

This exchange was a far cry from the 16 May 1946 memorandum by his predecessor, General Eisenhower, who had written:

There is a real need for one service to be charged with the responsibility for initially bridging the gap between the sailor on the ship and the soldier on land. This seems to me properly a function of the Marine Corps. I believe the Joint Chiefs of Staff should give serious consideration to such a concept. . . . I therefore recommend that the above concept be accepted as stating the role of the Marine Corps and that Marine units not exceed the regiment in size, and that the size of the Marine Corps be made consistent with the foregoing principles.

This statement was to haunt the Army later when Senator Paul Douglas, a retired Reserve lieutenant colonel, introduced it to the Armed Services Subcommittee holding hearings on Senate Bill No. 677 on 13 April 1951. Congressman Clare Hoffman had thoughtfully had the statement printed in House Report No. 961 of the 80th Congress, 1st session on 16 July 1947.

On 11 March 1948 the Key West Agreement had imposed a wartime 4-division ceiling on the Marine Corps, had restricted Marine tactical command to corps level, and had stated that the Corps was not to create a second land army.

Later that spring, Vice Admiral Arthur W. Radford, Vice Chief of Naval Operations, spoke at the MCROA conference banquet 29 May in Washington and his words reached wherever Marines, whether Regular or Reserve, were stationed. He said:

The strength and vitality of the Reserve components are of pressing importance— they are subjects which engage in this time the very careful attention of all who are concerned in the long-term defense of our national life—they are vital links in the chain of security. They give much needed depth to our forces. They make real contributions to the attainment of high standards of special skill.

Referring to the mothball or zipper fleet, he said that he had observed over a long period of time that there was no such thing as a "mothball Marine." He concluded his message, directed as much to the Marine Reserves fresh from the Capitol Hill battle as to the embattled but more muzzled Marines of the Regular service, by saying:

You Marines must not forget your tradition of radical military thought and experiment. Temper your imagination with your unequalled experience in the amphibious field, and you may again contribute a great quantity of practical theory toward our national security.

Wing and Division Staffs

The Reserves were trying to bring that practical theory into being and, early in 1948, a Reserve wing staff and 2 division staffs were formed in New York City. Brigadier General Karl Day commanded the wing staff, and Colonels Bernard S. Barron and Melvin L. Krulewitch headed the division staffs. This brought the total of VTU's to 31 in 26 cities early in 1948.

Six cities hit the 100 percent mark in the recruiting drive for Organized Ground units early that year, and it was announced that the Platoon Leader Course would be open in 200 colleges to potential Reserve officers that summer.

By March, there were 1,128 officers and 25,253 enlisted in the Organized Ground Reserve—75 percent of its authorized strength. The Volunteer Reserve stood at 54 percent with 37,885 enlisted. By this time, intensive recruiting had brought 17 members into the Organized Unit 100% Club. Plans were released for training 26,000 Organized Reserves, and chaplains were provided for units going to summer camp. Civilian correspondents were encouraged to accompany or visit their hometown units at camp.

The commissioning of VMF–232 in New York City, VMF–111 in Dallas, and VMF–231 in Akron brought Aviation Reserve squadrons up to authorized fighter-bomber strength of 27 in June. In addition, there were 8 ground-control intercept squadrons.

In July 1948 the Reserve districts were given authority to handle Reserve mobilization in the event of future emergencies. By August, the first postwar group of platoon leaders had finished summer training, and both ground and air Organized Reserve units were busy at summer camps and at air stations. On 23 July, the 19th Infantry Battalion under Lieutenant Colonel Lewis N. Samuelson took part in the first televised full-scale amphibious landing in an exercise at Onslow Beach, N.C.

Writing in the MCROA *Word* for September that year, Reserve Major Tim O'Mara, commanding officer of Company E, 13th Infantry Battalion of Tucson, Ariz., told of his pride in his unit. He had taken them to Camp Pendleton that summer where they had compiled an outstanding record. He said:

> During one of our weekly drill periods, a character crept into the armory selling encyclopedias. I made him a sporting proposition: if the first 3 kids in our company could so much as *speak* English, much less read it, I'd take a set.
>
> Naturally he lost, and nearly swallowed his cigar in the process. One reason he lost: he picked Indian, Chinese, and Mexican-Americans. That's the kind of outfit we've got here in the old Pueblo. But don't get the idea that they aren't good Marines, or that they can't be understood in English. Anyone familiar at all with the Corps will testify that too much windage is one of its vulnerable spots—and nearly always emanating from the wrong places. It would be a mistake, too, to imagine that lack of wind in these "foreign" kids meant a lack of the old Semper Fidelis spirit. A good number of them fought all the way from Guadalcanal to Okinawa—and without learning to parse one simple sentence!
>
> In our Organized Reserve company here in Tucson, a predominantly Mexican-Indian-Chinese locale (the whites around here will have to be fought for), we had to take what we could get, browns, yellows, whites. So far it's been all gold!

As a result of summer training of Organized units, the Director of Reserve stated that the military efficiency of the Reserve as a potential fighting force, able to take its place alongside the Regular service, increased 100 percent over 1947. General Clement praised the Regular units which hosted Reserve units. He also expressed pleasure with the 2,400 Volunteer reservists who took summer training, completing some 100 different courses at various posts and stations. Volunteer aviation reservists, training alongside the Organized aviation units, made up a quarter of the total under training.

. Back at Glenview, General Schilt was pleased with his Reserves. The Commander of Marine Air Reserve training commented that the speed, proficiency, and skill displayed by all hands had amazed observers and demonstrated that veterans had lost little, if any, of their wartime skills. The maneuvers proved that quick movements of Marine Air Reserve squadrons into combat could be accomplished from any part of the country in 24 hours and that Reserve pilots, ground officers, and enlisted personnel were capable of fulltime work under combat conditions to keep fighter squadrons operational. General Schilt also bowed in the direction of the Chief of Naval Air Reserve and his Training Command, as well as to the commanding officers of the 1st and 2d Marine Aircraft Wings and to Naval Air Station commanders; for, without their cooperation, the mission could not have been accomplished. The team was rounding into shape.

In describing the fierce competitive spirit of one group of "weekend warriors about 1948," one Marine general told of a St. Louis reservist who put his Corsair into a turnip patch, wheels up, on a forced landing. The general reported: "The aircraft was hauled some 20 miles back to El Toro, the mud cleaned out of it, the engine and propellor changed, the necessary 'runin' time accomplished, and that aircraft was back in the air within 24 hours."

Sergeant David L. Hendricks, an accountant from Paragould, Ark., was so pleased with summer training that he wrote his 8th District Director that the training gave the men with prior military service the chance of review and also gave the men with no prior service the opportunity of living under field conditions and firing weapons which they would never get to fire except on a training program of this kind. He also praised the night problems and daily routine drills as well planned and executed. This comment from the ranks echoed the official state-

ment of the 2 general officers responsible for the Reserve.

Trophies Announced

Four trophies were announced by Marine Corps Headquarters for Organized Ground units: 1 for the unit having the highest percentage of annual drill attendance, another for the unit with the highest percentage at summer camp, and 2 for the best unit newspapers, both printed and mimeographed.

The drill attendance trophy was named in honor of William McK. Fleming, a Reserve first lieutenant killed in action at Cape Gloucester. A former member of New York's 1st Battalion, Fleming had been awarded the Navy Cross and Bronze Star. The late Sergeant Lawrence H. Flynn, a former member of Boston's prewar 2d Battalion who was killed in action at New Georgia, was memoralized in the trophy for the unit with the best summer camp attendance. He had received both the Navy and Army Silver Star medals.

Staff Sergeant Solomon I. Blechman, one of General Denig's wartime Marine combat correspondents, died of wounds received on Guam. The trophy for the best Organized Ground newspaper printed by letterpress or offset process was named after Blechman, who held the Bronze Star.

Another combat correspondent, Sergeant John Barberio, who was killed on Iwo Jima, was honored in death by the trophy for the best mimeographed paper published for 6 months or more by an Organized Ground unit. A Marine Corps Reserve public affairs unit today conducts the annual judging for the best unit newspaper.

Barberio and Blechman are 2 of the Marine combat correspondents who lost their lives in World War II who are honored by a bronze commemorative plaque in the office of the Marine Director of Information. Presented by the Marine Corps Public Relations Association, now called the Marine Corps Combat Correspondents Association, the plaque honors 7 sergeants and 1 captain whose "last by-lines were written on white markers in the Pacific during World War II."

Promotion and Policy Boards

The first peacetime Reserve selection boards picked a whopping 7,480 officers for promotion. These included 19 colonels—several who eventually earned stars; 38 lieutenant colonels; 546 majors; 2,747 captains; 4,126 first lieutenants; and 4 chief warrant officers. Lieutenant Colonel Jacob M. Goff of Richmond, Va., was the first inactive Reserve officer to accept his promotion appointment. The promotions underscored the necessity to realign the Reserve lineal list to correct certain wartime inequities. These included certain spot-promoted officers, naval aviators who during the war were advanced at a rate faster than their ground contemporaries, and officers not promoted on active duty who were given a promotion on transfer to the inactive list. The law prohibited the reduction of any officers in rank; hence the Corps devised a system of marking time for the officers promoted out of line. A realignment date of 1 July 1945 was established. Because of the tangled situation following the war, Regular officers were promoted at a faster rate than Reserves.

In order to help alleviate the substantial "hump" problems caused by wartime promotions in the field grades, particularly since there were a great many more officers available for selection than were called for in Reserve mobilization tables, the boards selecting lieutenant colonels and majors for promotion made their choices on a "best fitted" basis from all available officers. The Board selected a given number from a much larger group. Company grade officers were selected on a "fitted" basis, starting from the top of the lineal list and proceeding downward until the mobilization number had been reached. This meant that field grade officers were competing among themselves for available openings and had a higher attrition rate and were considered passed over if not selected. Company grade officers had only to meet certain minimum requirements.

A Board was convened to handle this knotty problem and, in addition, was charged with clearing Reserve officer ranks of deadwood by reviewing the records of all officers and cataloging them in categories to show those who were over-age in grade, physically unfit, unsatisfactory, or of doubtful future value, including those disinterested souls who didn't answer their official mail.

The year was also a time of decision for Women Marines. On 12 June, President Truman had signed the Women's Armed Services Integration Act of 1948 (Public Law 625, 80th Congress) which meant that women could now serve in both the Reserve and Regular components of all 4 services (Marine Corps, Army, Navy, and Air Force). Although women had been admitted to the Marine Corps as reservists in 2 previous wars, this marked the first time that women reservists were allowed to serve as a permanent part of the peacetime Corps. It was also the first time women could be part of the Regular Establishment. Spelled out in numbers, the

Act provided for a maximum of 100 Regular Women Marine officers, 10 warrant officers, and 1,000 enlisted in a gradual buildup over 2 years. These Regular candidates were to come from Reserve Women Marines on active duty or from those with prior service who were not then on duty.

The second postwar Reserve Policy Board was convened at Headquarters that same month, with General Day serving as Associate Chairman under General Clement. Reserves on this vital board were Colonels John B. Jacob and Wells W. Miller, and Lieutenant Colonels Walter A. Churchill, John E. Fondahl, Frank C. DeSantis, Rolland F. Smith, and John R. Shively. Major Helen G. O'Neill, MCROA National Secretary, served as recorder. As a result of the Board's recommendations, more extension courses were opened to officers and enlisted Reserves. However, the recommendation that Volunteer Reserves be authorized to enroll in the Marine Corps Institute was disapproved as MCI already had its hands full with the Organized Reserve.

Another recommendation that was not approved would have placed Inspector-Instructors under the operational control of Organized unit commanders. Still another, disapproved, would have provided spot promotions for the Organized Reserve and CAD billets. A draft policy statement, however, was approved which called for active duty training at least once every 4 years for every Volunteer Reserve. Additional drill periods for administrative personnel and attendance at service schools were also favored. The Board only recommended. Actual approval came from the Commandant or the Secretary of the Navy.

Public Law 810

With the signature of the President on the Reserve Retirement Bill (Public Law 810) in June of 1948, Reserves of all services not only came of age but were here to stay. The bill held out nondisability retirement inducements for reservists with 20 years of "satisfactory Federal service" who arrived at age 60. It also spelled out the manner in which "points" were to be acquired. It was belated recognition of the essentiality of the Reserve program and placed Congressionally authorized incentives before those men and women who had chosen a second career or military avocation.

The same month, some two dozen Marine reservists led by Colonel Maas visited the White House and presented President Truman a gold honorary life membership in the Marine Corps Reserve Officers Association. This was at the heat of the Presidential pre-campaign fights and in honor of President Truman's long-time personal participation in and advocacy of a strong Reserve. In making the presentation, the former Republican ranking minority member of the House Naval Affairs Committee paid tribute to his Democratic President's activities in forming the first chapter of the Reserve Officers Association in Kansas City, Mo. An interesting sidelight of the White House meeting was the presence of the Director of the Bureau of the Budget, then Reserve Major James E. Webb, due to become better known in the early 1960's as the Administrator of the National Aeronautics and Space Administration, the man who would send Marine Lieutenant Colonel John Glenn into orbit in 1962.

A casual review of the 1948 *Reserve Bulletin* reveals such a variety of training and public relations activities as almost to defy logical classification. A motion picture to plug recruiting, "Centerville, U.S.A.," was produced. In Philadelphia, a street car named "Marine" was painted red, white, and blue, to stimulate recruiting. In Portland, Maine, Major Franklin J. Weeman, commanding officer of the 18th Engineer Company, donated a suit of clothes to the best recruiter. In New York City, Ford dealer Captain Ralph Horgan offered an automobile to the reservist in the 3d District who signed up the most Volunteer Reserves. Major John Apergis of Brooklyn won the car for "snatching" 412 boots or recruits. Governor Thomas E. Dewey gave him the keys to the car and the Commandant gave Horgan a Letter of Appreciation.

New York arranged for a dirigible to flash "Marine Corps" across the night sky. Philadelphia strung a 3-story banner high above the city streets during Marine Corps Reserve Week. The Women Marines celebrated their fifth Anniversary in February with ceremonies and cake-cutting parties. Film star Tyrone Power, a Marine reservist first lieutenant, swore in a group of Reserves on the Los Angeles City Hall steps during the Reserve Week that spring.

The Corps issued distinctive Reserve lapel buttons for the men and pins for the women with the letters USMCR below the gold Marine emblem. Enlistments were authorized by mail and 1,500 Volunteer recruiters received Certificates of Appreciation for their efforts. The 12th Infantry Battalion marched in downtown San Francisco in Saint Patrick's Day parade ceremonies and Hollywood starlet Janis Page was pictured with Camp Pendleton's Major General Graves B. Erskine, discussing summer camp in her capacity as Honorary Colonel of the Los Angeles 13th Infantry Battalion.

Governor Bradford of Massachusetts presented a large pot of Boston Baked Beans to the Boston Reserve Battalion prior to its departure for summer camp. On the August anniversary of the Guadalcanal landing, the 18th Infantry Battalion of Fort Wayne, Ind., donated 200 pints of Marine blood to the Red Cross. The Washington, D.C., MCROA–VTU also gave blood to the Red Cross, to the embarrassment of its President-Commanding Officer, who fainted and had to remain an hour afterwards.

On 10 November MCROA placed a Marine Corps emblem of flowers at the Tomb of the Unknown Soldier, beginning a ceremony that was to continue until erection of the Marine Corps Memorial at the other end of the Cemetery a few years later. Colonel Maas laid the wreath; and Reserves from the 5th Infantry Battalion, VMF–321, various area VTU's, and the Marine Corps League formed ranks in the noontime ceremony as the Marine Drum and Bugle Corps played and Corsairs from VMF–321 flew cover.

VTU 11–6, commanded by Lieutenant Colonel Franklin P. Adreon, produced the first television movie made by a branch of the military to be carried on video. The film, "Semper Fidelis," was shown by Station KTLA in Los Angeles as part of Birthday ceremonies. After 2 months of special effort, the 5th District had signed up 37 diversified specialist VTU's by the time of the Birthday. Another 23 were in the process of activation. Units ranged from basic infantry to pilotless aircraft, from ordnance to intelligence. One of the units was a division staff under Colonel William W. Stickney, destined to serve later as Reserve Deputy Director for several years and for 3 short periods as Director. A wing staff was formed under Colonel Maas.

Organized Reserve "Satisfactory"

The Secretary of the Navy's report for fiscal year 1948 (1 July 1947 through 30 June 1948) described the effectiveness of the Organized Reserve units as "satisfactory," since officer strength was at 89 percent and enlisted quotas were 110 percent subscribed. The report showed that the units had been trained in basic military subjects and were supplied with limited amounts of organizational equipment, so that it would take approximately 1 month to mobilize, equip, and integrate the Organized Reserve with the Fleet Marine Force. Like the ground units, aviation in mid-1948 would be able to mobilize within 30 days—placing 24 Reserve squadrons in the air on defensive missions.

The Secretary reported, further, that 142 officers and 1,237 enlisted men were on continuous active duty for the administration and training of Reserves. Ground units had more training site problems than did aviation, since the Air Reserve used the facilities of 22 Naval Air Stations and shared these training areas with the Naval Air Reserve.

By mid-1948, Organized Ground units had expanded from 29 to 106 training centers. More than half (56) were shared with the Navy, 23 were leased, and 27 federally owned. Basic skills were stressed in armory and summer field training since 60 percent of the Organized Ground Reserve had no prior military service. Aviation, however, emphasized unit training in flight operations—to maintain both the wartime flight proficiency of its aviators and the service and ground skills of its

war-trained mechanics. One thousand Volunteer Reserve officers and 300 enlisted personnel completed active duty for training in 68 scheduled courses of instruction, and 642 women reservists averaged 29 hours each in on-the-job training as unpaid members of VTU's.

An Executive Order on "Organization of the Reserve Units of the Armed Forces," signed by President Truman at the White House on 15 October, stated that the traditional national security policy of the Government was to place great reliance in organized citizens' forces supporting Regular Armed Forces "of minimum size consistent with National defense." The order stressed maximum effectiveness and the training of citizens who had completed a period of service in the Armed Forces.

The Secretary of Defense, along with the heads of the 3 military departments, was directed to proceed without delay, utilizing every practicable resource of the Regular Establishment to organize all Reserve component units required for the national security or for the training of individuals in the active Reserve, and to establish vigorous and progressive programs of appropriate instruction and training for all Reserve elements.

The Secretary was further directed to report back within 60 days on action taken; the current status of each Reserve force; programs or schedules initiated or proposed; and any legislation recommended as being necessary. The order also charged every citizen to do his utmost in aiding the development of effective Reserve components and urged every member of the Reserve or every person eligible "to take an active part in building up the strong and highly trained Reserve."

The Marine Corps Birthday on 10 November 1948 marked the occasion for swearing into the Regular Marine Corps the first group of 8 former Reserve enlisted women. A few days previous, the Commandant, General Clifton B. Cates, had sworn in the first 3 of 20 officers selected from wartime women officers applying for transfer to the Regular Establishment following passage of the Women's Armed Services Integration Act.

The trio consisted of Colonel Katherine A. Towle (who had succeeded Colonel Streeter in 1945 as the second wartime Director of the Women's Reserve); Major Julia E. Hamblet (who had served as Director during the transition period from November 1946 through November 1948); and First Lieutenant Mary J. Hale (the only Woman Marine who had served on continuous active duty throughout the entire interim period).

First "Toys-for-Tots"

As 1948 drew to a close, the Marine Corps announced a new public service activity—an annual Toys-For-Tots drive, to be conducted throughout the Organized Reserve. Conceived by Major John Hampton, 12th District Director Colonel Charles E. Shepard, Jr., and Major William Hendricks, a Warner Brothers public relations executive who is now (March 1966) commanding officer of the West Coast Public Affairs unit, this community "good turn" program has gladdened the hearts of millions of youngsters every year since who might not have had any Christmas toys but for the continuing voluntary efforts of personnel of the Marine Corps Reserve.

The November *Reserve Marine* noted that there had only been 4 Reserve generals, all brigadiers, in Marine history. In addition to Generals Waller and Day there were Evans F. Carlson and William J. Fox who had been promoted on retirement from their rank as colonel due to having been decorated in combat. Carlson had commanded the famous "Carlson's Raiders" and served as G–5 for the 4th Marine Division. Fox was an oldtime aviator and prewar squadron commander.

By the end of 1948, the rebuilding process was well along. The Reserve was in a higher state of readiness than anyone could have hoped for 2 years previously. Estimating that the Organized units would hit 75 percent attendance for the coming year, the Corps raised its sights from the 1948 high of 58 percent. And, the Reserves were convinced that the Corps meant business in wanting a ready force of trained manpower. Accordingly, they did their very best to measure up to the confidence placed in them by the Corps in assigning men, money, and material to the rebuilding program on a basis undreamed of in prewar days.

CHAPTER SIX

Setting the Stage

Highlights of 1949 were MCROA's January and October conferences; the October hearings of the House Committee on the Armed Services and the June introduction of legislation to guarantee a Marine Corps of adequate size for the future. This legislation consisted of identical House Bills (H.R. 5403 to H.R. 5457) by 55 Representatives where the rule is "one Member, one Bill" and S. 2177 by 4 Senators in the Senate. Nothing was to happen in 1949 on the so-called "Marine Bill", but the stage was set for eventual legislative action. During this same year, the Reserves got ready through stepped-up unit training for the drama of Korea that—as it turned out—was to be just ahead.

As the year began, decorations from the Iwo Jima Flag Raising Float placed in the previous week's Inaugural Parade by MCROA dressed up the Association's 29 January conference in Chicago. The new Commandant, General Clifton B. Cates, flew out in his personal plane and addressed the conferees, as did the Director of Reserve. The meeting theme was "interservice cooperation and understanding". Reservists pledged themselves to take the lead in their communities in honest efforts to make unification work. Programs for 1949 included all-service socials; joint meetings yearly of all Reserve units, so reservists of all services could understand and appreciate the problems and contributions of their sister services; and invitations to officers of other services, both

Regulars and Reserves, to speak at Marine Reserve meetings. On the political side, the conference called for new emphasis on civilian direction of the military establishments and for an Assistant Secretary for Reserves in the 3 military departments.

The Commandant reminded his audience that less than 4 years previously most of them had been on active duty, but that the tasks they were performing now in 1949 were no less important. He told them they were providing a large measure of the Corps' readiness for war or large-scale national emergency and that if the Regular services represented the hard shell of readiness, the Reserves were the solid core.

He further observed:

> You are also serving your country as citizens, and I like to think that you are better than average ones, bringing to the problems which face the citizen the same outstanding qualities of character and ability which have made you better-than-average military officers. I think that the record of the Marine Corps Reserve Officers Association fully justifies that feeling.

In summarizing Marine tasks, he included defense against enemy air and submarine attack; subordinate responsibilities for occupational duties; the delivery of atomic bombs; and the seizure of advanced bases for eventual offensive use. He concluded:

> There should be 1 guiding principle. . . . That principle is the principle of first things first. As we [Defense] reach into the public

126

purse for the largest peacetime appropriation in our history [$14 billion plus], I hope every American citizen will have that principle in mind. If the Marine Corps Reserve Officers Association can help the American citizen bear that principle in mind, the Association will be performing one of the most valuable of its many public services.

Maas Blasts Dissension

In spite of congratulatory messages to MCROA from President Truman, Navy Secretary John L. Sullivan, and Defense Secretary James Forrestal, all was far from being sweetness and light on the Reserve front, or the Regular either, for that matter. A hard-hitting speech by President Maas at the conference proved all-too-prophetic in the battle for the Marine Corps which soon followed. He warned:

> Never in history was there a greater need for unity, loyalty, and selfless leadership, yet we meet today faced with dissension, backbiting, and frequently a leadership of selfishness and greed even in our own military forces. Our enemies couldn't by design set the stage for their purpose better than we ourselves are doing. What do they see? Still all too much of a mad scramble to either hold blindly to outmoded traditions and weapons, or to greedily reach out and grab control of the weapons, personnel, and funds of sister military services, as if the battle were among themselves, instead of a common enemy.

He further charged that "bickering, backbiting, sly undercutting, exaggerated claims, slurs, and ill-concealed hostility among too many professional military leaders of all ranks" was causing disgust among Americans and gleeful jubilation among our enemies. He said this even applied to the attitude of the professional military toward Reserve components. He said too many Regulars consider reservists as outsiders, trying to "muscle in," as rank

seekers and parasites on their appropriations. He stated, conversely, that too many reservists have chips on their shoulders and too frequently take the attitude that all Regulars are "brass hats" interested only in holding down the Reserves. He blamed much of the situation upon the "imperfections in the unification law itself" as well as on the unyielding attitudes of too many individuals in the military service. Against this backdrop, Maas and the members of the National Council, together with the chapter presidents, urged MCROA to take the lead at the community level in promoting harmony and a spirit of live and let live.

General Clement, in a report to part of his Reserve officer constituency, told MCROA in frigid Chicago that the fiscal year 1949 manpower target was 141,739 Reserves. The Organized Reserve was scheduled to add 16,000 members for a total of 53,369 by 1 July, with 79 new Organized units on the drawing board. He pleaded for more help in locating armories, stressing that Reserves training during 1948 exceeded the entire Regular strength of 1937. "Never before in our history," he told delegates, "have we been so able to protect that trust placed in us by the American people."

Some of the provisions adopted in 1949 might seem strange today, but it was no laughing matter when resolutions had to be adopted opposing any change which would take from the Marine Corps its function as a combat component of the Armed Forces or stating emphatically that Marine Corps aviation was an integral part of the Corps in the fulfillment of its mission!

The Government reorganization bills then pending would have given the President power to make sweeping changes in the military without Congressional approval unless *both* House and Senate objected. For this reason, special provisions were made in the final bill which required any changes affecting the military to be sent separately to the Congress. On other legislation there was little controversy.

Miller First 810 Retiree

One such piece of legislation was the nondisability Reserve Retirement Act. Commenting on this Act, in *A Brief History of the Marine Corps. Reserve Officers Association*, MCROA Executive Secretary Colonel Tom Wert, said of Public Law 810, that it was the only legislative act ever written which provided longevity retirement pay for Reserve officers and that, "without question, had it not been for General Maas such legislation would never have been approved."

The first Marine reservist to retire under its provision was the colorful Colonel Harvey L. Miller, who reached his 60th birthday early in 1949 after 39½ years of Regular and Reserve service in both the Navy and Marine Corps. Colonel Miller had been the only Marine Reserve officer to command a regiment in World War II and one of the few to command a battalion in the early years of the war. For 2 decades prior to his official retirement, he combined his boxing skills and journalistic abilities with his Marine Corps Reserve activities to give dynamic leadership in the Washington area. Even after his retirement, he continued to maintain a full schedule at the University of Maryland in both athletic and journalistic activities and served for many years as Chairman of the District of Columbia Boxing Commission.

Referring to Colonel Miller in 1965, Brigadier General Charles Cogswell, a retired reservist who enlisted in Miller's battalion in 1933, said:

> Heinie Miller was one of the greatest leaders of men in the Marine Corps Reserve and the Marine Corps. He continually stressed the development of the "Professional Attitude" among his officers. All officers were required to take correspondence courses and failure to satisfactorily complete courses or maintain satisfactory progress meant an unsatisfactory fitness report, and eventual separation from the unit.

Younger reservists were also making news during this time. Lieutenant Colonel Sidney McMath was elected Governor of Arkansas and in January 1966 was selected as a Reserve major general. Major George Smathers, a young Congressman from Florida, took the lead in simplifying U.S. immigration laws. Today he is a Reserve colonel and a ranking member of the Senate Foreign Affairs Committee. Back in 1949, both were honored by the U.S. Junior Chamber of Commerce as among the 10 Outstanding Young Men of 1948. Major James E. Webb moved from his position as Director, Bureau of the Budget, to become Under Secretary of State; and a lieutenant colonel named Harry R. Van Liew (now deceased after reaching flag rank) caused quite a stir at Cherry Point when he flew his own plane down from New York to report for 1949 Reserve duty. President Truman, who was soon to attend a meeting of the Marine Corps League under less happy circumstances, received National Commandant Theus J. MacQueen and his son, Bruce, at the White House and accepted a gold honorary membership card in the League, along with the League's 1949 legislative program.

A bright ray that spring was passage of the Marine Reserve budget as presented to the Congress. The bill provided for an average of 50,772 reservists in a drill pay status. The total Reserve personnel was to hit 150,000, an increase of 21,805. It was expected the Corps would have 52 training centers for use by Reserve units and another 55 for shared use with the Naval Reserve.

General Silverthorn Heads Reserve

The Reserve Marine that May announced the promotion to Major General of Merwin H. Silverthorn who relieved General Clement as Director of Reserve on 3 May upon his completion of more than 2 years at the helm during a period of crucial urgency to the Reserve. General Silverthorn, once an Inspector-Instructor in Chicago, had been a reservist himself 31 years earlier. Taking over as Director, he noted that the first phase of a difficult operation had been completed and that the Reserve was now in a favorable position from which to launch continued efforts. "The Reserve will play a vital role in determining Marine Corps destiny," he said. "In peace as in war, the Marine Corps looks to the men of the Reserve for enthusiasm, initiative, and loyal support." Under General Clement, the Corps had expanded its Reserve from 38,403 officers and men to 123,000. But, there was still plenty of work ahead for all.

The Corps selected pilots from each Reserve squadron to check out the new jets the Marines were getting. These officers then returned to their squadrons to train their fellow pilots. Colonel Maas, representing Marine Reserve aviation, and Colonel Charles H. Cox, officiating for ground units, became members of the Defense Secretary's Civilian Components Policy Board that year and gave voice to Marine views at this newest advisory group which

is today known as the Reserve Forces Policy Board.

The Volunteer Reserve was moving forward with its VTU program and, on 16 March, a MCROA *Chapter Contact* featured "The VTU," written by Major Donald N. Carpenter. The article noted:

> Training periods for VTUs are 120 minutes. Leaders should schedule a variety of activity to hold the interest of the group and advance their knowledge of military skills. Wherever possible, it is considered advisable that VTU members learn their specialty by working with tangible training aids. Training and historical movies are also available. Advance planning is essential so that the proper manuals and training manuals can be arranged for in advance, so they will be on hand when required.
>
> The VTU program is new and all possibilities have not been explored. Individual commanding officers with a perfect setup for a meeting or with good ideas should write their Reserve Director so he can pass the word to others. This VTU plan of Reserve organization is a sound one. If it is carried out with customary Marine imagination and enthusiasm it will soon become another Marine activity of which our Corps can be proud.

Carpenter proved to be quite a prophet: The program today *is* a sound one, and it *has* taken imagination and enthusiasm to keep it current or ahead of the times during the decade and a half that have passed since 1949.

During 1949 Brigadier General Denig, also with Marine imagination and enthusiasm, conducted a preliminary survey to determine the feasibility of embarking upon a national fund-raising campaign for the Marine Corps League's Congressionally-approved war memorial. Eventually, General Denig headed the Marine Corps War Memorial Foundation which under new leadership, got the previously stalled drive back on track. His successors were

Major General Merritt A. Edson and Colonel Jean Moreau, both retired Regular officers, as Presidents of the Foundation which, with the considerable help of 2 Marine Corps Commandants and several "in house" fund drives, finally managed to finance the Marine Corps Memorial. Better known as the "Iwo Jima Memorial," sculptor Felix deWeldon's heroic bronze reproduction of Joe Rosenthal's famous flag-raising photo is now one of the Capital's most popular tourist attractions, just north of Arlington Cemetery. Colonel Arthur B. Hanson, who was selected as a Reserve brigadier general in January 1966, has served as President of the standby Foundation the past 9 years (1957–66).

The Blechman Trophy for 1948 was awarded to the 3d Infantry Battalion of St. Louis, Mo.; and the Barberio Trophy went to Company B, 15th Infantry Battalion, Corpus Christi, Tex. Lieutenant Colonel C. W. Stahl was commanding officer of the 3d Battalion, and Corporal W. A. Piel was editor of *The Dope Sheet*, its winning printed newspaper. Captain Richard C. Hedrick was skipper of the Corpus Christi unit and First Lieutenant Anton Froelich, Company Inspector-Instructor, was editor of its award-winning *Citmar*.

Company D, 13th Infantry Battalion, from Pearl Harbor, Hawaii, won the first Flynn Trophy that year with 80.9 percent attendance for 1948 summer training. Company D was formed in the spring of 1938 as part of the Los Angeles-based 13th Battalion. The Marine Corps League in the Hawaiian Islands had sent a delegation to Washington, D.C., to get an organized unit formed in the Hawaiian Islands and Major Glen H. L. Cooper was named the first commander. Their 1948

2-weeks annual training was on Maui, wartime home of the 4th Marine Division, in the old, unused National Guard Camp. The next year they trained at the Naval Rifle Range, Puuloa Point on Oahu and, in 1950, were flown by the famous Navy "MARS" flying boats to San Diego for training at Camp Pendleton where they were at the outbreak of the Korean War.

The report of Air Reserve training, released in March, showed a 38.8-percent attendance increase over 1948; a 57-percent increase in flying time; and a 3-percent increase—up to a remarkable 92 percent—in aircraft availability. In all, 1,497 officers and 4,671 enlisted men took part in 1948 Air Reserve training.

In April 1949, the first Organized Woman Reserve platoons were activated in Kansas City, Mo., and in Boston. In both cases, a VTU was the nucleus. One of the 2 Inspector-Instructors assigned to these pioneering units was First Lieutenant Ben Alice Day. (In later years she was to be better known in the Washington area as a Reserve lieutenant colonel, member of Public Affairs Unit 4–1, and the wife of the Assistant Commandant of the Marine Corps, Lieutenant General John C. Munn. In 1964, the Munns retired at the same time at Camp Pendleton, in the first husband-wife Regular-Reserve retirement ceremony in Corps history. The general had reached the retirement age for his rank. The colonel had completed her 20 years under Public Law 810, but had a long wait before drawing pay at age 60.)

Regarding a change in the mission and functions of the Corps, many Reserve officers had written intelligent and persuasive letters to their elected representatives in the Congress. One such letter to Senator

Brian McMahon from Major Philip N. Dumbrille of Stamford, Conn., referred to persisting rumors and "straws in the wind." A great believer in the superlative, the Major wrote:

> The U.S. Marine Corps is justifiably one of the proudest military organizations in the world and even a hasty examination of the record will disclose it as certainly the most distinguished service in this country from point of view of achievements, eternal readiness, and long-term planning. The morale and Esprit De Corps of the Corps is unexcelled and a cursory inquiry into the present preparedness of this service in any part of the world where its units are stationed today will reveal it as the Nation's foremost ready force.
>
> It is felt that you are probably cognizant of the above, but in the event that the press of business has prevented you from any thorough study of the situation, it is respectfully requested that you consult any of your unbiased sources of military information and I am sure that the facts will bear me out. It will also be noted that the taxpayer gets at least one and three-quarters fighting man for the 'same dollar expenditure as is obtained from any other service.
>
> This letter is written on behalf of a number of my friends and your constituents and we earnestly implore you to see that the U.S. Marine Corps is left alone to continue its matchless career and to function as the supreme amphibious power in existence today.

The Administration Bill

However, there were more than straws in the wind as the Regular Corps went about its business of establishing a *really Ready* Reserve. There was some serious question as to whether there would even be a Corps around in the future, let alone a need for a Reserve. So, while active duty Marines were officially unable to speak, the Reserves on the outside and "friends of the

Marine Corps" working with MCROA were far from silent.

On 20 April, a mass meeting of some 350 Marine Reserve officers heard Major General Edson, Colonel Maas, and others review the previous effort to absorb or destroy the Corps as they referred to the then-current Senate Bill No. 1269, authored by Senator Millard E. Tydings. Army Secretary Kenneth Royal had stated that the Secretary of Defense should be able to transfer the Marine Corps to the Army if he saw fit. This was cited as an illustration of the dangers in the Administration (Tydings) bill; another being the possibility of creating a "Super General Staff" with authority concentrated in the military. Both the Navy and the Marine Corps had testified against the bill in Executive Session and further testimony had been cut off.

Officially titled "The National Security Act Amendments of 1949," the Bill S. 1269 seemed, to many, to be just another version of what had been cut out of the Unification Act as originally proposed. At the same time, Consolidation Directive No. 1 (later revoked), signed on 14 April by William Frye for [the late] Defense Secretary Louis A. Johnson, prohibited any Regular, Retired officer, or Reserve on active duty from making public or private statements about the legislation. Among those who rallied to the Corps was Richard Tregaskis whose reporting from Guadalcanal and the Pacific had endeared him to the Marines for whom he had great admiration. His *Saturday Evening Post* story, "The Marine Corps Fights for Its Life" was reprinted by Marine Congressman Don Jackson of California and widely distributed by MCROA and the League to "Friends of the Marine Corps."

Collier's new editor, Marine reservist Louis Ruppel, also lent his talents and his magazine to the issue of Corps survival.

4th Marine Division Washington, D.C., Reunion

General Day in a communication to his wing staff in New York had reviewed the Tregaskis article and emphasized that an arm like aviation was developing so rapidly that competition was necessary. He pointed out the bargain rate of the individual Marine was a cost of $4,000 per year as against the Army average of $7,000 per capita. He stated that the Corps was the "only preventative for bureaucratic, comfortable, easy self-satisfaction" and, although in the light of today's world it may seem that he overstated the case, no one in the Reserve thought so then. Nor did the Marines in Congress.

That same June, the Fighting 4th Marine Division held its annual reunion in Washington. The timing was probably not accidental, for the Commandant, General Cates, had commanded the 4th at Tinian and Iwo Jima. The reunion gave the Marines a fine occasion to march in Washington, and the Reserves and former Marines of the 4th also found time for a boat ride on the Potomac, a style show, a wreath-laying at the Tomb of the Unknown Soldier, Memorial Ceremonies at the Arlington Cemetery Amphitheater, a banquet, and a business session.

The mysterious "national speaker of prominence" billed in early announcements turned out to be the fearless Admiral William (Bull) Halsey who kicked off a plea for a floor under the Corps at 6 percent of total personnel of the Armed Forces. His slogan was "Six Percent for Security" and he spoke to an overflow audience on the Washington Monument grounds almost within earshot of the White House and eyesight of the Capitol—2 of the 3 "battle" zones, the third being the Pentagon across the Potomac.

The salty Admiral told his enthusiastically partisan audience:

> Congress has placed a ceiling on the number of Marines. In addition to a ceiling, there should be a flooring that will see that the Marine Corps is perpetuated. In other words, it has been suggested to me by my many friends in the Marine Corps Reserve that 6 percent of the Army, Navy, and Air Force be a flooring of the Marine Corps so that we will always have a permanent Marine Corps of a proper size. What this country needs is legislation to see that there is a perpetual Marine Corps.

The Senate eventually passed Senate Bill No. S–1843, an amended version of the objectionable (to many) S. 1269 after the addition, during debate, of safeguards for Navy and Marine Corps aviation and amendments prohibiting transfer of personnel by the Secretary of Defense and limiting the number of officers serving in the staff of the Joint Chiefs of Staff.

In a June editorial in *The Word*, MCROA summed up an 8-paragraph "Box Score" by concluding that no convincing proof had been given that the legislation would produce either economy or greater unification and that no satisfactory figures had been drawn up to show where a billion or a billion and a half dollars could be saved. The Navy was having its troubles too, but this is a Marine story. Obviously, MCROA's work was unofficial and was not inspired by the Corps itself. The same should be emphasized regarding legislative activities of the Marine Corps League and of hundreds of Reserve Marines and former Marines exercising their American constitutional right of petition.

Marine Reserve Policy Board

The 1949 Marine Reserve Policy Board had met that May and one of its members, Colonel Horace W. Card, speaking to his fellow officers in Los Angeles some time later, said:

> There are many things being done for your benefit which lack of time and the desire to get on to other subjects prevents me from mentioning, but which you can ascertain by inquiry. It is pertinent to say that practically everything that can be done for you individually is predicated upon your own interest in the Reserve, your availability, and your ability as well as your desire to serve.
>
> We, as reservists, must realize that membership in the Reserve and advancement therein is not a one-way street; to be served we must serve. We can expect but little interest in ourselves if we do not exhibit a like interest and an active participation in the Reserve program, its mission and its problems, and the part we are expected to play.
>
> I can assure you that if any individual thinks that he is neglected by the Division of Reserve, or is forgotten by them, he has only to address a letter to the Director of Reserve, stating any problem that he may have or making any recommendation he believes appropriate, and his letter will receive the personal attention of an officer or several officers, including the Director himself, until an answer is provided.

Of the Policy Board itself, which had to have at least 50 percent Reserve membership, Colonel Card admitted many agenda items were somewhat less than "policy" in nature, saying:

> Annual boards have the virtue of overhauling policy and keeping it fresh and up to date and in step with progress in other branches of the military services and to keep it abreast of legislative changes.
>
> Now it happens that we just can't get away from the fact that a reservist is a civilian and that everything that he does as

a reservist must be reconciled with his position as a civilian; his economic status, his profession, his occupation, his social life, and his family affairs.

> The Division of Reserve is constantly faced with the problem of improving the education and training of reservists in the face of, and often in opposition to, the demands made upon them as civilians. Practically everything that we considered in our deliberations was affected in some degree by that problem, and the subjects we selected and recommended to the Secretary of the Navy as policy reflected the problem.

There were setbacks as well as advances in 1949. Summer camp attendance fell off from 54 percent in 1948 to 47 percent of authorized strength. Although 70 percent of eligible officers went to camp as against the previous year's 53 percent, General Silverthorn pulled no punches in voicing disappointment. While praising those who attended, he pointedly said that, with a bit more effort, many who stayed home could have gone. The first class of women to graduate from Quantico after World War II took their oath as new lieutenants that year. Seven of the 34 received Regular commissions, and the rest received appointments in the Reserve. The president of Ridder Publications of St. Paul, Reserve Major Herman H. Ridder, presented the Corps with a handsome trophy for the Organized Marine Corps Reserve Fighter Squadron and Ground Control Intercept Squadron judged the most efficient each fiscal year. The winners were allowed possession of the cup 5 months of each year and were given a smaller permanent trophy.

The third Saturday of each May was designated as Armed Forces Day by Defense Secretary Johnson, the first one to be 20 May 1950 the following year. The end result of this action was not only to discourage observance of the traditional Navy

Day, Army Day, and Marine Corps Birthday but to practically forbid the Regular services to do anything about these days outside their own families. Regular and Reserve organizations and VTU's were forbidden to initiate or participate in any public celebration aimed at publicizing the Birthday of the Corps. Social observances within the various units were permitted, including traditional cake-cutting ceremonies. The emphasis was on the word "public" and Regulars were specifically forbidden to act as speakers at MCROA, Marine Corps League, or other organization parties.

General Brice to Commander, Marine Air Training

On 1 June 1949 Brigadier General William O. Brice became Commander, Marine Air Reserve Training, relieving General Schilt who had built well during his pioneer tour as COMART. General Brice came to Glenview from Headquarters Marine Corps where he had been Assistant Director of Aviation. That fall the Corps selected 9 Reserve colonels and 11 lieutenant colonels. Three of the colonels were destined for eventual promotion to flag rank, Harry R. Van Liew, James E. Howarth, and John Lloyd Winston.

Through the second and third weeks of October 1949, the Navy and the Marine Corps presented their views before the Armed Services Committee of the House. There were 2 Marine spokesmen, Brigadier General Vernon E. Megee and the Commandant, General Cates. General Megee explained why close air support was essential to successful land combat operations and effectively emphasized the interchangeability of Navy and Marine aviators for carrier-based or close support

missions. The Commandant outlined the various steps, either taken or planned by the Administration, which were obviously aimed at carrying out the War Department General Staff demands that the Marine Corps should (1) be limited to units no larger than a regiment and reduced in total strength so as to have no more than 50,000 to 60,000 men; (2) no longer have the function of amphibious warfare, which was to be transferred to the Army; and (3) not be appreciably expanded in time of war. This last was of particular concern to the Reserves. For, if the Corps was to have no wartime expansion, there was no need for the backup force of a Reserve secret weapon.

The Commandant made the telling point that neither economy nor strategy seemed to lie behind stated intentions regarding the Corps, but rather the definite purpose of rendering it ineffective to carry out its mission either on the ground or in the air. Following his prepared testimony, he made additional recommendations, in response to questions from the committee. These recommendations called for a voice in discussions in matters affecting the Corps at both the Joint Chiefs and Department of Defense level and for 2 divisions of 6 fully equipped battalions, 2 wings having 12 fully equipped tactical squadrons, each air and ground arm having the necessary supporting service elements.

MCROA October Conference

In spite of legislation and the seeming safeguards enacted into military policy by the Congress and the Key West Agreements, the Corps wasn't taking any chances and, when MCROA held its 21–23 October 1949 weekend conference in Philadelphia, the Commandant read the same speech he had delivered a few days before to the House Committee. It was not only the safest speech he could deliver since it was privileged, but it was the strongest. MCROA reacted by expressing "its complete approval and confidence in the recent statement of the Commandant" in a press release given out in Washington by Colonel Maas the day following the conference.

Colonel Maas had keynoted the meeting with a warning that the destruction of the Marine Corps might well spell defeat for the United States in the event of another war, saying:

> Our history indicates that if the Marine Corps is destroyed as a combat organization, we are likely to enter World War III largely with weapons, tactics, and techniques developed to fight World War II. They will not be enough to win any future war. The current movement to preserve the Marine Corps as an integrated, well-equipped striking force is basically neither service rivalry nor pride in the Corps, but the deep conviction of people with knowledge that we must have what the Corps can give the Nation in order to survive as a democratic nation.

Citing the Halsey slogan, "Six Percent Spells Security," Colonel Maas said that an equal need was that "the law must provide that the Commandant of the Marine Corps sit with the Joint Chiefs during consideration of amphibious matters and on all other matters affecting the Marine Corps. Not until and unless these 2 things are done is this Nation assured of proper military security."

At the October conference, friendly letters from the President, the Secretary of Defense, and a new Secretary of the Navy, Francis P. Matthews, were read. The formal words of greeting prepared by speech-writing specialists were read and

published, but everybody kept their powder dry. Reserve Major Davis Merwin, an executive of the Bloomington, Ill., *Pantagraph* and former editor and publisher of the *Minneapolis Star*, received the first MCROA honor plaque for his "one-man education campaign to tear the blinders off Americans, make them see what they've actually got, and show them what they must have for a balanced defense." Merwin's articles and editorials had been welcome ammunition to those trying to tell the country what was happening and what might happen to the Corps.

MCROA's editorial, "Box Score No. 3," front-paged in its September *Word*, was so prophetic that it is reproduced as a sign of the effectiveness of the Reserves on the outside in pointing up dangers which Regulars could see just as well, or better, but couldn't discuss publicly:

> MCROA has kept faith in its pledge to promote cooperation and understanding among the services. Almost every chapter has invited Army, Navy, or Air Force officers to speak at meetings or has fall plans for such programs.
>
> Whether others have kept faith with MCROA and the USMC remains in doubt. At this writing no denial has been issued of David Lawrence's report that Marine Air will be cut in half during 1951. No denial has been made to the prophecy by Representative Hoffman on the House floor that danger lurks for the Corps in the recent Amendments to the National Security Act of 1949.
>
> Unless and until MCROA has better proof than is presently available to the contrary, we shall believe and expect the worst because the thinking of the Defense Establishment seems to be dominated by the Eisenhower-Bradley-Spaatz-Collins theory that the Marine Corps should never get bigger than a regiment.
>
> Unless and until Pentagon officials succeed in rendering Reserves incapable of speaking up, MCROA will continue to ask

why the Commandant isn't consulted on amphibious matters, why the Joint Chiefs can become a voting group where the Army and Air Force gang up on the Navy, and how the Defense Department dares to violate the express will of Congress by using its budget office to strip one service of the ability to perform its mission?

The Marine Corps does not yet have a Crommelin and MCROA has no desire to assume a martyr pose but its National Executive Council seriously questions the judgment of certain policies and individuals. We question no one's integrity and we violate no security but we predict that unless something is done to arrest the present tide of events, the following may well take place:

1. The Marines will suffer a 50-percent cut in planes in 1951.

2. Our battalion landing teams will be reduced drastically in 1951.

3. Our Reserve program will be emasculated so as to be ineffective by 1952.

4. Budgetary cuts in 1951 will make it impossible to provide flying time for Regulars and Reserves and hence in 1952 another request will be made for authority to transfer personnel within the National Military Establishment.

5. In the holy name of economy, "excess' Marine aviators will be transferred to the Air Force after a shotgun wedding.

6. Minus the personnel, funds, pilots, and weapons to handle its amphibious responsibilities, the Corps will have to default on its Key West assigned positions.

We hope we are wrong, for if we are right we may have lost the next war before it begins and will have arrived at a General Staff that brooks no independent thinking.

On 2 November 1949 just prior to the Corps Birthday, the embattled MCROA National Council, following a special session, issued a 1-page statement urging stronger Reserve forces in the fiscal 1951 budget. It said:

> The National Council of the Marine Corps Reserve Officers Association expects that the good judgment of the President, the Bureau of the Budget, and the Appropriations and Armed Services Committees of the

House of Representatives and the U.S. Senate will arrive at a 1951 budget for national defense which will give our country a balanced striking force in keeping with the needs of the times.

According to the testimony and recommendations of our military leaders, the real military strength of America lies in a small and highly trained professional establishment and a large and well-trained Reserve. We trust that if the President, the Budget Bureau, and the Congress believe the military budget must be reduced, the budget will permit an increase in the size of the Reserve and National Guard units.

Furthermore, we expect that, in the interests of economy, the Nation will be allowed to retain a Marine Corps worthy of its mission in this troubled world. We do not believe that any honest economy is served by substituting either Army ground units or Air Force squadrons for already trained and instantly ready Marine ground and air units, particularly since there is considerable proven economy in retention of existing Marine ground and air units.

Silverthorn Issues Status Report

At the exact same time (29 November–1 December), the Marine Corps was holding its conference of general officers at Headquarters Marine Corps. The Director of Reserve made a 9-page presentation, which highlighted Organized and Volunteer Reserve achievements and reviewed summer training just past and just ahead for 1950. He said that Reserve liaison and training sections were scheduled for 6 summer camp locations in 1950 to assist commanding generals in carrying out increased workloads resulting from Organized and Volunteer training.

General Silverthorn's report constituted a status report of the Reserve at the end of the third postwar year. Significant facts included:

1. The Reserve consisted of 127,475 officers and men.

2. There were 39,649 officers and men in the Organized and 86,585 in the Volunteer Reserve. The remainder were in the Fleet Reserve.

3. The Reserve was fully integrated with the Regular Establishment, with 168 Regular officers and 431 Regular enlisted devoting full time to the Reserve, and 387 Reserve officers and 2,273 Reserve enlisted on continuous active duty in the Reserve program.

4. The Air Reserve, with 1,617 officers and 5,068 enlisted in 41 squadrons, was at 95 percent of authorized Organized strength.

5. The Ground Organized Reserve was at 93 percent of strength in 100 separately administered units, with veterans making up 98 percent of its officers and 27 percent of its enlisted personnel.

6. The Volunteer Reserve was at 87 percent of strength (officers at 99 percent; enlisted at 83 percent). Of the Volunteer officers, some 98 percent were veterans, while 85 percent of the Volunteer enlisted could boast wartime service.

7. Summer camp attendance for Organized units was up 16 percent from 1948's 53 percent for officers, and down 8 percent for enlisted personnel.

8. Plans for 1950 summer training included expansion of airlifts of units to and from locations; minimum use of sea transportation to avoid loss of training time; permitting Volunteer reservists to attend established courses at the same time as Organized units; insistence by unit leaders on increased assumption of training responsibility at camp; increase in the administrative support taken to camp by ground units; and an annual spring pretraining conference for representatives of all Organized Reserve units.

The bugs were rapidly being worked out of the system; every possible plan was being tried to make it easier for enlisted reservists to accompany their units to camp or to go as individuals for Volunteer Reserve training. The decisions made in 1949 were so well-conceived and farsighted that today almost all of them are standing operating procedure, modified only as necessary to accommodate changes that are part of the process of growth.

As the year drew to a close, a number of pleasant facts came to light as reports were collected, reviewed, and tabulated. The Reserve airlift carried 8,243 reservists from home to camp and back with zero casualties and zero accidents. In compiling this impressive record, the Reserve pilots logged 6½ million passenger miles in 1,500 hours flying time in 260 trips, for actual plane miles of 260,386 or the equivalent of 10 times around the world and more. On some days, every plane from the 3 transport squadrons—VMR–152, VMR–153, and VMR–252—was in the air at the same hour. As a result, the Corps decided to continue and enlarge the airlift the coming year.

Out in Texas, Battery C, 2d 155mm Howitzer Battalion from Texarkana took the Lawrence H. Flynn Trophy for the highest summer camp attendance percentage—then an all-time record high of 94.9 percent—with 168 men of 177 making camp. As if to prove a point, the same unit—commanded by Captain Louis F. Graves, Jr.—won the 1949 William McK Fleming Trophy for the calendar year 1949 with 84.1 percent drill attendance.

By year's end, some 1,700 Volunteer Reserve personnel had applied for Marine Corps Institute courses and 700 had enrolled. Many applicants were ruled ineligible because of limitations on training opportunities in their functional fields. An indication that the Marines were taking their training seriously was the scope of the most popular courses applied for. They were: supply and mapping, Soviet Union geography, fundamentals of both radio and electricity, and refresher courses in military geography and mathematics.

There were no Reserves taking cinch courses!

In Wisconsin, on the shores of Lake Michigan, the 18th Infantry Battalion put Milwaukee's Company C ashore at nearby Racine as units of the 128th Air National Guard Squadron provided close air support with P–51 Mustangs. Prior to the simulated landing, three low-flying Douglas B–26 bombers put on a shore bombardment for the thousands of spectators gathered to see the Marines storm ashore. It was a 3-service show as the Wisconsin National Guard supplied reinforcements on D+1. The Marines were transported by the Wisconsin 32d National Guard Division.

At about this time across the continent, the Military Order of the World Wars was honoring Colonel Maas with its annual Medal of Honor award for having rendered the most outstanding service to the National Security during 1949. Maas was later to serve with distinction as the Commander in Chief of the Military Order, just as he was to become National Commander of the Disabled American Veterans and National President of the Blinded Veterans Association years later after loss of his sight from glaucoma, brought on by bomb blast and concussion suffered on Okinawa.

As if to underscore the year's activities, Chief of Naval Operations Admiral Louis E. Denfield reported that the Corps had enjoyed a "typical" peacetime year. To Denfield, who had been relieved as Chief of Naval Operations on orders from the President, the year had been anything else but typical or peaceful. However, he said of the Corps:

> Behind this small but highly integrated body stands an enthusiastic Reserve numbering 102,400 in the Ground Reserve and 22,075 in the Air Reserve, ready for quick inclusion into the U.S. Marine Corps should an emergency require it.

Before another 12 months rolled around, Denfield was proved a prophet of the first magnitude.

CHAPTER SEVEN

The Battle for the Marine Corps

The 3-year period which included the years 1950, 1951, and 1952 can best be told in 3 parts, rather than chronologically. The military part was the Korean War and the participation of tens of thousands of Reserves in that war. The political part was the battle for the Marine Corps, including the work of MCROA and many other Marine friends, both in and out of the Reserve, which culminated in passage of the "Marine Corps Bill." The third and more routine part of this 3-year chunk of Reserve history was the "back home at the ranch" story of what went on in the States in the Reserve program while the war and the truce were occupying Marines half a world away.

The Korean War is covered in the next chapter, although there are obvious references to it here for a war cannot be fought in a Stateside vacuum. This chapter will first give an overview of the Stateside developments, which were as important historically in their own way for the Reserves of all services, as was the legislation for the entire Marine Corps, treated in the second section.

In a way, there were really 3 "battles" during this 3-year period: the battle in Korea, the battle for a viable Reserve which is today's legacy of the 1950–52 trial by fire, and what has become known as the battle *for* the Marine Corps. In each "battle" there was much at stake: the honor of our pledged word in Korea, the future of a Reserve in the United States, and the future of the U.S. Marine Corps as a fighting arm of our country.

SECTION ONE

The year 1950 began routinely enough with the issuance in late January of the Annual Report of the Secretary of Defense in which Secretary Johnson said that America's strength made war unlikely, claiming that our readiness and military potential were "greater today than in any previous peacetime period in our Nation's history." The budget then in process of discussion for the fiscal year beginning 1 July included $19 million for Marine Reserve training. The continuous active duty budget was to be transferred for the first time to the Regular budget. This meant that the 226 officers and 2,038 enlisted reservists on full-time duty with the Reserve program would be paid out of the same funds as the 185 officers and 482 enlisted Regulars then assigned to the Reserve program.

The mission was the same, to "provide a trained force of officer and enlisted personnel in the Organized Reserve and a reservoir of trained and partially trained officer and enlisted personnel in the Volunteer Reserve for integration into and assimilation by the Fleet Marine Force of the Regular Marine Corps in the event of mobilization or national emergency." An official Headquarters Marine Corps "Statement on the Current Status of the Marine Corps Reserve," prepared for use toward the end of the fiscal year, indicated that "the entire Regular Establishment is in indirect support of the Reserves. During the summer months, this support constitutes the major activity of a large part of the Marine Corps." The statement pointed out that the pending budget allowed active-duty training funds for 90 percent of the officers and 72 percent of the enlisted in Organized units.

Before the summer ended, events in Korea had so changed all advance planning that Regulars found themselves in direct support of a larger body of Reserves, and Reserves found "active-duty training" funds provided for full-time active duty—period! The 1951 proposed budget called for a cut in volunteer Reserve active-duty training from 5,910 in fiscal year 1950 to 3,956 beginning in July. The Organized Reserve was stepping up its training, but had no knowledge it was getting ready for a cold hot war. A look at what was going on in one section of the country is revealing.

Lieutenant Colonel Joseph K. McCollum, who helped organize MCROA chapters in the South during the late forties and who was an assistant Inspector-Instructor of the 10th Infantry Battalion in New Orleans in the years immediately prior to the Korean War, supplied yellowed copies of literature sent out with drill notices and given to new enlisted reservists during early 1950. The literature included excerpts or reprints from articles written about the Marines. It was guaranteed to instill an esprit de corps in the men of the battalion as they read the proud history of those who had worn the uniform in years before them.

1950 Document Recalls Unit Pride

The 23-page document included not only a brief history of the Corps and of the Reserve, but also the high marks of New Orleans Marine Corps history. Recruits were informed that the first unit (the 310th Company) was organized in 1927—before many of them were born; that it became the 1st Battalion, 22d Reserve Regiment in 1930 and the 10th Infantry Battalion 2 years later; that its members were ordered to active duty 5 October 1940 and left New Orleans for San Diego 1 month and 2 days later. After being mustered into the 6th Marine Regiment and embarked for tropical duty, they were suddenly rerouted to Charleston, S.C., for emergency issue of nontropical gear and went to Iceland, serving there from 7 July 1941 until relieved in March 1942. The battalion was reactivated in November of 1946. Recruits interested in advancement were told that the 1950 Battalion Commanding Officer, Lieutenant Colonel James A. Moreau, had enlisted as a private in 1936!

The paragraph treating on New Orleans Marine history ended, quite matter-of-factly:

> Approximately 35 percent of the enlisted personnel who reported for the call of active duty with the 10th Battalion in 1940 were later to become commissioned officers, and 22 are now in the battalion. Their records speak well for members of the Reserve. This battalion has a fine and honored tradition to uphold; it is squarely up to you and the men in the battalion not to let our predecessors down.

During this pre-Korean period, the 10th had a drill platoon which drilled 4 times weekly and put on halftime drill exhibitions at area high school football games—all this in addition to their regularly scheduled, required training.

Commenting on the training given reservists during the 2 previous summers, and to some Organized units during the early summer of 1950, General Silverthorn said, years later, that "the nature of the training and the dedication of the men to get the most out of it paid off when the

units were mobilized and sent to Korea."
Organized reservists had not only *studied*
amphibious operations in several camps
during these 3 summers; *they had actually taken part in amphibious operations.*
That summer of 1950, 7 facilities offered
Volunteer reservists 150 courses and subjects, covering most of the military occupational specialties.

Summer camp wasn't the only matter
occupying the planners. In March, it was
announced that recommendations of the
Marine Reserve Policy Board had been
studied, and a policy for promotion of
Reserve enlisted personnel had been established, "insofar as practical," parallel to
that governing Regular promotions. The
newly instituted program included comparable eligibility requirements in length
of service and professional examinations.
Satisfactory Federal service in each grade
would be required when the program went
into effect in the Organized Reserve that
year and in the Volunteer Reserve in 1951.
The General Military Subjects Tests and
the Technical Tests were to be phased into
the system in 1951 and 1952. Organized
reservists would continue to take oral and
written tests locally under supervision of
Inspector-Instructors and commanding
officers of Organized units. Volunteer
reservists would take tests while on active
duty.

New extension courses were also offered
to sergeants and below as an aid to additional promotions. The courses were Primary A and B, paralleling the instruction
requirements for privates and privates
first class, and for corporals and sergeants,
respectively. The courses were the same
for Reserve and Regular enlisted. Reservists could earn retirement points by
completing them.

Banning Prepares Basic Students

Speaking to the Basic School class at
Quantico on 13 March 1950, Lieutenant
Colonel Virgil W. Banning, Officer in
Charge of the Training Branch of the
Division of Reserve, emphasized the mar-
riage of Regulars and Reserves in the
Corps of the future. A prime mover in
the training of which General Silverthorn
was and is so proud, Banning—a brigadier
general today (March 1966)—told his student audience:

> During your officer career, you will often
> be concerned with the Marine Corps Re-
> serve; and, in all likeliness, at some time or
> other you will actually be assigned to duty
> with the Reserve component of the Marine
> Corps. In fact, the Secretary of Defense
> recently announced that, henceforth, all
> Regular officers of the Armed Forces will be
> assigned, to the fullest extent feasible, to
> at least a 2-year tour of duty with the
> civilian components.

Quoting Defense Secretary Johnson directly, he went on:

> In time of mobilization for any future na-
> tional emergency, the officers and men of the
> civilian components will comprise the great
> bulk of the Nation's Armed Forces as they
> did in World War II. For the professional
> military man, in such a time, to weld these
> components and our Regular Establishment
> together into the most effective fighting force
> he must be intimately familiar with and
> understand the problems, state of training,
> and psychological outlook of the members of
> our civilian components. By the same token,
> our reservists urgently need the skilled
> guidance and supervision that only the pro-
> fessional military man can give.

Then, Banning reviewed the history and
background of the Reserve and the then
current state of training of reservists,
many of whom his Regular listeners would
lead into battle before the year was out.

That spring the first Ridder Trophy winners were announced. Reserve Fighter Squadron 142, of Miami, and Grosse Ile's Marine Ground Control Intercept Squadron 19 were judged best on the basis of combat readiness, combat proficiency, availability of equipment, drill attendance, esprit, and administrative and engineering excellence. General Cates presented the handsome silver trophy to Lieutenant Colonel Rolland F. Smith at Miami, and General Silverthorn made the presentation at Detroit. Each squadron retained the trophy for 5 months during the year that followed. At the time, it was announced that the GCIS squadrons were constantly ready for service as mobile components of the defensive radar screen around the Nation.

In his fiscal year-end report to the Navy Secretary in June 1950, the Commandant took pride in the reservists already at camp and in the plans to airlift some 10,000 Organized reservists before the summer training was completed, a 25 percent increase over 1949. He emphasized that for 14 consecutive weeks "the major part of the operational activities of the four Marine Corps transport squadrons have been directed toward the airlift of Marine air and ground reservists." He didn't say it, but it was generally recognized that the Corps was putting more time, effort, and money into its secret weapon, percentagewise, than any of the other services.

VTU and Marksmanship Up

General Cates reported that 221 Volunteer Training Units had been formed, with a strength of some 5,350 officers and enlisted personnel, and that target practice in the Reserve was expanding. Reservists, firing the pistol and carbine on the same course as Regulars, qualified approximately 51 percent of those who fired for record, even though time permitted only 3 days on the range. Some 75 units were regular participants in the gallery matches held during the previous year's fall-winter period, he reported. The result was a 98-point average improvement figure for rifle teams and a 163-point average improvement for pistol teams in the half-year period.

Reporting on the top shooting matches in which Reserve personnel had participated, he said:

> During 1949 the Marine Corps Reserve was represented on the United States International Pistol Team which fired at Fort Sheridan, Ill., and 2 were members of the United States International Rifle and Pistol Team firing at Buenos Aires, Argentina. A Marine Corps Reserve Pistol Team was entered in the National Pistol Matches fired at Fort Sheridan, Ill., during September 1949. This team placed fourth, winning over the regular Marine Corps team, and placed higher than any other Marine Reserve unit has ever placed. Two of the members placed fifth and sixth, respectively in the National All-Around Pistol Championship.
>
> In the recently concluded division matches of 1950, Marine Corps reservists continued to compete successfully by winning 7 places with the rifle and 7 with the pistol. As a result of the competitions, one shooter was awarded the coveted "Distinguished Pistol Shot" badge.
>
> For the third successive year, a member of the Marine Corps Reserve won the Eastern Division Pistol Match and for the second successive year a record-equaling score of 562 was fired. This score has been made only 3 times in Marine Corps competitions.

It was obvious that General Cates was proud of his Reserve pistol and rifle shots.

Women Have 13 Platoons

General Cates was also proud of his Woman Reserves. By February, Woman Reserve platoons had been activated in 13 Organized battalions. Each platoon rated 2 officers and 50 enlisted. Of the total authorized (26 officers and 650 enlisted), 24 officers and 595 enlisted were on board by the end of the fiscal year. The strength of the Volunteer Woman Reserve on 15 May 1951 was 500 officers and 835 enlisted. Training plans for 1950 placed the women on duty at their home training centers. They would have gone to posts of the Regular Corps for their 1951 summer training but, by that time, they were already on active duty.

General Cates concluded his report with the 19 May 1950 strength figure: 128,432 officers and enlisted personnel in the Organized and Volunteer Marine Corps Reserve.

While the Commandant was preparing his report, the Director of Reserve was addressing a letter to "Mr. Volunteer Marine Reservist, Everywhere, U.S.A." Featured on the front page of the March *Reserve Marine*, General Silverthorn's letter proved a lifesaver later in Korea for those who took his advice seriously. He said:

> The Marine Corps Reserve has planned for you up-to-date courses in the many important phases of training given Regular Marines throughout the year. You will have the opportunity to train with and under the expert supervision of Marines of the Regular Establishment.
>
> Whether you are a combat-hardened veteran of Marine campaigns, or of campaigns of other components of the Armed Forces, or a reservist with no prior military experience, you will find summer training a must. Marines are noted for their constant im-

provements in the techniques of modern warfare. It is essential that you, as a member of the Volunteer Reserve, be thoroughly familiar with these improvements so that, should an emergency arise, you will be fully prepared for active duty . . . .

> Keep in mind that summer training is, without question, the most important annual activity of the Volunteer Marine Corps Reserve. It is to your advantage, as a Marine, to participate in this all-important program.
>
> I'll be watching for you at summer camp.

That summer *The Reserve Marine* announced that educational and informational talks had been prepared for use by all Organized units and by Regular units at the various training locations "in an effort to maintain sound relationships and cooperation between Regular and Reserve Marines." The lecture stated: "The successful accomplishment of such objectives rests upon a true realization of training aims, social and military integration of Reserves and Regulars at training locations, and plain, hard work." The objective was the usual one of preparing individuals to fill FMF mobilization billets and to attain the highest practicable level of unit proficiency.

The reservists were urged to go to camp looking, acting, and working like Marines and were cautioned that glamour was no part of summer training. They were told: "Be prepared upon your return from camp, to answer affirmatively the question—'Could I now better serve my country in the event of mobilization?' If you can honestly say 'yes' to this question, you have accomplished your mission." The answers soon rolled back from the high hills and low valleys of Korea in a chorus of affirmation, "Mission Accomplished!"

Tribute to President

When the North Koreans violated the 38th Parallel on 25 June that summer, all Americans joined in support of their President. The recently promoted Brigadier General Maas, the first enlisted reservist to rise to stars, wrote President Truman on 29 June:

> At a time when your courageous and forthright action is being applauded throughout the peace-loving world, we of MCROA wish to express to you our most devoted support in this shining hour of our national life.
>
> This letter, which seeks and requires no answer, is written in behalf of our members who have never sought a fight but have never backed down from one when the alternative was dishonor. We are prouder than ever to have you as our only Honorary Life Member and as our Commander in Chief.

Maas concluded with a simple "God Bless You."

As the Nation prepared to go to war and as the Corps, its ability to respond as the force in readiness lessened due to cuts in its battalions and squadrons, had to call up its Reserves. Those who were not called did what they could. The Louisville Chapter of MCROA volunteered the services of lawyers in the unit to assist Organized reservists with legal problems. Then, MCROA asked all chapters to form special legal assistance committees.

General Maas wrote MCROA chapters in half a hundred cities that members of the Reserve:

> . . . who have not been called up and who may not be called for some time while the Corps builds up its strength in platoon and company officers, have a great responsibility to those now being called, particularly the Volunteer enlisted Marine.
>
> I call upon all chapters to spearhead

community programs aimed at making certain that these reservists now being called to duty will receive exceptional opportunities for employment upon their return. Many of the enlisted Marines will have no reemployment rights because they are not now working and have no work experience. In particular, we must make certain that no Marine wounded in the present conflict shall have any trouble in finding employment upon his return to civilian pursuits. We will not fail our wounded upon their return.

Maas also recounted efforts of individual MCROA members and chapters to help with legal problems, in recruiting, and other matters. In Washington, D.C., retired Reserve Captain John Pratt, who had lost an arm in the Pacific, headed a team of lawyers assisting Reserves called to duty. (In the mid-sixties, Pratt would be president of the Washington, D.C., Bar Association and MCROA's Judge Advocate.)

After the initial callup of the Organized Reserve on 19 July, it was only a matter of time before Volunteer reservists could expect to be called. The other shoe fell on 7 August, the anniversary of the Guadalcanal landing 18 years before, with the 2-paragraph Defense Department announcement that 50,000 Marines of the Volunteer Reserve would be called to extended active duty during a 6-week period beginning 15 August. A longer release the next day gave qualifying details.

The annual field training scheduled for July and August was discontinued and no units were ordered to training after 17 July 1950. The Volunteer Reserve training program was suspended the same week. The Corps changed promotion policy for Reserves that year so that in the future, whether on active duty or in an inactive status, officers would be considered for promotion by separate Reserve selection boards. Previously, officers on extended active duty competed with their Regular counterparts.

As families prepared for separation, those not yet called made plans for observing the 175th Birthday of the Corps on 10 November. The drive to raise half a million dollars for the Marine War Memorial was launched in October within the active-duty Corps, and all Reserve officers were asked to help recruiting personnel expand the Corps. In July, MCROA had advised it members to offer cooperation to recruiters "only after mutual consultation with recruiting people and only after being given a specific mission to perform. They have enough headaches without well-intentioned interference."

Memorial Drive Begins

On 18 September the Commandant released the first of several official communications on the Marine Corps War Memorial Foundation Drive, advising all active duty Marines of their opportunity to contribute to the Memorial the first 2 weeks in October. He gave the Foundation "unqualified endorsement" and commended it as worthy of "full support." He instructed all commands to prepare necessary plans for "a short and intensive campaign."

He also signed a Memorandum for all Marines, saying:

> Many Marines, for years, have wished that a fitting tribute to the Corps might be erected in the Nation's Capital. A number of former Marines and friends of the Corps have organized the Marine Corps War Memorial Foundation for the purpose of providing such a memorial. At my suggestion, the Foundation officers have agreed to begin their campaign within the Marine Corps and to offer to Marines the first opportunity to make this memorial a reality. . . . This project may well be one of the most important in our lifetime as Marines. It will serve as an eternal tribute to our fallen

comrades and as a perpetual reminder of the service of the Marine Corps to our country. The honor of making the first contribution within the Marine Corps has been accorded me. I hope that when the campaign shall have ended every Marine will proudly bear a membership card in the Foundation.

Four years later, after enough problems to warrant a separate story, the Memorial was dedicated on 10 November 1954 and turned over to the Department of the Interior. Today it is the scene of pageantry every Tuesday evening during the warmer months and of special parades for various reunions and for the annual 10 November memorial ceremonies. Three of the 5 Marines depicted in the heroic-size monument were Reserves (Cpl. Rene A. Gagnon, USMCR; Cpl. Ira H. Hayes, USMCR; and PFC Franklin R. Sousley, USMCR). The sixth member of the group was a Navy corpsman.

That fall the Pentagon, faced with the necessity of somehow emptying the "bucket of worms" that the Reserve callup had caused in all the services, fell back upon its own "secret weapon" and ordered General Maas to duty as chairman of a new Defense committee charged with the responsibility of finding a way to give the civilian soldiers (*and* their employers) a clearer picture of whether they'd be called to active duty and when. He commented:

> This means a lot of problems for the Armed Forces. No one is going to risk his civilian future to join units, and the only alternative to a decent Reserve is a huge permanent force which the Nation cannot afford.

He said that those not slated for callup deserve to know if they will be called and he called for definite "criteria for selecting reservists to be called other than military specialty requirements." Mass also advocated a set length of time reservists would have to serve in the absence of an all-out emergency. The recommendations were to go directly to the Civilian Components Policy Board for final recommendation to the new Secretary of Defense, George Marshall.

The committee charged itself with an early October deadline for completing its report, but it was many months before recommendations were either implemented administratively or, where legislation was required, passed after hearings in Congress. In December 1950, it was learned that the Defense policy would enable Reserves and Guardsmen to tell their employers just what their probable status was— employers who were holding off on promotions or on hiring until they saw what would happen to Reserves working for them. Maas said the policy "should satisfy both the young men and their employers because it basically requires the 4 services to make long-range plans so that they will be able to give Reserves and Guardsmen 4 months notice before being called." Although the specifics were still lacking, the Corps did advise that all remaining Volunteer reservists who would be mobilized by 30 June 1951 would be notified in advance of the month they could expect to report to active duty.

Headquarters said in December that, with the exception of a few needed specialists, captains of the Volunteer Reserve would not be called, nor would first lieutenants with initial appointment dates of 7 June 1944 or earlier. The announcement resulted from the high percentage of Organized Reserve officers who came to duty when called. More than 9 out of every 10 responded.

Marines Return as Correspondents

As a large number of World War II Marine combat correspondents and Public Re-

lations officers were covering the Korean War as civilian war correspondents, others working on newspapers and magazines and in broadcasting were reporting the homefront activities of Marines. Among those writing dispatches from the front were Lieutenant Jim Lucas of Scripps-Howard who was to win a Pulitzer Prize for Korean reporting, to add to the honors received from his beachhead reporting as a sergeant under fire on Tarawa.

Featured in all Scripps-Howard papers on 7 December was the Lucas interview with Major General Oliver P. Smith as he worked to bring his division out of Hagaru in spite of several Chinese divisions surrounding him. "I'm proud we haven't been broken," Lucas reported Smith as saying as he prepared for the historic attack in reverse. Others of the wartime combat correspondent group filing pictures and stories as civilian correspondents with the simulated rank of major were Keyes Beech, Tom Carson, Stan Tretik, and "the Jones boys" (Gene and Charlie), twins who gave up jobs on two Washington, D.C., papers to shoot pictures for NBC–TV Newsreel and become almost legendary characters at the age of 24. Publisher Dave Merwin also shoved off to do a series for a string of papers and to make reprints available to MCROA as it continued its work of giving the Congress and the people the facts about their Marines. *Life's* incredible Captain David Duncan was also back as a civilian photographer-writer. Lucas and Duncan, along with the late Marguerite Higgins of the *New York Herald Tribune*, were honored in 1952 by MCROA with *Non Sibi Sed Patriae* (Not for Self, But for Country) Awards for their reporting of the Korean War.

Father Redmond Helps Out

One of those working hardest back home was Captain Paul A. Redmond (Chaplains Corps), U.S. Navy Reserve, Retired. Better known to Marines as the "Raider Padre" in World War II, Father Redmond was director of Catholic Charities in Fresno, Calif., and National Chaplain of MCROA. He became a one-man organization in his area, seeing that neither the Marines who left Fresno nor their families were forgotten. On Christmas Eve, every Marine's child in Fresno received a present marked from "Your Dad." Delivered by a Marine in uniform, it was a reminder that Dad wasn't forgotten by the community.

Father Redmond also arranged for 300 baskets of food for needy families donated by the Elks to be delivered by Marine volunteers. There was also a Christmas party for children of area servicemen, with jeep rides furnished by the Air Force. Impressive ceremonies for Marines killed in action in the Fresno area were conducted with the cooperation of Army and Air Force units. Father Redmond's biggest headache, however, was caused by Marines who didn't write home about being wounded, and whose families, as a result, heard about it secondhand from letters written by other Marines.

Many Marine Reserves were either too old or too senior for Korea service, but many of them had sons, younger brothers, and nephews in uniform during the war that wasn't a war. One of these was Brigadier General John Carter who had 2 sons in the Corps, 1 a Reserve captain with the 1st Division in Korea and the other a staff sergeant at El Toro. A third Carter son, "born with an electronics bug," ended up in the Naval Reserve as an electronics mate, "all, naturally, Reserves!" according to the General.

Brigadier General Edwin A. Pollock, Director of Plans and Policies, testified before the Preparedness Subcommittee of the Senate Armed Forces Committee on 10 January 1951 that the Marine Reserve mission was appropriate "for the type of mission the Corps has had to accomplish" and placed stress on the fact that the Corps had not been "negligent" in its plans for partial mobilization of the Reserve. He said that the Corps was revising its program for the organization and training of the Organized Reserve ground component, but that mobilization had indicated no need to modify previous plans for aviation training.

He stated that lessons learned during the Korean buildup indicated the need for a new type of Organized Reserve program which would make personnel available "to immediately replace, and to augment where necessary, combat trained regulars assigned to the Security Forces."

Later, these Reserves would phase into the combat forces as procurement and training programs following M–Day would supply necessary replacements. Korea had stripped the Regular Security Forces faster than they could be replaced with properly trained Reserves. Training that past summer and fall for most of the Reserves had been "for real."

Department of Defense Issues Reserve Policy

The long-awaited Department of Defense Reserve Policy was finally issued on 18 April 1951 by Defense Secretary George Marshall. The 14-page policy had 43 separate items and was a landmark document hammered out by the Civilian Components

Policy Board members and the armed services. In his covering statement, General Marshall said:

> Department of Defense Policies on the Reserve Forces . . . are for the information of the members of The Reserve Forces and The American People.
>
> The establishment and maintenance of an effective and dynamic reserve force will be accomplished only by the full acceptance of responsibilities of all concerned. The Military Departments must provide appropriate plans and programs. The Reservist must exercise his right and meet his obligation to actively participate in these programs. Necessary support must be made available by the Congress, and the interest, approval and cooperation of the public is a prime prerequisite to success.

General Maas and his associates, Regular and Reserve, on the CCPB had done their work well. The report included policies already in effect, those which could be instituted administratively, and those which required legislation. Each section was followed by a statement indicating which action, if any, was necessary. Some 26 required legislation!

Progressive blindness had overtaken General Maas during the protracted hearings on the Armed Forces Reserve Bill which, finally passed, was called the Magna Charta of the Reserve Forces. He was one of the first to receive the new Armed Forces Medal which symbolized his last 10 years of Marine Reserve service. Marines may receive only one of the 2 available length of service medals for any 10-year period. Those having 20 years may wear both the Marine Reserve and the Armed Forces Reserve Medals.

On 13 June 1951, the Secretary of Defense abolished the Civilian Components Policy Board, and established in its place the present Reserve Forces Policy Board (RFPB). Because the RFPB, as it is known in the Washington alphabet language, is advisory, its papers are privileged and its members are under obligation to keep their own counsel on matters considered by the Board. A former RFPB member, Marine Reserve Major General George E. Tomlinson, was requested to summarize the Board's history as it pertained to its general mission and the Marine Reserve officers who rendered it distinguished service. The following brief historical summary, prepared by General Tomlinson at the time he was the senior Reserve general officer on the active list, is included in the history here because at this time the old CCPB changed names and Congressional action gave the country the Reserve it needed, thanks in large measure to the CCPB work.

The Reserve Forces Policy Board

The Reserve Forces Policy Board is a statutory Board established by law as, ". . . the principal policy adviser to the Secretary of Defense on matters pertaining to the Reserve components."

Major General Melvin J. Maas and Colonel Justice M. Chambers were 2 of the principal architects in shaping the National Security Act of 1947 which led to the appointment of a Committee on Civil Components by the Secretary of Defense. This committee made a comprehensive study of Reserve affairs. Based on its recommendations, the Secretary of Defense on 8 August 1949 created a Civilian Components Policy Board with the responsibility of developing, coordinating, and supervising the execution of the plans and programs of the Reserve Forces. Initially, this body served as an operational force as well as an advisory board although it gradually shifted into becoming strictly a policy adviser to the Secretary of Defense.

The Board is designed to operate as an integral part of the Secretary of Defense "Team," being housed in and working closely with the Office of the Assistant Secretary of Defense (Manpower).

The majority of the Board's members are themselves Reservists. They are high ranking officers with a history of long, continuous, and active participation in Reserve activities, and they are men whose military backgrounds prove they possess the necessary attributes for the effective representation of their Reserve components.

The Board may perform its basic mission in any of several ways: (1) It may, by Defense Department request, conduct research, compile information, render opinions upon which are based final and informed decisions. (2) It may, at the request of one branch of the military, perform similar studies, following with recommendations that are representative of the overall military posture. (3) It may serve as a screening board for the purpose of evaluating the proposals of the various, subordinate Reserve Forces policy committees.

The Board is available to provide a primary means by which the Secretary can bring into consideration the views of the non-active-duty Reservists. The Board contributes to decision making, to policy development, support, and understanding, and provides accurate conceptions of the attitudes of Reservists and of the bases and effects of these attitudes. It also serves as an informed source of information concerning the best way to accomplish directed or agreed ends, to check against hasty or undesirable action, and provides effective strength for gaining acceptance and support for Defense Department Reserve policies.

The Board consists of a civilian Chairman and 20 members, one of whom must be an active duty Reserve officer of general or flag officer grade appointed by the chairman, with the approval of the Secretary of Defense, and shall act as military adviser to the chairman and serve as executive officer of the Board without vote.

The other members of the Reserve Forces Policy Board consist of the Under Secretary of each military department, a Regular general officer of each military department, 2 Army and 2 Air National Guard general officers, 2 Army, Navy, Marine, and Air

Force Reserve general officers, and a Coast Guard flag officer who is not a voting member.

Marine Corps representatives on the Board and its predecessor organization include the following:

USMCR Ground Officers (appointed and term expired)

Colonel Charles H. Cox
    20 Sept 1949–3 Oct 1952
Colonel William W. Stickney
    12 Sept 1952–24 Nov 1958
Colonel George E. Tomlinson
    1 Dec 1958–24 Feb 1962
Colonel Charles F. Duchein
    27 Feb 1962–31 Mar 1965
Brigadier General Sidney S. McMath
    5 May 1965–

USMCR Aviation Officers (appointed and term expired)

Brigadier General Melvin J. Maas
    20 Sept 1949–31 Dec 1954
Major General Karl S. Day
    16 Dec 1954–1 Mar 1957
Colonel John Winston
    16 Mar 1957–21 Sept 1960
Brigadier General William H. Klenke
    5 Oct 1960–1 Jan 1964
Brigadier General Robert B. Bell
    2 Jan 1964–

The Board meets as often as the occasion demands, and upon the call of the chairman for one or more days at a time, usually 4 or 5 times each year.

The specific duties of the Reserve Forces Policy Board today are many and varied, ranging from developing and recommending policies dealing with the organization, training, activation, and supply of Reserve units to submitting recommendations on all new legislation or changes in existing law affecting the Reserve Forces. It develops and recommends policies relating to Reserve Officers Training Corps programs of the military departments, and finally, it prepares a report on the status of the Reserve programs of the Department of Defense for inclusion as a chapter in the annual official report of the Secretary of Defense to the President and Congress.

During the first half of 1951, surveys were conducted to determine the number of eligible Reserve women officers and staff noncommissioned officers available in event of further mobilization. Many women applied for active duty. The rolls were cleared of those women who were parents of minor children and thus ineligible to remain in the Reserve. The Commandant, in his June 1951 Annual Report to the Secretary of the Navy, announced that on-the-job training billets for women would be authorized at Reserve District Headquarters and, possibly, at Camp Lejeune and Camp Pendleton. An increased quota of active duty billets for women would also be established.

The Reserve Policy Board that year held lengthy discussions about the inequities of death and injury benefits going to dependents of some reservists and not to others due to a quirk in the law. A draft of a proposed bill was prepared by Colonel Card and left with MCROA and the Reserve Officers Association. The Congress eventually passed the Family Survivors' Equalization Bill which certainly originated in part from the Policy Board deliberations that year. As a result, Marine and Navy Reserves enjoyed the same dependency rights as did the Army and Air Force Reserves.

Thousands of Promotions

The Commandant reported, further, that the recent Korean emergency had greatly increased enrollment in the various officer procurement programs, both Regular and Reserve, and that reservists on extended active duty were being considered equally with enlisted members of the Regular Marine Corps in selecting men for the officer program. An Officer Candidate Course was established for men and more than 1,300 officers from all sources were appointed in the Reserve. From July to December 1950, Reserve Boards recommended some 6,630 Reserve officers, one-fourth of the total, for promotion. By mid-1951, more than 90 percent had been promoted and the remainder were waiting physical qualification. In the first half of 1951, promotion boards had recommended 1,987 officers for promotion, and the Commandant indicated that by the time the boards had completed their work, shortly after mid-1951, some 4,000 Reserve officers would have been recommended for promotion.

Enlisted promotions were also rapidly accelerated during the emergency. Because of the large number of reservists summoned to active duty, every effort was made to assist them to establish eligibility. Authority was granted to compute both active and inactive service in grade. Reservists without primary military occupational specialties were assigned promotable military occupational specialty numbers, providing they obtained satisfactory scores on promotion technical tests appropriate to their civilian or military skills.

The Civilian Components Policy Board worked long and hard to present some kind of agreed upon legislation to the Congress which would provide for a "ready" and a "standby" Reserve instead of the previous "Organized" and "Volunteer" nomenclature then being used. The Army and the Air Force opposed many of the more liberal personnel rights enjoyed by the Navy and the Marine Corps. The entire Reserve program was getting a rough going-over at the bar of public opinion during this period. Even the Marine Corps had its share of complaints.

So secure was the Corps, however, by the time the annual Marine Reserve Policy Board convened in 1952, the principal action taken was the recommendation that legislative action be taken to eliminate inequalities between the National Guard and the Marine Corps Reserve in the matter of induction liability. At this time, draftees who volunteered for the National Guard after 1 February 1951 were deferred as long as they served satisfactorily. No such provision had been made for deferment of pre-draft-age persons who enlisted after 1 July 1951 and joined an Organized unit of the Army, Navy, or Marine Corps Reserve components. This recommendation formed the basis for legislation making necessary amendments to the existing law.

Another development in 1952 was the announcement of policies for selection of both Reserve and temporary officers for integration into the Regular Marine Corps. By August, 38 Reserves—2 colonels, 28 lieutenant colonels, and 8 women officers—had been selected for integration. By the end of the year, 107 majors, 166 captains, and 524 first and second lieutenants who were either Reserves or temporary officers had been selected for integration.

Reactivation of the Organized Marine Corps Reserve Ground units began in November 1951. By 30 June 1952, 184 units had been reformed, and at year's end the total had risen to 197 units with a strength of approximately 500 Reserve officers and 5,000 enlisted men. Two-week annual field training was resumed for the Organized Ground Units in 1952, as 105 units went to the various training activities during the summer.

Organized Air Reserve units held their annual 2-week field training at their respective home air stations, as the busy situation at MCAS, Cherry Point, and MCAS, El Toro, precluded holding Reserve training there. Only the 10 fighter squadrons which never had been mobilized were at sufficient strength to train as units. Some 327 officers and 1,092 enlisted personnel participated in the annual 2-week training of the 10 squadrons. Organized aviation units had a total strength of 673 officers and 3,029 enlisted on 30 June 1952 and went to 893 and 3,760 by the end of the year. For the inactive Volunteer reservists, there was a complete schedule of 2-week training opportunities in 1952, as there had been in 1951.

As the unhappy year of 1952 dragged on to a stalemate in the far Pacific, Marines at home remembered their war dead and their widows and orphans in hundreds of ceremonies large and small. The Marine Corps Reserve Officers Association, in cooperation with Headquarters, Marine Corps and Regular and Reserves in the area held their traditional memorial services at high noon almost within bugle call of Headquarters.

The Memorial services that year at Arlington Cemetery featured Chaplain George A. Rosso, Captain, USN (ChC), as principal speaker. Father Rosso was later to serve as Chief of Chaplains and to tour the world visiting Marines everywhere. As 1952 CINCPAC Chaplain, his presence was symbolical of the still unresolved conflict in Korea. Colonel Burrows again was in charge of the historic ceremonies and Colonel Adams laid the wreath. An era was ending and peace of a sort was almost at hand.

SECTION TWO

While Regulars were making plans for hosting Reserves at camp, while Organized Reserves were completing drills, and while Volunteer Training Units were showing films and listening to lectures, Regular and Reserve problems were being reviewed by Congress and the Administration, and by the small band of MCROA officers operating with and through the "Friends of the Marine Corps."

At the 1949 national convention of the Reserve Officers Association, Colonel Maas, serving the Association as its legislative chairman, had been successful in having a resolution passed in favor of the legislation providing a minimum flooring on Corps strength. Following the convention, in the January 1950 issue of its authoritative monthly magazine, *Reserve Officer*, the Association featured an article for its predominantly Army, Navy, and Air Force readers: "Marine Battle Position 1950." Authored by MCROA's Executive Director, Major William P. McCahill, it received added stature by being inserted in the *Congressional Record* by Congressman Mansfield, who said:

> There are many Members of Congress who are aware of the attempts being made to reduce the duties and functions of the Marine Corps. We have noted with regret the language and budget estimates as they affect the Corps, but we have also noted with some satisfaction the statement by Secretary of Defense Johnson at his press conference when he unequivocally stated that the Marine Corps would maintain 2 divisions at reduced strength. This would indicate that more than 6 Marine battalion landing teams mentioned in the budget message will be considered.

McCahill began by writing:

> The Marine Reserve today finds himself in a peculiar role. He is on the defensive.

After almost making a fetish of the offensive spirit since 1775, the Marine of today is both baffled and belligerent over the role assigned to him in the peace of 1950. The Pacific champ almost has to apologize for being around.

Going on to note that Marines—Regulars and Reserves alike—had a "jaundiced eye cocked at recent developments in National Defense," he emphasized that Reserves didn't relish the role of defending a Corps whose history should have been defense enough, if defense be needed in an era of economy. The article continued:

> Marine Reserve officers have much more to do than to run down their sister services and their brother reservists. Yet, the professional publicists would have the Nation believe that we are essentially opposed to "unification," unable to give credit anywhere else but within our Corps, and violently antagonistic to the Army, the Air Force, and even the Navy at times.
>
> If a man strikes back after being pushed around, after being ignored, after being studiously insulted by inference if not in actuality, he isn't picking a fight. And yet, there are brother officers in the civilian reserve who resent the treatment the Corps has been getting in postwar policies almost as much as the Marines themselves. Generally, they are people who either served with or alongside Marines and are familiar with the way a Marine handles a dirty assignment nobody else wants.

He then reviewed recent legislative history and efforts of Marine sympathizers in the Reserve to assist the Corps through appeal to the Congress over the heads of the Administration. He reviewed for his non-Marine readers the recent statements of senior Army officers during 1949 Congressional hearings and closed the rather long and admittedly biased article by saying that "the Corps stands ready to discharge its responsibilities as in the past," concluding, "its future readiness is in the hands of the Congress and the American people. May they be as faithful to the Marines as the Corps has been to them."

Shortly thereafter, Senator Douglas read into the *Record* a document titled, "A Word About MCROA," which listed the objectives of MCROA for his Congressional colleagues. Paying tribute to Colonel Maas, Senator Douglas then said:

Many organizations with which we must deal here in the Congress of the United States serve various special interests, and their officers are highly salaried. Not only do the officers of MCROA not receive any salaries, but they have no special interests other than those of the Marine Corps and national defense. This particular type of interest is for the benefit of all citizens.

Like many organizations today, MCROA has drawn up a platform of its objectives and its accomplishments, both of which are outstanding. Many members of the Congress have frequently relied upon the recommendations, advice, and suggestions volunteered by MCROA representatives either in person or before the committees of Congress.

Because of its record since 1926, when it was formed, a record which brings us to the present and its endorsement of our bill, S. 2177, to provide for a minimum flooring on Marine personnel strength, I feel Marines everywhere and also those citizens interested in the nation's defense, should know more about this small professional guild of civilian Reserve officers.

The 1-page flyer "A Word About MCROA" briefly outlined the past work of the Association and quoted its original purposes and objectives as still the guidelines for its work:

To foster the advancement of the professional and technical skills of Reserve officers;

To promote the interest of Reserve officers in the U.S. Marine Corps and the interest of the U.S. Marine Corps in its Reserve officers;

To speak for Reserve officers before the committees of Congress on matters affecting the Corps, particularly in relation to personnel legislation;

To represent and assist individual members at Marine Corps Headquarters; and

At all times, to promote the interests of the U.S. Marine Corps in the broadest and most liberal manner, to the end that it may best advance the welfare and serve to preserve the security of the United States.

Among the activities listed in the flyer were an active campaign to have the mission and roles of the Corps defined by law; inclusion of Marines in every "joint military board, council, or commission"; disability retirement for Reserves; and the inclusion of the Commandant on the Joint Chiefs.

Chairman Carl Vinson of the House Armed Services Committee, who had worked so closely with Colonel Maas on the prewar Naval Affairs Committee, had introduced legislation on 6 March that year after extensive hearings and issuance of a special committee report which, among other things, would place the Commandant on the Joint Chiefs of Staff. This was no more pleasing to the President or Defense Secretary than were the bills establishing a floor under Corps personnel.

That March MCROA had sent an "Urgent" 1950 Chapter Contact to its Reserve officer members, asking them to cooperate in making Armed Forces Day a success and urging all chapters to make contact with the appropriate Service Commander named by Defense to coordinate the Day in the various areas and States. Chapters were reminded that the 1949 MCROA conference had pledged mutual interservice cooperation and understanding and were urged to make good on their pledge. Just 2 weeks before Armed Forces Day, MCROA held its first postwar national convention (previous MCROA gatherings had been conferences of chapter representatives).

Not surprisingly, Washington was the locale and speakers were several Congressional friends, including Senators Paul Douglas and Brian McMahon and Representatives Jackson and Mansfield. President Maas in a keynote speech told delegates that "the movement to abolish or whittle away the Marine Corps had failed. We have been assured by no less than our Commander in Chief, President Truman, and Secretary of Defense Louis Johnson, that an effective adequate Marine Corps, with its own air arm intact, will be maintained as an integral part of the United States security forces." The delegates from MCROA's 48 chapters in attendance were well aware that while it was good to have such assurances, it was better to have legislation. Consequently, several of the 32 resolutions adopted had to do with such matters as having the Commandant on the Joint Chiefs, having a personnel floor for the Corps, and, "when referring to all the Armed Forces, the term 'The Four Services' should be made official policy." Other resolutions called for authority for naval service officers to waive disability benefits temporarily in order to draw pay and allowances during training duty; recommended approximately the same distribution in grade for Reserve officers as for Regulars; objected to permitting Regular officers to fill Reserve CAD billets; opposed any change in basing lineal position on date of commission; and urged the Civilian Components Policy Board to "impress upon Defense Secretary Johnson the necessity for a strong campaign urging employers to grant mility leave to employees who are members of the civilian components."

That year a new MCROA post of Vice President Emeritus was established for Colonel Miller with the election of Colonel Justice M. Chambers as First Vice President. Colonel Chambers, a Medal of Honor reservist retired because of wounds received in combat, was a professional adviser to the Senate Armed Services Committee. That summer he was elected president of the 4th Marine Division Association.

Colonel Maas reported on the *POR-TREX* Operation at which he was an official observer and called for more Reserve involvement in all future Regular service joint operations—a recommendation, incidentally, which is today almost Standing Operating Procedure (SOP). He also called for more fair play by the Army and the Air Force relative to the lineal precedence of their Reserves when called to active duty. He subsequently authored a 1950 article in *The Reserve Officer*, "Why Penalize a Reserve For Being a Reserve," in which he pointed out that the Navy and Marine Corps used the date of original commissioning to establish precedence between Regulars and Reserves on active duty, while Army and Air Force reservists received credit only for time on active duty or active duty for training, thus placing all Reserves in positions junior to Regulars who had received their promotions years later.

Happy as he was over successes in staving off cuts to the Regular Corps, Maas was equally pleased at progress in the Reserve picture for all services. In a 15-page report, he told the 1950 MCROA convention delegates the year past had been, in his words:

> . . . a significant one of great progress for all Reserves. For the first time, we are given official recognition in the highest

echelon, for, I want to assure you that the agency set up by the Secretary of Defense in his office to see that the Reserves receive proper recognition and consideration, the Civilian Components Policy Board, is turning out to be a potent, genuine factor in the National Security Councils. This is not "just another board." The CCPB is a high-level agency, ranking just behind the Joint Chiefs of Staff. It is not a debating society. It is a powerful action board. It sets policy for the Services. On major matters, it is advisory to the Secretary of Defense, and its advice goes directly from the Board to him. On all other matters, its action is final, and establishes policy for the Army, Navy, Marine Corps, and Air Force. This Board, made up of 2 Reserves for each Regular, has never been overruled by the Secretary of Defense. Here at last, Reserves, is your opportunity to be heard by a really high-level agency in the military councils of the Nation.

This Board resulted from our long efforts to be represented in the highest councils. We now have it. At last you have the opportunity to have your views, go directly to the "top," to be given full, fair, and sympathetic consideration by your own representatives. Ladies and gentlemen of the Reserves, we have arrived! From now on it is up to us. With a President and a Secretary of Defense who themselves are Reserve officers, we are "in the family."

Mr. Truman's Famous Letter

At about the worst possible time, when everybody's tempers were already frayed, President Truman wrote his famous letter to Congressman Gordon L. McDonough of California in which he referred to the Marine Corps as a "police force for the Navy" and as having a propaganda machine "second only to Stalin's." The letter was inserted in the *Congressional Record* by Mr. McDonough on 1 September 1950 as the Marine Corps League was preparing for its national convention in Washington, D.C., and as Marines were

fighting and dying in defense of the Pusan Perimeter.

The cartoonists had a field day; a great many people, including the President, were embarrassed; and the Marine Corps received such a barrage of favorable adulation that MCROA officers were accused by war correspondent friends of masterminding the whole affair! It was a combination of circumstances which couldn't have been more helpful to the Corps if it had been planned. As it turned out, General Maas and others worked behind the scenes to find a quick way to help the Commander in Chief out of an embarrassing position, and the President himself manfully came before the assembled Marine Corps League Convention after sending them a message late the day before.

However, on 5 September, after 4 days of painful official silence, and before Mr. Truman's letter and appearance, MCROA had released a statement which General Maas was quick to point out was being issued in its role as "spokesman" for the Reserve and not for the Marine Corps.

He expressed "profound regret" at the necessity to comment on the exchange of correspondence between President Truman (whom he personally admired and respected) and Congressman McDonough. Maas began by saying that there must be a "monumental misunderstanding" involved in the Truman statement, but that MCROA is "acting on the asumption that the President actually read and signed the letter." Maas didn't say that Mr. Truman *wrote* it! Maas straight-facedly said that "neither in legislation or in history has the Marine Corps ever been named the 'police force' of the U.S. Navy except in a slang sense."

Relative to the "propaganda machine" comment, Maas said that the statement was "most unfortunate" and would be resented by Marines everywhere and "would not aid the morale of Marines fighting against Stalin's minions in Korea."

Again, playing it straight, Maas said:

> Our best information indicates that the public relations staff of the Marine Corps is disproportionately small in size to those of the other 3 services and everything the Marines release comes through the Department of Defense where there are 4 Marines on the public relations staff out of a total of some 227 personnel so assigned.

Maas set the record straight about the Marines going "into the Army" and being "a part of the Navy" and then endeavored to shift the blame partially off the President's embattled shoulders, saying:

> The fundamental tragedy of this ill-timed statement of the President is that it is quite obvious that there is no one available in high places to advise the President as to the mission and functions of the Marine Corps. It is quite evident that the President's thinking is only a reflection of the current Pentagon reactions to the Marine Corps.

He then shifted any blame for "propaganda" from the Corps to the people who had actually been involved in influencing public opinion over a period of several months and who were still doing it. The Reserve's arch spokesman observed:

> If any criticism can honestly be leveled at a "propaganda machine," it must be directed at those men of high purpose in the Congress of the United States and in the public life of the country and also at the many civilian Marines who believe so firmly in the truth of their Corps' motto "Semper Fidelis" that they feel constrained to strike out at any and all dangers to their Corps, and conversely, to their country.

Maas then closed by saying that nothing could so dramatically point up the "absolute necessity" of having the Commandant on the Joint Chiefs of Staff as the ex-

change of letters and "the misunderstanding on which it is so obviously based."

Almost lost in the barrage of statements, cartoons, editorials, articles, and letters favorable to the Corps were companion bills introduced in the House and Senate without fanfare or fireworks calling for a greatly expanded Corps, a Commandant sitting on the Joint Chiefs, and an Assistant Secretary of the Navy for Marines.

During this period, General Silverthorn had left the Reserve Directorship to become Assistant Commandant, with praises of Reserve officers ringing in his ears and a leather billfold gift from the MCROA National Council in his pocket. He was also made an honorary member of the Washington Chapter of MCROA, along with Colonel Bruce Hemphill and Lieutenant Colonel Banning who had relieved Hemphill as Director for the Washington-based 5th Reserve District.

1951 Begins Bright

As the war dragged on in Korea, things began looking up for the Corps in its problems with the Administration and the Joint Chiefs. A new "Marine Bill" (S. 677) was introduced 25 January in the new Congress by Senator Paul Douglas and 39 cosponsors in the Senate and 58 Representatives (H.R. 2001–2050 and H.R. 2056–2063) in the House. The list of those legislators who stood up to be counted, including additions to the original list, is recorded in Appendix E for the benefit of historians or the curious.

The Bill was "to fix the personnel strength of the U.S. Marine Corps, and to make the Commandant of the Marine Corps a permanent member of the Joint Chiefs of Staff." It read briefly:

> Be it enacted by the Senate and the House of Representatives of the United States of

Intelligence officer Captain "Tim" Hanson (far left) directs capture of Japanese prisoner, Roi-Namur, 1944.   Below, into boats for invasion of Saipan, Marianas, June 1944.

The inevitable! Using wrecked Jap tank for altar, chaplain reads prayers for 300 enemy dead on Saipan. Below, coral covered Orote strip and workhorse Corsairs, Guam.

Search and clear on U.S. soil, Guam, July 1944.   Below, 4th Air Wing plane takes wounded off Tinian, 1944.

Close air support for Marines at Peleliu, 1944.   Below, more support, tank variety, Peleliu, October 1944.

First flag raising atop Mt. Surabachi just before photographer Lou Lowery is shot at by Iwo enemy.

A dog's best friend sleeps on Iwo Jima ash, 1945.   Below, the reason for Iwo! First B–29 lands, February 1945.

USS Idaho *softens up Okinawa beaches, 1945.*   *Below, the last Pacific WW II beachhead, Okinawa, 1 April 1945.*

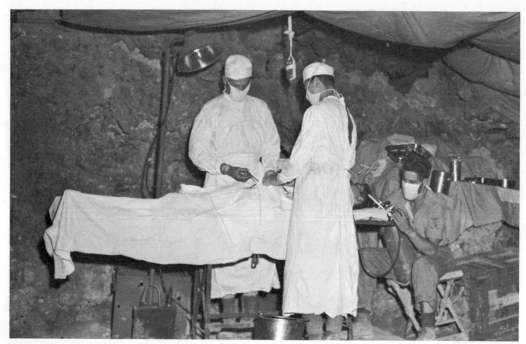

Navy doctors and corpsman operate in Okinawa cave. Below, helpless and abandoned, Okinawa granny finds friend.

Camp Lejeune's Woman Marine Reserve Band played for Victory ceremonies, such as Nimitz Day Parade in Washington, October 1945. Below, General C. B. Cates, CMC, swears in first group of Women Reservists as members of Regular Marine Corps, November 1948.

Photo courtesy Col D. L. Dickson

Same emblem, platoon formation, and rifle inspection for new postwar Reserve, 1945–1950 period.   Below, a new element in the postwar era as Woman Marine Reserve Platoons are established in 13 cities.   First Lt Ardath Bierlein, CO of the new Minneapolis platoon, tells members about their status as Marine Reservists.

Photo courtesy LtCol Elaine T. Carville

Meanwhile back at the White House, President Harry S. Truman receives MCROA
life membership card from Col Melvin J. Maas, 1948.   Below, Col Maas places
floral emblem at Arlington in honor of Marines who died in all wars, 10 November
1948.

BGen Robert L. Denig, wartime director of Marine Corps Information, presents plaque honoring combat correspondents killed in action to BGen John C. McQueen, USMC, one of his successors, during ceremonies at the National Press Club, Washington.

Photo courtesy *Leatherneck Magazine*

Summer camp at Lejeune, early 1950.   Below, 5th Infantry Battalion marches past Capitol after Korea callup, summer 1950.

Photo courtesy *Leatherneck Magazine*

Korea—the Pacific again, same ocean, another landing. This time it's Inchon, 15 September 1950. Below, old faithful F4U on call in Korea, 1950–52.

Forward Air Control vigil—Korea.   At right, supplies to Korean front.   Below, machine guns and tanks aid breakout from frozen Chosin.

Korea had everything, rice paddies in Central area.   Or: (below) gales and frozen trails in the mountains.

America in Congress assembled, That the first sentence of section 206(c) of the National Security Act of 1947 is hereby amended to read as follows: The U.S. Marine Corps, within the Department of the Navy, shall include 4 full-strength combat divisions, 4 full-strength air wings, and such other land combat, aviation and other services as may be organic therein, and the personnel strength of the Regular Marine Corps shall be maintained at not less than four hundred thousand.

Section 2. The Commandant of the Marine Corps shall be a permanent member of the Joint Chiefs of Staff.

However, it wasn't until 18 busy and sometimes bitter months later, 28 June 1952, that President Truman signed the compromise Public Law 416, which fixed Marine Corps personnel strength at a minimum of 3 divisions and wings and called for the Commandant to sit with the Chiefs only on matters affecting the Corps.

As matters moved toward the ultimate target, the hearings in the U.S. Senate, MCROA continued its education and information work. It honored the 2 freshmen Marine Senators who had left the House, Case and Smathers, with "Not For Self But For Country" Awards at a special Congressional breakfast, and named Major Arthur B. Hanson, Washington attorney, and Major Robert Mayo, Pennsylvania engineer, to its National Council.

Hanson played a most important role in the actual Senate and House hearings that resulted in passage of the Marine Bill. With Maas on duty with the Defense Department, General Day in New York as an American Airlines Vice President, Colonel Chambers on the Senate staff, and Major McCahill working for the President's Committee on Employment of the Physically Handicapped, it was obvious that someone had to carry out the "visible"

part of the Council's work in backstopping Senator Douglas in the Senate and Congressmen Mansfield and Jackson in the House during the actual preparation and presentation of testimony at the hearings. Hanson pitched in with vigor and intelligence and made a great contribution.

Senator Douglas in mid-March offered an amendment to his original bill, suggesting a ceiling on Marine Corps strength instead of the floor in the original proposal. The many cosponsors immediately fell into line, and the bill considered by the Senate the following month read "not *more* than 400,000" instead of "not *less* than." The first weekend in April, the Reserve Officers Association endorsed the "Marine Bill," acting upon a unanimous resolution of its Naval Affairs Committee. Colonel Charles Skeele, ROA President, received a letter from MCROA which thanked him for the favorable action, saying:

The fact that your Association National Executive Council, mostly composed of Army and Air Force Reserve officers, saw fit to approve this measure is but one of the many evidences that this Senate measure is truly one which the citizens of our country understand and support.

Senator Douglas followed up the momentum and, on 5 April, placed in the *Congressional Record* an 8-page, legal-size, single-spaced statement which he later presented to the Senate Armed Services Subcommittee. In it he outlined events leading up to introduction of the legislation, the testimony of the Army and Air Force in earlier hearings before the Congress, and the cutting down of Marine combat efficiency against the Commandant's protests prior to Korea. He then advanced arguments as to the national need for a Corps of 4 divisions and

4 wings and, finally, gave the background for the need for the Commandant's voice to be heard in the Joint Chiefs. His closing statement was understood by all Senators and Congressmen. He said:

> The Congress in carrying out its constitutional requirement to provide for the common defense, has indicated time and again that it desires a combatant Marine Corps. The executive branch of the Government has chosen to ignore the intent of Congress. We cannot stand idly by and see our defense structure weakened due to interservice rivalries and jealousies of the most petty nature.

Senate Passes Marine Bill

The Senate held hearings during April and an amended version, passed by unanimous consent on 4 May 1951, was sent to the House for action by Representative Vinson's Committee. Those testifying for S. 677 included Congressman James P. S. Devereux, a retired Marine general and Wake Island hero, who spoke for the Marine Corps League; General Day and Major Hanson for MCROA; former Assistant Secretary of the Navy for Air, the Honorable John Nicholas Brown; Governor Sid McMath of Arkansas; General Holcomb; and Congressman Mansfield. Senator Douglas read into the record a statement from General Vandegrift. The Navy, Army, Air Force, and Defense Departments opposed the legislation.

As passed by the Senate, the Commandant would not be a member of the Joint Chiefs, but a permanent consultant on all matters, with the opportunity of filing a paper for the Secretary of Defense and the President on matters pertaining to the Marine Corps. The Committee report spelled out that the Committee expected the Commandant to attend all sessions of the Joint Chiefs and to give them the bene-

fit of his experience and the experience of the Corps in their deliberations. It wasn't all that the proponents wanted, but it was much more than the opponents were willing to give. The Kefauver Subcommittee which held the hearings included Senators Stennis, Long, Saltonstall, and Flanders.

The House hearings which soon followed were recessed after 3 days. Congressmen Mansfield and Devereux had testified that they wanted "to meet the issue head on" and to "shoot straight from the shoulder" on a Marine Bill placing the Commandant on the Joint Chiefs as a permanent member. On 6 June MCROA's Executive Director sent another "Memo to Friends of the Marine Corps" to the key list of several hundred Marines and friends of the Corps in high places and in the media, saying:

> It would appear that Chairman Vinson is not as favorable to this legislation as we were led to believe by his introduction of H.R. 7580 on March 6, 1950, recommending Joint Chiefs status for the Commandant, and the unanimous report of his Committee which advocated the passage of this bill. It would further appear that an effort may be made either to delay passage of the bill or to load it with crippling and unacceptable amendments. We may be wrong. We hope so. But right now it appears that we are witnessing another "big stall" at a time when the Commandant could make a real contribution to the defense of our country and when additional Marine divisions and wings could help speed the day of world peace.

He then urged the "friends" to use their good offices with Members of the House. At the same time, a great many other individuals and groups were continuing and increasing their efforts in behalf of the Corps, generally without too much coordination or direction from anyone, although little happened that the Corps did not know about directly or indirectly. It was truly a citizen effort.

Finally, on 30 June 1951 the Committee on Armed Services of the House submitted its Report No. 666, 82d Congress, 1st Session (Appendix F) which put the Commandant on the Joint Chiefs and added considerable language to the first section of the bill, fixing the active duty enlisted strength at not less than 300,000, providing for a percentage of this figure for the officer permanent strength, and adding a safety clause suspending the strength limitation during time of war or national emergency.

Thus, the House Committee refused to accept the Senate's weak section about the Commandant and considerably qualified the section on Corps strength. The battle wasn't over, but quite a bit had been accomplished by mid–1951.

A few weeks previously, General Maas had stepped down as MCROA President to become Board Chairman at a meeting of Chapter Presidents which elected Colonel Chambers to head the Association. General Day moved up to First Vice President and Colonel Joseph P. Adams, a new member of the Civil Aeronautics Board from Seattle, Wash., became Second Vice President. He had for a long time been a Reserve squadron commanding officer in Seattle and is currently (March 1966) a retired Reserve brigadier general, a successful attorney, and airline association spokesman-representative. Brigadier General Douglas Peacher, at the 1965 MCROA Convention, reminisced about General Adams as typical of early Reserve leaders:

> Joe Adams was one of the faithful "City Fathers of the Marine Corps" prior to and after World War II. These men *were* the Corps in the home towns and frequently paid many bills for squadrons, battalions, or MCROA chapters out of their own pockets. Particularly was this true of MCROA presidents. These men were known as "Mr. Marine" to the hometown people and many times would be called by the parents of their enlisted Marines, a great many of whom wound up as lieutenants, captains, and majors in World War II as tremendous officers and the backbone of our units.

In response to a letter from Colonel Chambers, congratulating him upon his appointment as Commandant, General Lemuel C. Shepherd, Jr. said in January 1952:

> The past loyal support rendered by yourself and the Marine Corps Reserve Officers Association has been most helpful to the Corps in meeting the challenge of the past eighteen months where the Reserve component has played such a significant part in our accomplishments. I appreciate your offer of continued cooperation in our mutual interests and am looking forward to working with you personally in these matters. Certainly the Korean situation has reaffirmed our need for a large, well-trained and well-equipped Reserve component as an adjunct to our Regular Force.

A Maas Benediction

Maas, who had been the right man in the right place at the right time for a quarter of a century, left an eloquent testimonial for posterity in his farewell remarks as President (Appendix G). As he used his remarkable powers of oratory, undimmed by his total blindness, to conclude his brief remarks, there was hardly a dry eye in the room full of combat veterans. He wound up:

> I hand this challenge and this responsibility on to those who shall be selected today to carry on the direction of MCROA. As I say goodbye to you as your President, I wish to paraphrase, but slightly change, a recent farewell of a great American. Old Marines, unlike old soldiers, do not die; we don't fade away; we only step a pace to the rear. So as an old Marine, I do not "fade away" from you, but only step back so that I may better help from now on by pushing.

So as I step back to the ranks, I assure you that I shall always be in there backing up the younger Marines in the common job of preserving these magnificent United States, by always having a loyal fighting U.S. Marine Corps to lead the task force in our preservation.

The official record of the occasion was almost mute in the short majesty of its summation, "A rising vote of thanks and appreciation was tendered General Maas."

Just as the Presidency of MCROA passed from General Maas to Colonel Chambers, with General Day in the back-up First Vice President spot, Major Hanson moved into position to take over as Executive Director. It was a devastatingly effective brief prepared by Hanson that Congressman Mansfield placed into the House hearings. An amusing exchange took place during one of the hearings, following a statement by Admiral Forest Sherman to the effect that his commission strictly charged and required "all Officers, Seamen, and Marines under his Command to be obedient to his orders." His purpose was to show the command superiority of a naval officer over Marines. The next day Major Hanson showed his Reserve second lieutenant's commission to the Committee and pointed out the exact same language. This hardly increased the credibility of the Chief of Naval Operations before the Members of Congress.

Earlier, Major Hanson had been named Washington Liaison Officer for the Marine Corps League to handle contacts with the Marine Corps and Defense Department for the League and to advise League National Commandants. He had also served as Chairman of the Marine Subcommittee of the Reserve Officers Association Committee on Naval Affairs, heading up a panel of Marine Reserve officers who belonged both to ROA and MCROA.

Hanson's article, "Wake Up America!" in *The Reserve Officer* was a refutation of a previous story by Air Force Association President Harold Stuart which castigated Marine ground troops in Korea for supposedly requesting too much tactical air support. In relating the Stuart article to the battle on Capitol Hill, Hanson accused Stuart of "setting up a straw man designed to start a fight on a specific problem which is really a minor ramification of the overall problem of the air policy of this Nation."

The 1952 MCROA annual convention was held 23–24 May, in spite of the oil strike, with speakers including Navy Secretary Dan Kimball, General Pate, and Senator Douglas. Among those handling convention arrangements were Captain Dorothea Burton, Captain Emil Audette, Lieutenant Colonel Albert Jenkins, Colonel William Burrows, Major Jack DeChant, and the National Secretary, Major Helen G. O'Neill. During the bitter political battle, MCROA had reprinted and widely circulated a Navy League cut of an old Chinese proverb which featured the Chinese letter-characters and the translation, "The more you sweat in peace, the less you bleed in war." It wasn't too apt for, while the sweating was going on at the convention and before the Congress, the bleeding continued in Korea.

On 8 August 1952, Colonel Chambers signed the final "Memo to Friends of the Marine Corps," pointing out that the Commandant "sits as a co-equal member of the Joint Chiefs of Staff on matters of direct concern to the Corps" and that the "enlisted strength of the Corps is no longer tied to Navy strength."

He said further:

> This victory for a stronger America as embodied in the concept of a Marine force in readiness can be shared by the many friends of the Corps who proved so helpful in the months past.
>
> This victory, however, was won in the Congress . . . by Montana's Mike Mansfield, by Illinois' Senator Paul Douglas, by Maryland's General Devereux, by California's Don Jackson, and many others . . . .
>
> It has been both a pleasure and a duty to keep you informed in the months just past. We hope we have added something to the general fund of knowledge on matters Marine through these memos. We thank you from the bottom of our hearts for listening, and, for helping when and where possible.

Closing the legislative gap between the House Committee Report on 30 June 1951 and the signing of an amended bill on 28 June 1952, *A Brief History of the Marine Corps Reserve Officers Association* sums up the final act in the long drama thus:

> At long last the House Rules Committee, under the guidance of Congressman Howard Smith of Virginia, was able to obtain a hearing for the proponents of the bill who were led by Congressmen Mansfield, Devereux, and Clark Thompson of Texas, who had served as Director, Marine Corps Reserve, at the end of World War II. These gentlemen were ably assisted by the Minority Floor Leader Leslie Arends and many other Congressmen. As a result of this combined effort a rule was obtained and the legislation passed the House of Representative with only 31 votes against it.
>
> It immediately went to conference although, as many may recall, Senator Kefauver, as Chairman of the Senate Conference, was then conducting a campaign for the Democratic nomination for President. He called his Committee together primarily through the efforts and at the behest of Colonel Chambers, Colonel Hanson, and Congressman Mansfield and the historic Conference Report was issued and passed both Houses of Congress with sufficient time remaining so that if the President of the

United States carried out his threat to veto the bill there were still sufficient legislative days remaining to place this matter before the Congress for an override of the veto. Mr. Truman recognized the significance of his position and at approximately noon on June 28, a Saturday, he signed the bill into law in the presence of Mike Mansfield, with General Maas in the outer office of the White House and General Day and Colonel Hanson waiting the results in MCROA's offices two blocks away.

> Emphasis is placed on this monumental piece of work because it tested the strength and energies of MCROA as an organization and certain of its officers and members to a degree never before experienced. It also represented one of the greatest examples of quiet cooperation between Headquarters Marine Corps and the Association yet evidenced. Had it not been for the unswerving integrity and courage of General Clifton Cates and the acceptance of the burning need for this legislation by his successor, General Lemuel C. Shepherd, Jr., the great efforts put forth by MCROA and its friends in Congress could well have failed . . . the part it played in the development and enactment of this legislation has been one of MCROA's outstanding achievements to date for both Corps and Country.

Although there was no actual connection between the two events, 2 days after the signing of Public Law 416, Colonel William W. Stickney was appointed to fill a newly created Reserve officer post as Deputy Director, Marine Corps Reserve. A practicing attorney, Stickney had served in the Navy in World War I and had been commissioned in the Marine Corps Reserve in June 1930. Mobilized with the Organized Reserve, he served several units as executive officer during 1941. With the 1st Marine Regiment, he was operations officer and a battalion commander overseas in combat. For a short time he was law officer for the 1st Division before returning home for further assignment overseas with Fleet Marine Forces, Pacific, and the

2d Marine Division. Immediately before becoming Deputy Director, he had commanded Washington area VTU's and soon thereafter, he relieved Colonel Charles H. Cox on the Reserve Forces Policy Board.

The final chapter in the "Battle for the Marine Corps" was actually written in the 1952 anniversary edition of the MCROA *Word*—a 24-page issue for which Lieutenant Colonel Ted Drummond obtained sufficient pages of paid advertising to assure MCROA fiscal stability.

McNerney's Gallery of Marines

During the 3 years of the unification-Joint Chiefs-Marine Corps flooring hassle, one of the most effective "propaganda" artists was Major Eugene McNerney who contributed many cartoons to MCROA, including one which had John Q. Public looking at 4 pictures hanging in the "Joint Chiefs of Staff Gallery." The Army, Navy, and Air Force frames showed appropriate art, but the picture labeled "Marines" showed only the bare back of the canvas. Titled "The Picture That's Turned To The Wall," the cartoon had the civilian saying: "H-m-m-m, strange, they've been exhibiting since 1775. Wonder what's happened?" Another McNerney gem had the Commandant approaching 3 golfers with bags labeled for their services and saying, "Gentlemen, how about making this round a foursome?"

Featuring a McNerney Marine wielding "The Big Stick" against a "Semper Fidelis, 1775–1952" caption, the issue was a salute to those who had stayed hitched during the Congressional fighting of the previous years. It carried a number of tributes to the Reserves—from the Defense and Navy Secretaries; from General Shepherd; from Lieutenant General Graves B. Erskine of FMF, Atlantic, and Major General Edwin A. Pollock of the 1st Marine Division in Korea; and from National Commander Floyd L. Ming of the Disabled American Veterans, National Commander Lewis K. Gough of the American Legion, Marine Corps League Commandant John H. O'Brien, and Commander in Chief James W. Cothran of the Veterans of Foreign Wars.

General Shepherd's message reminded his Reserves not to let down their guard:

> During this past year, too, the people and the Congress of the United States have indicated their confidence in the Marine Corps. Their expression of faith in our ability to accomplish any task which may be assigned makes it mandatory that all Marines—in uniform and out—exert their uttermost effort to assure the constant readiness of the Corps.

A sign of the times was an article in the *Word* from the new Executive Assistant Administrator of the Federal Civil Defense Administration, Colonel Chambers, titled "MCROA and Home Defense" in which he called upon those who knew the horrors of war to lend their efforts toward protecting the homefront.

But, the finale to the drama was summarized on page 13 where Public Law 416 (S. 677) was printed. Beneath the short three paragraphs was the salutation, "In Grateful Appreciation, MCROA Salutes" and there followed the Roll of Honor of those groups who had helped: The Reserve Officers Association; the Military Order of the World Wars; the Disabled American Veterans; the Daughters of the American Revolution; the American Legion; the Veterans of Foreign Wars; the AMVETS; and the Marine Corps League.

Then followed a salute to the 10 stalwarts "who testified personally or by correspondence in behalf of S. 677," and a particular salute to the Members of the Congress who introduced the legislation "and who worked and fought for final passage." The last salute was reserved for the members of the Senate and House Armed Services Committee "for their diligence in obtaining all the necessary facts and their courtesy and consideration in listening to the supporters of S. 677."

The legislation, as finally passed and signed, reads today as it did then:

> To fix the personnel strength of the United States Marine Corps, and to establish the relationship of the Commandant of the Marine Corps to the Joint Chiefs of Staff.
>
> The United States Marine Corps, within the Department of the Navy, shall be so organized as to include not less than 3 combat divisions and 3 air wings, and such other land combat, aviation, and other services as may be organic therein, and except in time of war or national emergency hereafter declared by the Congress the personnel strength of the Regular Marine Corps shall be maintained at not more than four hundred thousand.
>
> The Commandant of the Marine Corps shall indicate to the Chairman of the Joint Chiefs of Staff any matter scheduled for consideration by the Joint Chiefs of Staff which directly concerns the United States Marine Corps. Unless the Secretary of Defense, upon request from the Chairman of the Joint Chiefs of Staff for a determination, determines that such matter does not concern the United States Marine Corps the Commandant of the Marine Corps shall meet with the Joint Chiefs of Staff when such matter is under consideration by them and on such occasion and with respect to such matter the Commandant of the Marine Corps shall have co-equal status with the members of the Joint Chiefs of Staff.

CHAPTER EIGHT

Korea

All the efforts that had been made to establish a strong Marine Corps Reserve in those first few years following World War II paid off much sooner than anyone had anticipated. On 25 June 1950 the North Korean Peoples Army (NKPA) swept across the 38th parallel into the Republic of Korea. What initially began as a war between the communist and free halves of Korea shortly involved the United States in the fourth most costly war in its history. It was a war which added new terms to the American vocabulary—such as "police action," "bug-out," "Pusan Perimeter," and "Frozen Chosin"—and new fame to the Marine Corps. And it was a war which saw the Marine Reserves of 1950–53 set a record that future Marine reservists will be hard-pressed to equal.

Within a few weeks after its initial onslaught, the NKPA had overrun a large part of the Republic of Korea. Even the commitment of United States air, naval, and ground forces then in the Far East and the establishment of a United Nations command under General Douglas MacArthur failed to stem the tide. By late July the United Nations forces were being compressed into a small area around the port of Pusan. Additional forces were urgently needed if a foothold was to be retained in Korea. But where would these reinforcements be obtained?

During July, General MacArthur repeatedly asked the Joint Chiefs of Staff for a war-strength Marine division with appropriate air support. Even then, he

was planning a bold blow that could relieve the pressure on the Pusan perimeter and turn the tide of the war. He envisioned an amphibious landing at Inchon, far to the rear of the advancing NKPA, to capture Seoul and cut its main supply route. But because of various factors, principally hydrographic conditions, the landing would have to be made in mid-September, only a few weeks away!

The Marine Corps, however, did not have a war-strength division. In fact, the ground forces in the entire Fleet Marine Force were insufficient to field a 22,000-man war-strength division.

On 30 June 1950 there were but 64,279 Marines on active duty, 97 percent of the Corps' authorized strength. Of these, 24,552 were in the Supporting Establishment, 3,871 on special or other assignment; 5,492 nonavailable (hospitalized, confined, or in transit status); 11,087 in security detachments; 1,574 afloat; and 27,703 in the Fleet Marine Force. Of the last group, FMFLant had 15,803 and FMFPac had 11,853.

Within FMFLant, the 2d Marine Division had 8,973 and the 2d Marine Aircraft Wing 5,297; within FMFPac, the 1st Marine Division had 7,779 and the 1st Marine Aircraft Wing 3,733. Under the cutback peacetime table of organization there was only 1 infantry regiment per division. Even these were below their modest authorized strength. For example, the battalions of the 1st Division's 5th Marines each had only 2 rifle companies and each company had but 2 platoons.

Thus, when the Joint Chiefs of Staff asked the Commandant, General Cates, about the Marine Corps' ability to provide a war-strength division, he replied this could not be done without recalling Marine reservists to active duty.

Reserve Strength June 1950

What was the strength of the Marine Corps Reserve at this crucial hour? By 30 June 1950, it had reached an alltime peacetime personnel high of 128,962 men and women, including 87,778 in the Volunteer Reserve, 1,316 in the Fleet Marine Reserve, and 39,868 in the Organized Reserve. Of the latter, 33,527 were in the Organized Ground Reserve and 6,341 in Aviation. The ground Reserve was at about 77 percent of authorized strength, and aviation at about 94 percent.

The ground personnel were distributed among these units: 21 infantry battalions; 16 rifle companies; 7 105mm howitzer battalions; 5 155mm howitzer battalions; 1 155mm gun battalion; 2 40mm gun batteries; 2 tank battalions; 3 amphibian tractor battalions; 1 amphibian truck company; 1 signal company (supplementary); 6 signal companies; 1 engineer battalion and 13 Woman Reserve platoons. Aviation personnel were in 30 Marine fighter squadrons (VMF) and 12 Marine ground control intercept squadrons (MGCIS).

Many of the Organized Reserve units, activated early in the post-World War II period, were well established. Others, such as the 6th 105mm Howitzer Battalion of Buffalo, N.Y., were scarcely "dry behind the ears" as units. Buffalo's howitzer battalion had been activated in February 1950, reached its authorized strength

3 months later, and was training with a 105mm howitzer borrowed from the New York National Guard!

The Callup

Faced with the need to provide additional forces in Korea immediately and with too few Regular Forces available, President Truman, with Congressional sanction, on 19 July 1950 authorized the Defense Establishment to call units and individuals of its Reserve components to active duty. The Marine Corps immediately began to order Organized Reserve units to active duty.

On 20 July, 22 Organized Ground units with a total strength of 4,830 were ordered to extended active duty. By 4 August, the entire Organized Reserve (Ground)—including the 13 Woman Reserve Platoons—had been ordered up. By 11 September, the last of the ground units had reported for duty. The schedule for the callup took into account the state of readiness of the various units, their nearness to their initial stations of deployment, and the facilities available to receive and care for them.

The first Organized units to report were the 13th Infantry Battalion of Los Angeles, the 12th Amphibian Tractor Battalion of San Francisco, the 12th Signal Company of Oakland, and the 3d Engineer Company of Phoenix, all of which checked in to Camp Pendleton on 31 July. At Camp Lejeune, the first units to arrive were the 5th Infantry Battalion of Washington, D.C. (which included companies from Lynchburg and Charlottesville, Va., and Cumberland, Md.); Company B, 6th Infantry Battalion of Reading, Pa.; and Battery C 1st 105mm Howitzer Battalion of Fort Lee, Va. These units arrived 1

August. From then on, units streamed into both camps.

At the same time that the entire Ground Organized Reserve was being called up, a sizeable number of aviation reservists were being mobilized. On 23 July 1950 personnel of the following Reserve squadrons were ordered to active duty: VMF–111 (Dallas); –123 and –241 (Los Alamitos); –141 (Oakland); –213 (Minneapolis); –221 (St. Louis); MGCIS–22 (Glenview); –18 (Los Alamitos) and –16 (Minneapolis). Of the 1,474 aviation reservists affected by these orders, 1,392 actually reported for duty at Marine Corps Air Station, El Toro, Calif. Of these air reservists, the then commanding general of the 1st Marine Aircraft Wing, Major General Field Harris, later said, "I will never forget the Texas squadron climbing out of the transport plane, whooping and hollering and waving the Texas flag; these boys were ready."

On 3 August 1950, personnel of the 9 remaining Ground Control Intercept Squadrons—MGCIS–15, –17, –19, –20, –21, –23, –24, –25, and –26—were ordered to duty and within 9 days were followed by VMF–232 and VMF–235 from Marine Air Reserve Training Command. These 2 VMF's were ordered to report as units, preserving their squadron designations. By so doing they brought the Marine Corps Regular Establishment total of VMF's to 18.

From late July through early September 1950 Reserve Training centers across the country were scenes of hectic activity. Harried commanders collected their scattered personnel and organized for the movement, all the time under pressure from phone calls and visitors. Not all of these concerned anxious parents and wives, as Volunteer Reserves often wanted to join up and go with units. Regulations didn't permit this, however. At Los Angeles, there were so many Volunteer reservists waiting hopefully outside the training center they were called the "Wailing Wall Gang."

When a unit entrained, there were the same scenes at railroad stations as a decade before. Once again, the families of the Organized Reserves saw their menfolk off to war. Woman Reserve platoons entrained as well. So, there were families (in some instances, husbands) seeing their womenfolk off to war!

Arrival dates at Camps Pendleton and Lejeune had been staggered so that each arriving unit could be received and processed before the next group arrived. As the units arrived they were billeted, processed, and classified. Units were then disbanded and their personnel employed where most needed, with every effort made to assign them to tasks which would best utilize their training and skills.

Less than 3 weeks before the first Organized Reserve units arrived at Camp Pendleton, the 1st Marine Provisional Brigade departed from the West Coast for the Far East under the command of Brigadier General Edward A. Craig. The brigade's principal elements were the 5th Marines and Marine Aircraft Group 33, both of which had been brought up to strength by stripping other Marine units of personnel and equipment. Even so, the 5th Marines departed with but 2 rifle companies per infantry battalion, and these companies had only recently acquired their third platoons.

On 25 July the Joint Chiefs of Staff directed the Marine Corps to build the 1st Marine Division to war strength, less 1 regimental combat team (RCT) and set 10–14 August as its date of departure. It would have as its 2 RCT's the 5th Marines (which would revert to it from the brigade when the division arrived off Korea) and the newly activated 1st Marines, commanded by Colonel Lewis B. (Chesty) Puller.

As the departure of the 1st Provisional Brigade left the 1st Marine Division with only 3,459 men, its manpower requirement was great and its time factor short. The division was filled out by many Regulars transferred to it from posts, stations, and the 2d Marine Division, and by a large number of reservists as well. A flood of these men poured into Camp Pendleton. At Camp Lejeune, meanwhile, thousands of Reserves arrived as thousands of Regulars departed for Camp Pendleton.

Assigning mobilized reservists to the 1st Marine Division was not what the Marine Corps desired, nor what it had planned. But the harsh necessities of the situation offered no other choice.

A major problem was the selection of reservists with previous training or military experience which made them best qualified for assignment to the 1st Division. Its imminent departure precluded the usual deliberative process of analyzing training records, interviewing personnel, and conducting practical tests. Criteria were used which balanced the need for rapid selection, the means available, and selection standards against the task to be performed.

Two categories of Reserves were established: combat-ready and non-combat-ready. Combat-ready included those who had been members of the Organized Reserve for 2 years and had attended 1 summer camp and 72 drills, or 2 summer camps and 36 drills, and veterans with more than 90 days service in the Corps. Reservists who did not meet these standards were designated non-combat-ready. Within this category was a subcategory called Recruit Class, in which were placed those who had less than 1 year of service in the Organized Reserve or poor drill attendance records. These standards represented the collective professional judgment of some of the most experienced Marine field commanders.

Although Reserve personnel in the combat-ready category were not trained as thoroughly as the Marine Corps desired, or as thoroughly as they would have been had time permitted, they nevertheless had the training required for combat assignment.

Before a reservist was placed in the combat-ready or non-combat-ready category, he was interviewed. If he considered himself combat-ready, this was not considered proof in itself. Reservists presented an overly optimistic picture of their previous training in their desire to be classified as combat-ready. Therefore, unit officers were also questioned about individual qualifications.

Any reservist, however, who believed he needed more training was removed, without prejudice, from consideration for immediate assignment to combat duty.

About 50 percent of the Reserve called up (including all officers) were placed in the combat-ready category. Of these, 2,891 were assigned initially to the 1st Marine Division.

As the 1st Marine Division (less a RCT), commanded by Major General Oliver P. Smith, approached war-strength and its date of departure for the Far East, the Commandant ordered it to activate a third RCT which would be ready to embark not later than 1 September 1950. Thus the 7th Marines (Reinforced) were activated on 17 August under the command of Colonel Homer L. Litzenberg who as a first lieutenant had been Inspector-Instructor to Philadelphia's 3d Battalion 19th Marines. Many of the combat-ready reservists were assigned to the 7th Marines. By the date of its departure for the Far East, reservists comprised 1,809 of the regiment's strength of 3,755. One of the 7th's battalion commanders was Major Raymond Davis, who but a few weeks before had been the Inspector-Instructor of the Reserve 9th Infantry Battalion at Chicago.

With all the Organized Reserve (Ground) units called up, and the 1st Division building to war strength, attention was then turned to the Volunteer Reserve. A review of Corps' assigned and projected commitments revealed that even with the Organized Reserve callup, there were not enough Marines available, particularly for providing rotation and replacement personnel for Korean operations. The Commandant, on 5 August, warned the Marine Corps Reserve Districts that approximately 60 percent of the Volunteer Reserve soon would be called to active duty.

Ten days later, the Marine Corps directed that "all male enlisted members of the Volunteer Marine Corps Reserve in the ranks of sergeant and below" be ordered to active duty with a 15-day delay. These men began arriving at Pendleton on 1 September. Meanwhile, on 18 August, MCR Districts had been informed of the need for approximately 2,650 company grade officers with combat specialties, and told that certain staff NCO's shortly would be ordered to active duty by name or MOS number. Headquarters ordered the first large group of Volunteer Reserve officers to active duty on 6 September. The next day, it directed Reserve District Directors to order to active duty quotas of Volunteer

Reserve staff NCO's with, or qualifying for, certain MOS numbers.

After 7 September 1950 Volunteer reservists for the most part were ordered to active duty only on the basis of individual orders. An additional quota of staff NCO's was called on 8 February 1951. Thereafter, the need for reservists diminished steadily until, in May 1951, only a few were ordered to duty. These latter were almost exclusively those whose delay period had expired, who volunteered for active duty, or who were ordered to duty to fill specific billets.

During October 1950, a peak month, 21,-343 Volunteer reservists (1,010 of whom were newly enlisted) reported for active duty. By May 1951 the number of Volunteer reservists on active duty reached 52,-305, up some 49,924 from the number on active duty as of 31 July 1950. Of the Volunteer reservists ordered to active duty, the Marine Corps found more than 80 percent available. Twelve to 15 percent of those nonavailable were physically disqualified; and the remainder were discharged for their own or the Government's convenience.

Many of the Volunteer reservists were shipped to Lejeune and assigned to the 2d Marine Division. By the end of 1950, 19,895 reservists were in that division. At least 80 percent of these were Volunteer Reserves! A substantial number of reservists assigned to domestic security forces were Volunteer Reservists. They also relieved Regulars from overseas security forces (on a man-for-man basis) for service in Korea. Volunteer reservists assumed important duties in training and replacement commands, in recruit training, in maintenance, and in a number of specialized tasks.

Volunteer reservists made up the bulk

of replacement drafts sent to the 1st Marine Division and 1st Marine Aircraft Wing late in 1950. Their availability made it possible for the Corps to initiate the first Armed Forces rotation program for personnel in Korea.

"Pusan Perimeter"

Even as the first Volunteer Reserves were being called up, the 1st Provisional Brigade was in action in Korea. All through August and early September, these Marines were the "firemen" of the "Pusan Perimeter" as they moved from critical point to critical point to meet and smash back North Korean (NKPA) breakthroughs.

The brigade had contained few, if any, reservists when it arrived in Korea. But, when it pulled out of the line to prepare for the Inchon landing, reservists were among its casualty replacements and in the third companies added to the infantry battalions.

With the Inchon operation at hand, the brigade was disbanded. The 5th Marines and other ground elements reverted to the 1st Division, with Brigadier General Edwin A. Craig becoming Assistant Division Commander. MAG–33 reverted to the 1st Wing, which, under the command of Major General Field Harris, arrived in the Far East early in September.

The Inchon-Seoul Operation

With the 5th Marines on the left, and the 1st Marines on the right, and the 7th Marines still en route from the United States, the 1st Marine Division stormed ashore at Inchon on 15 September. Within 2 days, the Marines captured the vital port and prepared to attack Seoul.

Part of the air support for the landings was provided by Marine Fighter Squadrons VMF–214 and VMF–323 operating from small aircraft carriers. Shortly after the Marines captured Kimpo Airfield between Inchon and Seoul, MAG–33 with VMF(N)–542, VMF–212, and VMF–312 moved in to furnish close air support for the final attack on Seoul. VMF(N)–542, a number of whose pilots were recalled Volunteer reservists, was the first of these to arrive. Other air units which moved into Kimpo were Marine Tactical Air Control Squadron 2 (MTACS–2) and Marine Ground Control Intercept Squadron–1 (MGCIS–1), both under MAG–33, and Marine Observation Squadron–6 (VMO–6), which was attached to the division.

In the attack on Seoul, the 1st Marines advanced along the main route from Inchon, the 5th Marines on the left, and Army and Republic of Korea (ROK) elements on the right. On 22 September the 7th Marines landed at Inchon and swung around to the left of the 5th Marines to attack Seoul from the northwest. About 30 percent of the 7th Marines were reservists, and two of these, Captains Richard R. Breen and Richard H. Sengewald, commanded D/2/7 and I/3/7 respectively. Captain Breen won the Navy Cross and Captain Sengewald, the Silver Star.

Among the Marines who distinguished themselves during the Seoul-Inchon operation there were, in addition to Captains Breen and Sengewald, a number of other reservists. On 21 September, Private First Class Albert H. Collins won the Navy Cross posthumously, just 45 short days after leaving Tulsa, Okla., for Camp Pendleton with his unit! Seven others earned the Silver Star: Corporals William T. Davis, Billy D. Webb, Anthony

Pitts, and Robert W. Ingram, and Private First Class Cecil Wedworth, all from the 1st Marines; Private First Class Gene H. Lease of the 7th Marines; and Captain Robert E. McClean of VMO–6. The awards to Wedworth and Lease were posthumous.

After much bitter fighting on the outskirts and in the city, the NKPA forces were driven from Seoul by 28 September. In the week following the Marines, Army, and ROK forces cleaned out the area and advanced to key points inland. The division ceased operations on 7 October, but MAG–33 squadrons provided air support for the Army and ROK forces for several more days.

The Inchon-Seoul operation, spearheaded by a Marine division about 20 percent of whose personnel were Reserves, was in all respects extremely successful. The ROK capital had been recaptured. Most important of all, with their main supply routes to North Korea cut, the NKPA forces pressing hard on the Pusan perimeter broke into a wild and disorganized retreat. The United Nations forces pursuing them captured thousands of prisoners and the NKPA rapidly ceased to be an effective force.

The Chosin Reservoir Campaign

After the close of the Inchon-Seoul operation, the 1st Marine Division embarked at Inchon and sailed to Wonsan on the North Korean east coast, where it landed 26 October. MAG–12, including VMF–312, VMF–212, and VMF(N)–513, moved to Wonsan to furnish air support for the Division, along with the carrier-borne squadrons VMF–214 and VMF–323. About half of the Marine air missions during the next 6 weeks were in support of non-Marine units.

From Wonsan, the Division advanced northwestward to the Chosin Reservoir and Yudam-ni in the mountains of north-central North Korea. But instead of scattered, disorganized NKPA resistance, the Marines and other United Nations forces all along the front ran into large Chinese Communist Forces (CCF) armies. These, along with the snow and bitter cold of the Korean winter, and the rugged terrain, would test the Marines—Regular and Reserve alike—as severely during the Chosin Reservoir campaign as ever men had been tested in the long history of the Corps.

The 7th Marines spearheaded the advance of the Division. At Sudong on 2 November, this regiment (by now 34 percent of its men reservists) engaged the 124th CCF Division. After a 4-day battle, the CCF fell back, beaten in the first decisive defeat inflicted on a Chinese unit in Korea!

At Sudong, 2 reservists—Staff Sergeant Archie Van Winkle and Sergeant James I. Poynter—won the Medal of Honor. Van Winkle, the first reservist to win the Medal of Honor in Korea, less than 100 days earlier had reported to Camp Pendleton with Company A, 11th Infantry Battalion, Seattle. Another reservist, Sergeant Earl F. Peach, won the Navy Cross at Sudong. Poynter's and Peach's awards were posthumous.

From Sudong the Marines advanced northward through Koto-ri to Hagaru on the southeastern edge of the Chosin Reservoir. General Smith set up his headquarters at Hagaru, and Marine engineers constructed an airstrip there. The 7th Marines and 5th Marines advanced to Yudam-ni at the western tip of the reservoir, with the 1st Marines stationed at

Hagaru and points back along the main supply route.

Between 27–29 November, the 9th CCF Army Group, employing at least 6 of its 9 divisions, struck the Marines at several points. The CCF encircled the division and nearby elements of the Army's 7th Division. The main supply route—a narrow winding road through the mountains back to the port of Hungnam—was cut in several places.

Many experts were ready to write the division off as lost; others thought that the only way to save it was to airlift it out, leaving its equipment behind for the enemy. Instead, the Marines fought their way out through the frozen, snow-covered mountains, bringing with them their wounded, their equipment, and most of their dead. On 13 December the last elements of the division arrived at Hungnam and, except for the process of embarking, the epic of "Frozen Chosin" came to an end. In the campaign, the Marines so severely mauled the 9th CCF Army Group that it was subsequently withdrawn to the rear for several months to recoup its losses.

In the breakout from "Frozen Chosin," Marines fought endlessly in bitter cold and snow against overwhelming numbers of doggedly determined Chinese troops, producing more than the normal share of heroism. Many heroic acts were performed by reservists. Private First Class Hector A. Cafferatta, Jr., called up with the 21st Infantry Battalion of Dover, N.J., on 6 September, played an important part in F/2/7's heroic stand at Taktong Pass between Yudam-ni and Hagaru, and was awarded the Medal of Honor. Another 13 reservists were awarded the Navy Cross for actions during this campaign: Captains Morse "L" Holladay, Commanding Officer, Headquarters Company, 1st Serv-

ice Battalion; and Samuel S. Smith, Jr., Commanding Officer D/2/5; First Lieutenants Welton R. Abell, Commanding Officer, F/2/7; John Yancey, Bernard W. Christofferson, Harrison F. Betts, Horace L. Johnson, Jr., and Chester O. Penney, Jr.; Sergeant John H. C. Hamby; Corporal Jack V. Williams; Privates First Class Russell J. Seldal and Charles H. Monroe, Jr., and Private James P. Gallagher. Corporal Williams' award was made posthumously. Lieutenant Yancey's Navy Cross was his second. He had earned the first at the Lunga River on Guadalcanal, almost to the day, 8 years before.

A major factor in the breakout from the Chosin Reservoir was the close air support of ground units, principally by Marine fighter planes. The airlifting in of supplies, landed at Hagaru or airdropped to units, was also important in the Chosin story. Marine transport aircraft played a vital role, as VMR–152 carried more than 5,000,000 pounds of supplies to the front and evacuated more than 4,000 casualties between 1 November and 25 December.

More Air Reserves Mobilized

Because of the success of the Inchon-Seoul operation and the possibility the war would soon end, the initial mobilization of Air Reserves had not been so extensive as that of Ground reservists. But Communist China's entrance into the war and the reverses it inflicted on the United Nations forces in November and December 1950 changed the picture.

As a result, on 3 January 1951, the Joint Chiefs of Staff authorized the Marine Corps to increase the number of its fighter squadrons from 18 to 21. Eight days later, 9 Reserve VMF's were ordered to report to duty. Six of these—VMF's–112, –143, –144, –215, –234, and –321—were mobilized as personnel; and 3—VMF's–131, –251, and –451—as units, preserving their squadron designations. Of the 1,900 aviation reservists affected by these orders, 1,637 actually reported on 1 March 1951. As of that date, the Corps had its newly-authorized 21 VMF's in active service.

In summary, by 1 March 1951, 20 of the 30 MARTCOM fighter squadrons and all 12 of its GCI squadrons had mobilized. Of the 6,341 Marines in the Organized Aviation Reserve, a total of 5,240 had been ordered to active duty. Of these the impressive number of approximately 4,900, or nearly 94 percent, actually reported to initial stations of deployment. At this time there still remained 10 well-trained fighter squadrons under MARTCOM, ready for almost immediate field employment. Although these units were not called up, it is noteworthy that MART-COM enabled the Corps to meet its Korean War aviation manpower requirements and still have 10 combat-ready squadrons in reserve, after having met all the requirements.

Many Volunteer Reserve aviators recalled were World War II aviators. Their recall resulted from the very small number of Marine pilots, Regular and Reserve, coming out of flight training between World War II and the first part of the Korean War.

Marine Operations in Korea During Early 1951

Following its embarkation at Hungnam at the end of the Chosin Reservoir campaign in December 1950, the 1st Marine Division returned to South Korea and en-camped at Masan, about 40 miles west of Pusan. There it rested and reorganized for the last few days of 1950 and the early part of January 1951.

Marine air units meanwhile flew air support missions for the other United Nations forces which were under heavy CCF attack near the 38th parallel early in January. Joining the Marine air units at this time was the first Marine jet fighter squadron to operate in Korea, VMF–311.

The 1st Marine Division moved to the Pohang-Andong area in mid-January, where its mission was to destroy North Korean guerrilla forces operating in the area. A reservist, Lieutenant Colonel Robert L. Bayer, commanded the 2d Battalion, 7th Marines, during the "Pohang Guerrilla Hunt." Another reservist, Private First Class "R" "J" Elliot was awarded the Navy Cross posthumously for his actions during this period.

The division moved into the east-central front in February 1951, taking part in "Operation Ripper",. "Operation Killer," and numerous other offensives and counteroffensives. In continuous operations from Wonju to the Hwachon Reservoir the enemy was driven back 40 miles. By late fall, the United Nations forces had pushed the CCF and NKPA forces well beyond the 38th parallel, except in the extreme west.

Beginning near Wonju on 21 February, the Marines, with the 1st Korean Marine Corps (KMC) Regiment attached, advanced through Hoeng-song, Hongchon, and Chunchon to the Hwachon Reservoir. On 22 April, a massive CCF offensive which routed the division on the Marines' left flank caused them to pull back some. But the CCF offensives were soon stopped with great Chinese loss and the Marines resumed the attack, advancing past the Hwachon Reservoir to the "Punchbowl" by June.

During much of this period, 2 of the 5th Marines battalions were commanded by Reserves: 2/5 by Lieutenant Colonel Glen E. Martin and 3/5 by Major Morse "L" Holladay. Lieutenant Colonel Martin won the Silver Star 3 times and Major Holladay was awarded it twice during this period. In addition, reservists commanded 5 of the division's rifle companies during most of the first half of 1951. These were Captains Frank N. Mazver, E/2/5; Samuel S. Smith, Jr., D/2/5; and Thomas J. Bohannon, A/1/1; and First Lieutenants Alfred Thomas, I/3/7; and Horace L. Johnson, B/3/1.

Reservists distinguished themselves individually during the operations that began with "Operation Ripper" in February and ended with the Division at the "Punchbowl" in June. Three won the Medal of Honor during this period: Technical Sergeant Harold E. Wilson and Privates First Class Herbert A. Littleton and Whitt L. Moreland. Several others won the Navy Cross, including First Lieutenants George S. Sulliman (posthumously) and Lucian L. Vestal; Second Lieutenants Patrick T. McGahn, Jr., Harvey Nolan, and Paul N. McCloskey, Jr.; Sergeants John Chinner, Jack F. Larson, John L. Fenwick, and William B. Lourim (posthumously); Corporal Earl B. Bratback; and Privates First Class George W. Elmore and Earnest J. Hightower.

About 50 percent of the enlisted strength of the division during the first half of 1951 were reservists. By June this also held true for division officers. (In April, the figure for Reserve officers had been about 32 percent.)

As the Marines and other United Nations forces pushed the Chinese and North Koreans northward during this period, Marine air was flying close support or harassing enemy supply routes. There were notable performances by a number of Reserve aviators, including First Lieutenants Walter Jung, James H. McCleery, James L. Frazier, and Robert W. Taylor and Captains William J. Rainalter and Arthur W. Wagner—all of whom won Silver Stars. Awards to Lieutenants Jung and Frazier, and Captain Rainalter were posthumous. VMF–312 was commanded during much of the first half of 1951 by 2 reservists: Major Frank H. Presley and Major Edward J. McGee. (Presley was the son of Marine pilot No. 8, R. A. Presley.)

To provide better support for the ground troops, MAG–12 moved to an airstrip near Hoengsong, and eventually to Airfield K–18 at Kanhung on the east coast. Added to Marine air strength in Korea early in the year were MGCIS–3 and Marine Air Control Group 2.

In April 36.5 percent of the 1st Marine Air Wing's enlisted strength and more than 51 percent of its officers were Reserves. By June, when the Marine air units were taking part in the Far Eastern Air Forces' "Operation Strangle," the enlisted reservists were under 31 percent, but the percentage of Reserve officers was about 57.

The Phaseout Program

While the battle was still being fought in the Inchon-Seoul area and reservists were still reporting for extended active duty, Headquarters Marine Corps had already begun planning to phaseout the reservists. By March 1951, a preliminary plan had been worked out. About 1 month later the release plan was announced.

For enlisted personnel the plan gave first priority for release to those on the following categories:

AA: Members of the Volunteer Reserve who had served on active duty for 12 months or more between 7 December 1941 and 2 September 1945.

A: Those Marines who had served for a period of 90 days or more between 7 December 1941 and 2 September 1945 in the Army, Navy, Marine Corps, Air Force, Coast Guard, Public Health Service, or in the service of any country allied with the United States in World War II.

B: Those not in category AA or A who had served for a period of 12 months or more between 16 September 1940 and 24 June 1948 in the same services as listed in category A.

C: Those not in category AA, A, or B who had completed 3 years of active duty or more prior to 1 July 1951.

D: Those not in category AA, A, B, C, or F, who would be 26 years of age or older prior to 1 July 1951.

Second priority was given to category E, which included those not falling in categories AA through D. These were Marines with some service—but not qualifying for categories AA through C—who were less than 26 years old prior to 1 July 1951 and had not enlisted and been assigned to active duty prior to 16 August 1951.

Third priority was assigned to category F which was made up of enlisted Marines with no prior service who had enlisted and been assigned to active duty subsequent to 16 August 1951.

For officers, the plan provided that those, except second lieutenants, in categories AA, A, B, or C, were to be released in

chronological order of date assigned to active duty. All other officers, including second lieutenants, were to be released upon completion of 21 months of current active duty tour. All second lieutenants who qualified for categories AA through C and who were subsequently promoted to first lieutenant were released with other officers in those categories.

The phaseout plan was placed in effect in June 1951. During the first month 2,106 enlisted and 77 officer reservists were released from active duty.

Along with the phaseout program the Corps, in June 1951, announced that enlisted reservists on extended active duty could reenlist in the Regular Marine Corps at their Reserve rank. By 2 November 1951, 2,000 had made this transfer, including 325 master sergeants.

By 2 November 1951, more than 21,000 other enlisted reservists and 400 officers had been phased out. A year from that date another 51,112 enlisted and 4,211 officers had been phased out, most of them by 20 June 1952.

There were some other releases, mostly enlisted hardship cases, particularly those in the lower paygrades with more than 3 dependents.

Korean Operations, Summer-Fall 1951

The 2-year-long Korean truce negotiations began in June 1951. After the United Nations forces completed their highly successful offensive, the fighting slackened to large-scale patrol activity. The 1st Marine Division went into Corps reserve, but the 1st Marine Aircraft Wing, now commanded by Major General Schilt, kept busy. Much of its efforts were devoted to participation in the Far Eastern Air Forces' "Operation Strangle."

Two reservists, both commanding fighter squadrons, particularly distinguished themselves during July: Lieutenant Colonel Harry Reed, commanding VMF–312, led a strike against the North Korean capital despite very bad weather and heavy antiaircraft fire. Killed in the attack, he was awarded the Silver Star posthumously. The same day Reserve Major Frank S. Hoffecker of VMF–311 led 17 of his jets in a very difficult but successful strike. Major Hoffecker received the Silver Star, but was killed a month later leading another strike.

During the latter part of 1951, Reserve Major Edward J. McGee, executive officer of VMF–312, and Reserve Captain Robert W. Hamilton of VMF(N)–513 were awarded the Silver Star.

By September 1951, the number of Reserves in the 1st Marine Aircraft Wing made up 61 percent of the officers and 20 percent of enlisted personnel. At the end of 1951 the figures stood at approximately 58 and 19 percent, respectively.

The large number of Marine Reserve aviators in Korea in the fall of 1951 resulted in an interesting Marine Corps Birthday celebration by MAG–12, as later related by Lieutenant General Mangrum:

Marine Air Group 12 at K–18 (Kangnung) observed the 176th Marine Corps Birthday with as much of the usual tradition as possible in the middle of maintaining a round-the-clock schedule of combat missions beyond the lines. Enough butter and sugar were scrounged to produce beautifully ornamented cakes for enlisted, non-coms, and officers' messes, which I cut in that order as commanding officer. By the time I appeared at the officers' mess a large black cardboard "R" mysteriously had been added to the USMC in the icing on the cake. And the crowd waited for me to notice it. I was able to say that I had spent more time in the Reserve than anyone present had spent in the Marine Corps. Spirit was tremendous!

A significant air development during 1951 was the arrival in Korea of the Marine Helicopter Transport Squadron 161. Until that time VMO–6, which flew both helicopters and light planes, had carried casualties, evacuating nearly 2,000 wounded Marines in its first year in Korea. HMR–161 immediately became of great assistance to ground troops fighting hard around the "Punchbowl" in September. Another important air development was the arrival in October 1951 of VMF–121, the first Marine squadron to be equipped with AD–2 Skyraiders. The 1st Wing made a 78-plane fly-over the division on 10 November.

When the 1st Marine Division returned to the front lines in late August 1951, it began an offensive which carried it beyond the "Punchbowl." In this operation Reserve Lieutenant Colonel Foster LaHue (in 1966, to become military secretary to the Commandant) was in charge of the 3d Battalion, 1st Marines. Another reservist, Lieutenant Colonel John E. Gorman, became commander of 1st Battalion, 1st Marines on September 15. Of the division's 27 rifle companies, 16 were commanded by reservists at the start of the operation. These were First Lieutenants Calvin R. Baker, A/1/1; Richard S. Kitchen, Jr., B/1/1; Harold R. Connolly, G/3/1; Herbert M. Anderson, H/3/1; Norbert D. Carlson, I/1/1; William G. Robinson, G/3/5; Bruce E. Meyers, H/3/5; Dean F. Johnson, B/1/7; Thomas W. Burke, D/2/7; Robert W. Schmidt, E/2/7; Don G. Phelan, F/2/7; Dwight A. Young, H/3/7; Richard L. Shell, I/3/7; Captains Ralph V. Harper, E/2/1; William L. Wallace, E/2/5; and Robert C. Hendrickson, G/3/7.

Both Lieutenant Colonels LaHue and Gorman earned the Silver Star during this fighting as did Captain Victor Sawina (posthumously), a reservist who commanded D/2/5. Lieutenant Colonel Gorman was also subsequently awarded the Legion of Merit. Three Reservists won the Medal of Honor (posthumously) during the bitter fighting in September 1951: Second Lieutenant George Ramer, Corporal Joseph Vittori, and Private First Class Edward Gomez.

During the last half of the year, the number of Reserve officers in the division increased from about 50 percent in June to 63 percent at the end of the year. Meanwhile, the number of enlisted Reserves in the division declined, due in large part to the phaseout program. Still, during the heavy fighting north of the "Punchbowl" in September, they comprised nearly 44 percent of the division's enlisted strength. By the year's end, this figure stood at about 30 percent.

At the conclusion of the division's successful offensive in September, it took up position along Line *Minnesota*, north of the "Punchbowl." This began a long p e r i o d of position warfare, lasting through to March 1952. No large scale attacks were made by either side, but there was much patrolling.

By 30 December 1951, not a Marine who had arrived in Korea prior to the preceding January was left among the division's 1,495 officers and 23,040 enlisted men in Korea. On 11 January 1952, Major General John T. Selden relieved Major General Gerald C. Thomas as commanding general of the division. (General Thomas had relieved General Smith the preceding April.)

Among the air units, HMR–161 was continuing to prove the value of the helicopter. In October it airlifted to the front a battalion (3/7) which was due to relieve another battalion there. Four days later, it airlifted 19,000 pounds of ammunition to a beleaguered ROK unit and evacuated its worst casualities. During November it moved 2,002 personnel and 149,477 pounds of cargo back and forth to and from the front. VMO–6, using its helicopters to good purpose, evacuated nearly 1,100 Marine casualties during the last half of 1951.

In December 1951, Reserve Sergeant Albert Ireland was wounded in fighting beyond the "Punchbowl." It brought Ireland his ninth Purple Heart: 5 had been awarded him in World War II; 4 (including this wound) were received in Korea. Ireland was also awarded the Bronze Star for his actions in Korea.

Marines Move to Western Front

In March 1952, the 1st Marine Division moved from east-central Korea to the extreme west of Korea. Shortly thereafter it moved into the front, occupying positions along Line *Jamestown,* just north of the Imjin River and southeast of Panmunjon where the truce talks were being held. The demilitarized route for the United Nations negotiators led through the Marine lines. It was a key position since it guarded the best routes of advance from North Korea to Seoul, and indicated the high regard which General James A. Van Fleet, the United Nations commander in Korea, had for the Marines.

The terrain was rugged, hilly, and friendly to the CCF. The latter held the high ground, and had considerably more manpower. The "no man's land" between the 2 forces varied in depth from 0 to 2,000 yards. As had been the case during

October 1951 through March 1952 on Line *Minnesota*, patrolling was carried on very extensively. The patrols were mostly squad size, with platoon-sized patrols occasionally used. Patrols larger than this were rare.

Although the truce talks went on at nearby Panmunjon, fighting as furious as at any time earlier in the war flared up intermittently. There were heavy CCF attacks on Marine positions on Hill 122 (*Bunker Hill*) in August 1952; at the "Hook" in October 1952, and on outposts *Vegas*, *Reno*, *Carson*, and *Dagmar* in March 1953. Then, in the waning moments of the war, the CCF made one last heavy attack on outposts *Berlin* and *Esther* on 25–26 July 1953.

Two reservists, Corporal Duane E. Dewey and Private First Class Billie J. Bowerman distinguished themselves in patrol actions during April and May of 1952. Dewey was awarded the Medal of Honor and Bowerman the Navy Cross.

During 1952, there were also shifts in the location, composition, and even some designations of Marine air units in Korea. A second jet fighter squadron, VMF–115, arrived from the United States at Airfield K–3, Pohang, on February 25. In April, shortly after the 1st Division had moved to the western front along the Imjin, MAG–12 also moved to the west coast. MAG–12 and most of its operating squadrons were stationed at Airfield K–6 Pyontaek, about 40 miles south of Seoul; VMF(N)–513 at K–8, Kushan. In March, VMF–312 was redesignated VMA–212. Four reservists commanded squadrons for the the usual 3-month tours each during 1952. These were Lieutenant Colonels Richard L. Blume and Henry S. Miller, VMF–323; Robert L. Bryson, VMA–212; and John R. Burnett, VMF(N)–513.

A reservist with VMF(N)–513, First Lieutenant John A. Andre, became the second night fighter ace in Marine history when he shot down a YAK–15 at night. It was his first kill in Korea; during World War II, he had shot down 4 Japanese planes at night in the Philippines. Other Reserve aviators whose actions were particularly noteworthy during 1952 were Second Lieutenant Donald L. Parks, who was awarded the Navy Cross posthumously, and Captains Elmer R. Foster, John S. Sutherland, and Thomas S. Moore who received the Silver Star.

Bunker Hill and The "Hook"

Colonel Walter F. Layer, a Reserve, assumed command of the 1st Marines on 27 July. In addition, reservists commanded 4 of this regiment's rifle companies and its antitank company when it became heavily engaged at Bunker Hill in August. These were Captains Robert W. Judson, Sereno S. Scranton, John H. Lauck, and Douglas S. Ashton of A/1/1, B/1/1, D/2/1, and G/3/1, respectively, and First Lieutenant Bernard C. Kearns of the Antitank Company. Captain Scranton played a particularly significant part in battle and received the Silver Star. Colonel Layer subsequently received the Legion of Merit.

Patrol and outpost actions during September and early October resulted in 3 reservists being awarded the Navy Cross. These were Second Lieutenants John G. Word and Phillip J. Burr, and Private First Class Adolfo Benavides.

The CCF launched heavy attacks on the "Hook" late in October. (The "Hook" was a salient in the 7th Marines sector, poorly suited for defense, but very important to the Marine positions.) Four Reserve second lieutenants were among those distinguishing themselves in this bitter fighting. Two of these, Sherrod E. Skinner, Jr. (posthumously) and George H. O'Brien, Jr., won the Medal of Honor. Second Lieutenant Martin L. Givot and David L. Hyde both were awarded the Navy Cross, posthumously.

After the "Hook," there were no heavy CCF attacks on Marine positions until late March. Nevertheless, there were many hard-fought small patrol and outpost actions in which reservists distinguished themselves. The Medal of Honor was won by Second Lieutenant Raymond G. Murphy. First Lieutenants David K. Fauser, William C. Britt, and William J. Livingston, and Technical Sergeant Joseph W. Dailey all earned the Navy Cross.

Early in 1953, a detachment from VMF (N)–542 equipped with F3D Skyknights arrived in Korea. Major William T. Stratton, Jr., a reservist, scored the first jet night kill in aviation history flying one of the Skyknights. He and Master Sergeant Hans C. Hoglin, his airborne intercept operator, tracked and shot down a YAK–15 deep in enemy territory. Another Reserve aviator, First Lieutenant Dale G. Gough of VMA–121, distinguished himself and received the Silver Star.

Final Months Along the Front

Marine outposts *Vegas, Reno, Carson,* and *Dagmar* were the objectives of heavy CCF attacks late in March 1953. *Vegas, Reno,* and *Carson* were three hills about 1,500 yards in front of the 5th Marines' main line of resistence (MLR). *Dagmar*

was in front of the 1st Marines. Reservists played an important part in these actions. Lieutenant Colonel James H. Finch commanded 2/5; Major Joseph Buntin was executive officer of 3/5; and Captain Ralph F. Estey commanded F/2/7. Captain Estey and Second Lieutenant Benjamin F. Murray I/3/1 both received the Navy Cross. Lieutenant Colonel Finch was awarded the Legion of Merit for his handling of 2/5 during March through May, and Major Buntin was awarded the Silver Star.

Throughout April the Marine front was comparatively quiet, except for small patrol actions. The division was relieved and went into Corps reserve in May. In July, it returned to the line. Truce was a few weeks away (27 July), but they were to be bloody weeks. Trying to gain terrain features for bargaining purposes at Panmunjon, the CCF staged heavy attacks.

During this last month of the war, in addition to Lieutenant Colonel Andrew Geer commanding 2/5, Reserves commanded several of the division's rifle companies. These included Captains James K. McCreight, B/1/7, and John J. Zulkofske, H/3/1; and First Lieutenant Kenneth B. Turner, I/3/7.

On 25 and 26 July, the CCF launched attacks on outpost *Berlin* and *East Berlin* in the 7th Marines sector and outpost *Esther* in the 1st Marines sector. And, as ever since the landing at Inchon nearly 3 years before, there were Marine reservists participating in the action. When the battle was over and the Marine lines had held, Sergeant Robert J. Raymond had won the Navy Cross (posthumously) ; and Captain Zulkofske, First Lieutenant Robert A. Fleischner, Second Lieutenant

William H. Cowie, Jr., and Private First Class Phillip C. Brohen (posthumously) had earned the Silver Star.

And so, on 27 July 1953, what had initially been conceived as a "police action" and what had become the fourth costliest war in American history, ended in an uneasy truce. Some 33,629 Americans died in battle in Korea—4,267 of them Marines. And, the Marines counted another 23,744 wounded in the war that was not a war!

Unhappy as many were with the stalemate in which the Korean War ended, the Communists failed in their original purpose of crushing the Republic of Korea and dragging it behind the Iron Curtain. The Communists failure was due, in no small part, to the Marine air-ground team.

In turn, the Marine air-ground team successes—particularly during 1 9 5 1— owed much to the mobilized Reserves. As in World War II, they proved themselves as leaders—from the fire team through the regimental level on the ground, and at the squadron level in the air. Once again, they demonstrated their proficiency at various staff levels, as attested by the number of reservists in staff billets who were awarded the Legion of Merit. In addition, Reserve Major Walter R. Harris was 1 of the 5 Marine officers who received the Legion of Merit for leadership and conduct as prisoners of war.

Above all else, the Marine Reserves proved themselves in combat, both as individuals and as a group. The 13 Medals of Honor, 50 Navy Crosses, and over 400 Silver Stars awarded individual reservists attest their bravery. The victory of the 7th Marines (more than a third of whom were Reserves) at Sudong in November 1950 over a CCF division, and the success of the division in the spring and summer of 1951, when about one-half of its strength was Reserves, are indicative of the Reserves' overall performance in battle. In the air, according to the Honorable John F. Floberg, Assistant Secretary of the Navy for Air at the time, every third airplane that flew over Korea on a combat mission was flown by an activated Navy or Marine reservist. Of all 1st Marine Aircraft Wing combat sorties in Korea, 48 percent were flown by Reserves.

The performance of Reserves in Korea is best attested by some of the Marine commanders under whom they served there.

General Lemuel C. Shepherd, Jr., Commandant of the Marine Corps from 1952 to 1956 and Commanding General of Fleet Marine Force, Pacific, in 1950, wrote on 17 November 1964:

> . . . if it had not been for the mobilization of the Reserve to bring the remaining units of the [1st] Division to full strength, I would not have been able to recommend to General MacArthur that he request the assignment of the 1st Division to the Far East Command for his desired employment at Inchon which turned the tide of defeat to one of victory, to the lasting glory and prestige of the U.S. Marine Corps . . . .

Lieutenant General Craig from retirement wrote:

> As Assistant Division Commander of the Division commencing at the Inchon landing and continuing until February 1951, I came in contact with the thousands of Reserves serving with the Division . . . . They had a can do spirit, no griping, not afraid to go forward under fire and take the consequences . . . . They endured hardships probably never encountered by Marines in the past and always acquitted themselves in the highest traditions of the Corps. I was proud to be serving with them . . . .

Retired Lieutenant General Field Harris, writing of the Reserve aviators he commanded in the 1st Marine Air Wing, said :

Now they were cold-blooded professionals skilled in instrument flying and spent hours planning their attacks and briefing themselves on flak installations. As a result in 1950 and 1951 our operational losses, excluding those caused by enemy ground fire, were the lowest I have ever seen and under the worst possible conditions. These squadrons shuttled back and forth between carriers and makeshift airfields without incident. . . .

Last, no higher praise could be given than the 1st Marine Division's former commander, retired General O. P. Smith, who later said :

When I was detached from the Division in April 1951, 51 percent of the Division was composed of Reserves, and in my opinion it was a better division than the one I brought to Korea. . . .

CHAPTER NINE

Rebuilding—Again

The years from 1953 through 1960 were primarily years of rebuilding the Reserve following its involvement in the Korean War. And, as after World War II, the rebuilding proved a real challenge. With all Organized Ground units, a great many Air units, and a considerable number of Class III reservists on duty during the Korean emergency, the callup had created a measure of resentment in some areas, as evidenced in editorial comment during and immediately after Korea. Young men listened to recruiting talk with divided attention, asking themselves, "Is it worth the gamble?" Prior-service reservists, too, sometimes found themselves torn between loyalty to Country and Corps and reluctance to place personal commitments—family responsibilities, chances for job advancement, and schooling—in jeopardy again by remaining in the Ready Reserve, subject to another callup. And, some Members of Congress, hearing the complaints of vocal constituents, hesitated to support measures designed to strengthen the Reserve program and to make it more attractive to career-minded citizen soldiers. Here, then, were some of the "hidden costs" of Korea—costs not fully realized until the rebuilding operation got underway.

During much of this period the role of the Reserve was determined by Public Law 476 and its amendments—the Armed Forces Reserve Act of 1952. Once again, Congress provided for a Marine Corps Reserve with the now familiar section: "The

Marine Corps Reserve is the reserve component of the Marine Corps." The Act called for a Ready Reserve, a Standby Reserve, and a Retired Reserve. The Ready Reserve was to consist of units or members liable for active duty in time of war, in time of national emergency declared by the Congress or proclaimed by the President, or when otherwise authorized by law. The Standby Reserve was to consist of units or members (other than Retired Reserve members) or both, liable for active duty only in time of war or national emergency declared by the Congress, or when otherwise authorized by law. The Retired Reserve was to include members whose names had been placed on the Reserve Retired list subject to certain specific conditions. The Act provided, again, for a Marine Corps Reserve Policy Board to advise the Secretary of the Navy on Reserve matters. At least half of the Policy Board members were to be Marine reservists. Yet another provision of the Act dealt with what had come to be known, in Marine Corps jargon, as "Tombstone Promotions." Officers who had been commended in combat could be promoted to the next higher rank when transferred to the Retired Reserve. Although the 1952 Act was to be considerably amended in the years ahead, it did provide a basis upon which the Marine Corps was able to begin rebuilding its Reserve, again.

Upon the reactivation of Marine Corps reserve units at the end of the Korean con-

181

flict, the women's platoons were again established, beginning in January 1952. The first authorized was the Woman Marine Classification Platoon of Boston, attached to the 2d Infantry Battalion. Within the year there were a total of 14 Women's Reserve units in existence, spanning the country from New England, to Florida, the Midwest, and Pacific Coast.

In addition to the pre-Korea's women's platoons in 13 major cities, new ones were also formed. (Appendix H) At peak strength, there were 20 Women Marine Reserve units (1 company in Boston and 19 platoons). And, in one case—Philadelphia—2 women's p l a t o o n s in the same city. The women reservists were given a thorough indoctrination in basic military subjects plus specialty training in 1 of 5 Marine Corps occupational fields (administration, supply, classification, disbursing, communication). They participated in the annual Christmas Toys-for-Tots drive and other local civic programs, such as Armed Forces Day parades, TV fund-raising drives, or historical pageants. As with the men, the high point of their activities was the summer 2-week training period at a regular Marine Corps post or station.

For the Air Reserve, the Marine Air Reserve Training Command continued to carry out its assigned missions, the most important for this period being the recruiting of replacements for squadrons of the Command. The experience and lessons learned in Korea helped greatly in expanding and improving the Air Reserve program. Modern jet aircraft and the latest in equipment were to become an integral part of Marine Air Reserve training; with more modern aircraft and equipment to support the program, training

activities for all MARTCOM units were greatly enhanced.

The 17 Air Reserve Training detachments, previously known as Marine Air Detachments, were under the control of MARTCOM and staffed by personnel of the Regular Establishment. These detachments administered, supervised, and coordinated the active training of the individual reservist. They worked closely with the host Naval Air Station or Naval Air Reserve Training Unit, to provide aircraft and training facilities for Marine reservists—facilities, in most cases, shared with the Navy.

To strengthen MARTCOM further, within 2 years 5 Marine Air Reserve Groups would be established within its Class II organizational structure. These Reserve Groups would provide trained staff officers for mobilization needs of Marine Aviation. Their mission would be to train Reserve officers in various staff functions in peacetime, thus providing capable officers, trained and experienced for billets on Marine Corps aviation unit staffs on M–Day. Unlike the 48-paid-drill squadrons, the groups were to have 24 paid drills. Group billets, generally, would be filled by field grade officers.

The keynote of the future of the Reserve program was sounded by Secretary of Defense Charles E. Wilson who stated early in 1953 that the security of the Nation will depend

> . . . even more upon the Reserve forces in the future . . . the Reserve forces must become more than ever an integral component of national defense to supplement the Armed Forces on short notice.

At the same time, Marine Corps spokesmen again raised the now decades-old cry of the Reserve that budgetary limitations would force reductions in the standing forces, thus placing greater importance upon the Reserve which itself was grossly underfinanced. Foremost among these voices was that of General Maas. He said:

> In the future, great emphasis is going to be placed on Reserve forces. Standing forces will probably be reduced. This is in keeping with Secretary of Defense Wilson's plan for keeping the cost of defense within the purchasing power of the Nation's pocketbook.

Within the Reserve, steps were being taken to reduce operating costs. In April the 3d, 11th, and 13th Marine Corps Reserve Districts were eliminated. The remaining districts extended their jurisdiction and became Marine Corps Reserve and Recruitment Districts, combining the 4 major activities of enlisted recruitment, officer procurement, Reserve activities, and public information.

Colonel Krulewitch Heads New York Attack

The major effort of the Reserve was concentrated on rebuilding and retraining both Ground and Air units—again. During the summer of 1953, a total of 42 Marine Air squadrons trained at El Toro or Cherry Point. On the ground, one 1951 training program was accentuated, cold-weather training at Camp Pendleton. The actual site for this training was at Pickel Meadows, near Bridgeport, Calif. Here the scope of winter training was stepped up to take in all reservists: officers and enlisted men, Organized and Volunteer. Organized units expanded their summer training activities and many undertook special training operations. One of the most spectacular of these training exercises was the amphibious assault of 600 Marines on Willets Point, Long Island Sound. Twelve Organized units, including Air units, participated in this *Operation Vol-*

unteer under the command of Colonel Mel Krulewitch. Colonel William W. Stickney, Deputy Director, Marine Corps Reserve, observed the 2-day operation and commented that it was carried out in excellent fashion.

In December, the Commandant set forth new regulations for enrollment in the Platoon Leader Class. Designed to strengthen the PLC program, the new regulations covered physical and academic qualifications and the enrollment of discharged veterans and Volunteer reservists.

Perhaps the most important single item in the area of public information and community relations for 1953 was the tremendous kickoff given to the annual Toys-for-Tots campaign. Since its inception the Toys-for-Tots campaigns has provided a thread of continuity which greatly enhanced the excellent public image of the Marine Corps Reserve. The fourfold purpose of this, the outstanding military community relations program in the Nation was:

> To enrich the lives of culturally and economically deprived children;
>
> To make the people of the community more aware of the Marine Corps Reserve, together with its aims and purpose;
>
> To create a favorable climate for Marine Corps recruiting—Regular, Reserve, and officer procurement; and
>
> To bring the individual reservist face-to-face with his community and to help train him in the responsibilities of citizenship.

The Year 1954

Bolstered by the excellent public relations results of the 1953 Toys-for-Tots campaign, the 1954 Reserve program was off to a flying start with community prestige and a greatly improved concept of training which included many long-range implications for Volunteer reservists.

Emphasis was placed upon both amphibious and ground warfare techniques. The scope of training was expanded by the addition of Reserve Junior and Senior Courses, two 2-week condensations of the 9-month Regular Junior and Senior Courses of the Marine Corps Schools. Enlisted reservists were given almost unlimited on-the-job training opportunities—not just during summer training, but for 15-day periods at any time the opportunity could be created, particularly with FMF units at various command levels. Organized Reserve training, both Ground and Aviation, consisted again, of 2 phases—48 drills and an annual 15-day period of active duty for training. For Aviation units, the training syllabus paralleled as nearly as possible the training program of similar type squadrons of the Regular Marine Corps, and was adjusted to meeting changing needs.

There was some concern during this year regarding a relatively low state of readiness in both Ground and Aviation—a state of readiness attributable to several factors: rapid turnover of non-prior-service enlisted men; reluctance of prior-service personnel with obligated service to affiliate with Organized units; relatively low personnel strengths; and, in Aviation units, the adverse affect of high average age and rank of pilots. In fact, the major problem confronting the Reserve during 1954 was how to maintain a stable structure, sensitive to mobilization requirements, in view of the rapid turnover of personnel within the Organized units. The instability which resulted from such turnover hampered the units because it resulted in consistently low personnel strengths and made a progressive training program more difficult. To house its 239 Organized Ground units, as of 30 June

1954, the Marine Corps had a total of 230 training centers, either jointly owned with the Navy, federally owned, or commercially leased. Plans for further construction and alterations to the existing facilities—to accommodate accelerated training requirements—were scheduled for the following year.

Jim Lucas Honored Again

Among the first newsworthy items involving reservists in 1954 was the announcement that Long Island University had named former Marine combat correspondent, Reserve Captain Jim G. Lucas, to receive the 1953 George Polk Memorial Award for distinguished foreign reporting. Early in the year Captain Lucas had received the first award of the Ernie Pyle Memorial Fund. These 2 honors were added to a long list of awards, including the Marine Corps Reserve Officers Association's Non Sibi Sed Patriae Plaque, the Omar Bradley Gold Medal of the Veterans of Foreign Wars, and a citation by the American 7th Division. About the same time the name of another reservist, Sergeant Henry I. Shaw, appeared as winner of the enlisted men's portion of the Marine Corps Association's 1953 essay contest. Sergeant Shaw's essay, based on personal experience and observation, dealt with the necessity of making better use of assistant small-unit leaders.

Also early in 1954 Marine Ground Control Intercept Squadron 17, commanded by Major Martin A. Landenberger, won the coveted Marine Air Reserve (Ridder) Trophy and was judged top MGCIS in the Nation; and Marine Fighter Squadron 141 of Oakland, Calif.—commanded by Lieutenant Colonel Leon Sparrow—carried off the Pete Ross Safety Trophy.

Special training activities conducted by Reserve Ground and Air units during 1954 attracted widespread public attention. On 7 March, more than 200 members of the 2d 155mm Gun Battalion paralyzed the heart of Miami Beach in a surprise attack which caught even the police on the beat, flatfooted. Creating the biggest traffic jam in Miami's history, the reservists captured the center of the city—including a beautiful young girl who "happened" to be attired in Marine garb, complete with pistol, but with nonregulation tropical short shorts. Needless to say, the entire operation was a well-publicized success. A month later more than 100,000 people witnessed the 1954 annual military inspection of New Orleans Marine and Naval Air reservists. As their part in the program, pilots of Marine Fighter Squadron 143 of the New Orleans Marine Air Training Detachment—led by their commanding officer, Major Carol Bernard—participated in a simulated carrier-style takeoff of Navy and Marine fighter planes to open the aerial review. On the ground hundreds watched Technical Sergeant John Trepagnier of the same detachment field strip and assemble the mixed-up parts of a BAR, a .45 caliber automatic pistol, and an M–1 rifle, while blindfolded.

In observance of the 15 May Armed Forces Day, the 23d Special Infantry Company, commanded by Major John A. Steiner, conducted an amphibious assault in Tacoma, Wash., as part of a combined operation with all the other forces. As with the Miami and New Orleans operations, the civilian populace turned out in large numbers—this time more than 7,000 strong—to witness the highly successful landing.

July and August brought 2 more Reserve amphibious landing exercises and *Operation Alert*, a Marine Air Reserve effort which involved 28 fighter squadrons and 12 Marine air control squadrons. This operation was considered a model for the development of a constantly combat-ready air fighter force. It stressed precision flying, gunnery, rocket-firing, and bombing—and concentrated additional heavy emphasis on the training of ground crew personnel in the task of keeping aircraft combat-ready. The first of the amphibious landing exercises (at Seal Beach, Calif.) brought into action the 15th Rifle Company, the 21st Special Infantry Company, the 5th Signal Company, VMF–123 and VMF–241, and the 5th Automatic Weapons Battery. Major Theodore Tunis, who was in charge of this exercise, noted that it was carried out in a realistic manner and that the training objective of reducing pillboxes and bunkers was attained. In the second of these fall amphibious landings, reservists of the 15th Infantry Battalion in Hawaii carried out a well-planned and expertly executed raid, complete with UDT and beach reconnaissance, on the Keawakapa-Wailea coast of the island of Maui.

The raid of the Maui coast was, in effect, frosting on the cake for Oahu's 15th Infantry Battalion. By attaining the highest percentage of field training attendance among Organized Ground units of battalion size, the 15th won the Annual Field Training Award for 1954—the Joseph Vittori Trophy—besting the 2d 155mm Gun Battalion of Miami, Fla.; the 1st Engineer Battalion of Baltimore, Md.; the 2d Infantry Battalion of Boston, Mass.; and the 13th Infantry Battalion of Washington, D.C. For the highest percentage of field training attendance in units of company and battery size, the 1st Engineer Field Maintenance Company of Baltimore won the Lawrence H. Flynn Trophy; and, on the distaff side, the Woman Marine Classification Platoon (WMCP) of the 2d Infantry Battalion of Boston carried off the Katherine A. Towle Trophy.

Problems, Problems

Throughout 1954, national interest focused from time to time on Reserve problems and the need for stronger Reserve forces. In an executive session presentation to the Senate Committee on Armed Services in January, Secretary of Defense Wilson had reported on the need for improving the Reserves. In March the committee chairman, Senator Leverett Saltonstall of Massachusetts, announced in a report to the Senate that the Reserve forces of the country were suffering from a serious manpower shortage. Although he spoke in relatively general terms, his comments touched on several basic problems facing the Marine Corps Reserve—imbalance in ranks, shortages of pilots and skilled technicians, undefined responsibilities and opportunities, and lack of acceptance and support of the Reserve program by civic groups and the public at large. Another problem, the feeling among many in Washington that the atomic age marked the obituary of the Marine Corps, was the subject of remarks made by Congressman James T. Patterson, speaking to the Marine Corps Reserve Officers Association at the 1954 convention. The Congressman, a Reserve lieutenant colonel, told his banquet audience in the New York City Astor Hotel on 22 May 1954:

> We Marines have a long history of being written off—and of continuing to survive. The Corps survived the Barbary pirates. It survived the best the rulers of Germany and Japan could throw against it. The

Corps even survived the remarks of a former American President. I know the Marine Corps will also survive the advent of atomic weapons.

Congressman Patterson's position as a member of both the Joint Committee on Atomic Energy and the House Armed Services Committee lent more than ordinary credence to his prediction. Subsequent events have proved that his position was, in fact, well taken.

In a major change of command in June 1954, Major General John C. McQueen turned the Reserve directorship over to Brigadier General Joseph C. Burger. Departing, General McQueen said:

> During my tenure I have enjoyed the cooperation and exceptional enthusiasm from all the citizen-Marines with whom I have had contact. Many times over I have been impressed with the truth of the old Marine Corps slogan "Once a Marine, always a Marine." Although I am leaving my official position in the Reserve Program, I will carry with me an active interest in reservists . . .

Women Reserves Honored by McQueen

Earlier in the year, General McQueen had paid tribute to the women of the Marine Corps Reserve in these words:

> Eleven years ago the Marine Corps Women's Reserve was established. The mission at that time was to take over numerous essential tasks in order to relieve men who were badly needed on the fighting fronts. Today, more than a decade later, the mission has been altered only to the extent that Women Marine reservists must stand *ready* to accomplish the same undertaking they performed so efficiently during World War II and the turbulent years thereafter.
>
> The value of these dedicated women to the Marine Corps has never been measured alone by the great numbers of additional fighting men made available in times of severe emer-

gency. An extremely high quality of patriotism, coupled with an illustrious record of serious and loyal devotion to duty in the finest traditions of our Corps, have gained them the enviable reputation they enjoy today.

To the 1,364 Women Marines in Organized units and the Volunteer Reserve, and to those still serving on active duty, I extend my congratulations on your 11th anniversary as Marines.

Unique among the Reserve events of 1954 was a petition by the legislative branch of the Government of American Samoa for the reactivation of a Marine Corps Reserve unit in the islands. Although the petition was denied, it recalled the original Samoan Reserve Battalion, formed shortly before World War II.

And, once again in 1954, reservists—both as individuals and as teams—won many high honors in marksmanship. At the National Rifle and Pistol Matches, Marine Corps Reserve Team Number One carried off the Roumanian Trophy Team Match. In winning this trophy—originally presented by Queen Marie of Roumania in 1919 for AEF competition at Le Mans, France—Team Number One established a new match record, besting the previous record set by the Marine Corps Reserve team in 1939. Further reflecting the high caliber of Reserve marksmanship in 1954, Reserve Lieutenant Colonels Philip C. Roettinger, Harry Reeves, and Emmet O. Swanson won berths on the United States International Rifle and Pistol Team that year.

Marine War Memorial Dedicated

The highlight of Marine Reserve public affairs of 1954 was the formal dedication of the Marine Corps War Memorial in Washington, D.C. On 10 November, the 179th Anniversary of the founding of the Corps, the Commandant presented the Memorial to the American people in impressive ceremonies witnessed by the President and Vice President of the United States and a host of "representative citizens." The crowd of more than 7,000 who came out for the formal dedication foreshadowed a remarkable interest which was to make this, in years to come, one of the most popular of all meccas for visitors to the Nation's Capital, ranking with the Lincoln Memorial, the Washington Monument, and the Capitol Building itself. Arrangements for the dedication ceremonies were made by 2 Reserve officers, Lieutenant Colonel McCahill and Captain Stephen Tripp, chairman and vice chairman, respectively. Marines—Regular and Reserve alike—from all over the world had contributed to this tribute to the uncommon valor which had been the common virtue of their comrades in arms down through the years of our country's history.

Aside from its appeal to patriotism, the statue represented a remarkable feat in sculpture. Famed sculptor Felix G. W. de Weldon had spent nearly 9 years on this faithful, over-lifesized reproduction of Associated Press photographer Joe Rosenthal's Pulitzer-prize-winning photograph of 5 Marines and a Navy corpsman struggling to raise the American flag atop Iwo Jima's Mount Suribachi. About midway through this 9-year labor, Sculptor de Weldon was visited in his Washington studio by Photographer Rosenthal. Standing dwarfed by the nearly completed plaster model of the scene Rosenthal had caught for posterity, de Weldon beamed appreciative thanks when Rosenthal called his work "Magnificient," and added, "Without your picture, Mr. Rosenthal, this would never have been possible." Rosenthal countered: "Without those Marines, there would have been no picture."

The Year 1955

Most important to the Marine Corps Reserve program in 1955 was major legislation, enacted or implemented during the year, to strengthen the Reserve components of all the Armed Forces. The first step in this direction came with the implementation of Public Law 773, 83d Congress—the Reserve Officer Personnel Act of 1954, popularly known as "ROPA." Enacted into law on 3 September 1954, to become effective on 1 July 1955, it applied to Reserve officers not on active duty and those on active duty in connection with the Reserve program. It provided for officer promotion, precedence, constructive credit, distribution, retention, and elimination. Insofar as it pertained to the Marine Corps Reserve, ROPA continued in effect most of the existing provisions governing Reserve officers. One such provision required reservists to maintain an annual minimum of 27 retirement points to remain in an active status. Other provisions authorized 5 general officers; required selection boards and other boards convened to consider officers pursuant to ROPA to have at least 50 percent Reserve members, if practicable; and established criteria for promotion zones and definitions, duties, and reports of selection boards.

A second major legislative measure, the Reserve Forces Act of 1955 (Public Law 305, 85th Congress), changed the Reserve picture considerably. Signed by the President on 9 August and effective on that date, the Act amended much of the existing law affecting the Marine Corps Reserve as contained in the Universal Military Training and Service Act and the Armed Forces Reserve Act of 1952. It pointed up the necessity of keeping the Ready Reserve *really ready for active service*, through a system of continuous screening and involuntary transfer to the Standby Reserve. It further provided for the training of reservists on a planned basis; almost doubled the Nation's Ready Reserve manpower ceiling (from 1.5 million to 2.9 million men); established an obligation for Reserve participation; and authorized presidential mobilization of 1 million Ready Reserves in an emergency proclaimed by the President.

Military obligation for young men over the age of 18½ years who had completed 6 months of active duty was reduced from 8 years to 6. They were required to join an Organized Reserve unit upon release from active duty—and to remain active in the Organized unit, drilling once a week and attending 15 days of summer training each year for the remaining period of their obligated service. During this time they remained deferred from the draft. But, a provision that put teeth into the law warned that failure to participate satisfactorily in training duty could result in involuntary orders to active duty for a period not to exceed 45 days. In addition, this Act of 1955 made provision for possible future implementation of a Three to Six Month Training Program if the Ready Reserve could not otherwise be maintained at a level considered necessary in the interest of national security.

Reflecting the continuing need to make the Ready Reserve really ready, the 1955 Volunteer Reserve training schedule provided formalized training for more than 2,500 Volunteer Reserve officers and approximately 1,500 enlisted Volunteer reservists. An estimated 2,600 Volunteer reservists attended 15-day periods of active duty for training. While not organized into individual combat and support type units which trained as an entity, the Volunteer Reserve, nevertheless, did constitute a large portion of the immediate 1955 Reserve strength prepared to augment the Regular Establishment on call. Growth of the Volunteer component during the year paralleled that of the Organized Reserve. By 30 June 1955 the Volunteer Reserve had approximately 21,000 officers and about 108,000 enlisted personnel. Included in this total were 133 VTU's. The Organized Reserve had 42,174 members in 286 units, including 42 Aviation units and 19 Women Reserve platoons.

Interest and participation in the 1955 summer maneuvers for Aviation units was heightened by an exchange of training locations between East and West Coast units. East Coast squadrons were airlifted to El Toro; West Coast units flew across country to Cherry Point. This criss-cross maneuver provided valuable experience in troop transportation.

Ground Staff Groups Formed

Nearly 10,000 reservists from some 68 Organized units trained at Camp Lejune under a program that included specialized training for selected officers and enlisted men in amtracs, tanks, communications, and air delivery. Recruit training was available on request to privates. The 1955 training schedule included a number of special refresher courses, given for Reserve officers by the Army at Fort Benning, Fort Knox, and Fort Sill. And, a new type of Organized Ground unit was added to the program in June with the creation of Staff Groups,

designed to train field grade officers in staff functions and procedures and noncommissioned officers in duties that exist within staff agencies. Twenty-four paid drills were scheduled, and each group would attend field training as a unit. Finally, participation in cold weather training at Pickel Meadows was encouraged again. By June 1955 the Marine Corps had 234 training facilities for its Organized Ground units. No additional Reserve facilities were planned for 1956.

Although many of the personnel problems of the preceding year had eased, some serious ones persisted. The officer rank structure in Organized units remained unbalanced, particularly in Aviation squadrons. The training of specialists was complicated by limitations on active duty for training. There were so many new developments in radar, electronics, communications, and other specialized fields that Reserve specialists could scarcely be brought up-to-date with 15 days of training. To solve this problem, plans for 1954 included 30-, 60- and 90-day training tours for specialists in these fields.

General Burger set 3 additional goals for the year: to increase the size of the Reserve; to improve its capability for quick employment; and to continue to maintain the high quality of the individual reservist. Continued study and resulting recommendations of the Marine Reserve Policy Board helped in attaining these goals.

In the 1955 National Rifle and Pistol Matches, Marine reservists topped all comers to carry off the famed Rattlesnake Trophy, symbolic of the top Reserve team in the country, and won more than a hundred medals—double the number credited to any previous Reserve team. The team, under coaching of Captain Joseph Hankins, had won the trophy in 1937, '38, '39 and '40.

The 2d 155mm Gun Battalion of Miami won the Vittori Trophy for top attendance honors at annual field training; the 1st Engineer Field Maintenance Company of Baltimore retained possession of the Flynn Trophy; and the Woman Marine Classification Platoon of Boston took the Towle Trophy for the third straight year. Upon the detachment of General Burger, General Stickney served as Acting Director from 4 January to 11 March 1956 until Brigadier General Thomas G. Ennis arrived from Korea to become Director. General Burger, on departure, summed up his personal feelings about the Reserve:

> I depart as Director, Marine Corps Reserve, with the knowledge that great progress has been made in building a bigger, better, and stronger Reserve. This could not have been accomplished without the full cooperation and unswerving loyalty of our Regulars and members of our Reserve.
>
> I believe in the importance of the Reserve because experience has proven that a strong Reserve is necessary for the Marine Corps and for the defense of our beloved country.
>
> I have been impressed with the high motivation of all who belong to the Reserve and those Regulars who work with them. Building and maintaining a Reserve is not an easy job and our success so far is because all those have given unsparingly of time and talent.

The Year 1956

Continued emphasis on improving Reserve mobilization capability and strengthening the training program marked 1956. On every appropriate occasion, General Stickney, who had received his star in September 1955, voiced his conviction that such terms as "Weekend Warriors," "Thursday Night Soldiers," and "Civilian Marines" should be junked; that those

pseudo titles and the kind of thinking that went with them were obsolete in the age of the atom; that it was time for the public to assume a more adult approach in its attitude toward reservists; and that reservists should be thought of, not as quasi-amateurs, but rather as quasi-professional military men. Speaking to the Advanced Research Group in Quantico, he emphasized the increasingly dominant place of the Ready Reserve in the Armed Forces; the fact that it must be immediately available for call in any emergency proclaimed by the President or declared by the Congress; and the importance of maintaining the highest possible state of readiness at all times. This goal, he said, would be attained by establishing a screening process to eliminate excesses in grade and skill requirements needed for a balanced force; by further screening out all Ready Reserves possessing critical civilian skills needed by industry in wartime, providing those skills exceeded Reserve wartime requirements; and by eliminating from the Ready rolls all reservists whose call to service would result in extreme personal or community hardship and those who could not meet age requirements or prescribed standards of physical and professional fitness. He explained that the new concept was the outgrowth of a need for fair-sharing of available skilled manpower between the military forces and industry and an ever-increasing necessity for a *trained* and *ready* Reserve, and that the course upon which the Marine Corps had embarked would indeed produce "a Reserve that is, in fact, trained and ready; one that can be counted upon to respond immediately and effectively when needed."

To tighten and strengthen the Reserve program, the Department of Defense eliminated pay for Standby reservists on active duty for training and created uniform training categories and pay groups. Under the new provisions, the Marine Corps Reserve had 6 training categories:

Category	Annual periods of inactive duty training	Annual active duty for training
A------------	48----------------	15 days.
B------------	24----------------	15 days.
D----------	None------------	15 days.
G-----------	No Training------	None.
H-----------	None------------	30 days.
I-----------	Officers' Training Programs.	None.

The Armed Forces Reserve Act of 1952 was the basis for a new policy, announced by the Commandant in 1956, establishing 4 recall priorities for Ready reservists. Topping the list and subject to first call were reservists with less than 2 years of active service; scheduled for last call were combat veterans and students. Readiness, however, was not to be scaled to recall priority; the Marine Corps share of the overall service-callable Ready Reserve was approximately 246,000; the Marine Corps aim was to fill every one of those 246,000 slots with a completely ready reservist. The tempo of the training program for attaining this aim was set by the Commandant in March, when he said:

> Experience has proven that attendance at drills is in direct proportion to the effectiveness of the training program. A successful drill period is a training period; fast moving, highly organized, and disciplined, without distraction or interruption from the main purpose. Administrative details pertinent to individuals must be accomplished at a time other than the scheduled training periods. Strenuous efforts to achieve the above *will result* in increased drill attendance and growth.

Three months after becoming Director in March, General Ennis described the Reserve as being in the middle of a campaign with dual aims: to build stability, personnelwise, into the Organized units; and, to bolster drill attendance. He pointed to the Six Month Training Program—a feature of the Reserve Forces Act of 1955—as the most effective source of support for the stabilizing effort. Impetus for the drive to improve drill attendance was provided by setting firm drill percentage requirements and by fostering unit competition for the annual attendance trophies.

General Ennis Wants Really Strong Reserve

Speaking of the need for stability in the Organized units, General Ennis told a joint meeting of the Otho L. Rogers Chapter of MCROA and Washington-Baltimore VTU's that the Marine Corps Reserve was a D–Day force that must be ready. He stated:

> We want a big hard core of trained reservists, not a small hard core! Last year we lost 14,000 individuals from Organized units for nonattendance. Meanwhile, we're trying for a Ready Reserve to meet Marine Corps mobilization needs. The Marine Corps Reserve can be brought up to an even keel with personnel attrition, and the Six Month Training Program is the best method available to accomplish this goal.

To improve the training of individual reservists, the Commandant approved a plan allowing Organized reservists who missed unit training to make up the absence with alternate training dates or by training with another Organized unit. Organized units also got at least 4 days of additional active duty for training by conducting local field exercises. Among the first units to benefit from this new training feature were the 9th Special Infantry Company of Greenville, S.C., and the 3d Cargo Company of Charlotte, N.C., which participated in a 2-day combined maneuver with the National Guard, Air Force Reserve, Army Reserve, and Naval Reserve units. Reservists living temporarily overseas were also given training opportunities. The large number of reservists serving with Government agencies and private industry overseas had created a need, long recognized, for supplementing the correspondence courses available for their training. A new policy, initiated in 1956, set up certain conditions under which training was to be permitted in foreign countries which allowed the United States to maintain troops of the active military forces (other than Military Advisory Assistance Group or attache personnel) within their boundaries.

A further refinement of the training program was the broad expansion of the winter training program. This expansion was desirable because of the availability of training facilities which would not otherwise have been used fully and, more importantly, because many reservists could best adjust their personal affairs to participate in training during the winter season. To draw back inactive status lieutenants, flight training and 2-year tours of extended active duty were made available to them during 1956.

Other items on the 1956 training agenda included Reserve Officer Training Courses at Camp Pendleton, Coronado, Quantico, and Little Creek. These courses covering diverse phases of amphibious warfare and ground combat tactics constituted an integral part of the training cycle concept for reservists. From Quantico, too, came a series of 2-day presentations (Advance Base Problem XIII) illustrating Marine Corps future concepts and projections of developments in landing force techniques—an instruction team traveling to Newport, R.I.; Fort Knox; Fort Bliss; Fort Sill; Coronado; and El Toro; and on to Hawaii, to tell this most important story. Attendance, established by quota for each district, was limited to majors and above with Secret security clearance. The training program drew other help from Quantico: the 1956 catalog of Marine Corps Schools included courses on tactical and general military subjects for which reservists could enroll and earn retirement credit—1 point for each 3 hours of estimated student effort. The Reserve Liaison and Training Group (RL&TG), established in 1954 at Quantico, provided VTU's with valuable training materials on request that included lessons on military subjects currently being studied by Regular officers.

Volunteer Training Unit Seminars

In the 3 years following formation of the RL&TG, training available to Class III reservists had been expanded and the VTU growth rate had outstripped that of the larger, more numerous Organized units; the number of VTU's had doubled in the 3-year period ending 1 July 1956. The 38 new units activated during 1956 brought the number of Volunteer units engaging in regularly scheduled training to 198. VTU seminars, held in the various districts, pointed up the fact that too many reservists were not familiar with the Reserve training policy. A substantial improvement in the Volunteer training program was the clarification of the concept of progressive active duty training instruction for 2 successive years at formal schools, with a third year devoted to appropriate on-the-job training (OJT).

The enthusiasm with which Class III reservists entered into the VTU program was further evidenced by unit projects undertaken outside regular drill periods to aid the overall Reserve training effort. Most interesting among these extracurricular activities were: a field problem organized by VTU(G) 8–11 in Midland, Tex., for the local OMCR organization; a military law presentation, including a Moot General Court Martial, staged by Colonel William J. Burrows' law VTU(S) 5–8; an NCO Training School, established and operated by VTU(G) 8–19 in Lubbock, Tex., for the local OMCR unit; a slide presentation and narrative explaining the VTU program, prepared by Rhode Island's VTU(G) 1–21 for local TV stations; and construction of an outdoor rifle range by members of VTU(M) 8–31 of Weslaco, Tex., assisted by several local former Marines.

Air Class III's to MARTCOM

During 1956, Class III Air reservists were administratively transferred from the various Marine Corps Reserve and Recruitment Districts to the Marine Air Reserve Training Command. This action was designed to speed up the processing of training applications and to provide closer integration of training within the Air Reserve. Some 23,000 Volunteer reservists were thus integrated into the comprehensive Air Reserve training program. The major effort of that program was *Operation Able*, which involved more than 4,000 reservists from 25 detachments. The rapid transition to jet aircraft was reflected in the fact that 80 percent of the aircraft used by the 30 fighter squadrons and 12 air control squadrons participating in *Operation Able* were jets—150 of them the latest "Cougar Jets."

For the first half of 1956—and indeed for the entire year—the Commandant's Report to the Secretary of the Navy for Fiscal Year 1956 provides an excellent summary of Reserve activities:

There were no major changes in the Marine Corps Reserve during the period of this report. The Director of Reserve, as the Commandant's staff agent, continued the supervision of Ground Reserve affairs through district directors who administered the Volunteer (Class III) program in addition to supervising Organized Reserve Ground activities, to which Inspector-Instructor staffs were assigned.

The Commander, Marine Air Reserve Training, through Air Reserve training detachments, exercises control over Organized Reserve Aviation units. In fiscal year 1957, he will assume control over aviation specialists now carried on district rolls. This will produce a better functional alignment within the Reserve.

During the fiscal year 1956 there were consolidations, deactivations, and redesignations, all made in the interest of administrative and operational efficiency. Plans have been made to convert 90mm AA gun units to the 75mm Skysweeper weapon in fiscal year 1957. One new Woman Marine administrative platoon and 12 staff groups were formed. The present troop list includes 244 Ground and 47 Aviation units.

The Marine Corps has made a successful start on the Six Month Training Program established by the Reserve Forces Act of 1955. During the year, 3,189 men joined under this program and 1,368 actually began training. This training takes place at Regular bases, and no distinction is made between these men and any other under training. The return of these young men to Organized Reserve units, where they serve the balance of their 8-year obligation, will do much to reduce the excessive turnover and resultant reduced training level in the Organized Reserve.

Two aspects of the Reserve program are of primary importance. First is the matter of mobilization. The Reserve exists to provide the Regular Establishment with trained personnel. The nature of Marine Corps operations is such that this critical action usually takes place in a time of stress and confusion. Any mobilization in the future, full or potential, promises to occur under greater difficulties than known before. The Marine Corps is therefore making a full and objective examination of its Reserve mobilization requirements and methods. The goal is a detailed plan which will stand up under the most difficult conditions. The Marine Corps Reserve must consist of, and furnish when called upon, the skills and numbers needed to put the total establishment in the field in accordance with plans.

The size and training requirements of the Marine Corps Reserve are of equally grave concern. The structure of Reserve Forces as established by current law, the phasing of obligated periods, and the training requirements set by statute will bring about a peak in mandatory participation during the period 1960–62. Strengths, turnover, the need for training facilities, and Regular training base requirements will combine to make demands on the Regular Establishment which, if not foreseen and provided for, will seriously affect the force-in-readiness capability of the Corps.

The Commandant concluded that Reserve strength and stability, and the need for training facilities, were under constant and careful study. And, as noted before, so they were! The entire Reserve training program for 1956 reflected the beneficial results of that continuing study.

The Year 1957

Through 1957, *Readiness* continued as the watchword of the Reserve. Emphasis on personnel stability in Organized units and improved drill attendance as means to that readiness increased. The Six Month Training Program, backbone of the stabilizing effort, was proving its worth. In February the Marine Corps announced that, beginning 1 April, the only recruits to be taken into its Organized Reserve would be 6-month trainees. The "open" enlistment was almost gone. The immediate move to limit enlistments of men without prior military service strictly to the 6-month program resulted from a Department of Defense order designed to build the Reserve forces upon *trained* Ready reservists in Organized units. But the action also reflected confidence in the 6-month program, for which the Marine Corps had already exceeded its enlistment quota. Noting that curtailment of "open" enlistments—those which involved no active duty requirements—meant that the quota for 6-month trainees would probably be raised, General Ennis said the program was "the way to attain stability in drill pay units."

Four months later General Stickney—serving as Director, Marine Corps Reserve, for the second time in as many years—noted that while certain sacrifices had been necessary and training for certain categories of reservists had been cut back to accommodate the Six Month Training Program, the plan was now definitely "on the rails" and the Reserve was heading toward the long-sought destination of stability in Organized units. This confidence was general. For example, Colonel Robert O. Bisson, Chief of Staff of MARTCOM, had commented at MCROA's early-May military conference in New Orleans:

> Because of the Six Month Training Program, in the not too distant future the Marine reservist will be of the same caliber as his counterpart in the Regulars—they will both be professionals.

Reservists, he stressed, must be first-string players—the Reserve had no room for bench warmers. General Stickney had told MCROA that, thanks to the Six Month Training Program, the Reserve was now ready to train as a unit; that Reserve units were, in fact, training with units in which they would serve in time of war; that, should war come, the reservist—being familiar with his unit—would be able to say "I've been here before!"

General Shapley Makes Changes

Some of the most drastic changes to the Reserve program were instituted during Major General Alan Shapley's 1957–58 assignment as Director. Despite the fact that he had never before served in a billet connected with reservists—other than serving beside them in World War II and Korea—he quickly ordered fundamental changes to strengthen the program. In a 3-pronged move to increase the responsiveness of Reserve officers to mobilization needs, requirements were tightened up as age in grade was reduced; the Inactive Status List was slashed—to conform to Department of Defense criteria designed to limit the ISL to reservists who could not participate for good and sufficient reason, but who would be *needed* by the services to fill specific mobilization requirements; and participation in an active status was made a prerequisite to eligibility for selection.

Under this new policy, age-in-grade limits for the Ready Reserve were established at: 50 for lieutenant colonels; 45 for majors; 40 for captains; and 35 for lieutenants. If the Ready Reserve was to be truly ready, realistic age-in-grade requirements were an absolute necessity. Calling 46-year old captains and 58-year old lieutenant colonels to active duty to meet FMF requirements in the early stages of an

emergency was regarded as highly undesirable. Reducing the age-in-grade limit forced some officers out of the Ready Reserve earlier than they would have preferred; but it did not deny them any benefits previously earned or the right to continue to participate in training, without pay, as members of the Standby Reserve.

The rationale behind the measures affecting the Inactive Status List was even more compelling. There were 11,287 officers on the ISL—far more than needed to fill emergency billets. A weeding out of nonessentials and self-determined nonparticipants was imperative. The tightening of eligibility-for-selection criteria stemmed from the grade limitations feature of ROPA; the Reserve officer "hump"; and the need to encourage more active participation by Reserve officers in Reserve training activities.

Prior to this time, the only eligibility factor for consideration for selection had been that prescribed by law: active status at the time of selection and promotion. This had permitted officers to remain inactive during a large portion of their time in grade and then to become eligible for consideration by returning to active status just in time for selection board action. To be eligible for consideration under the new concept, an officer was required to have been off the Inactive Status List for at least 2 years. Cutting the ISL resulted in the earlier retirement or involuntary separation of several thousand nonparticipating officers who, while indicating that they valued their Reserve status, were contributing little to the posture of the Reserve. And, the new eligibility-for-selection criteria proved most effective in stimulating officer participation in Reserve training activities.

Nonperformers Sent to Class III

Meanwhile, the individual drill attendance records of all Class II reservists were being closely monitored. "Drill or Be Dropped!" sternly warned a headline in the July issue of *The Reserve Marine*. "An attendance record that isn't up to standard can easily earn the holder a ticket to the Class III Reserve as the Corps clamps down on 'nonperformers.'" The story under the headline explained that, for the first time in its history, the Reserve was now confronted with the problem of a "full boat"—finding itself in almost the situation of the old lady who lived in a shoe, with nearly too many people. Unlike the shoe-dweller, the article went on to relate, the Corps knew what to do about the situation.

District directors were instructed to cut nonperformers from the rolls. The Organized Reserve had reached peak strength; only 3,000 men could be added during the fiscal year just beginning; during the same period, some 8,000 6-month trainees would be enrolled. That meant, according to *The Reserve Marine*, some 5,000 men, in all probability, would lose their drill pay status during the year. Regarding continued recruiting as vital to the maintenance of a vigorous drill pay Reserve, Headquarters had told the district directors that, in screening records of present members, they should consider for immediate transfer to the inactive Reserve, any reservist who did not have a drill attendance mark of at least 90 percent, plus attendance at the most recent period of annual field training. Although this instruction was rescinded within the year, it had the desired effect of making commanders more "drill-attendance-conscious" and resulted in increased attendance throughout the Organized ranks. The Ground Reserve, in particular, reported "Planned Performance Estimates Exceeded," every month for a period of some 8 months.

The stepped-up emphasis on attendance was matched—and more—by efforts to make the training offered worth the attending. More and varied training programs, for both Organized and Volunteer units, were set up as long-range objectives. The goals, consolidated in a 31-page document by the Training Branch, Division of Reserve, were to be accomplished over a 5-year period. This report formalized the training mission of the Ready Reserve: to provide progressive individual and unit training that would maintain a level of proficiency commensurate with mobilization requirements and make possible the integration of individuals into the Regular Establishment without further training in the event of mobilization.

Four prime objectives were established for Organized units:

> (1) To establish training programs as required to enable Reserve drill pay units to attain a level of proficiency comparable to similar type units of the Regular Marine Corps;
>
> (2) To open training programs which would enable members of Ready Reserve units to qualify in the T/O billet assigned, and to require all personnel not in the determined-critical fields to accomplish such qualification within a definite period of time;
>
> (3) To establish billets in a greater variety of occupational fields, within each drill pay unit, either by the formation of new type composite units or by adding different type platoons to existing units, for the purpose of providing appropriate training for mandatory participants returning from active duty; and
>
> (4) To provide recruit and basic training programs for all Ready reservists enlisting as members of drill pay units, and to require

completion of such training within a definite period of time.

For the Class III program, a goal of 475 VTU's with a total membership of 10,500 called for the doubling of the number of VTU's—up from 240 units with an overall membership of 4,500—in the 5 years ahead. Three other VTU objectives were spelled out in the long-range planning:

(1) To provide a monitored training program for VTU meetings, using prepared lesson plans and courses made available through the facilities of the Reserve Liaison and Training Group at Quantico;

(2) To organize VTU's into military specialty units—eliminating, to a large extent, the general type units which comprised the bulk of the existing 240 units: and

(3) To establish annual field training periods for all specialist units, marksmanship units, and those remaining general units whose personnel composition would permit the scheduling of appropriate training.

These were ambitious goals—ambitious as were the 1957 training course schedules—and, like those schedules, the goals would be subject to some retrenching. For example, the VTU annual field training periods were, for the most part, to go by the boards. But, again, the very fact that the goals were established demonstrated the grave concern with which the Marine Corps viewed its responsibility to ensure, for any future mobilization, a level of Reserve readiness such as it had never before been permitted to contemplate, let alone attain, in a "no-war era."

33,000 Go to Camp

Evidence of the effectiveness of the all-out effort of Organized unit commanders to ensure maximum participation, more than 29,000 Class II Ground and some 4,000 Air reservists turned out for annual summer training exercises in 1957. The Ground field training program featured the first full-scale amphibious landing conducted by the Reserve since 1951 and the first assignment of infantry units to train at Marine Corps air stations. For Air reservists, the highly successful criss-cross airlift was repeated—East Coast squadrons training at El Toro, West Coast units at Cherry Point.

General Shapley, who had taken over from General Stickney in August, was at Camp Pendleton for a first-hand appraisal of the September amphibious landing exercises. He expressed satisfaction with Reserve combat readiness, noting that units from all parts of the country could be brought together and, in less than a week, fused into a compact fighting force. The *San Diego Union*, in a commendatory editorial on the landings, observed: "It is to the Nation's advantage that the transition from inactive to active can be effected so quickly and so well."

The summer training maneuver of the Air Reserve (*Operation Vigor*) drew similar praise from Brigadier General Frank C. Croft, Commander of MARTCOM. This operation gave fighter pilots training in cross-country navigation problems and practice in the Marine Corps specialty, close air support. Ground crews were busy keeping the planes in the air and attending various schools and training sessions in techniques and weapons. Radar men and technicians of the air control squadrons worked on the latest radar gear as the eyes of the fighter squadrons, directing them to intercept "enemy" planes. Several Reserve pilots completed instrument flight training in the new F9F–8T Cougar (Transonic 2-place jet). Instruction that normally took 3 weeks was compressed into a week and a half of intensive training.

92 Choices

Besides annual field training, eligible Class II and III reservists had additional training opportunities. Two- and 3-week courses at 5 of the 1st Marine Brigade's service schools were open to enlisted reservists living in the Hawaiian Islands. A 2-day presentation (Advance Base Problem XIII) was offered to majors and above with Confidential or higher security clearance—with alternate training sites at the Infantry School at Fort Benning, and the Antiaircraft Artillery and Guided Missile School at Fort Bliss, Tex. The 1957 Reserve formal course schedule offered 92 choices, ranging from formal NCO Leadership classes through OJT in a wide variety of military specialties for enlisted personnel. Reserve officers had options for the 2-week Reserve Junior and Senior Courses, for formal specialty courses, and for 2-week periods of OJT in military specialties not available as formal school classes. New courses in supporting arms and shore party organization and operations were available to both officers and staff NCO's; and, again, the cold weather training program gave reservists training in the techniques of mountain warfare training and the use of cold weather clothing and equipment. And there were other "special" programs: the 10-week Officer Candidate Course and the Platoon Leader Classes at Quantico; the first WR Noncommissioned Officer Leadership Course, also at Quantico; opportunities for Repeated Training Duty Without Pay; and expanded training schedules in Volunteer Training Units. Although training opportunities for overseas reservists were somewhat curtailed this year, in every other respect 1957 could be dubbed a "Banner Training Year."

The Year 1958

Economy dicated the end of an era in 1958 as all 18 Woman Marine platoons were deactivated. The move, prompted by a cut in Reserve training funds, reduced the number of women in drill pay status from 630 to 227. The 227 who remained were affiliated with male Reserve units. The Woman Marine platoons had provided a colorful chapter in Marine Corps Reserve history. They came into being in 1949. When the Korean War began, the platoons were mobilized with their male counterparts and distingushed themselves when 98 percent actually came on active duty. This was the first time in the history of the United States that both men and women were mobilized for war. Upon deactivation of the platoons, personnel were afforded opportunity to affiliate with male units, if appropriate billets were available and authorization for such duty was approved by the district director and unit commanding officer.

While the Women Marines were attending their last drills, Sergeant John R. Brown, Jr., who had become one of the country's leading air aces during World War II, once again donned his greens as a Marine Corps reservist. In the 19 years between his enlistments, Sergeant Brown had kept busy—rising to the rank of lieutenant colonel in the Air Force. Upon his return to the Marine Corps Reserve, he was assigned to the 62d Infantry Company of Harrisburg, Pa.

Additional attention came to the Marine Corps Reserve when, in Philadelphia, the fifth member of a prominent family joined the Marine Corps Reserve. Richardson Dilworth, Jr., was sworn into the PLC program by his father, Philadelphia Mayor Richardson Dilworth, a Reserve lieutenant colonel. Young Dilworth followed in the footsteps of 3 brothers and a half-brother.

Examples of Reserve "devotion to duty" in 1958 were perfect drill attendance records made by Master Sergeant Robert H. Hickman and Staff Sergeant William Gordon. Master Sergeant Hickman, a Jackson, Miss., letter carrier, was brought to Washington for a Meritorious Mast with the Commandant, General Randolph McC. Pate. A veteran of both World War II and Korea, Hickman had maintained a perfect drill attendance record for 10 years. Staff Sergeant Gordon of the 11th Rifle Company, Freeport, N.Y., a New York State Trooper in civilian life, regularly traveled 250 miles each week to make Monday evening drills. A veteran of the Pusan Perimeter and the Chosin Reservoir with the 1st Marine Division, Staff Sergeant Gordon also had a 100-percent drill attendance record for the year.

Another reservist, Major Richard J. Hardaway, brought new honors to the Marine Corps Reserve during the 1958 Marine Corps Rifle and Pistol Matches at San Diego. The 35-year-old Californian won the Corps highest shooting award, the Lauchheimer Trophy, and set a new record doing it. A mainstay of the Reserve Rifle and Pistol teams which fired in the National Matches at Camp Perry, Ohio, Major Hardaway won the trophy by scoring a 571x600 with the rifle and 559x600 with the pistol.

Another Marine Corps record was broken in 1958 by a reservist, when Private First Class James S. Lapcevic, of Pittsburgh's 12th Infantry Battalion, broke a school mark at Camp Lejeune's PFC class. Private Lapcevic scored a 95.90 to set the record.

On the quiet campus of Eastern Baptist College in St. Davids, Pa., 15 members of VTU 4–18 (Intelligence) commanded by Captain Robert N. Burrows, an associate professor of English at the college, studied the Russian language. Two other VTU's were also engaged in studying Russian; another, Chinese; and yet another, Turkish.

Ballance Board Reviews Reserve

The entire structure of the Reserve also came under careful study in 1958. A special Headquarters panel, directed by Colonel Robert G. Ballance, Assistant Director, Marine Corps Reserve, investigated several major problem areas, such as reorganization of troop lists, problems of new weapons, and procedures for emergency mobilization.

The "hump problem" which plagued the Regular Establishment during 1958 also affected Reserve captains who were eligible for promotion. Only 31 officers of 1,182 could be selected for promotion during the fiscal year.

The state of readiness of the Reserve was not bad, however. In fact, the Marine Reserve was the only branch to receive an "Excellent" readiness rating in the Annual Report of the Secretary of Defense on Reserve Forces. Speaking of the Marine Corps Reserve, Defense Secretary Neil McElroy told the President:

> Fiscal year 1957 was a signal year for the Marine Corps Reserve. Not only did it achieve the highest total strength ever attained, but it did so concurrently with the initiation of a rigid screening process designed to eliminate nonavailables or noneffectives from the Reserve . . .
>
> The overall estimate of the state of readiness of the Marine Corps Reserve may be termed excellent at the end of fiscal year 1957. This is not meant to imply that all mobilization needs can be met, but . . . the Marine Corps Reserve can more than meet its stated mobilization requirements. All officers have completed tours of active duty

and over 200,000 enlisted personnel have met or exceeded minimum requirements for deployment overseas.

Helicopter Squadrons

A major change, designed to increase readiness, occurred in 1958 when 12 operating helicopter squadrons were activated. The squadrons—located at Minneapolis; Oakland and Los Alamitos, Calif.; Seattle; New Orleans; Columbus, Ohio; Willow Grove, Pa.; Dallas; Glenview; Jacksonville, Fla.; South Weymouth, Mass.; and Brooklyn, N.Y.—were assigned dual training roles. These were to upgrade the flying skills of 'copter pilots and train nonflying members in essential maintenance and supply operations; and to provide exercise in vertical envelopment and helicopter support methods for the mutual benefit of both Ground and Air Reserve units.

Another major change—from once-a-week drill meetings to "back-to-back" weekend drills—was strongly advocated for Organized Ground units during 1958 by General Shapley. Visiting Organized Reserve units throughout the country, General Shapley pointed out that weekend drills made it possible for units to schedule more field problems, range firing, physical conditioning, and overnight bivouacs. Although there were individual cases of hardship when units changed from the 2-hour drills once weekly to the 1-weekend-a-month plan, the units found they had gained substantially in 4 areas: attendance, administration, training, and morale. In addition, units found it easier to interest new recruits in 12 meetings a year instead of 48, and the once-a-month drill schedule brought in reservists with prior service who had previously felt they lived too far away to attend weekly meetings.

One of the greatest improvements under the new system came in unit administration. With once-a-week drills, an average of 10 percent of administration had been handled by Reserve personnel. Under the new drill schedule, with more time for company clerks to instruct and supervise on-the-job administration training programs, most units handled 80 percent or more of their administrative requirements. By mid-1958, more than 40 ground units had adopted back-to-back drills.

Man on the Move

Living up to his motto that you can't command from a desk chair, General Shapley, in his first year as Director, had visited over one-half of his Organized Ground units. To do this he traveled 58,860 miles, stopped in 26 States, and spent 153 days on the road. When informed that he unquestionably had set a travel record as Director, the General admitted that he had "gotten off to a pretty fair start."

Several changes that would affect VTU's in 1959 were announced in July 1958. They covered reorganization of type units; the number of units an individual could join; minimum size of units; participation of Standby reservists; unit training schedules; and wider participation in language units. In the new VTU Ground organization, there would be no more general type units. All VTU's would specialize in one of 12 areas: ABC Warfare; Civil Affairs and Military Government; Communications-Electronics; Engineering; Guided Missiles; Intelligence; Law; Logistics; Operations and Training; Ordnance; Personnel and Administration; and Public Information. Marksmanship and Language VTU's would be permitted upon approval of the Commandant.

Another major change in the Reserve program occurred in late 1958 when the ratio of officers to enlisted in the Organized units was changed from 1-to-15 to 1-to-20. More than 800 officers thus lost their drill pay status. The new officer-enlisted ratio for the Reserve corresponded more closely to the FMF ratio of 1-to-19. In ground units, majors were reduced from 395 to 214; captains, from 1,060 to 645. The new directive also limited tours of duty for all Organized unit commanding officers to 2 years.

Summing up the year in his *Marine Corps Reserve Notes* of 23 December, General Shapley reported that more and more units had changed to multiple drills and 64 units had held a combination of single and double drills. Eighty-two units did not hold multiple drills. He said:

> This has been a good year for the Reserve in spite of the fact that we have had such severe budgetary restrictions. We have accomplished many things that are good. I will not attempt to enumerate them for, frankly, there are too many, but it gives me a deep sense of personal satisfaction to realize that the Reserve Program is far and above the best program in the Armed Services. . . .
>
> I have a feeling that the morale is as high now as it ever has been. You people make morale and when morale is high our accomplishments can be unlimited—so stay in there and continue to pitch.

The Year 1959
"IMPROVE—
TRAINING
PROFICIENCY
QUALITY
BENEFITS"

"Forecast for '59," in the January issue of *The Reserve Marine*, expanded on this checklist of Marine Corps Reserve New Year's Resolutions with Headquarters

predictions as to how the objectives would be attained. Improved and advanced unit training and air-ground exercises would keep Ground elements fully occupied. Squadrons would work in the direction of greater flight safety and proficiency through a stepped-up training program necessitated by advances in weaponry and warfare techniques and made possible by the high level of training completed during the previous year. Through improved training Headquarters was also aiming, as a side benefit, for reduction in enlisted turnover in the Air Reserve. The Six Month Training Program would remain the recruiting mainstay for Organized units, with a goal of roughly 7,000 top quality recruits for the year. Here, the Reserve could be highly selective, since far more young men than could be accommodated were waiting to be enrolled. Annual field training would be limited to trained personnel; only those who had completed 6 months of training would be eligible for summer camp. Thus, the necessity for 2 levels of instruction at training commands would be eliminated and training funds could be conserved.

In spite of an unusually austere training budget, Headquarters was determined to maintain the previous year's momentum in all its training programs. Class III officer training would take the brunt of any unavoidable cutback but here, too, quality training for selected individuals would be stressed.

The brightest spot in the year's training picture lay in the continuing improvement and expanded range of specialist courses provided by the Reserve Liaison and

Training Group at Quantico. These courses would serve as a base on which Organized units could develop additional advanced specialty training and, supplemented by a new "VTU Starter Kit," would provide a complete training syllabus available to VTU's on request.

Forecast as "probably the greatest advance the Marine Corps Reserve will make in 1959" was increased training in vertical envelopment tactics. The Air Reserve was slated to have 21 helicopter squadrons by midyear; vertical envelopment instruction would be emphasized at annual field training; and the subject would be a major topic at drill sessions and in the VTU's as well.

Training facilities, too, were due for improvement. The training center at Portland, Maine, was scheduled for rehabilitation and, within the year, construction would be completed on 6 new centers—located at Raleigh, N.C.; Wilmington, Del.; Fort Schuyler, N.Y.; and at Reading, Forty Fort, and Eddystone in Pennsylvania. Other projected facility improvements included contract awards for 4 additional centers, plus building additions that would give the Marine Corps Reserve exclusive use of 3 existing centers. Also on the boards were 6 rifle ranges, 24 additional classrooms, and 4 buildings for vehicle and artillery maintainence. With better training facilities in prospect, improved drill attendance was anticipated. Goals were set for 80 percent average attendance at unit drills and at least 78 percent attendance of each Organized unit at annual field training.

Efforts were also being made to increase disability benefits for the Reserve as Headquarters got solidly behind legislation to provide disability and other benefits to Reserve personnel injured while traveling to or from authorized inactive duty training.

An ambitious forecast, this. But the milestones already passed on the Rebuild Trail had been ambitious too—and the goals set and attained since Korea lent confidence to the 1959 effort.

Commandant Calls Reserve Vital

"There is no precept more valuable to the Marine Corps than the one prescribing the vital importance of a readily available and highly qualified Reserve." So said the Commandant, General Pate, in introducing the Marine Corps portion of the 1959 National Reserve Training Program to the House Armed Services Committee.

And, in his salute to the Reserves of the Armed Forces, President Eisenhower called a Ready Reserve a major consideration in National defense planning. "Despite great scientific advancements" the President's message went on, "the ultimate security of our land will always depend upon an alert citizenry."

In such a climate, it is not surprising that the entire Marine Corps Reserve Inactive Duty Training Program, covering as it did the vast majority of all Marines in Reserve, was subjected to close scrutiny during 1959. Regulations governing all aspects of the program were consolidated into one Marine Corps Order in which significant policy changes appeared. Five categories of inactive duty training were listed in the Order: Associate Duty with the Organized Reserve; Appropriate Duty; Repeated Training Duty; Correspondence Courses, and—the workhorse of the Class III program—the Volunteer Training Unit.

Members of the Ready Reserve were eligible to participate in all phases of the Inactive Duty Training Program. Members of the Standby Reserve, if not on the ISL, were eligible for Appropriate Duty and Repeated Training Duty, but not for Associate Duty. Under certain conditions, they were also eligible for VTU membership. For personnel of the Standby Reserve of the ISL, the only training available was that offered in correspondence courses, which were open to all members of the Reserve—except the Retired Reserve—regardless of status or rank.

Three objectives formed the criteria for Associate and Appropriate Duty assignments: to maintain and develop the military skills of the individual; to increase mobilization potential; and to further the state of readiness of the Reserve. Attainment of retirement credits was not included in the objectives, but—since no reimbursement for pay, allowances, travel, subsistence, uniforms, or any other expenses was authorized—retirement credits were recognized as a means of compensation incidental to satisfactory performance of duty.

Class III members were assigned to Associate Duty with Organized Air and Ground units to fill differences between manning levels and T/O strengths. They filled actual billets and attended drills throughout the year, just as did the Organized members, but without pay and allowances. During the year, approximately 200 Class III officers were trained in Associate Duty status.

Appropriate Duty Doubly Beneficial

Of particular significance during this period of reduced funds was the ever-increasing activity designated as Appropriate Duty. Most flexible of all the categories, Appropriate Duty opened a wide range of activities to inactive Reserves throughout the United States and overseas. Appropriate Duty cost the Marine Corps nothing immediately, except retirement points. It could be performed almost anywhere, at any time. During 1959, a significant number of Volunteer Reserves performed Appropriate Duty, on their own, participating in military instruction that would improve their own proficiency—or giving the Marine Corps and the Reserve valuable service in recruiting, officer procurement, and public information activities; conducting specialized instruction of Reserve organizations of all branches of the Armed Forces; serving as observers at field exercises; and participating in parades and ceremonies. Imagination was the only limitation on this program. Further, it permitted every military establishment, from the smallest detachment to the largest FMF command, to contribute to the vital task of maintaining a ready M-day force in Reserve.

Five types of Repeated Training Duty were authorized: participation as a shooter in rifle and pistol competition; participation, by members of Organized units, in field exercises outside regularly scheduled drills; active participation in Organized unit field exercises by Class III members assigned as umpires or augmentation personnel; participation in flight operations; and assistance in connection with local civil disasters. Repeated Training Duty orders could be issued for 1 year's duration, with a 6-day limitation on any one training assignment, or on a one-time basis to cover single periods of 1 week.

Correspondence courses offered by the Quantico Extension School and by the Marine Corps Institute provided additional training opportunities for upwards of 5,600 Reserve Marines in 1959. More than

500 officers and 1,200 enlisted took advantage of the Extension School offerings, while approximately 720 officers and 3,200 enlisted enrolled in institute courses.

But by far the largest measure of inactive duty training came through participation in the VTU program. Volunteer Training Units, located throughout the United States, formed the Corps' second largest continuing training program for its Reserve—second only to that of the drill pay Organized units. Counterparts of the Organized units, the VTU's provided the backbone of the Class III training program, year in and year out. During 1959, more than 290 Ground and Aviation units boasted of attendance by approximately 3,700 officers and 350 enlisted personnel. Each unit was required to hold at least 24 meetings a year—each meeting of at least 2-hours duration. No discussion of the VTU's would be complete without a word of praise for the body of individual members responsible for the program's continuing success. Serving without monetary remuneration, they devoted countless hours to attendance and many more to preparation of instruction, which in most cases was given by the members themselves.

The New, New VTU

Pointing up the importance attached to this form of training, a special board, composed of VTU officer experts from each of the 7 Reserve and Recruitment Districts and MARTCOM, was convened at Marine Headquarters in March 1959, to study all aspects of the VTU program. The group, headed by Colonel Harry N. Lyon, Commanding Officer of San Francisco's VTU(G) 12–1, was given wide scope in which to operate, the only limitation being that the VTU program must re-main a nonpay operation. Pursuing the mission of revitalizing this particular phase of Reserve training, the board tackled such matters as VTU administration and requirements; training syllabus; the problem of diversified occupational specialties within VTU's; the number of members required for formation of a unit; the types of units needed; chain of command setup for Air officers participating in ground units, and vice versa; officer fitness reports; promotional opportunities for enlisted members; and Standby Reserve participation in the program.

Of the Board's 21 recommendations, covering practically every facet of the VTU operation, 13 were unconditionally approved and incorporated into the new *Reserve Training Standing Operating Procedures* (RESSOP). One definite mission was spelled out for the VTU program: "to increase the mobilization potential of Class III reservists." To accomplish this mission, 3 tasks were given:

> To promote the highest state of readiness consistent with a volunteer program, using available training media; to encourage the participation of inactive reservists of all ranks; and to encourage and guide Class III reservists toward increasing their professional value and promotion opportunities.

Causing the most furor in the reorganization scheme, was the subject of Standby participation. The final word, as published in RESSOP, was: "Standbys can be members *only* if they are precluded from Ready Reserve status because of age in grade or physical fitness." One further restriction was placed on Standby participation: "No Standby may serve as a commanding officer of any VTU."

The number of members needed to form a unit was reduced. RESSOP decreed:

> A minimum membership of 10 is desirable. In no case will a unit be activated with

fewer than 4 members. Actual membership requirements once a unit has been established will be set by district directors. Primary consideration will be the type of unit and the military/civilian backgrounds of the members.

Gone were the old "General units." Fifteen types of specialist units were authorized. Units without enough members with appropriate specialist backgrounds were permitted to continue as Staff units. and many of the former General units fell into this category. Membership standards for the Intelligence-Language units were tightened, and the percentage of field grade officers permitted in these units was limited. Membership in more than 1 unit was no longer permitted. Units were required to hold 24 training sessions per year (the old minimum had been just half that number); and, at least 50 percent of unit training was required to be selected from a Training Material Index prepared to meet specific VTU needs. The purpose of this latter requirement was to ensure a certain degree of cohesion and uniformity in the training of all units, and to make available the very latest information on Marine Corps tactics, techniques, and doctrines.

Besides these inactive training opportunities, a few assignments to active duty with pay were available to Class III members. Budgetary considerations limited these assignments to what was called "the hard core of the Ready Reserve." Young officers newly released from active duty—recognized as offering the greatest mobilization potential for the longest period of time—got first crack at these assignments. Class III aviators could go to formal schools. Qualified helicopter and transport pilots were encouraged to apply for training in their occupational specialties,

and Aviation ground personnel were offered on-the-job training at MARTD's, Marine Corps Air Stations, and certain formal schools.

Class III programs were not alone in their struggle with fund strictures. Ground units of the Organized Reserve were caught in the budget squeeze play as well. Two paid drills were cut from the 48 scheduled for the fiscal year ending on 30 June.

Announcing this curtailment, General Shapley said: "We made every possible effort to avoid having to cut out the 2 drills, but it had to be done to make ends meet." He went on to define 2 factors which had contributed to the cutback. Many military aircraft had been diverted from the previous year's AFT airlift to carry troops to Lebanon; this meant training funds had to be used to purchase commercial airlift for many units that had been scheduled to use military aircraft. The other item reflecting on the situation was a happier one: the Organized Reserve drill and AFT attendance had been flourishing. Reserve strength had risen above that planned for the year, and anticipated dropouts among 6-month trainees had not materialized.

In other words, the Reserve was doing better than expected in both its attendance drive and the quality of its recruiting. The price of this over-success was a temporary curtailment of planned activity for the 48-drill units, since the budget had been unable to foresee these developments. The program for the 24-drill units, having already been pruned, was not touched. Nor were Aviation units cut, because safety requirements dictated otherwise. "In fact," General Shapley went on, "we'd give aviators more flying time if we could."

Readiness Improved

For Class II members, multiple drills and the most comprehensive schedule of AFT yet seen in the Reserve marked the way to improved readiness. A sampling of the activities through which drill pay units sought to improve their proficiency is drawn from the pages of *The Reserve Marine* of the time. Examples:

On the multiple drill side, some 600 men representing 4 Reserve units—the 6th Infantry Company, Cumberland, Md.; the 13th Infantry Battalion, Washington, D.C.; the 1st 105mm Howitzer Battalion, Richmond; and the 5th Staff Group (Ground) from the Nation's Capital area, which did the staff planning for the operation—got a taste of the war of the future in *Operation Vigilance* at Quantico, where they saw little change the role of the individual rifleman. In *Operation Razorback*, Texarkana's 2d 155mm Howitzer Battery joined forces with the 10th Infantry Company, of Shreveport; Little Rock's 6th Rifle Company; and the 92d Infantry Company from Fort Smith, Ark., to make up the 4th Marine Reserve Battalion which wiped out "aggressor elements" during a 2-day campaign in Camp Robinson, Ark.

Operation Ready-Reserve, a combined air-ground amphibious assault on Johnson's Island in Sandusky Bay, Lake Erie, brought together more than 500 men of the Marine and Naval Reserve and Ohio National Guard. Members of Brigadier General Walter A. Churchill's VTU 4–36 of Toledo and Major Carl Stahley's VTU 4–2 of Cleveland served as umpires for the joint exercise.

Texas was the scene of *Operation Big Splash*, in which 3 Marine Reserve units teamed up with Air Force, National Guard, and Coast Guard contingents to assault Galveston Island under the watchful eyes of some 5,000 interested fellow Texans. In another all-Texas show, a hundred men of Houston's 6th Infantry Battalion slogged and sloshed across 40 miles of previously uncharted, rain-swollen streams and mudholes in a 2-day trail-blazing trek through the swampy jungle of the Big Thicket between Houston and Beaumont. This strictly volunteer, no-pay, weekend problem was led by Volunteer Bill Daniel, prominent Texas attorney, cattle rancher, and brother of Governor Price Daniel.

For yet another "on-your-own" effort, the boondocks of the Lakehurst Naval Air Station, 50 miles east of Philadelphia, provided the locale for *Operation Yapon*, a weekend battle practice planned by the 4th Staff Group of Philadelphia with the aid of neighboring unit commanding officers and inspector-instructors. Participating in *Operation Yapon* (spell it backwards for effect), were the 39th Infantry Company, Atlantic City; 69th Infantry Company, Eddystone, Pa.; 68th Infantry Company, Camden, N.J.; a battery from the 3d 155mm Howitzer Battalion, Trenton, N.J.; elements from the 2d Depot Supply Battalion, Philadelphia; supporting elements from the 1st 155mm Howitzer Battalion; Philadelphia's 4th Staff Group; and VTU 4–15, Wilmington, Del. *Operation Yapon* was designed to test the efficiency of an independent reinforced battalion against an enemy company. At its close Colonel Philip L. Mossburg, Commanding Officer of the Staff Group, seconded Battalion Commander Lieutenant Colonel Guy L. Wharton, summing up the exercise:

> The purpose for our presence here is readiness. If every man here can go back to his

unit feeling he is better prepared for combat, then *Yapon* served its purpose.

Highlight of the AFT program on the East Coast was *Operation Nailivic* largest Reserve training exercise in the history of Camp Lejeune, where more than 2,000 air and ground personnel from 10 States practiced air-ground coordination tactics, emphasizing the use of helicopters and conventional landing craft. Reserve infantry, artillery, tank, communications, amphibian tractor, and truck units—along with 6 Marine Air Reserve units—took part in the 2-day coordinated assault which was the culmination of months of detailed planning between Colonel Mossburg's Staff Group and Lieutenant Colonel John L. McCalla's Marine Air Reserve Group 25 from Willow Grove, Pa.

Across the Nation, 16 Ground and Air Reserve units combined forces in the desert around Marine Corps Base, Twentynine Palms, to field *Operation Handyman*, described as "the largest air-ground exercise in Reserve history." *Handyman* was the brainchild of the New Orleans 8th Staff Group and Marine Air Reserve Group 18. A helping hand came from Regular units from Force Troops, Fleet Marine Force, Pacific; the 1st Marine Division; and the 3d Marine Aircraft Wing. Preparations for *Handyman* included construction of a 700-foot landing strip for use as a prime objective of attacking forces during the operation and as a demonstration site following the skirmish.

In the air MARTCOM's 2-phased active duty training program featured *Operation Ready Reserve* in which, under the leadership of newly appointed COMART, Brigadier General Frederick E. Leek, Reserve squadrons from the eastern section of the country conducted 2 weeks of intensified training at Cherry Point, while their western opposites operated from El Toro. In this operation MARTCOM personnel were able to put into actual practice many of the lessons learned during monthly weekend drills at their home stations. Intelligence personnel studied new developments in reconnaissance and intelligence-gathering techniques, including a new jeep-helicopter patrol method in which a helicopter acted as scout for a road-bound jeep patrol in ferreting out the enemy. In another "first" for *Operation Ready Reserve*, MARTCOM conducted a competitive exercise in gunnery, rocketry, and bombing for its pilots. The 235 pilots taking part logged 7,473.7 hours of valuable flight time to improve their combat efficiency. Gunnery, bombing, and strafing were part of the training syllabus. General Leek summarized the training in a message to the Marine Air Reserve:

> Your record this past year reveals that you have developed the skill, confidence, and moral fibre that truly makes you important members of the Marine Corps great air-sea-ground team: America's force in readiness.

"Excellent to Outstanding"

Reports from host field activities indicated the success achieved during the year through training exercises of this nature. A typical evaluation read:

> The training, readiness, and general performance of the company as to appearance and military bearing, promptness, cooperation, attention to duty, ability to conduct training, improvement shown during training, and progress toward accomplishment of their mission was excellent to outstanding in all respects.

Although improvement in training and proficiency was the year's predominant theme, there were other interesting and significant happenings to record for 1959. When General Shapley left the Division of Reserve in November to become Commanding General, Marine Corps Base, Camp Pendleton, General Stickney assumed duty as Director of the Reserve for the third time. He served in that capacity for 2 months (from 5 November) before going to inactive duty on 1 January 1960, at which time Brigadier General William T. Fairbourn moved up from Deputy to Director.

"Reserves are Professionals"—Stickney

Again, as in 1956, General Stickney voiced his conviction that Reserves are professionals. Writing in the *Marine Corps Reserve News and Views* of 2 December 1959 he declared:

> Our greatest mission presently is the professional approach. We have outgrown our amateur standards. We have been praised by both the Secretary of the Navy and the Secretary of Defense as the outstanding military Reserve of the Nation. We must not only maintain this reputation but improve upon it each day. I do not want any officers in the Reserve who have but the pride of wearing the Eagle, Globe, and Anchor or the desire of knowing what the Marine Corps can give them. Rather the question must always be, "What can you give the Marine Corps?" The Marine Corps in turn will pay back in direct proportion to what is given. Further, with our present low manning levels, we cannot afford to take in any enlisted personnel other than the best obtainable. They must be Marine minded, they must know their full obligation of service and they must be in the best of health both in mind and body if we are to achieve our basic mission.

Again, in *News and Views*, he pointed out:

> ... we have a Marine Corps Reserve of well over 300,000 and 311 well-trained units in our organized structure. That's a far cry from the handful of men back in 1918.

We have traveled a long and rocky road but we surely have gained a lot of ground, particularly in the past few years. We have been proclaimed by the Secretary of Defense, and others in high places, as the best Reserve of all components. This we not only intend to keep, but to become just a little better each day. There are those who think that someday we will lose our Marine Corps. But we have something that money and single-suiters cannot buy and that can be summed up in just one word, "love." Love of country, love of the Marine Corps, and love of those good Marines on our left and right when we are in combat. . . .

During 1959 the 9th District Headquarters moved from Chicago to Kansas City. The closing of a number of Naval Air stations forced the transfer or deactivation of several Marine Air Reserve units. Some of the personnel of these units found new homes in Air VTU's.

Officer promotions were few and far between as the effect of the "hump" continued to be felt in the Reserve. Tombstone promotions came in for a new, critical appraisal; recommendations to eliminate them altogether were being studied. Nineteen former Reserve enlisted men were commissioned Reserve second lieutenants under the so-called "at home" program.

Under a program designed to relieve a critical shortage of Regular legal officers, Reserve lawyers got a chance to serve as trial and defense counsels for general courts-martial, upon certification by Headquarters Marine Corps. In lieu of advanced infantry training, occupational field training was offered 6-month trainees who had completed individual combat training.

Judge Fisher Retires

A 1959 retirement ceremony brought a nostalgic note to the year's chronicle when Brigadier General Carlton A. Fisher accepted an official Marine Corps Seal presented by General Stickney during retirement ceremonies in Buffalo, N.Y. Back-dropping the presentation was a near-lifesize photograph of *Private* Fisher (now a Supreme Court Justice for the State of New York) as he had looked at Parris Island in 1917, when the Marine Corps Reserve was barely a year old.

More than 200 members of MCROA—representing 40 chapters—journeyed to Washington for the Association's 33d annual military conference. Highlighting the 2-day meeting were briefings by members of the Commandant's staff—briefings designed to bring the conferees up-to-date on the status and needs of the Corps. Resolutions adopted by the conference urged statutory support for a 200,000-man Marine Corps and pledged Association support for a vigorous helicopter assault construction and conversion program.

As a part of a giant reorganization scheme, 129 Class II units were redesignated to bring them and their training missions more in line with those of the FMF. Two features of the new structure were the organization of reconnaissance units and the elimination of 155mm howitzer battalions. All of these latter units were broken down into gun batteries. A number of former infantry companies became rifle companies. Seven newly-formed antitank companies were slated for outfitting with the Corps' newest mobile tank destroyer, the ONTOS, which—mounting 6 106mm recoilless rifles—was capable of being airlifted as part of the Corps' "travel light and hit hard force."

Had the emphasis on drill attendance paid off? In fiscal year 1959, it took a better-than-perfect average to win a trophy for Class II drill or AFT attendance. Each of the 4 units cited as tops in the Corps went over the 100-percent mark, and so did 7 runners-up! For the third consecutive year, the James Poynter Trophy went to the 1st Service Battalion of Memphis. Their final average was 106.9 percent. Runners-up were Philadelphia's 1st 155mm Howitzer Battalion, with 102.8 percent, and the 1st Weapons Battalion of Forest Park, Ill. The William McK. Fleming award went to the 13th Rifle Company of Santa Monica for a 108 percent record. Raleigh's 4th 155mm Howitzer Battery finished second with a 104.3 mark, closely followed—at 103.5—by the 43d Infantry Company from Great Lakes. The hard-charging 1st Weapons Battalion, which had pressed for the Poynter Trophy, carried off the Vittori Trophy with its 109.8 AFT attendance average. Runner-ups were Dallas' 1st 4.5 Rocket Battalion and Baltimore's 1st Engineer Battalion, with averages of 100.4 and 96.8, respectively. With an almost unbelievable 125.1, Captain Charles W. Collier's 27th Infantry Company from Columbus, Ohio, outstripped the competition for the Lawrence H. Flynn Trophy, 10 points ahead of the 28th Infantry Company of Lafayette, La., and followed—at 112.6—by the 7th Rifle Company of Dover, N.J.

Jane Blakeney Honored

Mrs. Jane Blakeney, a World War I Woman Reserve who had subsequently served the Corps with distinction for many years as civilian head of its Decorations and Medals Branch, was honored by the Marine Corps Combat Correspondents Association for her monumental book, *Heroes U.S. Marine Corps, 1861–1955*. Privately published after her retirement, Mrs.

Blakeney's 620-page reference book was inscribed to her late husband, a Marine Corps Reserve Major.

Making the presentation on behalf of the Association during its annual reunion in Washington was the Commanding Officer of VTU (PI) 5–21, Lieutenant Colonel John A. DeChant.

Community service was not neglected in 1959. The Reserve was on hand to lend assistance during a New Jersey epidemic of equine encephalitis, and participated in the Harpers Ferry (W. Va.) reenactment of the capture of John Brown. Toys-for-Tots crossed the Pacific when Headquarters approved the request of 4 Reserve officers living in Japan to conduct a toy drive for children in the typhoon-stricken Nagoya area. And, Camp Pendleton opened its gates to boys between the ages of 15 and 17 for the 6th Annual Devil Pup encampment. Conceived in 1954 by Lieutenant Colonel Richard F. Hyland's VTU 12–5 of Beverly Hills as a 5-day training program for Los Angeles youths, the encampment had proved so successful that, with Headquarters approval and the cooperation of Camp Pendleton officials, the unit had continued it as an annual project—expanding to a 10-day exercise open to boys from all over southern California.

At the opposite end of the age-scale, the closing weeks of the year saw 20 Marine Reserve general officers—both retired and active—join more than a hundred admirals of the Navy in a 2-day Pentagon meeting, described by Secretary of the Navy William B. Franke as "designed to provide a much clearer picture of where the Navy (and Marine Corps) stands today and what it faces tomorrow." Agenda for the gathering included intelligence briefings on the current situation, discussions of Navy and Marine Corps posture, and topical legislative problems.

The roster of Reserve Marines attending read: Lieutenant Generals Karl S. Day and Bertrand T. Fay; Major Generals L. W. T. Waller and Melvin J. Maas; Brigadier Generals Joseph Knowlan, Carlton A. Fisher, Samuel F. Zeiler, Philip G. Strong, John W. Scott, Gooderham L. McCormick, Robert N. Fricke, Arnold D a n e, Walter A. Churchill, Charles H. Cox, James E. Howarth, Jr., George E. Tomlinson, Harry R. VanLiew, and John L. Winston; and Brigadier Selectees William H. Klenke, Jr., and Harry N. Lyon.

The level of intelligence presented at these briefings made clear the special confidence reposed in the Reserve. The stature of the officers attending was equal evidence that this confidence was merited.

The Year 1960

A new decade—a new Commandant—a reaffirmation of the Corps' reliance on and confidence in its Reserve.

> The readiness of the Marine Corps Reserve is at an all-time high. Never before has our dependency upon the Reserve been more worthy of that dependency.

So said General David M. Shoup in his first official message to his Headquarters staff officers 3 days after taking the oath as 22d Commandant of the Marine Corps.

The new Commandant went on to highlight the steps by which the Reserve had reached this state of readiness, and closed with the admonition: "We must in the years ahead nurture and maintain these valuable assets to the strength and security of our Nation."

Contrasting with this confidence in the immediate state of Reserve readiness, however, was a mounting concern over an anticipated decline in R e a d y Reserve strength. General Shoup spelled out the reasons for concern in his 1960 "Posture of the Marine Corps" statement before the Senate Armed S e r v i c e s Committee. Through the next several years, he reported, the enlisted Ready Reserve stood to lose more than a hundred thousand members. During the same period, about 230,000 of its 8-year obligors would be due for release. Other factors calculated to speed the decline included limitations on 6-month enlistments—"our only direct input into Organized units from civil life"—and a marked reduction in personnel being released from active duty to the Reserve.

Problems and More Problems

The Commandant then dwelt at length upon the urgency of beefing-up the technical training of the Volunteer Reserve. Predicting that the enlisted Ready Reserve would drop from 194,000 to 90,000 by the end of fiscal year 1963, he pointed to the non-drill-pay units as the primary source for meeting mobilization requirements in such critical fields as electronics and aircraft maintenance. The 6-month training tour could not include sufficient formal schooling for qualification in these highly technical fields; therefore, for the future, more of the limited training budget would have to be funneled into technical training if the objective of achieving and maintaining optimum readiness for mobilization within the now familiar strictures on money and manpower were to be attained.

To meet this objective would be no simple task. The bulk of the Reserve personnel budget provided for training the drill pay Reserve, since it would augment the Fleet Marine Forces for immediate

post M-day commitments. The vast majority of total mobilization billets, however, would have to come from the Volunteer Reserve. The crux of the problem: how to keep the Volunteer Reserve healthy and virile, to fill the lion's share of mobilization requirements, with only a fraction of the training funds? Nothing short of full exploitation of all resources would even approach an acceptable solution.

To meet this challenge, the new Director of the Reserve, General Fairbourn, pressed the three-pronged attack which had produced tangible gains in the Class III sector during the previous years. The screening-out process—purification of the ISL—was closely monitored and extended. The screening-in process—enforcement of the mandatory participation provisions of the 1955 amendments to the Armed Forces Reserve Act of 1952—was tightened. And efforts were concentrated on making the VTU program—already the nucleus of an effective training apparatus—bear a large share of the training mission of the Volunteer Reserve.

Other new measures were undertaken in the continuing drive toward immediate "response ability" for mobilization. One such development was the issuing of advance M-day orders to selected officers enrolled in VTU's. These hip-pocket orders gave the recipient ample forewarning as to exactly how soon he would be needed, where he would report, what billet he would fill, and what sort of preparation would stand him in best stead in the event of mobilization. Further, they served as a priority gauge for determining who should be trained, and in what measure. By pinpointing actual mobilization billets, they provided realistic standards for matching VTU training to actual mobilization needs. Finally, and by no means least significant, the orders sparked a certain pride of profession in the officers who carried them. At training sessions, shoulders squared and heads were held noticeably higher as these officers responded "Here, Sir," to the VTU commander's checkoff of specially designated reservists.

Throughout 1960, requests for active duty for training—*with or without pay*—were screened closely, with the individual's mobilization potential being the primary criteria for duty assignment. Factors determining this potential were: projected mobilization requirements for the individual's rank and occupational specialty; age in grade; physical risk classification; amount and type of training and duty previously completed; and caliber of previous performance. Emphasizing the importance of instant availability when needed, Headquarters did not normally consider favorably applicants who were not available for recall within the first 30 days of mobilization. There was one additional determining element: training performed must enhance the individual's ability to perform the duties of his occupational specialty and—in the case of holders of advance mobilization orders—the duties of his assigned mobilization billet.

For those who met the criteria, a variety of training was available. Appropriate Duty assignments included a 2-week course in Communist Strategy, offered by the Foreign Service Institute in Arlington, Va. Field grade officers were afforded opportunity to increase their understanding of the economic, military, and political requirements of national security through National Security Seminars, taught by faculty members of the Industrial College of the Armed Forces. In a 15-stop swing around the country, the Quantico Landing Force Instruction Team

brought to Reserve officers and senior NCO's the most up-to-date Marine Corps thinking in doctrine, strategy, and tactics through a series of Advanced Base Problem demonstrations.

Correspondence courses from the Marine Corps Extension School and the Marine Corps Institute provided those unable to participate in other training opportunity to retain and enhance their military proficiency. The 1960 syllabus paralleled the level and type of tactical instruction presented at Quantico's Basic, Communications, Junior, and Senior School courses.

A few paid training billets were included in the Class III program. Among these were: slots at the 2-week Naval Justice Course at Newport, R.I.; a limited number of openings in the Military Intelligence Officer Course at Fort Holabird, Md.; and, for one Associate Duty officer per drill pay unit, opportunity to attend summer camp with his unit.

At midyear, Headquarters announced that all Organized units except the Air Reserve Groups and Staff Groups would perform 48 drills in fiscal year 1961 and that the groups would be allowed 24 paid drills. The authorization included drills conducted as field exercises and, for each unit, a maximum of 2 drills on a single-drill-pay basis to participate in local parades. (All others were to be multiple drills.)

Marines "Battle" Guard

Without exception, 1960's field exercises were well-planned and well-attended, and in postmaneuver evaluations won "Well Done's!" Noteworthy among the weekend problems was a joint Marine Reserve-National Guard set-to staged by the 83d Rifle Company of Huntington, W. Va., and neighboring National Guard Special

Service Forces. Huntington's 83d chose a cold, rainy Sunday morning to tangle with the National Guard aggressors. The realism of the maneuvers kept the police switchboard swamped with calls about "all the shootin' up in the hills." Guardsmen, outfitted in commando garb and civilian clothes, used guerrilla tactics in an attempt to rattle the Marines.

More than a hundred shivering spectators in the area—many from other services, Regular and Reserve—watched the action from a nearby hilltop. Guerrilla forces, using a civilian delivery truck, cut off the last truck of the Marine convoy on its way to the assembly area. The surprised Marines were "captured," but later overpowered their captors. The commanding officer, Major Sidney B. Garland, turned around and began a search for his lost vehicle. Guerrillas then ambushed the command jeep amid a fierce fire-fight. Area residents frantically called the police, who—of course—had given the action prior clearance. A local radio station carried news flashes throughout the day, reporting the progress of the battle. Two TV stations ran film clips that evening and the following day. Absolute realism was sought and achieved. Air National Guard spotter planes went aloft to provide strafing runs and even dropped propaganda surrender leaflets. The Guard's mission was to hit and run. Several guardsmen were disguised as farmers leading cows. Not expecting this type of action—which added to the problem's value—the Marines, caught off guard, found that 2 of their vehicles had been driven off by infiltrators who had simply melted into the crowd.

"Nothing like it has ever been seen around here," was the comment of most observers. To veterans among the Marines, however, the hit-and-run tactics were reminiscent of many other such actions. The commanding officers of both participating units were quite satisfied with the results. "It provided excellent training for both outfits," commented Major Garland, while the National Guard commander expressed admiration for the precision and effectiveness of the tactical formations and maneuvers of the Marines.

In another weekend problem, *Operation Sharkbite*, northern California Reserve units staged a combined land-sea-air assault on Tiburon Peninsula, Calif. Members of the 14th Rifle Company and VTU 12–44—both of Kentfield, Calif.— planned this operation. Other participating units included the 2d Armored Amphibian Company, Treasure Island; the 4th Supply Company of Stockton; Alameda's 6th Communications Company; and the 1st Air Delivery Company of San Jose. Enemy forces came from Sacramento's 6th Truck Company, and helicopters in the operation were flown by pilots of the MARTD, NAS, Oakland.

Operation Jay Husker, at Fort Riley, Kans., brought together the 73d Rifle Company of Wichita and the 86th Rifle Company of Lincoln, Nebr., pitted against aggressors from the 101st Rifle Company of Topeka. The Marines were helicopter-lifted to the combat area by the 19th Aviation Company of the Army 1st Division, or ground-transported in vehicles furnished by the Army, the Air Force, and the Kansas and Nebraska National Guards.

Fifteen hundred Ohio and Michigan Air and Ground Reserves battled it out in *Operation Cold Steel* on Johnson Island in Lake Erie. Air support came from Lieutenant Colonel Edwin Piotrowski's VMA–231 of Grosse Ile, Mich. Skindivers and rubber-boat teams of Company A, 2d Reconnaissance Battalion of Toledo, moved a mile over Sandusky Bay under cover of darkness to cut aggressor lines of communications on the island. They even laid an underwater telephone line to the mainland, so their battalion commander, Major David D. Thompson, had rapid intelligence reports direct from the objective area. Captain Charles A. James of the 11th Infantry Battalion, Cleveland, brought his reconnaissance squad on a 48-mile march from the home armory to Johnson Island, to give the Toledo recon men a hand in gathering preassault intelligence. Another Grosse Ile squadron, HMR 773, commanded by Lieutenant Colonel John J. Rolfes, sent a helicopter to St. John's Lutheran Church in Toledo to "heaven-lift" Reverend Robert W. Menter to the island to conduct church services. Other participants in the exercise included Lieutenant Colonel A. F. Mackin's Cleveland VTU and VTU members from Grosse Ile, commanded by Brigadier General W. H. Klenke, Jr. Aggressors were members of the 72d Rifle Company of Lima, Ohio, commanded by Captain D. E. Naylor. Overall director of the maneuver was Lieutenant Colonel Charles Whitacre, Jr., Commanding Officer of MARG 13, Toledo.

Colonel James F. Coady's 4th Staff Group of Philadelphia planned *Operation Res-Ag-Fex*, a combined air-ground exercise at Indiantown Gap, Pa., for 4th District Reserve units. Harrisburg's 62d Rifle Company made up the aggressor force. Also involved were units from Folsom, Philadelphia, Pottsville and Williamsport, Pa.; and Trenton, N.J. Air-lift to positions behind aggressor lines was provided by helicopters from NAS, Willow Grove, Pa.

Another Paper Mobilization

Proving that originality needs only imagination, *Resmobex–60* was undertaken in April 1960 following a priority dispatch from Marine Headquarters to each district director. The only Reserve participants in this 2-phase exercise in mobilization were members of Organized units designated as Mobilization Stations. One such station was activied in each Reserve district. Its mission was to process Class II members, equal in number to the Class III's normally processed in a 1-day period during actual mobilization. Until the activating dispatches were received, not even the directors knew when the exercise would be kicked off. Mobilization stations, on signal from their district directors, became operational for a day; gave physicals; briefed troops on assignments to reporting stations in the FMF; and handed out orders. Although they never got past the training centers' front doors, the Class II "selectees" did everything but ship out.

Resmobex, Phase II, carried out solely at MARTCOM and District Headquarters offices, began with arrival of new orders—with entirely new requirements—from Washington. The criteria bore no relationship to any anticipated mobilization requirements, but served to test data processing procedures used to scan records for certain skills. This paper-tiger aspect of *Resmobex* involved the writing of orders for individuals selected by electronic processing to fill specific billets. In an around-the-clock push to meet deadlines, MARTCOM and District Headquarters personnel typed, multilithed, and processed thousands of orders—right up to where mailing would take place under actual mobilization conditions. But that was as far as the orders went. Fortunately, nobody dropped the completed orders in the nearest mail chute.

The 1960 training story included a most successful Annual Field Training Program. Following the steady line of hardnosed improvement of past years, Class II units reported and performed in the best shape ever. More than 40,000 Ready Reserves, from 311 Organized units, took part in the summer program. Host activity personnel from Parris Island to Camp Pendleton admired the maximum efforts the Reserves exerted to make the most of their summer training. Once again, Camp Lejeune had the largest overall turnout: 10,000 plus. On the West Coast, *Operation Charger* at Twentynine Palms, Calif., drew some 4,000 for the largest single encampment.

Operation Charger got underway in April, when Colonel Douglas J. Peacher brought Chicago's 9th Staff Group to Twentynine Palms for a 3-day, on-site, pretraining conference. The master battle plan was drawn to include artillery barrages, infantry attacks, spearheading tanks, air strikes, vertical assaults by helicopter, and a final simulated atomic blast. Four months later 13 Ground and 9 Air Reserve units from 7 Western States put *Charger* in motion. Aggressor troops from the 25th Rifle Company of Gary, Ind., infiltrated desert installations spread across an area 50 by 15 miles. With temperatures across the desert wasteland soaring above 120° for nearly 3 days, the Reserves pushed to their final objective, an airstrip dubbed "Sears Field." (Colonel Peacher is a Sears-Roebuck Vice President.) Assault forces launched a three-pronged attack against the air field, then fell back to "dig in" as a simulated atomic blast ripped the position. A mushroom-

ing "cloud" swirling up from the hot Mojave desert floor brought the coordinated air-ground exercise to a close.

Marine Air Reserve Group 12 of Glenview, Ill., helped Colonel Peacher and his 9th Staff Group plan and execute *Operation Charger*. Lieutenant Colonel Miles P. Patrone served as commander of troops, and his Chicago-based 9th Infantry Battalion provided the backbone of the infantry elements. Other Reserve units taking part in the exercise came from San Diego, Sacramento, Long Beach, and San Jose, Calif.; Glenview, Rockford, and East Peoria, Ill.; Phoenix, Ariz.; Chattanooga, Tenn.; San Angelo, Tex.; and New York City.

Charger Gave "Maximum Training"

"The operation was designed to give maximum training to all participating Reserves," reported Operation Director Peacher. With characteristic word-economy, he continued: "We feel that we accomplished our mission."

Two vignettes—lifted in toto from *The Reserve Marine*—wrap up the 1960 training tale. The first concerns Toledo's 2d Reconnaissance Battalion, already mentioned in connection with *Operation Cold Steel*. The second illustrates a point made earlier, in the discussion of Appropriate Duty training: "Imagination was the only limitation on this program."

> Members of Toledo's 2d Recon Battalion, not content with paddling rubber boats through the surf, have turned to subsurface tactics in an effort to qualify as well-rounded reconnaissance men. Thirty-five of them just completed a 10-week special skin diving and SCUBA course at the local YMCA. The training is expected to pay off during day-and-night exercises calling for hydrographic and beach reconnaissance. During their course, the Toledo Reserves learned the

proper use of swim fins, masks, and snorkel equipment; progressed to diving physics and physiology; and wrapped it up with sessions on the SCUBA (Self-Contained Underwater Breathing Apparatus).

MCB, Twentynine Palms, Calif.—Some 125 Marine officers and Staff NCO's here will read of new developments in missile and space travel with more understanding since attending a 3-day seminar on the subject— its past, present, and future. Conducted by 7 Marine Reserve officers of VTU 12–3 (Intelligence), each of whom is an authority in guided missiles or related fields, the seminar was designed to review the world's current and planned missiles. In addition to local personnel, those attending the seminar included officers and men from MCAS, El Toro, and Camp Pendleton. Anyone attending who possibly believed lectures on the present Marine Corps guided missiles were forthcoming, was instead introduced to more than 300 missile systems, subsystems, and space vehicles. Through the use of posters, pamphlets, handouts, photographs, still slides, movies, and a running commentary, such subjects as space communications, budgetary problems, and logistics of missiles were explained. Every military specialty represented at the seminar, which included infantry leaders through jet pilots, could find problems related to his job alone, only on a larger scale. Lieutenant Colonel John H. Roscoe, officer in charge of the missile section of VTU 12–3, commented that this visit of the members was, in effect, repayment for their visit here earlier this year. At that time, local missilemen conducted a 2-day presentation of the Corps' missile tactics and techniques for the San Francisco area visitors.

Off the training newsbeat, 1960's principal Reserve headlines mirrored a now-familiar pattern: Major Command Changes; Legislative Action; Policy Board Results; The Promotion Picture; MCROA Speaks; Quality Recruiting; Attendance Records and Awards; Community Service; Faces in the News; and A Look to the Future.

The post of Deputy Director of the Reserve, vacated by General Fairbourn when he moved into the Director's chair on 1 January, was filled later in the year by Colonel Owen M. Hines, long a mainstay of the Reserve team. Still later Brigadier General Louis B. Robertshaw replaced General Leek as COMART.

Amendments to ROPA (the Reserve Officer Personnel Act of 1945) reduced the permanent authorized strength of Marine Reserve officers from 29.500 to 24,500; authorized a 100-percent increase in active Reserve general officer strength (from 5 to 10); provided for the "extension" of active status majors and above with constructive service time, who had previously faced retirement or discharge before reaching 20 years of satisfactory Federal service; and established a 1-year minimum waiting period before officers returning to active status could be considered for promotion.

The Marine Corps Reserve Policy Board, headed by Major General Churchill, batted well over the .750 mark. Acting on the Board's recommendations, Secretary of the Navy Franke directed the Commandant to increase the program of indoctrinating troops in the objectives and operating techniques of democracy and communism; to continue required, adequate, and equitable training for the Reserve insofar as training could be funded without detriment to the budgetary requirements of the Regular Establishment; to develop, maintain, and properly budget for a definite and adequate training program for senior Reserve officers, and to continue to make assignments to available training billets on the basis of relative priority for mobilization; and to require of Selective Service reimbursement for Marine Reserve officers assigned to

Selective Service Augmentation billets. Secretary Franke disapproved only one of the Board's recommendations: to increase the authorized Organized strength to 80,000–90,000. However, h i s disapproval was cushioned with a promise of continued efforts to obtain an increase to 55,000 Organized Reserves by fiscal year 1964. Of the 11 administrative topics presented by the Board (requiring only Commandant of the Marine Corps acceptance), eight were approved. Significant among those approved were recommendations to (1) process junior Reserve officers for discharge only after 8 years of commissioned service; (2) provide drill pay Reserves opportunity equal to that afforded Regulars for promotion to pay grades E–3 and E–4; and (3) assure the availability of sufficient officer training billets to meet known requirements, and order maximum Class III personnel to active duty for training with full pay and allowances.

The 1960 promotion picture was colored by the ROPA amendments and Policy Board recommendations. Besides making room at the top through the increase in general officer strength, Congress fixed a stable promotion base—the permanent *authorized* strength (24,500) replacing the previous *actual-strength base* which had fluctuated around 22,000. The "equal opportunity" recommendation of the Policy Board improved promotion chances of inactive duty enlisted personnel; and, as an outgrowth of a recommendation relating to maintaining current data on individual Reserves, promotion questionnaires designed expressly to provide selection boards with up-to-date information were circulated to all Class II and III officers on inactive duty.

Peacher To MCROA Presidency

Meeting in Chicago during Armed Forces Week, MCROA members sent President Eisenhower a pledge of continuing support in the fight against international communism, and named Colonel Peacher to take over the gavel from outgoing National President Brigadier General John L. Winston.

Peacher had served a Regular enlisted hitch from 1929 to 1933, joining the Reserve at Bremerton Navy Yard after 3 years at sea as a sergeant. Commissioned in March 1936, he became a Reserve brigadier on 1 January 1964.

By scoring 158 and 156, respectively, on the General Classification Test, Privates James K. Martens and Roy H. Geiss led all 6-month trainees and supported the frequently voiced proposition that all Marines are created superior, or—at least—that Marine recruiters know a good man when they see one. Meanwhile, on the individual attendance front, 66 members of the Marine Air Reserve Detachment, Floyd Bennett Field, Brooklyn, won commendations from their Detachment Commander, Lieutenant Colonel Robert F. Whitten, for 100 percent drill attendance records for the year.

The attendance trophy winner roster for 1960 read:

Poynter Trophy_____	1 s t Service Battalion, Memphis (3d consecutive award).
Vittori Trophy_____	8th 105mm Howitzer Battalion, Los Angeles.
Flynn Trophy_____	3d Antitank Company, Midland, Tex.
William McK. Fleming Trophy.	3d Reconnaissance Company, Great Lakes.

To the perennial support given through their Toys-for-Tots campaigns and Devil

Pup Encampments, Reserves added a third community service project in 1960. Citing the aid Reserve Colonel Ted Watson had given to the 17-day March of Dimes hike through South Carolina, Congressman L. Mendel Rivers praised all Marines, Regular and Reserve, who had backed this effort. The Congressman's remarks, recorded in the *Congressional Record*, read—in part: "The Marines ask for the hard jobs, the difficult jobs, the unusual jobs. The Marines accomplish the impossible." Also honored for community service, was First Lieutenant Gene Slagle, of the 6th Engineer Company of Knoxville, named Young Man of the Year by the Jaycees of Harriman, Tenn. His citation dwelt on community contributions as a Marine Reserve officer, a Scoutmaster, and an active member of several fraternal organizations.

Stickney and Wert Retire

The long arm of the retirement law reached into the Reserve in 1960 and drew out 2 long-time stalwarts. Reserve rolls lost—and the Retired List picked up—the names of Major General Stickney, three-time Director of the Reserve and its ranking officer on active duty, and Colonel Thomas R. Wert, the Corps' last World War I combat veteran on active duty. Colonel Wert had enlisted in the Corps in May 1917, a month after the U.S. entry into World War I. Commissioned after action at Verdun, and mustered out in 1919 with a wound stripe and a commendation that brought a Silver Star, he had hung up his uniform until the opening of World War II. Then, as a captain in the Reserve, he was back in action at Saipan and Iwo Jima, where he was awarded the Bronze Star. Staying with the Reserve

after that war, he took command of Battery B in Chattanooga's 4th 155mm Howitzer Battalion in 1947, and, in August 1950, led his Tennesseans to Camp Pendleton when they were mobilized for the Korean War. With another war under his belt, in April 1952 he reported to Headquarters where he served with distinction in the Division of Reserve as Head of the Liaison and Information Branch until his retirement. Nor did retirement end this career of service to Country, Corps, and fellow Reserves. Today, as MCROA's Administrative Secretary, Colonel Wert continues to personify the Association's objectives in action.

Two programs inaugurated in 1960 were expected to help in getting the right men to the right place in the right job at the right time. Advance mobilization orders were to become the vehicle for pinpointing exact mobilization requirements and ensuring that training to match those requirements received top priority, although this program was later modified. A comprehensive review of military occupational specialties was also begun in 1960. The following year would bring increased emphasis to this effort, with an expanded review of Reserve occupational specialty assignments and the establishment of categories of skill deterioration to serve as additional criteria for training and assignments. The years of rebuilding had been rigorous, but rewarding!

Drafting his second annual State of the Corps message as 1960 drew to a close, General Shoup chose to say of the Reserve: "I have complete confidence in (their) competence to be a part of the Fleet Marine Forces for combat duty, or to perform any other tasks to which they might properly be assigned."

Relief troops board transport 'copters, Korea 1952. *Below, more rice paddies, but the Korean chapter closes.*

Women Reservists of Boston's award-winning platoon that carried off top honors in national pistol and rifle championship match receive medals from Col Albert Creal. Below, the right fit for lady Marines in the Reserve platoons, 1952–1958 era, here modeled by Baltimore Reservists.

Reservists of the Columbia, S.C., 89th Rifle Co., FMF, spend 90 percent of their time in the field. Below, Mr. Marine Corps Reserve retires—MajGen Maas (left) receives commendation letter and his second star upon retirement from Commandant Lemuel C. Shepherd, Jr., 1 August 1952.

Reserve Cold Weather training, Pickel Meadows.   Below, scuba diving demonstration by SSgt Walter Webb at Reservist hometown pool, Mobile, Ala.

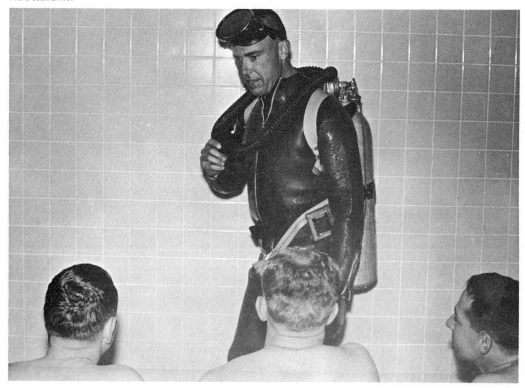

Photo Leatherneck

Mobile Reservists in Air Force C–119 yell "Recon, recon, all the way" en route to jump zone. Below, Corpsman J. G. Dodd (right) of the Mobile I–I staff has made more than 50 jumps. At right, Kalamazoo, Mich., Reservists go up and over at summer camp training.

Photo Leatherneck

USMC Photo A275287

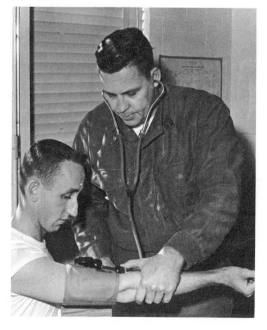

Photo Leatherneck

Col Irving Schechter, former CO, 1st Staff Group, Brooklyn, squints into weekend sun during training.   Below, I–I, SgtMaj Theodore Bollack briefs Brooklyn area Reserves leaving for Parris Island boot training.

Photo Leatherneck

Photo Leatherneck

At Willow Grove, Pa., a Reserve CO gives squadron pilots a preflight briefing. Below, ejection seat of Reserve jet is "ejected" at Willow Grove for inspection, while (right) aviation Reserve mechanics work on a big one.

Photo Leatherneck

Photo Leatherneck

Photo Leatherneck

Camden, N.J. reservists search for the "enemy" during winter exercises. Below, weapons platoon sergeant Donald L. Davidson calls on Korea experience to demonstrate how to secure prisoners by tying opposite legs with belts.

Photo Leatherneck

Reserves at Cherry Point use OH–43D helicopters in summer training. Below, jets like these A–4 series are also used at Cherry Point in buddy system refueling.

Roanoke Marine Reserves adopt classic pose for a 1960–61 Reserve "A" Sign recruiting poster. Below, whether they train at the home armory or on a field exercise, Marine Reservists have the opportunity to attend religious services.

Richmond's Reserve artillery batteries do everything but fire at their training center. Gun drills are run often.   Below, into the Pacific surf from LCU during Reserve amphibious exercises at Coronado, Calif.

Coming ashore at Onslow Beach during exercises in 1964.   Photo used at New York World's Fair.

Location: almost anywhere. Time: before Christmas as Toys for Tots scores again, in 1964.

Reservists of Reno's 49th Rifle Company get field action as two members designated as "aggressors" are searched for weapons. Below, Col Paul "A" Noel, Jr., CO, MARTD, Los Alamitos, inspects radar gear with SgtMaj A. W. Wiberg. At right, Reservist works under supervision of trained Regulars at Los Alamitos.

Photo courtesy MARTC Digest

World War II ace and Medal of Honor winner, "Pappy" Boyington, talks with Col Robert F. Conley, CO, MAG–11, at Danang air base, Vietnam, 1965. Below, 'copters like these, many piloted by young Reserve officers, keep men and materials moving in Vietnam.

Photo Leatherneck

Air, ground, and sea combat readiness of modern-day Marine Reserve is depicted in 1966 design concept for all recruiting and informational materials.

CHAPTER TEN

Today and Tomorrow

The Year 1961

Economists were calling them the "sizzling sixties," and to Marines, on guard throughout the Caribbean, the Far East, the Mediterranean, and the South China Sea, that was a just description of the times. Communist forces had invaded Laos at the close of 1960, and a powerful Marine force moved in 7th Fleet ships to the South China Sea, alert for possible employment. Early in 1961, a Marine helicopter squadron was sent into Thailand to help provide logistical support for the Laotian Government. Trouble was brewing in Southeast Asia. At home, Marine Reserves had a terse and stirring answer. From 100 billboards along the Nation's highways, from 1 million matchbooks, from envelope stickers, and A-frame signs on city sidewalks, the word went forth in big red capital letters. The word was "READY."

General Fairbourn, as Director of Reserve, remarked:

> Perhaps hammering this word into the public consciousness may make Reserve recruiting a little more difficult, but those young men we do get know they are joining an outfit that is primed for National defense. Maybe people should have known better, but when the Marine Reserve was mobilized for Korea, a lot of citizens dipped their pens in vinegar and protested. Not the Reserves themselves, but friends and relatives in many cases figured the Marine Corps was not playing the game.

One reason for widespread unfavorable public response during the Korean mobilization had been lack of understanding. Few had been prepared for the rapid, large-scale callup of Reserve forces. This time, the Marines aimed to make certain the public knew how it stood. The message was unmistakable and quite accurate; seldom had one word so eloquently summed up the status of Americans in Reserve.

Speaking to members of the House Armed Services Committee in March 1961, General David M. Shoup, Commandant of the Marine Corps, reported that Organized Reserve strength would stand at 45,000 by the end of the fiscal year and attain an end-strength of 45,500 during fiscal year 1962. He said all training, including that of the Volunteer Reserves, was directed toward meeting the requirements of the Marine Corps in time of emergency, and that Organized units were putting increased emphasis on advanced field exercises and combined air-ground operations. Virtually all units performed multiple drill field problems regularly, he pointed out, and under this system, the percentage of time devoted to training per drill had more than doubled.

It was a time when gratifying reports of attendance, success in training, and devotion to duty were arriving at Marine Corps Headquarters daily from the 232 Ground organizations and 86 Air units in the field. The Inspector-Instructor for 2 companies in Brooklyn, New York, submitted the following for fiscal year 1961: 2d Communications Company, with 12 officers and 221 enlisted, recorded drill attendance of

219

94 percent, annual field training attendance of 98 percent, with 99 percent of all its shooters requalifying with the rifle and 39 percent shooting expert. Upon reading the report, General Fairbourn observed that "reports from other units, and my own personal observation, indicate that such quality is a rule rather than an exception." The Nation's largest Organized Marine Corps Reserve unit, Houston's 6th Infantry Battalion, won the February monthly drill attendance award in its home district with a Class II drill attendance of 97 percent. Manning level strength of the Texas unit stood at 22 officers and 430 enlisted.

The individual resolve of a great number of individual reservists played a major part in successes such as these. Lance Corporal Andrew C. Hyman, a nonmandatory participant in the Reserve, and a member of the 89th Rifle Company, in Columbia, S.C., flew 4,000 miles one way from a temporary job in Fairbanks, Alaska, to make a scheduled drill of his unit. Sergeant John Nawoichyk, a resident of New York City and a member of Marine Attack Squadron 217 which drilled at the Naval Air Station, South Weymouth, Mass., was accustomed to making the long trek to meetings. Since he was employed by a major airline, he received a company rate for travel, but he made 1 drill under almost impossible circumstances. Nawoichyk left New York's Idlewild airport 17 hours before drill was to start on a regular New York-to-Boston flight which was scheduled to continue on to Shannon, Ireland. A storm over Boston changed the flight plan, and the plane landed at Gander, Newfoundland, for refueling. Nawoichyk remained there, and after an hour caught a flight back to Bos-

ton on a plane that had stopped for refueling on its regular flight back to Boston from London. The weather over Boston remained poor, however, and Nawoichyk, soon found himself back at Idlewild. This time he caught a bus for Grand Central station where he boarded a train for Boston, but switch trouble developed and the train was delayed for 2 hours. An aunt living in Boston drove him to South Weymouth where he arrived 1 hour late for drill, bearing a wild tale for the sergeant major.

Throughout the Organized Reserve, attendance at drill was 89 percent for 1961, up from 81 percent the previous year. Annual field training attendance increased proportionately, with 94.4 percent of all officer members and 92.8 percent of all enlisted members attending, and 18 units boasting 100 percent summer camp participation. Without doubt, much of this success was tied closely to the new 6 month Reserve program which filled the ranks of units throughout the country with college graduates—some with M.A. and Ph.D degrees—and well-trained Marines. More than half of the Organized Reserve was composed of these recent active duty personnel in 1961, and their contribution of spirit, interest, and know-how paid high dividends. "The Six Month Training Program has given us a more solid air of professionalism in our lower ranks than we have ever known before," Brigadier General Joseph L. Stewart was to write some years later as Director of Reserve. He remarked further:

The 6-month trainee, as a group, is a fine physical specimen, with a high GCT and in general perhaps a better basic quality for a Marine than those in the Regular Marine Corps. He is trained the same in boot camp; and the remainder of his 6-months active duty and the Reserve training program does a better job of keeping him ready than we have ever known before.

New Weapons

Six-month trainees were among the first to become familiar with the M14 rifle and M60 machinegun, as the Marine Corps issued these new weapons to recruit depots and infantry training regiments on a priority basis. The 2 weapons were phased into these units during the first 6 months of 1961, but the Organized Reserve would have to wait for several years. Following distribution to recruit depots and ITR's, the new rifle and machinegun went to the FMF. An interesting result was that many longtime Reserves received their first instruction on the M14 and M60 from the junior men in the unit—the newly reported Marines fresh from 6-month training. While the old hands were learning something new, they were unlearning something "old." With a stroke of the pen Commandant Shoup abolished the 8-man squad drill which had been reintroduced soon after the end of the fighting in Korea, and Marines again marched according to the Landing Party Manual. No longer would they have to worry about who would pivot, who would stand still, and who would take 2 paces to the rear.

For those few old timers who could recall when the 8-man drill was standard years ago—when Reserve members drilled in street clothes and carried dummy rifles—an announcement concerning 3 organized units in California took on special significance. On 1 March, the 3— located in Pasadena, Fresno, and San Jose—were redesignated as missile batteries, soon to be armed with the powerful 17-foot-long surface-to-air HAWK.

The units formerly had employed the 75mm "Skysweeper" conventional antiaircraft weapon. The newly redesignated missile batteries were labeled assault units, and were capable of complete air transportability. Their new weapon was designed specifically as a defense against low-flying, supersonic aircraft, and normally carried a nonnuclear warhead.

The switch was in keeping with a policy to realign training of Reserve units with comparable Regular units in the Fleet Marine Forces, and members of the California batteries already had received some preliminary indoctrination on the HAWK during the previous summer training at Twentynine Palms, Calif. Two enlisted specialists from each unit were assigned to extended technical training in HAWK fire control procedures, and Regular Marines, members of the 2 active HAWK battalions at Twentynine Palms, spent many hours during the year at the California armories, introducing the Reserves to their new missile. The 3 units went to Twentynine Palms for annual field training during the same increment and the instruction they received, which included actual firing of a "bird," went a long way toward readying these units for possible mobilization.

Since 1959 more than half of the Organized Ground units had been reorganized or redesignated to achieve the goal of providing a Reserve force capable of stepping into the ranks of the Regulars. In early 1961 Marine Air Reserves embarked upon a 3-year program with a similar objective—integration of Air Reserve units with units of the Regular Establishment. The program began with *Operation Co-Mate* in 1961 and continued with *Operation Unity* in 1962 and *Opera-*

tion Climax in 1963. The program included broad plans and policies for integration and deployment. During *Co-Mate*, which became effective in July, Marine Reserve Fighter Squadron 215 from the Naval Air Station, Olathe, Kans., integrated into Marine Aircraft Group 14 at Marine Corps Air Station, Cherry Point.

The objective was to parallel Reserve training more closely with the syllabus of Regular squadrons. It also was designed to help bring the pilots of both Regular and Reserve squadrons into closer association and to enable them to acquaint each other with their capabilities. In those cases where the Reserves and Regulars flew the same planes, the objective was to have the Reserve pilots perform their active duty training side-by-side with compatible squadrons in the Regular establishment. During the year additional Air Reserve units integrated with the Regulars under the new system. A Reserve jet squadron from Olathe, VMF–113, came under the operational control of MAG–33, a Regular unit at MCAS, El Toro, Calif.; and the training of its pilots roughly paralleled the training set up for VMF–215 at Cherry Point. In addition, 8 helicopter squadrons were integrated with MAG–26 at Marine Corps Air Facility, New River, N.C., on the East Coast, and with MAG–36 at Marine Corps Air Facility, Santa Ana, Calif., in the West. A number of Reserve Marine air control squadrons also were linked with their Regular counterparts and integrated into ground control operations at various air stations.

As a result of *Co-Mate*, HMR–767 of New Orleans, Louisiana, became the first Reserve helicopter squadron in history to become c a r r i e r-qualified. T h e unit merged for 15 days with Regular Squadron HMR–361 at Santa Ana, and pilots, mechanics, and other personnel were integrated as if they were replacements. Arrangements were made by HMR–361 for landings aboard the U.S.S. *Princeton* on the first day of training. The carrier landings served a twofold purpose, according to an administrative officer of HMR–767. They gave the Regulars confidence in the ability of the Reserves, and they stimulated the enthusiasm of the Reserves by providing a new and valuable training experience. Because of the flat terrain around New Orleans, pilots of HMR–767 had been unable to train in rough area landings. The mountainous country of California, however, enabled the "bayou pilots" to obtain valuable and badly needed experience in landing in such terrain. In the case of the Louisiana unit, none of this training could have been accomplished at the home station, even if it had lasted for 6 months instead of 15 days. Practically all the other Reserve units participating in *Co-Mate* took advantage of the opportunity to correct training inadequacies that could not be corrected at home.

The Marine Air Reserve Training Command arranged for an operational readiness inspection (ORI) of the selected squadrons at their active duty training sites. The ORI, conducted by officers of the Regular Establishment, was based on the exact inspection given Regular units. The objective was to obtain a better working knowledge of the Air Reserve and its potential for mobilization. An important factor was that the integrated training was not designed for summer exercises alone. It was set up as a continuous program to be carried on throughout the year to facilitate the sharing of up-to-date technical information, training, and operational procedures between members of the two components. The result of the ORI, generally, indicated a high state of unit readiness.

More than 40,000 members of the Organized units, Air and Ground, spent part of their summers at annual field training, participating, in most part, in 2 extensive air-ground exercises. *Operation Patriot*, at Camp Lejeune, featured more than 2,500 Reserves. Rifle companies, antitank units, artillery battalions, truck companies, engineer units, and infantry battalions joined with Reserve attack and fighter squadrons in 3 days and nights of action. Aggressors were members of a Reserve reconnaissance battalion who did their utmost to quell the Marine Expeditionary Brigade composed of a dozen Ground units. On the West Coast, Reserves from 13 Ground units and 9 Air units took to the desert in 100-degree-plus temperatures for *Operation Inferno* at Twentynine Palms. There, the Marine Expeditionary Brigade fought across the desert floor and saw its enemy go up in smoke when a simulated nuclear blast ended activities for the aggressor. Remarkably few Reservists fell out with heat prostration, an indication of good conditioning and good training. An incident that will be most recalled by those who trained at Twentynine Palms that year was a flash flood that thundered down mountain passes to take a heavy toll of trucks and equipment.

Reserves Check Mobilization Readiness

Summer exercises at Camp Lejeune coincided with the final phase of *RESMO-BEX–60*, the Reserve Mobilization Exercise. Reserves from 13 Organized Ground units actually reported to Mobilization

Personnel Processing Centers (MPPC's) at Lejeune, Camp Pendleton, Cherry Point, and El Toro. Purpose of the exercise was to find out how well Organized Reserve units would mesh with the FMF, and to determine any weak points in Reserve training, in order to adequately train individuals for performance in the FMF upon mobilization. Reserves reporting to Camp Lejeune and Camp Pendleton were evaluated by their opposite numbers in the Regular Establishment. The final phase simulated a general mobilization of Reserves by COMART and district directors, plus the reception, processing, and assigning of Reserves by the MPPC located at each of the 4 bases. Each district and MARTCOM prepared mobilization orders for members scheduled to take part. To alleviate possible concern in the minds of recipients and their families, orders were clearly marked "Constructive Orders—Not to be Executed—For Exercise Purposes Only." The participating organizations traveled to camp in groups, as they normally would do if mobilized, and were assigned, on an individual basis, to Regular units on each base.

One of the most significant developments of *RESMOBEX* was that the Reserves, though they had been taking part in multiunit exercises back home, were not used to a continuing problem, where one objective was secured, the unit consolidated, and the next objective was sought. In some cases, they were not considered physically prepared for a long offensive operation. The Regulars also reported that many junior NCO's displayed weakness in leadership, and a number were found lacking knowledge in such fundamentals as hand and arm signals, cover and concealment, and small unit tactics. On the other hand, the Regulars reported the Reserve generally were cooperative and hard working, the Staff NCO's "performed admirably," and most of the younger Reserve Marines in grades E–1 and E–2 displayed high competence. The mobilization phase of *RESMOBEX* for Ground units was followed later in the summer by similar air exercises at MCAS, El Toro, and MCAS, Cherry Point.

20-Year Plan Released

Reserve officers got a somewhat clearer picture of what the Corps planned for them as Headquarters announced a Reserve Officer Training Program which outlined a plan of participation for Reserves who wished to remain trained and ready over a 20-year combined active duty and Reserve career. The Reserve career plan, promoted by General Fairbourn even before he became Director of Reserve, stressed the individual officer's readiness for mobilization. The plan provided guidelines of what was expected of all officers, whether they chose active participation and hoped to eventually qualify for Reserve retirement pay, or elected to drop out of the program somewhere along the line.

The major significance was for Ground officers who were encouraged to rotate into and out of Organized units and VTU's. They were told, geography and money permitting, they would be given a chance at the best training and be required, also, to take turns earning their points the "hard way." It was a share-the-wealth approach, aimed at giving an opportunity to some Reserves who had been shut out of training duty or command positions because of the active participation of some individuals who had early "locked on" to choicer billets, especially in Organized units. A normal plan would have the officer serve 3 years on active duty, 3 more in a VTU, followed by alternating periods of additional active duty for professional and occupational field training.

There was no real change for Organized Reserve pilots who were advised that they might be able to switch to the Volunteer Reserve and back into Organized units, but that such opportunities were considered slight. "Now there is a training program for the guidance of all Marine Reserve officers," General Fairbourn told the Navy Section of the Reserve Officers Association meeting in Washington. "I don't expect that any Reserve officer will be able to follow this plan to the letter any more than a Regular officer follows his career plan down the line. But at least we have a plan—something to shoot at—and the closer an individual can come to this plan, the better he will serve his Corps."

The 1961 Marine Corps Reserve Policy Board tackled the confusion surrounding the role and structure of Volunteer Training Units and recommended to the Commandant that he consider changing most VTU's to staff type organizations and establish a long-range training program. The Division of Reserve staff study attached to the recommendation revealed interesting new thinking on the role of these 277 Volunteer units:

> Our 1959 belief that we could effectively retrain officers in specialist fields through the VTU medium, with supporting assignments to active duty for training, has proved unsound. Additionally, giving VTU members priority of assignment to paid periods of training has not appreciably increased the training effectiveness of the parent VTU's. From the Division's standpoint, this failure is attributed to:
>
> a. The complete flexibility presently allowed, both to the individual forming a unit,

and that required by the district director in his approval of the type unit to be activated. For example, if 4 Class III majors—all 0302's and all schoolteachers in civilian life—desire to activate a Guided Missile unit, they are free to do so.

b. Our inability, both at the district and HQMC level, to determine with any degree of validity when VTU participation alone justifies an officer's reclassification. With benefit of hindsight, it is fallacious to attribute to the VTU program the capability of retraining reservists in any specialist MOS, particularly when the Regular Establishment requires formal schooling and/or extended OJT for qualification, or retraining, for the same MOS.

The best indicator of the task we set for ourselves 2 years ago, and by its inherent design, the near impossibility of its accomplishment, are the following factors:

(a) Our long delayed abolishment of the specialist language VTU's, some of which we had supported with paid instructors and paid unit-ACDUTRA periods for 5–6 years. These 11 units, at time of deactivation, were costing us $50,000 a year, yet had not qualified one officer, by Navy standards, as a language officer.

(b) The specialist unit preferences of our present VTU members. Our latest statistics indicate that of 252 Ground units, 110—or 43 percent—are of staff type.

VTU Rules, Roles Revised

Based on this reasoning, and other information, such as the failure of district directors to control the training of VTU's in their districts, the conclusion reached by the study was that neither the VTU program, nor any other volunteer inactive duty training program, in itself possessed the capability of retraining an officer from an MOS assigned while on active duty. The study recommended that the philosophy of the VTU program as a retraining vehicle be rejected; that all specialist type VTU training activities, except marksmanship, be eliminated; and that a pro-

gram of controlled training be instituted for all units except marksmanship units. Under the proposed reorganization and subsequent controlled training, members of VTU's would take tests, supplied by Quantico's Reserve Liaison and Training Section, to ascertain the level at which a unit would commence its planned schedule, and then embark on a 4-phase training cycle corresponding to Phases I and II of both the Reserve Junior and Senior courses.

Several other rulings from Headquarters changed the complexion of the VTU's somewhat during the year. The Commandant decreed that Standby Reserves no longer were eligible for VTU membership, and that Ready Reserves who were members would have to attend at least 75 percent of the meetings scheduled by their parent units to retain affiliation.

President Kennedy asked Congress for additional appropriations to aid in speeding modernization of the Marine Corps and raising its Regular strength to 190,000 men; and, in August, Headquarters announced a plan offering 2-, 3-, and 4-year tours of active duty to 2,500 enlisted Marine Reserves as part of the enlarged force authorized by Congress. Corporals and below were given priority in applying for the voluntary active duty program, and applications were considered from all inactive duty enlisted members of the Marine Corps Reserve, as well as all trainees on 6-month active training duty. At the time, there were 208,000 in the Ready Reserve and 27,000 in the Standby. Of the Ready Reserve total, 44,000 were members of Organized units. Those accepted for extended active duty were required to serve a minimum of 2 years, and would retain their Reserve status. Six-month trainees who chose EAD were to return to an inactive, "no training" category after completing their tours. Late in the year the Commandant announced that the 190,-000-man strength would be reached by the end of 1961, 6 months ahead of schedule. Reserve EAD's provided a major portion of the manpower increase, he reported.

Later, in explaining the response from the Reserves to a member of the press, General Fairbourn reported:

> About 3,400 men had responded to this program to meet a 2,500 requirement. Based on this response, initially only single enlisted men in the grades of E–4 and below were accepted. Later this restriction was relaxed to the extent of applying the same dependency criteria as is applied for Regular enlistments. I reported that we had accepted about 1,500 6-month trainees undergoing training who had either volunteered for extended active duty or enlisted in the Regular Marine Corps. The reporter asked why our Reserve program seemed to be so effective, and I replied that it was due to several recent changes in the program: the 6-month training, the multiple drills, and our administration of involuntary active duty for training for disciplinary purposes. He asked where the volunteers would be sent, and I replied they would be assigned generally in the same manner as recruits are assigned. That is, those from west of the Mississippi to FMF, Pacific, and those in the eastern part of the country to FMF, Atlantic. He queried as to whether we contemplated any involuntary call of units or individuals, and I replied that we did not contemplate any involuntary recall since the Marine Corps was more fortunate than other services because our buildup started earlier. It actually started with President Kennedy's first add-on to the fiscal 1962 budget. While this was a modest increase of 3,000, it nevertheless set the machinery in motion to permit steady achievement of the strength of 190,000 Marines on a voluntary basis.

Not Enough Ships

Because of the buildup a large number of Federal employees in key Government jobs were dropped from the Ready to the Standby Reserve, for mobilization only in case of all-out war. The Department of Defense urged Reserve unit commanders to screen records of Federal employees who were members of their units "to insure that those who are members of the Ready Reserve will be available for active duty within 30 days of mobilization." Some 3,000 key Federal workers, all of whom had been labeled more essential in their civilian jobs than to their Reserve positions, were shifted to the Standby by the end of 1961.

A key problem of the Marine Corps, which touched the Reserve and their employment after any possible mobilization, was neatly summed up by Commandant Shoup when he told Congress early in 1961, "We have more fight than we can ferry." Also testifying was Vice Admiral John S. McCain, Jr., former Commander Amphibious Group Two, who said he'd have to "leave 49 percent of the Marines on the dock" if the whistle blew. Navy planners said if they had the money, they would urgently seek a 2-division, 2-wing lift. But the most eloquent plea for increased attention to lift capability appeared in remarks to the House of Representatives by Congressman Thomas N. Downing of Virginia, who noted:

> The Secretary of the Navy recently announced a decision to augment the Marine Corps, thus providing a nucleus and framework for a 4th Marine Division. This is, in my opinion, a significant step forward toward providing our country with adequate forces for limited war. Throughout our history, a ready Marine Corps had played an important role in our continued efforts to preserve peace by being strong. The record of the Marine Corps speaks for itself. . . . I am considerably concerned about the Navy's capability to move the Marines to trouble points. The record shows that we

have amphibious lift of only 1½ Marine Division/Wings, or about one-third of a total realistic requirement. As [the late] Mark Watson recently reported in the *Baltimore Sun*, "The United States has the best amphibious fleet in the world—for 1 regiment. But it won't carry 2 divisions." It appears that our amphibious ship Navy has been sadly neglected in recent years. . . . The decision to bolster our Marine Corps was incisive and forward looking. But it was merely the first step. The next step, which must begin right now, is to provide the Marines with modern Navy ships which will guarantee their being moved and sustained in any place on earth where communism might throw down the challenge.

As 1961 drew to a close, it was clear to Department of Defense planners that the Marine Reserves could be mobilized faster than they could be transported to trouble spots, but increased Pentagon and Congressional concern indicated there soon might be a solution to the problem, labeled by General Shoup as "listlessness about our liftlessness."

Late in 1961, the world situation was neatly summed up in a terse sentence on page 1 of a Washington, D.C., daily paper: "Today would be a heck of a time for the meek to inherit the earth." But the Marines were ready. They had the plans and the training and 15,000 additional men in ranks. The expanded force was enough for 3 full-strength air wings and 3 full-strength divisions with an extra battalion thrown in for rotation between the 3d Division on Okinawa and the 1st Division in California. This 190,000-man Corps would provide the headquarters for the 4th Marine Division—ready to be filled out as a fighting division with Reserves should the President issue a call to arms.

The Year 1962

Marine reservists needed only to review the messages of Marine Corps general officers in the early sixties to sense the country's awakening to the needs for currentness and reorganization to meet all exigencies. The Commandant exhorted the Corps to be prepared to fight "in any type of war," and, as he stressed training, research and development, economy of men and equipment, and speed of mountout, he spoke to his Reserve, indistinguishably from his Regulars. "In the future, as so often in the past, it will be the Reserves on whom we can count for the additional ready strength required when the chips are down. . . . Stay ready. If you are mobilized, it will be fast. You will be needed—and needed badly."

Around the globe, Marines were active on the frontiers of freedom. Late in the spring of 1962, 3,000 combat-ready Marines landed in Thailand within hours after President Kennedy announced this country's decision to assist the Thai in protecting their territorial integrity. This powerful Marine air-ground team remained near the threatened northern border of Thailand for 2 months, and was quietly withdrawn in July when its presence on the scene of crisis was no longer needed. These Marines were provided by the 3d Marine Division and 1st Marine Wing. This division/wing team, based on Okinawa and Japan, had been operating in the Far East with the 7th Fleet since the close of the Korean conflict, and its forward posture and strategic mobility made it instantly responsive to the recurring contingency crises in Southeast Asia.

In much the same fashion, a Marine helicopter squadron moved into South Vietnam in early 1962. Its mission was to support that country's operations against insurgent forces threatening the legally constituted government. Then, in late October, Marine Corps units were alerted for a possible move to the Caribbean area to play a vital role in this country's quarantine of Cuba. In connection with the Cuban crisis the Secretary of the Navy ordered extensions in service of Marines whose tours would have expired before 28 February 1963.

As the adversary's style became better understood, Department of Defense planners incorporated an awareness of the need for dealing with guerrilla warfare. Counterinsurgency training became a major part of military training for Regular and Reserve forces alike. In June 1962 Lieutenant General John C. Munn, Assistant Commandment, aptly called to the attention of the Marine Corps Combat Correspondents Association in Allentown, Pa., that before Mao was taking China from Chiang, and Castro, Cuba from Batista, Marines were employing know-how in counterinsurgency with the Colonel Commandant fighting Indians in Florida, and later with Medal of Honor winner Christian Schilt and comrades fighting bandits in Nicaragua.

"As I see it," General Munn told the correspondents, including many reservists:

> . . . the 1960's may turn out to be the decade of the guerilla as far as military news is concerned. Events in Southeast Asia, in Africa, and in the Caribbean bear this out. There is an increasing nationwide realization of the importance of guerilla and counterguerrilla warfare. Numerous books and articles are appearing on the subject, kindling the public imagination as if it were something new and sensational. Counterguerrilla operations are neither new nor sensational to Marines. Marines participated in counterguerrilla operations in Haiti as well as on the other side of the same island in Santo Domingo. These men were neither specially picked nor specially trained for these operations. They were trained to be Marines and to fight as Marines. Many of you will recall from first-hand experience that a considerable part of the fighting that the Marine Corps did during World War II—particularly on Guadalcanal—was essentially patrol warfare in the jungle, for which the experiences in the "Banana Wars" were excellent preparation. Probably no force in the world today is better equipped, experienced, and organized for counterguerrilla operations than the Marines.

The philosophy of the Corps for the sixties—Ready—was the same as ever, with only the necessary adaptations to fit the contemporary scene. In his annual message of 4 January 1962, Commandant Shoup admonished his Marines to "get out into the kinds of geography in which you are likely to have to fight. Get out in the rain, snow, cold, and darkness similar to where you might have to do battle. Get used to the field mice, screech owls, coyotes, and katydids." The philosophy for the Corps pressed hard on the psychological capital of its reputation. Emphasis was placed on the Marine Corps' known qualities as a fighting machine. Marine generals, in all their addresses, urged reservists to be more than proud of this image—to sustain it.

Early in 1962, Secretary of Defense Robert McNamara indicated in his "posture" statement to Congress that he wanted the Marine Corps ready to go with 4 division-wing teams—one of them to be formed of Ready Reserves—for the next 5 years. In asking the legislators for $1,148,400,000 for the fiscal 1963 Marine Corps, McNamara noted the Marine Reserves were "trained and manned to be able to fill out the 4th Division/Wing team in a relatively short period." The budget again provided for 45,000 Ready Reserves. Of these, 42,000 would get 48 drills and 15 days active duty for training. Noting the Secretary's mention of Marine

Reserve capabilities, Commandant Shoup pointed out the need to change the structure of the Reserve forces to match changes in the Regulars. "Some units," he said, "will be combined to provide more nearly the numbers and types we need for completing the mobilization of a 4th Division/Wing Team."

Organized Reserve Reorganized

The mention of structural changes was a hint of things to come; for, in April, the Commandant formally announced a major reorganization affecting nearly half of the 218 Ground units and all 86 Aviation units then participating in the Organized Reserve program. The move grouped units into major elements to form a 4th Marine Division and a 4th Marine Aircraft Wing within the Reserve structure. Ten Ground units, all of them rifle companies, were deactivated on 1 July, the date that reorganization commenced; and in large part, the reservists who met with these units were shifted to nearby organizations. Fifty-three others became 4th Marine Division units. Of the remainder, 84 were reassigned as Force Troops units and 56 remained in augmentation status (a nucleus of trained reservists to strengthen all FMF units on mobilization). Of the Aviation units affected, 40 went to form the 4th Aircraft Wing, and 38 squadrons were assigned to train individual reservists.

The new structure gave individual reservists a stronger sense of identification with the Regular Marine Corps, and a "division pride" that had been lacking under the old system. Marine Reserves now could identify themselves as members of the 23d, 24th, or 25th Marines, the 14th Marines (artillery), or one of the various support units of the 4th Marine Division. The division, disbanded following World War II, had established quite a record for itself in the Central Pacific by taking 4 beachheads—all bitterly opposed—in less than 13 months. Formally activated in August 1943, the 4th had tasted combat at Roi and Namur, Saipan, Tinian, and Iwo Jima. Some 81,000 Marines had seen action with the "Fighting Fourth" and 17,722 had become casualties. The division received 2 Presidential Unit Citations and a Navy Unit Commendation. The 4th Marine Aircraft Wing was 1 of 5 wings organized for service during World War II and was deactivated shortly after the war's end. Its 3 air groups were originally positioned on Hawaii, Midway, and Samoa, with the mission of providing air defense, search and patrol, air-sea rescue, and shipping escort duties. A year later it moved to Samoa, then to the Ellice Islands, and on to Tarawa in December 1943. The 4th served in the Central Pacific until after the Japanese surrender, neutralizing bypassed Japanese-mandated bases.

The designation of Marine Reserve units as elements of an air-ground team was aimed at enhancing realistic long-range training and providing for rapid unit response in event of mobilization. The reorganization placed further emphasis on unit training, and the 4th Division entered its 1962 training year with the objective of providing not a smattering of well-trained, separate units—but a single team, working together to build mobilization efficiency.

The changes, perhaps, were dictated in part by the requirements of the times. But certainly, many lessons bearing on the decisions were the result of the massive and unprecedented mountout which occurred in the fateful summer of 1950 when the Marine Reserves headed for Korea. Although the Reserves rallying to support the requirement of Korea appeared, were processed, and embarked with incredible dispatch, the problems of adapting to organizational need, the administrative backup, and many other factors made it apparent that streamlining was in order for the jet and missile-minded Marine Reserve of the sixties.

Van Stockum Takes Over Reserve

In June 1962 Brigadier General Ronald R. Van Stockum, winner of the Bronze Star at Bougainville and a former director of the 4th Reserve and Recruitment District, became the 25th Director of the Marine Corps Reserve. "No matter from which side one looks at it, the Reserve organization presents a promise of hard work," he wrote in his first Reserve Column for the *Marine Corps Gazette*. "But reorganization gives the Reserve for the first time a longer range training goal at which to aim. The Reserve knows where it ought to be 5 to 8 years from now."

MCR Mobilization Teams Authorized

Without a doubt, the most significant aspect of the reorganization was a basic change in mobilization procedures. Under the new planning, the mobilized 4th Division/Wing team, plus selected Force Troops units, were geared to be on station of initial assignment somewhere within 5 to 30 days, depending on factors of distance and the world situation. Shortly following the announcement of reorganization, Headquarters reported that 80 teams of specially trained reservists would man mobilization stations across the country should the Reserves ever be mobilized.

Reserve mobilization teams consisting of a Reserve officer and 3 enlisted reservists—all Class II's—were formed to train in mobilization procedures. They trained at training centers used by organized units and spent 2 weeks on active duty each summer, sharpening their techniques of arranging for medical examinations of Ready reservists called for active duty as individuals, screening service record books, and providing travel to Marine Corps bases. Thus, the Marines retained their capability of recalling reservists who were not part of the 4th Division/Wing team, either as individuals or on a unit basis as the Division of Reserve announced that a combination of both procedures probably would be used.

In the event of mobilization, weapons and materiel for units would come from stockpiles specially earmarked at Barstow, Calif., and Albany, Ga. Division and Wing reservists would carry training level weapons and equipment with them and draw the extra materiel needed to fill out their tables of equipment.

The Class III reservists weren't excluded from the mobilization picture. Early in the year, "hip pocket" orders, similar to those issued to officers a year previously, were mailed to a number of Class III enlisted Ready reservists in all ranks who had certain military skills. They specified where the man was to report and authorized any transportation required to carry out the orders. The timing was based on M–Day: some orders called for early reporting following nationwide mobilization for all-out war; others authorized delays up to M-plus-30 days. The orders did not apply to partial mobilization. Reservists were told the main reason for the issuance of advance orders at the time was to provide them with the knowledge that they were considered priority people, and as such would be underway in short order following general mobilization. Thus, they would be better able to prepare their families and employers for such an eventuality. The orders for enlisted personnel were to remain in effect for the remainder of the reservist's Ready Reserve obligation—a departure from the officer plan which put a 2-year effectiveness on orders.

While Marine Corps Headquarters was making news with major changes in plans and policies, individual Marines and single units added new luster to the history and traditions of the Corps. A young lieutenant colonel from Cambridge, Ohio, became America's first orbital astronaut and the latest in a long list of Marine Corps heroes as he spent nearly 5 hours in space on 20 February. John H. Glenn had been commissioned a second lieutenant in the Marine Corps Reserve in 1943. His career as a Naval Aviator had included 59 missions in the Marshall Islands campaign and 90 combat missions as a jet pilot with Marine Fighter Squadron 311 and as an exchange pilot with the 5th U.S. Air Force in Korea. He had integrated into the Regular Marine Corps as a captain in March 1946.

Another Marine pilot who achieved fame as part of America's space team joined the Class II ranks. First Lieutenant Wayne E. Koons, a Marine helicopter pilot who snatched America's first astronaut from the sea, joined VMA–233, an Air Reserve squadron at the Naval Air Station, Norfolk, Va. Lieutenant Koons, who made the historic pickup after Commander Alan Shepard's suborbital flight in May 1961, joined the staff of the National Aeronautics and Space Administration's Project Apollo at Langley Field,

Va., where he helped develop recovery methods for the project.

Elsewhere, individual heroes enhanced the image of Marines in reserve. In Pueblo, Colo., Lance Corporal Silvano Peralta, a member of the 5th Antitank Company, climbed through a window and billowing smoke to save the life of 1-year-old Lynette Nielson, trapped in her burning home. In Pottsville, Pa., the 63d Rifle Company closed its training center in July as one of the units deactivated as a result of reorganization. But, days before the closing, the inspector-instructor and a unit gunnery sergeant had recovered the body of a local miner from a caved-in mine shaft. "This voluntary action at considerable personal risk will leave the Marine Corps remembered in Pottsville long after the deactivation of the 63d Rifle Company," noted General Van Stockum.

When high tides driven by gale winds smashed into the East Coast in March, the 39th Rifle Company of Atlantic City, N.J., carried rations, stood guard against looters, loaned ponchos and blankets to civilians who were without heat, directed traffic, and helped residents of the area dig out their cars and houses, buried under sand following 9 days of the storm. And, after the fury of Hurricane Carla swept from the Gulf of Mexico into Texas in September, the 3d Amphibian Tractor Company of Galveston used 5 amphibian tractors to rescue and evacuate wounded, bring in doctors, and deliver food. The position of the Marine Reserves was one of Instant Samaritans. They did not solicit rescue business, but they stood by to help when recruited by proper authority in emergencies. By giving quick and expert aid in time of need, the Reserves enhanced their reputation as a ready, well-disciplined force.

The dedicated work of hundreds of inactive (Class III) Reserve officers contributed materially to the growth and success of the Marine Corps in 1962. These men, tried and proved on the battlefields of World War II and Korea, successful in their civilian pursuits, and leaders in hometown civic affairs, generally were not paid or rewarded in any material way, except for the satisfaction of accomplishment and the knowledge they had contributed service to their Corps. They worked in many active-duty-for-training assignments, as members of the Marine Corps Reserve Policy Board; as staff officers of major operations, such as the combined air/ground exercises at annual field training; as members of promotion boards; as specialists in civic affairs and public information.

One group of inactive reservists, VTU 12–36 (now PAU 12–1 of Santa Monica, Calif.) won a coveted Academy Award during the year for production of the film, "A Force in Readiness." The movie presented the Navy-Marine Corps team in vivid detail as a deterrent to enemy aggression. Another unit, VTU 1–1 (now PAU 1–1 of New York City) conducted an effective Writing and Photography Clinic for informational services personnel of the Regular Marine Corps. In Washington, D.C., members of VTU 5–21 (now PAU 4–1) took the first tentative steps of a 3-year project to produce a complete history of the Marine Corps Reserve.

"No study of the Marine Corps Reserve would be complete without recognition of the voluntary contributions of time and dedicated effort made by continuously 'active' members of the inactive Reserve," Major General John P. Condon wrote later from retirement: "The value of these many individuals throughout the country,

prominent or not in their communities, is invaluable in keeping alive the Marine Corps image. Their dedicated effort in behalf of Marine Corps interests, direct or indirect, gives real substance to the phrase, 'Once a Marine, always a Marine!'"

Training of Reserve/Regular Integrated

In his 1962 message to Marines, the Commandant left no doubt that the Corps would train, train, train. Training is "so obvious—so often proved in combat," General Shoup noted:

> ... yet so many times our thinking strays from the age-old truism that proper training is the very foundation of all military success .... To develop in your men the requisite psychology of willingness to tangle with any enemy, foreign or domestic, to steep them in the hot oil of determination is the ultimate goal of all training. This is the way to win battles.

Of the Reserves, the Commandant noted, "there will be more emphasis on mobilization training at home armories. I also intend to have more Reserve units integrated with Regular units during a summer training period."

As the Commandant specified, Marines got out into the boondocks. The 86th Rifle Company of Lincoln, Nebr., marched nearly 8 miles to a training area where they patrolled in 2-degree weather and snow driven by 20-mile-an-hour winds. The 13th Infantry Battalion of Washington, D.C., devoted nearly half of its training to night problems, working in the hills of Quantico with the Regulars of the mobilization-designated 22d Marines. Out in the rugged area of Wisconsin's Kettle Moraine State Park, where large iron ore deposits drive magnetic compasses berserk, the 96th Rifle Company of Milwaukee, Wis., waded through a night problem relying for direction on good reconaissance and an 1897 map—the newest they could find. "Of course we didn't have instant tropic jungles for straining our training in all home armory areas," General Fairbourn had reported:

> Guerrilla forces were usually lacking as training aids. But the Reserve does have darkness, and darkness is a trusty test of unit control. The company commander who hits the objective during the dark of the moon has control.

In a typical district order, 4th District reservists were told that, subject to training needs of the particular unit and availability of training areas, "it is desirable that each unit conduct at least 2 overnight field exercises each training year" and that in addition, "as many other periods as possible should be spent in the field." The order also specified that staff groups and Volunteer Training Units were encouraged to participate in as many field exercises as possible, either as umpires or as control groups.

Operation Unity, the 1962 version of the integrated training program for air reservists, placed even greater emphasis on combined training than had its predecessor, *Co-Mate*, in 1961. During the 1962 maneuvers, Air reservists merged with Regulars from throughout the United States and Puerto Rico. Marine Air Reserve Group 20 from Norfolk reported to Headquarters, FMF Atlantic, in October, for on-the-job training in FMF headquarters staff billets. A Marine attack squadron from Jacksonville, Fla., VMA–144, became the first MARTCOM unit to train outside the United States for summer maneuvers when it deployed in July to Roosevelt Roads, Puerto Rico. During the summer, air reservists trained with their Regular counterparts at MCAS, Cherry Point; MCAS, Beaufort; MCAF, New River; MCAS, Yuma; MCAF, Santa Ana; MCAS, El Toro; and MCB, Twentynine Palms.

The new year saw many changes in equipment for Marine Air Reserve units. MARTCOM acquired its first transport squadrons in January as detachments at Grosse Ile, Minneapolis, and Seattle began flying the R4Q aircraft. In June Reserves from Olathe, Kans., began transitioning into the F4D "Skyray," the first afterburner jet in the command. New Orleans pilots got a new aircraft when they replaced their FJ "Furies" with the photo version of the swept-winged "Cougar." By the end of 1962 all prop-driven aircraft, except the R4Q's and helicopters, had been phased out of MARTCOM.

In July, to coincide with the formation of the 4th Marine Division in reserve, MARTCOM began organizing a Marine aircraft wing within the command. The major elements of the 4th Wing were Marine Wing Headquarters Group 4, Glenview, Ill.; MWSG–47, Los Alamitos, Calif.; MAG–41, Dallas, Tex.; MAG–42, Alameda, Calif.; MAG–43, Willow Grove, Pa.; MAG–44, Minneapolis; and MAG–46, Groose Ile. MAG–41 and MAG–43 were primarily fighter groups, while MAG–42 was an attack group. MAG–44 was designated as the command's transport group and MAG–46 was a helicopter group. In all, the Air Reserve under the command of Brigadier General Louis B. Robertshaw at MARTCOM was composed of 17 detachments. The detachments trained 21 fighter and attack squadrons, 11 helicopter squadrons, 4 transport squadrons, 1 photo squadron, 30 supporting units, and 10 Marine Air Reserve groups.

The first opportunity for the new 4th Division/Wing team to perform an air-ground exercise came with *Operation Trident*, a 3-day exercise at Camp Lejeune which involved the largest complement of organized Marine reservists ever to stage such a training exercise on the East Coast. Nineteen separate units from 18 eastern States participated. Some 3,000 reservists, including Marine Air Reserve squadrons from Willow Grove, Pa.; Glenview, Ill.; and Floyd Bennett Field in New York, made up a Marine Expeditionary Brigade. MAG 26 from New River provided helicopter airlift of troops and supplies during vertical envelopment maneuvers. In addition to the *Trident* Marines, 8,000 other reservists trained at Camp Lejeune under the supervision of Reserve Liaison personnel headed by C o l o n e l Robert Port.

In the West, some 10,000 Marine Reserves trained at 6 installations including Twentynine Palms, scene of *Operation Tiger*. Like its East Coast counterpart, *Operation Tiger* was an aggressor-opposed, umpire-controlled air-ground maneuver for Air and Ground units task-organized as a Marine Expeditionary Brigade in a non-nuclear situation. Brigadier General Charles F. Duchein, commander of the 8th Staff Group of New Orleans, served as Marine Reserve Expeditionary Brigade Commander for *Tiger*, perhaps the largest Reserve exercise yet conducted.

For the first time in history, Marine ground reservists went outside continental United States to conduct annual field training. Six ground units, including more than 1,000 reservists, were involved. The 10th Engineer Company of Portland, Maine, was the first unit to fly to Puerto Rico, where it was ferried to the island of Vieques, for its 2-week on-the-job training with D Company, 8th Engineer Bat-

talion, Force Troops, FMF, Atlantic. Three engineer companies, an engineer battalion, and a provisional company from the 13th Infantry Battalion, also journeyed to Vieques for AFT.

The Reserves tested the new mobilization teams during summer exercises at Lejeune, Twentynine Palms, and Camp Pendleton. East Coast teams spent a week at their respective district headquarters, then went on to Lejeune for the second week where they processed some 1,700 incoming Reserves. West Coast teams spent a week at district headquarters, then returned to local mobilization stations at home armories. Mobilization Personnel Processing Centers at Pendleton and Twentynine Palms received and processed more than 1,500 Reserves during the test periods.

In 1962 the Regular Establishment concentrated its Research and Development efforts on improving the short airfield for tactical support (SATS), developing helicopter-transportable weapons for fire support, and improving tactical communication. Other projects under study included a rocket-boosted artillery weapon, a new family of helicopters, hydrofoil amphibious support vehicles, drone-reconnaissance aircraft, and improved missile systems. But, for the Reserve, the emphasis was on the individual and how he fitted into the newly reorganized Marine force in readiness. In his January message, the Commandant had said, "I have no trouble finding people to handle machines. The problem is to find people who can handle people. Concentrate on Marines. They'll handle the machines." The Reserves concentrated on Marines in 1962 as they trained for efficient manpower management, for leadership under unusual and trying circumstances, and for a new type of warfare.

The Year 1963

The Marine Corps took advantage of relative world peace in 1963 to continue the development of new techniques, weapons, and equipment. Improvement of the current family of amphibious assault vehicles was carried on, together with the testing of radically new land and water vehicles that could play major roles in future amphibious warfare operations. By year's end, distribution of the new family of 7.62mm rifles and machine-guns—the M14 and the M60—to Fleet Marine Force units was completed. Marine Aviation attained the capability of operating high-performance aircraft from airfields no longer than 2,000 feet, utilizing the SATS. The vertical assault concept was bolstered when work began on the new CH53A heavy-assault helicopter, which with its maximum capacity of 63 Marines was to be the largest of its type in the free world. The addition of a seventh amphibious assault ship (LPH) and 2 amphibious landing docks (LPD's) to the Navy during 1963 provided the Marine Corps with an increased capability for vertical and surface amphibious assault operations.

Americans were fighting a helicopter war in Vietnam, and one squadron of the 1st Marine Aircraft Wing was engaged in airlifting troops and cargo in support of Vietnamese operations against the Viet Cong guerrillas. The conflict was billed as the "War of the Future," with hundreds of helicopters lifting troops into airphibious assaults—the type of combat which Marine planners expected to see in future conflicts with aggressive communism.

Continuing world unrest had kept the Corps in a high state of readiness. As trouble brewed in Cuba late in 1962, a battalion landing team of the 1st Marine Division was airlifted from Camp Pendleton to Guantanamo Naval Base. The battalion was ready to move out just 5 hours after receiving orders to deploy. The same day, a BLT of the 2d Marine Division was flown to Guantanamo from Camp Lejeune and the following morning, a third BLT from ships of the ready amphibious squadron in the Caribbean began landing across the beaches. Regimental and provisional brigade headquarters were set up. Marine aircraft squadrons were embarked in carriers, and others were poised at various bases. Three days after the initial call, 5,000 well-organized Marines had taken up stations at Guantanamo fully ready to execute any mission assigned the brigade-size unit. Significantly, the Reserves had not been called.

"The Marine Corps Reserve is a reserve in a literal sense," Commandant Shoup noted in his "State of the Corps" message in January 1963. "It is not unlike the reserve division available to a corps commander. It is something to be committed at the vital moment. For the Marine Corps in recent crises, that moment was not quite reached. If it comes in the future, the Reserve will be called. Only when combat casualties exist or are imminent will I ask to call our Reserve."

At the turn of the year, the Marine Corps could count 124,253 Ready reservists. Of these, 43,745 were in Organized units, serving in most cases as the major nucleus of the 4th Marine Division and the 4th Marine Aircraft Wing. Their role had been well-defined in the Commandant's message: "Stay ready. If you are mobilized it will be fast. You will be needed—and needed badly." Their importance to the Nation's safety was further defined by the Secretary of Defense Robert McNamara:

> The requirement for active duty general purpose forces is influenced by the size and character of our Reserves. To the extent that our Reserve units can be brought to bear in a timely manner, the requirement for active forces is reduced. But to be fully effective, certain portions of our Reserve forces must be maintained at a high level of readiness, since, as we have seen, a quick response on our part to communist aggression can do much to forestall the need for a much greater military effort later, when the military situation has already deteriorated. Thus there is a great premium on highly ready Reserve forces which can be used to augment quickly our active forces.

Centralized Control Stressed

The division/wing concept was the focal point of Marine Corps Reserve organization, and increased efficiency was its greatest advantage. An example was the 2d Battalion, 24th Marines, in the Chicago area. The commanding officer and inspector-instructor, operating out of a central Chicago headquarters, controlled subordinate companies in Forest Park and at Great Lakes, Ill., as well. Centralized control applied to training, supply, fiscal, and administration matters, thus conserving manpower. The need for retraining in certain "hard skills" was one of the problems of the reorganization because it was expected that a rapid commitment to combat would provide little time for post-mobilization training. Commanders were quick to request special schooling for their units, and the on-the-job training phase of Reserve 6-month training received increased emphasis.

New equipment and new techniques were introduced to provide more realistic training for Reserves. Heavy artillery units conducted annual field training at Twenty-nine Palms, and light and medium artillery units arrived periodically. Specialist units—the type normally found in the force service regiments and service battalions—conducted more practical work and actively assisted the Regular host units in fulfilling daily requirements. The 3d Motor Transport Maintenance Company of Sacramento, for instance, repaired 76 tactical vehicles under supervision of the supply depot repair division during AFT at Barstow. Reservists from reconnaissance, Anglico, and air delivery companies received jump training at Fort Benning. Tracked vehicle units phased through the tracked vehicle school at Camp Pendleton on a regular basis. With the arrival of relatively more sophisticated aircraft—particularly the F4D and the F8U afterburner fighter craft—the number of flight hours for Reserve pilots and air crews approached an average of 120 hours a year, providing increased safety and proficiency opportunity.

34,000 Ground Reserves at Camp

As in past years, 2 major ground exercises were conducted, 1 on each coast. These were planned, staged, and staffed by Organized Ground and Air Reserve Units. Each exercise provided an excellent opportunity for combined training of Reserve Ground and Air in conjunction with the Regular Establishment. At *Scorpion*, in the California desert, and *Unity*, under the tall pines of Onslow County, Reserves put their year-long armory training to work in the field under searching eyes of the Regulars. In all, 34,075 reservists went to summer camp, participating not only in giant manuevers but in specialized training at Coronado, Parris Island, Pickel Meadows, Yuma, Little Creek, and Vieques.

Amphibious training received special emphasis as 3,300 reservists from 10 States attended 2-week training periods at the Naval Amphibious Base, Coronado, where ship-to-shore techniques and helicopter operations were stressed.

Marine Air Reserves trained at 13 sites during the summer months, and continued their training at home. In the words of General Robertshaw:

> A significant contributing factor in the fine performance of the Marine Air Reserve during their year's summer training has been the use of additional Inactive Duty Flying Training periods for Organized Marine Corps Reserve aviators and crewmen. These periods have helped to attain and retain pilot and aircrew readiness at the highest level to date.

Nearly 1,000 Marine Air reservists, operating from MCAS, Cherry Point, and MCAF, New River, supported the combined air/ground exercise at Camp Lejeune; and an equal number—flying from MCAS, Yuma; MCAF, Santa Ana; and MCAS, El Toro—supported the operation at Twentynine Palms. The 3 light antiaircraft missile batteries received summer training at San Nicholas, Calif., where they fired the HAWK missile with live ammunition. They operated on staggered schedules and were integrated for training and support with Regular LAAM batteries from Twentynine Palms. Following summer training, Brigadier General Hugh M. Elwood, a World War II ace, relieved General Robertshaw as Commanding General, MARTCOM.

A number of units distinguished themselves with outstanding achievements at annual field training. Marine reservists from the 5th Motor Transport Battalion at Memphis qualified 98.9 percent of the unit during summer rifle training at Camp Lejeune, as 50 percent plus qualified as "expert." Leading the Tennessee shooters was Captain Reginald Germany with a score of 246. The 5th Truck Company from Charlotte, N.C., with 195 members at Camp Lejeune, qualified 100 percent on the rifle range, with fewer "expert" shooters.

Sharpshooting wasn't limited to annual field training, however, as 3 Marine reservists won major individual awards at the National Shooting Matches at Camp Perry, Ohio. Colonel Emmet O. Swanson, Reserve Team captain, won the National Service Rifle Senior Championship with a score of 773–44V's. Colonel Swanson was selected to continue as team captain through 1964. Reserve First Lieutenant Robert J. Maguire received a plaque as the high Marine shooter in the National Trophy individual rifle matches at the 1963 National Matches, and additional recognition as high Reserve shooter. Captain Leonard C. De Jong was awarded a plaque at the National Matches for the highest score from the 200-yard line. An air control reservist, Private George A. Cordingly, Jr., while serving as a recruit in the Six Month Training Program at Parris Island, blazed a score of 241 with the M14 rifle to tie the recruit range record and become the highest recruit shooter for 1963.

Marine reservists have built a tradition of solid attendance at drills, often overcoming near impossible handicaps, and 1963 was a banner year for individual records. Gunnery Sergeant George C. Ribley may well have established the record for distance traveled to attend field training. A member of Company B, 4th Tank Battalion, from Mattydale, N.Y., Sergeant Ribley was transferred by his civilian employer to Huntsville, Ala., in March 1963. When his unit departed for summer training at Camp Pendleton, how-ever, Ribley's family still lived in Syra-cuse, N.Y., and Ribley was still attending his unit's drills. To join the unit for camp, he flew 1,050 miles from Huntsville to Syracuse, then another 3,000 miles with Company B to reach Camp Pendleton. Master Sergeant George E. Harper, of Garner, N.C., had logged more than 67,000 miles commuting to drills by the end of 1963. He did it by attending drills at the Naval Air Station in Norfolk, a distance of 200 miles from Garner. Harper main-tained a 100 percent attendance record for 10 of his 13 drill years. Reserve Master Sergeant Robert L. Fulgham completed his 10th consecutive year of perfect drill attendance with Marine Attack Squadron 233 at the Norfolk Naval Air Station. Sergeant Fulgham, squadron ordnance chief, received a Certificate of Merit from Lieutenant Colonel Russell F. Fiske, unit commanding officer, who himself had logged 12 years of 100 percent attendance at Air Reserve drills. In New York City, First Sergeant William F. Oehl completed his 15th consecutive year of perfect drill attendance. He served as sergeant major of Marine Attack Squadron 132 which drilled at the New York Naval Air Sta-tion. And Company D, 4th Amphibian Tractor Battalion, West Palm Beach, Fla., maintained a perfect attendance figure for an entire quarter to become one of the few Marine Reserve units ever to make such a record. In addition, the unit had a 100 percent record at annual field training for 3 consecutive years.

The year 1963 also marked the retire-ment on 1 November of Chief Warrant Officer Harry W. Warner, a reservist for more than 30 years. Among other things, in those 30-odd years, Mr. Warner had missed only 1 summer training camp,

not counting his period of active duty service during World War II. His final answer to the question of how he felt about leaving the active Reserve is, perhaps, not Gung-ho; but it undoubtedly reflects the attitude of many reservists—"He is well paid that is well satisfied."

The Harder It Is, The Better They Do

As in the other years, Marines with the real problems in reaching weekend drill sites for training seemed to thrive on the challenge and maintain the best attendance records. One Marine with a good record, Corporal Glenn Jenkins, of Bunnell, Fla., undertook a 50-mile hike to his monthly session with Marine Attack Squadron 142 at Jacksonville, but ran into difficulty with police after covering about 35 miles. Jen-kins started at about 5 a.m. from his home to reach the Naval Air Station at Jack-sonville the next morning by 7:30 a.m. However, at about 8 p.m. that evening, he was picked up by a Putnam County squad car for violation of a law which prohibited walking county roads after dark. The Reserve Marine got a free ride for the re-mainder of the distance to his station while police explained the law to him. The 56th Rifle Company, Bellingham, Wash., claimed the record for the average number of miles driven to weekend drills by company officers. The officers, Captain Howard S. Roehl of Edmonds, Wash. (170 miles); Captain John R. White of Issaquah, Wash. (210 miles); Captain Richard S. Brownrigg of Portland, Ore. (536 miles); and 1st Lieutenant Arthur J. Hawker, Jr. of Bellevue, Wash. (180 miles), all maintained 100 percent drill attendance during the year.

Marine reservists continued their tradi-tion of community service during the year.

In Kalamazoo, Mich., Private Donald Rininger, who had enlisted in Company B, 6th Engineer Battalion, only 2 weeks earlier, jumped into the Kalamazoo River to rescue a young boy who had fallen in and appeared to be drowning. He pulled the child ashore and applied artificial respiration until the boy revived. Rininger was recommended for the Treasury Department's Gold Life Saving Medal. In Eugene, Ore., Company B, 5th Engineer Battalion, which already had established enviable good will between its community and the Marine Corps Reserve through a series of community projects, accepted responsibility for (1) removal of an old dam on the nearby McKenzie River which obstructed the flow of the river and caused it to change course; (2) rejuvenation of a Campfire Girls camp; and (3) leveling and grading a number of roads and sites for city parks. Reservists of the 14th Engineer Company, Peoria, Ill., designed and constructed a timber trestle bridge across a creek at the entrance of Neighborhood House Camp, a nonsectarian camp for underprivileged children near Chillicothe. A creek flowing across the entrance to the camp had often flooded following heavy rains, marooning persons inside the camp. Contractor estimates for a bridge had ranged upwards of $10,000. To finish the 78-foot-long bridge in time for the 1963 camping season, the unit was placed on split drills during several months during early summer.

Uniforms made Marine news in 1963, and the biggest shock was the announcement that black shoes, black socks, and black gloves would replace the dark brown Marine accessories. In his request that these items be standardized, the Commandant informed the Defense Supply Agency that, on the shoes alone, direct savings of $106,644 in fiscal years 1964 and 1965 would be realized. Women Marines would use black shoes, gloves, and handbags. During the 2 years, the black gloves for men and women would save $56,054, the Commandant reported. Black accessories were already in use by the Army, Navy, and Air Force. Reserves were given specific instructions for the changeover. Dress shoes and cap frames could be dyed black by the individual, and dyes were made available at some posts and stations. Brown socks were authorized until January 1967. Brown gloves (which could not be dyed satisfactorily) could be worn with black shoes and black cap frames until January 1965. Women Marines were to complete the changeover to a new style black handbag by the end of 1966. Black buttons and emblems for both men's and women's uniforms were decreed at a later date.

Reserve captains on active duty were required to possess the evening and mess dress uniforms, Headquarters announced in July. Previously, only field grade officers had to have these uniforms. A month later the Commandant approved Marine Corps Uniform Board recommendations on male headgear. Thereafter, company grade officers were required to possess only one cap frame, with black leather visor, worn with both service and dress uniforms. Gone was the white helmet liner of the M.P.'s—replaced by the cap frame and white cover. And, the campaign hat was to be issued to drill instructors and Marine Corps rifle and pistol team members only!

While Marine reservists were making the style changes, Philadelphia's 10th Motor Transport Battalion officers held a formal mess night, observing the traditional procedures of formal dress, a fife and drum corps, guests of honor, and a ceremonial entry of the roast beef to the tune of the traditional refrain, "The Roast Beef of Old England." General Van Stockum, Director of Reserve, was the honored guest. All the diners wore full formal Marine dress. Honor guards stood smartly in blues outside the dining room, the wine servers were attired in Marine Corps period uniforms, and the fife and drum corps played as the members of the mess filed into the room and the roast beef was wheeled into the hall. Following the dinner, there were the traditional toasts, speeches, singing, and good fellowship.

Policy Board has High Average

The 1963 Reserve Policy Board recommended 12 policy changes, 11 of which were approved, in whole or in part, by the Commandant. Two new promotion plans were specified, one providing a means whereby "exceptionally well-qualified Reserve corporals may be promoted at about the fourth anniversary of their initial enlistment," and the other providing "Class II Woman Marine reservists opportunity for promotion to the grades of E–3 and E–4." The Commandant referred for additional Headquarters study a recommendation to "alleviate the shortage of staff noncommissioned officers in the Organized Reserve by special promotion procedures and positive effort to retrain present noncommissioned officers in their specialty." The Commandant also approved measures: (1) to promote physical fitness of Reserve personnel by distributing instructional material on conditioning exercises; (2) to give extra retirement credit points to VTU commanding officers for performance of duties in connection with scheduled instruction periods; and (3) to conduct unit training of Organized Marine Corps

Reserve units with the Regular Establishment. The Commandant disapproved the Policy Board's suggested new VTU concept which would have provided for:

> A pilot training program to be known as the "Organized Reserve Training Class," similar in concept to the present Volunteer Training Unit Program, and oriented toward anticipated mobilization requirements but incorporating mandatory participation by lieutenants and junior captains, paid drills and emphasizing training of junior officers; such program to be extended in event it proves successful.

Marine Corps directives on Reserve officer skill deterioration in primary MOS, and Reserve officer career training programs required that the Reserve officer maintain over a span of his inactive commissioned years a balance between MOS refreshers, amphibious staff p l a n n i n g courses, and Junior and Senior level doctrinal training. The reasoning was based on mobilization planning. The very scope of mobilization requirements had made obsolete any program which allowed independent pursuit of specialization, Headquarters reasoned. On the other hand, Headquarters pointed out, periodic MOS refreshers were necessary as a minimum to ensure that the individual was equipped to meet any challenge suddenly thrust upon him by a partial or general call to duty. Officers applying for active duty for training, who had been training along one line of specialization, were required to "get in step" with the career training program. Those not applying for training which they had gone too long without were informed that they would be assigned to the course they needed, rather than the course applied for—unless they advised within 10 days that they could not accept such orders.

Physical fitness and weight control programs were extended early in the year to include Reserves. Although commanders always had been charged with keeping their troops in good physical condition, there was no previous requirement for testing Reserves. Now Organized Reserves would be required to take the standard Physical Readiness Test annually, either at home armories where facilities existed, or during annual field training. Other classes of reservists were to be tested at the nearest Organized Reserve training center or during active duty training. Women Marines were included and all under age 40, regardless of rank or assignment, had to participate.

Requests from reservists for formal instruction were the highest in history, and new courses reflected new thinking. An ambitious program of retraining certain Class III Ready Reserve Officers in the new HAWK missile air defense system began at Twentynine Palms for first lieutenants through lieutenant colonels with appropriate MOS's. After successful completion of a 4-week qualification course, all student officers not on MARTCOM rolls were transferred to that command. Other new courses for Reserve officers included a 2-week artillery refresher course at Fort Sill, Okla., and a 2½-week amphibious reconnaissance course for company grade officers at Coronado.

Women "20-Years Old"

The Women Marines were 20-years old in 1963, having first answered the call to "Free a Marine to Fight" in February 1943. Their Director, Colonel Margaret M. Henderson, said:

> We have become truly a part of what we uphold as the finest military organization in the world. What may lie before us no one can foretell, but I know that the patri-

otic desire to serve our country and our Corps is uppermost in every Woman Marine's heart and binds us as closely together now as it did 20 years ago.

Woman Marines were serving at every major post and station in the United States, in Hawaii, and on special assignment in Europe in 1963. They were assigned duty in 26 occupational fields, including personnel and administration, operational communications, intelligence, logistics, drafting and surveying, disbursing, photography, aerology, aviation operations, and informational services. In some Organized Reserve units, such as Chicago's 2d Battalion, 24th Marines, they held administrative posts. Seven Reserve "Lady Leathernecks" were promoted to lieutenant colonel in 1963, 5 were selected for major, and 7 for captain.

One year after the reorganization of the Marine Corps Reserve which provided predesignated units of a 4th Division/Wing, General Van Stockum reported on the new team:

> The morale is high. The Reserve organization has been extremely popular with these men and they are finding in the division that units congeal into true battalion structure. Major cities with battalion headquarters draw in the outlying companies in nearby towns, giving tactical and administrative entity comparable to that found in the Regular Establishment. The obvious economies in command have correspondingly increased morale within the battalions. Reservists have a strong sense of "belonging" to a growing unit. During the year of new awareness of the division and wing and their mission, the Reserve has stressed the continued importance of units outside the air-ground team organization. These are the separate battalions and companies which reinforce the existing three Regular divisions. When the commanding officers of these separate units express concern at being outside the 4th Division and on the "second team," I inform them that they

are first stringers—and actually may be the first to fight in event of mobilization. In the final analysis, with the first anniversary of the 4th Division/Wing team behind us, the capability for unit response to a mobilization call exists today. Further honing will produce an even finer edge on this capability.

The year 1963 was a year of growth, refinement, and consolidation. It was a year following a major reorganization in which the Marines in reserve took to their new tasks determined to carve a new tradition of readiness. It was a year that looked to the future, as Marine Reserve Captain Ronnie W. Cunningham, jet pilot, was named an Astronaut and assigned to duty at NASA's Manned Spacecraft Center at Houston, Tex. It was the year that 65 girls spent the night at the armory of Montgomery, Ala.'s 38th Rifle Company when hotels were jammed for an upcoming inaugural parade; the year that a Marine corporal found 2 rifles with the same serial number in an armory at Cherry Point; and the year that Master Sergeant Catherine G. Murray became the first enlisted Woman Marine to retire after almost 20 years of active service.

It was a year of hard work, determination, and at least one courteous retort that became a Reserve classic. In the 6th Motor Transport Battalion of Port Newark, N.J.—a unit composed largely of college graduates in a number of professions and fields of business—Major V. Bruce LaSala, Battalion S-1, having trouble with a large number of personnel wandering in the training center corridors during drill, stepped into the hallway to intercept one of the men. "Say lad, what company are you from?" he asked a young Marine, who promptly answered, "Dun and Bradstreet, Sir."

The Year 1964

By early 1964 Marine Reserves had established a firm reputation of readiness, had become known throughout the land as servants of the community as well as the Nation, and were enjoying an increasingly warm reception on Capitol Hill where $35 million was authorized for Marine Reserve activities. The Corps had a new leader, General Wallace M. Greene, Jr., a graduate of the Naval Academy, named the previous year by the late President Kennedy as the 23d Commandant of the Marine Corps. Attention of Marine reservists was focused on Vietnam where, throughout the year, Marine ground advisors trained Vietnamese Marines for combat operations against Communist forces. A Marine helicopter squadron played a large part in airlifting Vietnamese troop and cargo into combat areas and supporting ground operations against the Viet Cong. And, Marine aviators trained their Vietnamese counterparts for missions against the Communists. The Commandant noted:

> This is a tough, dirty war being fought in southeast Asia, reminiscent of the jungle fighting early in World War II. Regretably, the biggest difference between the 2 wars is on the home front. Only a relatively small segment of our population seems to be aware that American men are dying on foreign shores, just as they were in the 1940's.

To best ensure quick response to any crisis which would project Marines ashore to protect the national interest, 3 reinforced battalions were constantly afloat in widely separated areas. A landing team had been on hand in the Mediterranean since before the Korean War. A special landing force cruised with the 7th Fleet in the Western Pacific, and a third unit was afloat in the Caribbean, ready on very short notice for one of several contingency plans.

Basic to the strength of the active force was the increasing use of the helicopter as all Marines were trained in vertical envelopment. The Navy provided new helicopter carriers to expedite this technique, and each LPH could carry a landing force of nearly 2,000 Marines with a squadron of 24 helicopters.

To do battle against the guerrilla and the insurgent, the Corps stated a formal requirement in 1964 for a new counter-insurgency (COIN) type aircraft, designed specifically for air support of limited war operations. This airborne equivalent of the "jeep" was to be a twin-engine, turbo-prop craft—carrying 6 passengers or 3,000 pounds of cargo, and flying as slow as 100 knots on jungle search missions. Ruggedness, simplicity of operation, and the ability to operate from rough clearings and jungle roads were considered necessary qualities.

The Corps also announced plastic canteens which would reduce cost and weight; a new helmet liner, made by bonding layers of ballistic nylon with synthetic resin, which was more comfortable and provided some ballistic protection; and a foxhole-digging kit with which a field Marine could blast a hole about 20 to 36 inches deep and about 2 feet in diameter within minutes. As usual, these items were all to be supplied to the Reserves as soon as possible.

The biggest Reserve weapon news was the modification of the M50 ONTOS anti-tank weapon into the M50A1 for certain Reserve units. Companies A, B, and C of the 4th Antitank Battalion, in Rome, Ga.; Tulare, Calif.; and Amarillo, Tex., received the tank-killer. Improvements to

the ONTOS, in service since 1955, included a more powerful engine, a night-firing capability which utilized a left- and right-azimuth scale, elevation quadrant and range card procedures for night firing, and improved, longer track life. The M50's destructive features remained: 6 106 recoilless rifles, 4 50 caliber spotting rifles and the 30 caliber machinegun.

Early in the year the Marine Corps announced that the Army and the Atomic Energy Commission had developed a nuclear projectile which could be fired from any 155mm artillery piece, and had a similar range, about 8 miles. Training devices were provided for artillerymen learning the techniques of assembling and firing the nuclear round. A "duplex" cartridge which fired 2 bullets instead of 1, thereby significantly increasing a soldier's ability to hit his target at close range, was developed and adopted for Marine use. The cartridge was similar in appearance to the conventional round. However, a second bullet was nestled behind the visible one for successive projection, and was designed not to follow the first but to proportionately displace itself in order to increase the radius of the strike area. When fired, the first bullet traveled the line of fire and the second followed a path which was slightly off-course.

Leathernecks had been wearing uniforms made from kersey wool material for more than 150 years when the Marine Corps announced, late in 1962, that it was making available through cash sales outlets new winter service uniforms made of a serge material. The new greens retained the color and style of the existing uniforms, and were authorized for wear by enlisted personnel and officers.

New materials and equipment are highly desirable—if they get to the troops—and in a speech to a Navy League group in San Diego, Calif., in mid-1964, Reserve Brigadier General Klenke noted that the Reserve forces were in no way slighted. He said:

> I am proud to be able to tell you that the Marine Corps is now procuring its equipment on the basis of 4 division/wing teams. This means that the Reserve is or soon will be as well-equipped as the Regular forces. This is tremendously important in the event of mobilization, but it is also extremely significant in our training. Our Regulars can mesh with our Reserves in training, providing the latest and best in technical instruction because the family of weapons is identical. The Regulars and Reserves can—and we're bending every effort to increase the amount of this—actually train together in the air, and on the ground, in joint exercises of various sizes.

Combined Exercises—Year Round

The concept of combined exercises which had proved so effective during annual field training the past few years was applied to training for individual units, and unit exercises showed surprising realism. The 4th Division/Wing team was expected to be ready to go in a short time following mobilization, but units had only 39 days available each year for training. To make training as realistic as possible, many units combined and joined hands, getting out of the classroom into the field for joint operations.

One weekend drill turned into a full-scale air-ground-artillery exercise for Washington State reservists during October. Units from Seattle, Bellingham, Tacoma, and Yakima got together for a joint exercise at the Army's Yakima firing center. Planning for the operation was done by 2 Seattle Volunteer Training Units. Marine Transport Squadron 353 started the maneuver by picking up members of Bellingham's 56th Rifle Company

and flying them to a municipal airport near the training site. Observers from Tacoma's 23d Rifle Company and communicators from the 4th Shore Party Battalion, Seattle, also were flown in VMR–353 transports. Five choppers of Marine Medium Helicopter Squadron 770 were on location in Yakima to ferry troops from the municipal airport to the exercise area. A vertical assault lift carried riflemen into the maneuver area on the desert where 1 of Yakima's 8-inch howitzers was in position. The infantry unit consolidated the position defending the howitzer and then received impromptu instruction on the weapon from battery NCO's. The Ground reservists practiced antiguerrilla warfare that night as members of the Bellingham Rifle Company attempted to infiltrate battery lines. Lieutenant Colonel S. Frank Leis, Commanding Offcer of the Seattle Marine Air Reserve Training Detachment, said the operation was an example of what can be done by Reserve units, working together, combining their varied missions for realistic training on home grounds rather than depending on summer training alone.

Marine reservists from Canton, Ohio, held a live-firing exercise at Quantico to sharpen their shooting eyes and to get the additional benefits of training away from their home armory. The 110 members of the 6th 105mm Howitzer Battery, Force Troops, were airlifted aboard C–119's at Grosse Ile, Mich. Pilots of VMF–221, Memphis, made what was billed as the "longest cross-country flight of a Marine Air Reserve squadron utilizing air-to-air refueling," when they flew from their home station to Nellis AFB, Nev., and returned during a weekend drill. The 2-day exercise began on a Saturday, when two 4-plane flights of AF–1E Furies left

Memphis for a rendezvous point with refuelers near Oklahoma City. Awaiting the Memphis pilots at 20,000 feet were 2 C–130F Hercules refuelers from the 3d Marine Wing. Each Fury was allotted 10 minutes to complete the fueling operation. As the fighter aircraft streaked on to remain overnight in Nevada, the tankers headed for Amarillo, Tex., to await Sunday's operation. The return leg was a repeat of the previous day's maneuver, using a refueling point just east of Amarillo. "The exercise has provided a good indicator of Marine Air Reserve capability," said Lieutenant Colonel James R. Weaver, Squadron Commander.

Jackson, Miss.'s 2d 105mm Howitzer Battery landed 6 artillery pieces on the shore at Gulfport, Miss., in a weekend exercise which tested the unit's ability to transport the weapons with amphibious vehicles. Some 100 Jackson reservists joined forces with members of Company C, 4th Amphibian Tractor Battalion of Gulfport, in *Operation Rollback*, a defensive action against a hypothetical enemy force which threatened an amphibious landing in the area.

Copperhead and Sirocco

Operation Copperhead, the 1964 Marine Reserve air-ground exercise at Camp Lejeune, involved more than 2,000 reservists in a 3-day exercise. The problem was set up this way: *Copperhead* took its name from an unfriendly—and imaginary—island south and east of the friendly South American country of Conifer, which had successfully ousted an alien-controlled government and established a government friendly to the United States. Copperhead had landed aggressor units on Conifer's soil and was believed to be moving toward the provisional capital and a strategic airfield. Conifer asked the United States for help, and the Marine unit was airlifted from the States and prepared to disperse the aggressors with the assistance of helicopter, attack, fighter, and support aircraft of the 4th Marine Air Wing.

The Reserve Marine Expeditionary Unit was commanded by Colonel Richard A. Vanderhoof, of Cincinnati, Commanding Officer of the 3d Staff Group from Dayton, Ohio. Reserve Provisional Marine Air Group 1 was headed by Lieutenant Colonel Maurice D. Russell, Commanding Officer of Marine Air Reserve Group 7, based at Andrews Air Force Base, Washington, D.C.

Major General Alpha L. Bowser, Commanding General at Camp Lejeune, was Exercise Director and was assisted by Lieutenant Colonel George A. Bickerstaff, of Richmond, Va., Commanding Officer of the 6th Staff Group there. Bickerstaff also acted as Chief Umpire as his Staff Group had prepared the Operations Plan for *Copperhead*.

Marine Air Reserve units operating from Cherry Point during the exercise were Marine Attack Squadron 134 of Los Alamitos, Calif.; Marine Fighter Squadron 124 of Memphis; Marine Photo Squadron 4 of New Orleans; and Marine Air Control Squadron 20 and Marine Attack Squadron 144 of Jacksonville, Fla.

Operation Copperhead got underway with air strikes by Reserve units under operational control of Provisional Marine Air Group 1 and a daylight landing by helicopter and amphibian tractors of companies of the 3d Battalion, 25th Marines, 4th Marine Division, from Ohio under command of Lieutenant Colonel Ray Jorz of Cleveland. Aggressor forces were formed from the 3d Infantry Battalion of

St. Louis, Mo., commanded by Lieutenant Colonel Earl F. Voelz. Umpires were attached to all friendly and aggressor Ground units and to all Air units. They controlled the problem by assessing damage suffered by troops under air or artillery attack, indicated by smoke bombs, and ruled on casualties suffered by patrolling and attacking units in the 15 square miles of scrub pine zone of operations.

Operation Sirocco was an air-ground field exercise conducted at Twentynine Palms during the 1964 annual field training period. The mock war, involving 1,400 reservists, was waged over a large portion of the 1,000-square-mile Marine Corps Base. Extensive unit training in weapons, tactics, and leadership preceded the exercise. *Sirocco* had 3 objectives: to indoctrinate units in the Marine Expeditionary Unit (MEU) concept; to train and test small unit leaders; and to improve the readiness of the individual Marine through participation in an airground team exercise. Nine separate Reserve units took part. The main infantry force was made up of units from the 3d Battalion, 24th Marines. The 6th Communications Company of Alameda, Calif., and the 4th 105mm Howitzer Battery of Madison, Wis., provided support. The objective of the MEU was capture of an aircraft and rocket base located near the center of the desert camp. Some 300 troops from Reserve units on 2-weeks duty acted as aggressors.

A giant Reserve field artillery group exercise was conducted at Twentynine Palms during the summer, and, for the first time in the history of Reserve field artillery shoots, an entire Regular battalion (the 3d Battalion, 11th Marines) also participated. Reserve units involved in the exercise were the 3d 155mm Howitzer Battery of Con-

nellsville, Pa., the 4th 8-inch Howitzer Battery of El Paso, and the 8th and 9th 155mm Gun Batteries of Oklahoma City.

In all, 26,844 Marine reservists were trained during the summer, with nearly one-third of them on duty at Camp Lejeune. Units were afforded a wide variety of training, including desert warfare at Twentynine Palms and mountain warfare at Bridgeport, Calif. Engineers built housing units at Vieques and put together a combat town at Camp Pendleton. Amphibious training also was featured at Landing Force Training Units on both coasts. Nine Reserve units—about 4 percent of the total number of Marine summer trainees—flew to Puerto Rico for training at Vieques. One unit, the 6th Rifle Company of Little Rock, Ark., engaged in extensive field problems and served as aggressor forces against a Marine Expeditionary Unit of Regulars. Late in the training period, the unit observed a bomb and rocket demonstration given by VMA–322, the Reserve Air unit from South Weymouth, Mass.

Stewart for Van Stockum

Early in the year Brigadier General Van Stockum, who had served as Director of Reserve for 21 months, was reassigned as Commanding General, Landing Force Training Unit, Pacific, at Coronado, Calif. His relief was Brigadier General Joseph L. Stewart, holder of the Silver Star and former Commanding General, Marine Corps Base, Twentynine Palms, Calif.

General Van Stockum wrote in his "Reserve Report" in the *Marine Corps Gazette*:

A basic school classmate and friend of long standing, General Stewart already has made a significant contribution to the Reserve through his fine training program at Twentynine Palms. He is taking up one of the most challenging and rewarding assignments a Marine general officer can hold— for there is yet much to be done to improve our mobilization readiness.

General Stewart toured summer training facilities during annual field exercises and noted the continuing need for combined training. He reported:

> From my observation, I believe there are 2 significant lessons apparent from these exercises: we need more Reserve air-ground training on a regular and continuing basis throughout the year, and we need increased integration of training of all types, such as tank-infantry and artillery-infantry. Dispersed as we are in 211 training centers, we need to seek every means possible to train with other units of the air-ground team, particularly during annual training duty.

In a subsequent report General Stewart noted the continuing support provided Ground units by various Reserve Air organizations throughout the country. During the summer 80 Marine Reserve Ground units were airlifted to 15 active duty training sites throughout continental United States, Hawaii, and Puerto Rico. The 4 Reserve transport squadrons flew 2,765 flight hours, making 110 individual airlifts for Aviation and Ground units alike. Well-planned and diversified programs of individual and unit training were climaxed by the large air-ground exercises. Air support for *Copperhead* was provided by Reserve Aviation units deployed at MCAS, Cherry Point and MCALF, Bogue Field. Marine Air Reserve units operated from MCAS, El Toro; MCAS, Yuma; MCAF, Santa Ana; and MCB, Twentynine Palms, in support of *Sirocco*. Twelve Reserve helicopter squadrons, operating from both land and sea, flew over 8,000 hours—a creditable record, representing an average of 49 hours per pilot during the 2-week periods each squadron was deployed. Day and night carrier operations were conducted aboard ships of the Atlantic and Pacific fleets. HMM–764, Los Alamitos, became the first Air Reserve unit to deploy to Hawaii, operating from MCAS, Kaneohe. HMM–769, from Alameda, participated in high altitude and mountain training in the Sierra mountains.

Increased proficiency in bombing, rocketry, and air-to-ground gunnery was stressed by Reserve attack squadrons operating out of MCAS, Yuma; NAAS, Fallon, Nevada; NS, Roosevelt Roads; and MCAS, Cherry Point. At NAAS, Fallon, attack squadrons from Alameda provided close air support for the 23d Rifle Company of Tacoma, Wash., in an exercise at Hawthorne, Nev. Fighter squadron training stressed air-to-air gunnery and air intercepts. The first Reserve squadron to be equipped with F–8 Crusaders (VMF–112 of Dallas) deployed at MCAS, Beaufort, for 2 weeks of intensive training in their new aircraft. Controllers of Reserve air control squadrons, training with Regular Marine Corps units, made more than 860 intercepts. And the Air Reserve's 3 HAWK missile batteries underwent training at Twentynine Palms.

9,000 Hours—No Accident

Air Reserve units won an array of honors and awards during the year as the intensive training and continued affiliation with Regular units began to show results. The Marine fighter squadron that had recorded the second highest number of confirmed kills during World War II (VMF–221 of Memphis) completed its eighth straight year of flight operations without a single mishap. It was a record unequalled in Marine Air Reserve history. The unit reported that total hours flown during the accident-free period were estimated to be in excess of 9,000.

Marine Fighter Squadron 611 of Glenview, Ill., received the Chief of Naval Operations Safety Award for outstanding safety during the year, and VMA–322, South Weymouth, Mass.; VMR–234, Twin Cities, Minn.; and HMM–772, Willow Grove, also were selected as winners of the top CNO safety award. The Air reservists competed for the award in 4 categories: attack aircraft, jet; fighter aircraft, jet; propeller-driven aircraft; and helicopters. It was the first time that a Chicago area Reserve unit had won the Chief of Naval Operations award since Marines became eligible in 1955. The Marine Air Reserve Training Command broke its own record for consecutive accident-free days of flight operations for the third time in 2 fiscal years when it passed 130 days in March, on Friday, the Thirteenth!

In a move to give Reserves additional contact with Regular units, the Marine Corps embarked on a trial program early in 1964 in which Reserve officers were used as umpires to observe and assist in evaluating exercises of Regular units. At the request of the exercise director for *Winter Nite*, conducted at Twentynine Palms in February and March, 50 Reserve officers were furnished to act as umpires. General Stewart reported:

> Their performance in the umpire role was excellent. It brought about a recommendation for future exploitation of the use of citizen Marines to avoid stripping units of their Regular officers to do the job. We expect to use several hundred such Reserve umpires this year in other exercises to the benefit of Regular and Reserves alike.

General Stewart also announced that Reserve units would be augmenting and participating with the 1st Marine Division at Camp Pendleton in May and September division exercises in 1965.

Two Reserve officers were selected for promotion to major general and 2 for advancement to brigadier general in 1964. President Lyndon B. Johnson approved the report of the selection board, and Brigadier Generals George E. Tomlinson of Washington, D.C., and John L. Winston of Gladstone, N.J., advanced to two-star rank. Named brigadier generals were Colonels Russell A. Bowen of Los Altos, Calif., and Douglas J. Peacher of Evanston, Ill.

An equally significant if somewhat typical promotion story, in the eyes of reservists of Montgomery, Ala., was that of Reserve Captain James E. Nelson, Commanding Officer of the 38th Rifle Company. Nelson had joined the company 9 years previously—as a private. Commissioned through the Platoon Leader Class, he had served with the 2d Marine Division at Camp Lejeune and the 3d Division on Okinawa, returning to his former Reserve unit as a platoon leader.

In New Orleans, Marine Reservists helped reunite 96 children lost during the Mardi Gras, thus continuing a long-time tradition of Marine Corps Reserve service to the community. In Roanoke, Va., members of the 5th Engineer Company completed construction of a mile-long road which linked 2 dead end roads and gave dozens of school children more convenient school bus service. The company also built 5 sleeping cabins and a troop meeting house at a local Girl Scout camp and built picnic benches for use at a recreation center for the needy. Members of the inspector-instructor staff of the 61st Rifle

Company in Lexington, Ky., provided marksmanship training at the Bluegrass Council Scout camp—an 8-week program which involved more than 1,200 boys each season. Each Marine assigned to the task spent an entire week at the camp as a staff member. Marine Corps rifle range techniques were employed.

Elsewhere during 1964, reservists participated in 2 important rescues. Captain Grady V. Gardner, Inspector-Instructor of the 56th Rifle Company in Bellingham, Wash., a volunteer member of the Bellingham Mountain Rescue Council, helped save the life of a northern California woman who was injured while climbing the 8,000-foot Shark Fin Tower about 100 miles southeast of Bellingham. Captain Gardner and his rescue party climbed 4,000 feet to the woman after a helicopter failed to reach her in the foggy weather. A helicopter crew from HMM–722, stationed at MARTD, Willow Grove, was on a training maneuver when it got a call to pick up a Navy doctor and proceed to a quarry near Swarthmore, Pa., where a man had fallen 50 feet from the top of the quarry to a 5-foot-wide ledge. After a number of attempts to drop a line to the man had failed, the rescuers lowered a litter and the victim was fastened to the metal basket. A cable was thrown from the helicopter and fastened to the litter, and the man was lifted slowly to the top.

Toys-for-Tots, 17 Years Old

Without a doubt one of the most successful community relations programs ever conducted by an organization is the Toys-for-Tots program, sponsored annually by Marine reservists which by 1964, in its 17th year, had spread to 200 major communities. Over 16 million needy children had received approximately 45 million toys collected during this period. In 1963, the Marines collected 3,515,264 toys and distributed them to 1,147,813 children who were made a little happier at Christmastime. As 1964 campaigns various Marine Corps districts had their own special promotions. In the 14th District, the campaign kickoff was in the form of an open house where the Honorable William Richardson, Lieutenant Governor of Hawaii, proclaimed December "Hawaii's Toys-for-Tots Month." In the 12th District, Mayor George Christopher of San Francisco designated 1 December to 20 December "Toys-for-Tots Days." In the 1st District, more than 2,500 toys were collected in Yankee Stadium while the New York Giants met the Washington Redskins. Other dignitaries issued proclamations launching the drives in their areas. The vast number of children who are made happier each year, of itself, would be all the justification needed for the Toys-for-Tots program, General Stewart noted:

> But the fact that it serves as a natural catalyst to draw together the citizens and the Marine reservists of a community is an additional benefit representing good will that cannot be measured in terms of toys alone.

Of 10 recommendations made by the 1964 Reserve Policy Board, the Commandant approved 7. One of the 7 approved was a recommendation that Reserve promotions from corporal to sergeant be based on Reserve needs rather than on the percentages computed by the needs of the Regular Establishment. The Commandant followed the Board's recommendation in disapproving a plan by which commanding officers could temporarily promote Reserve NCO's beyond the rank of corporal.

As recommended by the Policy Board,

the Director of Reserve turned down a proposal to permit staff NCO's in the Fleet Marine Corps Reserve to join Organized Reserve units, drill for pay, and earn additional retirement credits. In vetoing such use of the 20-year men, the Board called for increasing the on-board staff NCO strength in Organized units.

In a speech to the Naval Affairs Committee of the Reserve Officers Association in October, General Stewart touched on a manpower problem faced by the Reserve:

> We are authorized to have a strength of 45,500 in the Organized Reserve. This gives us only a 70- to 80-percent manning level in our units, and we have been seeking to obtain an increase in order to meet our mobilization requirements. While this effort has not been successful in preceding years, we are still shooting for an ultimate Organized strength of about 59,000, acquired in annual increments, which would put our manning levels to 100 percent. We are asking for 48,000 in fiscal year 1966 as the first increment.

In addition to a general shortage in numbers of personnel, General Stewart noted that the Marine Reserve did not have sufficient young company grade officers and experienced junior NCO's:

> These shortages amount to about 400 company grade officers and about 10 times that many prior-service sergeants and corporals. This does not mean that the billets are empty. It does mean that the wrong ranks are in the spaces, since we find more senior officers filling the company grade officer billets and more junior Marines filling the NCO billets.

But, he concluded, despite personnel problems, there were few problems related to lack of leadership or lack of morale. Marine reservists knew their mission and their leaders knew their jobs.

> Of all our traditions, the spirit of the whole, the oneness of the Corps within its

Regular and Reserve Establishments, is the most outstanding. Our Regular Establishment must be supported by an efficient and well-trained Reserve which has often been referred to as the Marine Corps "Secret Weapon." The Marine Reserve has well earned that title. It is a substantial operation that is, and always has been, highly motivated and always prepared and ready to answer its country's call to arms.

Perhaps the essence of this close relationship is best expressed by the very brief remarks of General Holland M. Smith, when called to the platform to receive a standing ovation at the 1964 Marine Corps Reserve Officers Association National Military Conference in Boston. With tears in his eyes, the 83-year-old crusty Fleet Marine Force, Pacific, Commanding General of World War II looked at his Reserve audience and said from his heart, "I promise you this. Until this twilight zone deepens into darkness, my memory of you will go hand in hand with my fervent prayer for your happiness and health." The "Amen" of the audience was almost audible.

The Legacy of General Maas

On the minus side, the year 1964 also witnessed the departure from the scene of Major General Melvin J. Maas, a man who had become a legend within his own lifetime, popularly known as "Mr. Reserve," and a real friend of all Marines everywhere. General Maas died at the Bethesda Naval Hospital on 14 April 1964 after a long illness. He was buried with full military honors at Arlington National Cemetery. He was survived by his wife, Katherine, his son Joseph, and 3 daughters, including Major Patricia A. Maas, a Regular Marine. Joe had gone into the 6-month program while in his teens and has his honorable discharge.

A great deal was written and said about General Maas, in the White House, in the Congress, and in the Corps. In the front-page editorial "A Bright Spirit Passes," in the May *Word*, Colonel Hanson summed it up for the Marine Corps Reserve:

> No one person in the history of our country has ever devoted himself more selflessly to his Nation and the people of his country than did Mel Maas. Without fear, he faced up to many, many crises in legislation and in war which would have turned lesser men's heads aside.
>
> Mel Maas is more responsible for the creation of the Reserve Forces of this Nation that saved this country from defeat in World War II than any other American, living or dead. His foresight and intestinal fortitude forced acceptance of the Reserve principle upon those unwilling to face up to the matter.
>
> We will not go into the many fields which Mel served so ably but we state to all who are members of the organization which he founded in 1926, to all of you members of MCROA, that although this bright spirit has passed from our physical scene, the memory of his dedication and the thought that we might let him down should serve to keep each and every one of us on the firing line to maintain the ideals which he established for us.
>
> May God rest his soul. May we inherit a touch of his courage to carry on the work with which he ennobled his fellow countrymen.

General Greene's statement also referred to his spirit. He said: "General Maas' spirit will forever be a shining example to all Marines present and future."

The Year 1965

More than 20 times since the close of World War II, the Navy-Marine Corps team had demonstrated America's determination to preserve world peace. In Lebanon, Thailand, and Korea, the Marines went ashore to forcibly represent our interest. In the Formosa Strait and in Cuban waters, mere presence of the fleet deterred aggressive action. The Marines fought again in 1965—in 2 widely separated corners of the globe. They achieved heartening success in Santo Domingo where the 4th Marine Expeditionary Brigade, an 8,000-man force, protected American interests in the battle between rebels and counterrevolutionaries. It was the fifth landing by U.S. Marines there since the first landing in 1800 when Captain Dan Carmick's troops from the U.S.S. *Constitution* went ashore at Port au Platte, overran a shore battery, and captured HMS *Sandwich*, a British frigate in possession of the French. By the time the modern-day Marines had withdrawn in June 1965, they had been in the island country for slightly more than 1 month and had stood sentry duty, exchanged sporadic rifle and machinegun fire with the rebels, and assisted in protection of the civilian population. "Our fire discipline was good. . . . I'm very proud of all the Marines . . . their conduct and their attitude," said the Brigade Commander, Brigadier General John G. Bouker, a 1936 Platoon Leaders Class graduate and a former Deputy Director, Marine Corps Reserve.

In Vietnam Marines fought harder and achieved less against a tenacious Viet Cong guerrilla force. The year opened with a small detachment of Marine advisers supporting the ground and air operations of the South Vietnamese. It closed with the commitment of much of the 1st and 3d Marine Divisions and supporting air wing—the III Marine Amphibious Force—fighting a full-scale war in that far-off land. Americans used a new term in discussing conduct of the Vietnam fighting: "escalation." As had been the case in Korea, the war in Vietnam often was described as largely different from anything modern-day Marines had experienced before. Some Marines were wounded by sharpened bamboo stakes embedded in the ground near pathways and roads. At least 1 Marine cut himself on an ice cream cone—and later learned that guerrillas were freezing glass slivers and selling the ice to parched troops in the field. The enemy was everywhere—and often nowhere to be found. It was a frustrating war, calling for new disciplines and new training—for Regulars and Reserves alike, for many of the younger Marines were Reserves serving out an active duty part of obligated service.

Although the Ready Reserve had not been called by year-end, training had been intensified and a number of reservists had been invited to apply for extended active duty. And—for the first time since the Korean War—the Marine Corps turned to the draft. "The current commitments of the Marine Corps present compelling reasons for accomplishing the buildup, from 193,000 previously authorized to 223,000 Marines as soon as possible," Commandant Greene said in requesting 4,050 draftees in November. The buildup, authorized in August 1965, added a requirement of 30,000 new Marines to the original recruitment objectives of 36,000 personnel for the year. The demand was beyond the capabilities of Marine recruiters on such short notice, even though 757 Reserves volunteered for extended active duty the first 2 months.

During hearings before the House Armed Services Committee on 18 August,

the Commandant indicated that he saw no reason to have the 4th Division/Wing Team sitting around on the West Coast waiting for an assignment. When there was a positive job for them to do, he added, he would ask that they be called—and was certain they would respond quickly and well.

An information bulletin, released by Headquarters Marine Corps at about the same time, was particularly significant to reservists:

> There are 2 basic ways to effect a quick buildup of forces such as that presently required: mobilize the Reserve or draw from the civilian manpower pool as rapidly as possible. The Marine Corps Reserve unquestionably has the capability of meeting the increased strength requirement. However, the Reserve is not being utilized at this time because a partial mobilization to fill this support role would largely destroy its capability to respond to its primary mission of providing a ready combat force in the form of the 4th Division/Wing Team.

In August the Commandant put out a call for Reserve officers to voluntarily request extended active duty by way of a Standard Written Agreement (SWAG) to assist in the buildup. All officers whose date of original commissioning as a second lieutenant was 4 June 1955 or later were eligible to request a 1-year tour. By the end of October, 183 had signed up. Recruit training at Parris Island and San Diego was shortened from 12 to 8 weeks. The reduction was accomplished by intensifying training and increasing training hours each week, in much the same fashion as 8-week training programs had been tailored to meet the increased manpower requirements of World War II and Korea.

Manpower continued to be a problem area for the Reserves. General Stewart had told a Reserve luncheon audience in Philadelphia in April:

> Our Organized Reserve strength of 45,000 gives us only 70- to 80-percent manning level in our units. We actually need—to meet our commitments—something in the nature of 59,000, gained in incremental steps. We had hoped that we would be able to go to 48,000 this fiscal year and reach 59,000 by 1970. Because of this, we do not have certain additional 4th Division/Wing team units that we need—such as headquarters elements, some service and supply elements, the growth in existing units, or some additional combat support Force Troops units needed in support of the Marine Corps four division/wing team force structure.

Prior-Service NCO Percentage Up

Another type of manpower problem—shortage in certain types of personnel—was partially solved during the year, not by action of the Secretary of the Navy, but by hard-working recruiters and Reserve Liaison and Training officers in the field. Organized units long had been short of prior-service NCO's and young officers. Prior-service NCO's stood at 20 percent in 1963. By 1964 this figure had jumped to 26 percent, and a realistic goal of 30 percent was set for 1965.

Two orders from Headquarters gave strength to improved recruiting of prior-service NCO's and officers. One established a sound recruiting program within the Reserve. The other revised an existing order, strongly reemphasizing the indoctrination program for Marines being discharged or released from active duty. Headquarters also issued several new pamphlets pointing up what a Reserve career had to offer. Every NCO and young officer leaving active duty at a major installation was briefed by a Re-

serve Liaison and Training officer with complete information on the Reserve program. The program worked quickly and well for officers, but lagged somewhat with NCO's. More NCO's with "hard skills" were needed, primarily because of the increasing issue of new, complex weapons and equipment to the Reserve.

General Stewart pointed out:

> The "hard skill" electronics, engineer specialist, or aviation mechanic represents the most difficult training problem we have in the Reserve program, due to the lack of time available to train the 6-month enlistee. If we can retain the technical talents of Regulars as they leave the Regular service, it will be a useful accomplishment. Every prior-service NCO who joins an Organized Reserve unit represents a savings to the Marine Corps of about $20,000. This is what it takes—as a sort of mean average—to bring a new Marine up to that NCO's level. We don't expect to fill the entire Reserve with prior-service Marines, but we do want as many as we can use, and we do want to save as many of those $20,000 bills as possible.

At Headquarters, G–1 section planners took a look at the possibility of shortening time-in-grade requirements for promotion of some junior officers. Considered was the selection of some captains in their fourth year of commissioned service. Time-in-grade requirements for warrant officers in grades W–2 and W–3 were cut from 6 to 4 years. Promotion time from W–1 to W–2 remained at 3 years. Headquarters was attempting to balance warrant officer grades within the rank structure, while increasing the number of warrant officers in all grades from 1,500 to 1,750. At the time 1,300 of the 1,500 warrant officers were in the 2 lower grades.

A new detachment was added to the rolls of the Marine Air Reserve Training Command—but it had a slightly different name and a completely different mission. The new unit, called Marine Air Reserve Missile Training Detachment, was located at Twentynine Palms and was formed of some 75 Regular Marines who had the mission of providing equipment, maintenance support, and training support for all elements of the 4th Light Anti-Aircraft Missile (LAAM) Battalion. The Regular Marines added 3 LAAM batteries as new units in 1965, each to form a fourth firing battery for one of the Corps' 3 HAWK-firing LAAM battalions. The addition of the fourth battery to each battalion provided 2 to 3 times more coverage than the previous 3-battery formations. Defense in depth was thus provided, regardless of the direction of the attack. The new alignment also provided increased capability to cope with possible enemy saturation raids.

Reserves Get ADP Pay System

The Reserves received good pay-check news on two separate fronts. In August President Johnson signed into law a billion-dollar pay bill which affected the retirement and drill-pay rates of reservists, as well as the pay checks of Regulars and reservists on extended active duty. Some 1.5 million reservists and retired personnel were affected. In addition to increases ranging from 6 to 22 percent, the bill included provisions which provided a variable reenlistment bonus to men shipping over for the first time in critical skills, provisions for regularly bringing military pay up-to-date through Presidential study each year, and complete overhaul of the pay structure every 4 years. During the summer, the Reserves adopted a centralized personnel accounting system com-

pletely compatible with the Regular system. Located in Kansas City, Mo., the automatic data processing installation was designed to relieve about 190 Marines; to save about 1.2 million dollars annually; to provide virtually up-to-the-minute personnel data; to afford smooth administrative transition in the event of mobilization. More important—to the drill-pay reservists, at least—it would mean they would be getting paid every month instead of every quarter.

General Stewart noted:

> While our personnel have been trained and ready to go, our personnel accounting has been a little archaic and out-of-step with the Regulars. It has been decentralized to districts and the Marine Air Reserve Training Command; it has been slow—with data running as much as several months behind actuality—and it has been burdensome.

Now, data would be as up-to-date as the latest unit diary.

Also up-to-date were the 50 Class II Reserve officers performing appropriate duty with pay with the Selective Service System. The Corps has 75 billets for Reserve officers who would report to the Selective Service System in event of mobilization. Today there are 11 Reserve officers serving on extended active duty with Selective Service. Two Marine Reserve Selective Service units, 1 in Houston and another at Pittsburgh, Pa., provide training opportunities in these areas. Other Marines serve with Selective Service training units of the other services.

A support weapon shelved by the Corps in 1956—the 60mm mortar—returned to service with Marine forces in Vietnam. This lightweight weapon, often called the company commander's personal artillery, had been replaced by the 81mm mortar which had double the range of the 60mm.

However, the smaller weapon had the advantage of being easy to carry on patrol. It was put into operation with few difficulties—spare parts and ammunition had been stored in dumps in the United States since the phase-out. At that time a number of Marines, lamenting the loss of a favorite weapon, had said, "Wait until the shooting starts; the 60 will be back."

An experimental, lightweight green uniform, which could be worn throughout the year in some climates and as a warm-weather uniform in warmer areas, was started on a testing cycle which could result in adoption as an official uniform as early as fiscal year 1973. The uniform, made from a new 8½ ounce polyester-wool material, was issued to officers and enlisted personnel at several stations for wear-testing. Marines accepted a new combat boot during the year—the same boot that the Army was using. Adopting the new boot, with its enlarged eyelets and round laces, resulted in economy in logistic supply and procurement.

Not all equipment development in 1965 was as routine as mortars, boots, and uniform materials. A new turbine-powered hydrofoil amphibian vehicle, specifically designed to provide improved performance during amphibious assault operations, was delivered. The vehicle, capable of operating overland on wheels or through the water on the hull and hydrofoils, was designated the LVHX–1, or Landing Force Amphibious Support Vehicle, Hydrofoil. Designed to operate from a "mother" ship 50 miles offshore to inland logistic support areas, the vessel could "fly" through rough seas at up to 35 knots, or drive overland at speeds up to 40 miles per hour.

The trend toward combined arms training was intensified in 1965 as Organized

Reserve units from coast to coast shared training periods, often at remote areas, to sharpen their mobilization readiness. Organized units trained with equipment as modern as their Regular counterparts, and major items were scheduled for modernization along with the Regular FMF. Flame tanks, 90mm gun tanks, ONTOS, and LVT's had the latest modifications applied. Newly introduced equipment was provided Organized Reserve units as soon as possible after the Regular forces were equipped. An example was the 155mm self-propelled howitzer (M–109) which was delivered to the FMF in August 1964. Two months later, the general support artillery battalion of the 4th Division—at Birmingham and Chattanooga—had it.

General Stewart told the national conference of the Marine Corps Reserve Officers Association, meeting in Washington, D.C., in May:

> One of my major goals since becoming Director of the Marine Corps Reserve has been to increase air-ground training during the year, not just at annual field training, in order to weld the Reserve into a truly great air-ground team. We have established tactical air control parties in 5 of our infantry battalions throughout the country and MARTCOM is providing well-qualified naval aviators from attack squadrons on a temporary duty basis to act as air liaison/forward air controllers. These organizations are required to plan and participate in at least one local air-ground exercise annually. We have had several of these exercise already, and they have proved highly successful.

Six Organized Ground Units to MARTCOM

General Stewart also announced that in line with further refinement of the Division/Wing Team, 6 Organized Ground units had been transferred to General Elwood's command to help in the manning of aviation support units such as Marine air base squadrons and headquarters and maintenance squadrons which had been hampered by authorized strength limitations. In May a communications battalion, a motor transport battalion, 2 engineer companies, a motor transport maintenance company, and an engineer maintenance company were transferred. "This will greatly increase the capabilities and readiness of aviation support type units," General Stewart said.

Intense realism was the byword in unit training during the year, and throughout the country, reservists departed their training centers to battle weather, difficult terrain, and tenacious aggressor forces, usually composed of other Reserve personnel.

Nearly 1,000 Marine reservists sharpened their air-ground skills in *Operation Scarecrow* against a "guerrilla force" dug into the hills west of the Naval Auxiliary Air Station, Crow's Landing, Calif., early in February, in one of the year's first combined exercises. The 2-day exercise, testing the abilities of units of the 23d Marines from San Bruno and Stockton, against a small force of guerrillas in a mountainous region, proved this type of combat required rigid training. Air units in training at the Alameda Naval Air Station, Alameda, Calif., and Marine Attack Squadron 133, Headquarters and Maintenance Squadron 42, Marine Air Base Squadron 42, Medium Helicopter Squadron 769, and Marine Air Traffic Control Unit 72 also participated. The missiles of Battery D, 3d LAAM Battalion, San Jose, kept the guerrilla air force in check.

Nearly 1,000 Marine reservists of the 1st Battalion, 24th Marines, from Toledo, Ohio, and the southern Michigan area,

traveled to Fort Custer near Battle Creek, Mich., to participate in *Operation Lancer* in early April. Battalion Commander Lieutenant Colonel Harold W. Thompson announced the overnight problem would consist of a battalion-size maneuver to test the reservists' combat readiness. The operation began with 1 platoon of each of the battalion units being airlifted into a designated area. As the battalion moved through the problem toward its objective, it was opposed by aggressor forces from Company B, Toledo. Near-zero temperatures and a heavy blanket of snow provided further obstacles.

In April, 3 Missouri units combined forces for a weekend exercise at Fort Leonard Wood, Mo. Heavy rains just prior to the maneuver caused deep mud, swollen streams, and poor visibility, creating a rugged test of the abilities of participating units to engage in large-scale unit tactical training. The 3d Infantry Battalion, St. Louis; 12th Rifle Company, Springfield; and 30th Rifle Company, Kansas City, attacked an aggressor unit dug into the rolling and heavily wooded countryside that makes up most of the terrain of the giant base.

During a storm which dumped 6 inches of snow on the Delaware Valley, Battery L of the 3d Battalion, 14th Marines, Trenton, N.J., conducted outdoor occupation-of-position and gun drills. The unit then moved out on a 30-mile motor march to a nearby firing area where frozen ground and chill winds created dozens of new problems—including new challenges for the forward observers in adjusting live fire. An April amphibious landing at Rodeo Cove in Marin County, Calif., topped off a 2-day operation by San Francisco Bay area reservists from the 2d Armored Amphibian Company at Treasure Island.

After departing the LST *Polk County*, the 10 LVT's churned toward the beach and established defensive positions ashore.

POW Training Increased

For a day and a half in May, Marine reservists of Company M, 3d Battalion, 23d Marines, were subjected to indoctrination, interrogation, and other harassments which they might have to undergo if taken prisoner of war. The purpose of the drill was to emphasize responsibilities of leadership among prisoners—indispensable to POW organization. The unit had conducted numerous classes on escape, evasion and survival, and the Code of Conduct. The realistic training, which took place at a ranch some 20 miles from the unit's training center at San Rafael, Calif., included physical training in search techniques, interrogation, and POW camp organization. Members of the county sheriff's department assisted the "camp commander" in interrogation of "prisoners."

Troops of the 41st Rifle Company, Durham, N.C., staged a realistic 2-day escape and evasion exercise in March at nearby Camp Butner, a deactivated World War II Army camp. Members of the University of North Carolina NROTC staff took part in the exercise as interrogators and officers in charge of the POW compound. The aggressor forces were members of a mythical enemy nation known as the "Peoples Democratic Republic of Chi-Nam." One hundred reservists were turned loose in squad-size units without weapons and instructed to remain in a 2-square mile area and try to avoid capture by the Chi-Nam forces. As the "victims" were captured and brought into the POW compound, they were introduced

to the "cramped position" pit, a hole in the ground covered with logs; various signs and banners written in oriental-type characters; and abusive treatment. They were searched; pushed around; tied up; made to stand, sit, or lie in uncomfortable positions; and then placed in the stockade. From time to time, they were given lectures and ordered to sign confessions. "The invaluable knowledge derived from such a realistic exercise will be retained for a long time and will serve as important guidance if the Marine should one day be captured," said Major Willard E. Cheatham, Inspector-Instructor of the 41st.

Despite the new emphasis on field exercises, Marine reservists needed good armory facilities, and 192 such training centers were used in 1965. The plant account for Marine Corps-exclusive Ground centers amounted to about 16½ million dollars; and, if shared facilities were prorated out, some 40 million dollars worth of facilities were used. Buildings in use ranged from one that had been a Confederate hospital during the Civil War to modern structures built specifically for Marine Reserve training. Thirty new facilities had been built since 1959, and 4 new buildings or additions to existing buildings were under construction. The Marine Corps Reserve had obtained long-range approval of expenditures of one and a half million dollars a year for new construction, with 46 additional new structures planned for the next 5 years.

Experience gained in the weekend exercises and drills was put to test during the summer in several major air-ground problems. The largest of these, *Yellowjacket*, was a MEU landing exercise conducted across the beaches and in the swamps of

Lejeune. Some 2,000 Reserves took part in the 3-day problem. From Ohio, Toledo's 1st Battalion, 24th Marines, and the 1st 105mm Howitzer Battery from Richmond, Va., combined with a battalion from the 2d Marine Division, were landed by helicopters. Over-the-beaches air support was furnished by Marine Air Group 43, 4th Marine Aircraft Wing, from Willow Grove, Pa. Aggressor forces for *Yellowjacket* included elements of the 13th Infantry Battalion, Washington, D.C.; the 5th Engineer Company, Roanoke, Va.; the 89th Rifle Company, Columbia, S.C.; the 7th Truck Company, Charlottesville, Va.; and the 5th Communications Company, Greensboro, N.C. The 6th Staff Group of Atlanta conducted planning for the operation. Attack elements provided security for an American airfield in a mock country torn with civil strife. The landing force also was charged with maintaining communication lines and destroying aggressor forces on order.

Although part of the activity was purely paperwork, 22 Reserve units actually participated. Supporting the Ground forces, VMA–131 of New York and VMA–322 of Boston operated from a SATS site at Bogue Field, N.C., to furnish close air support. Photo reconnaissance was provided by VMJ–4 of New Orleans, flying RF9J–2 Cougars. HMM–771 of Boston with UH–34D's and supporting helicopters flew tactical helicopter troop lifts from the carrier *Guadalcanal* to designated landing zones. They set up operations ashore at MCAF, New River, and provided continued helicopter missions in support.

On the opposite coast Reserves from the 2d Battalion, 24th Marines, from the Chicago area, teamed with Regulars from the 1st Marines for *Crazy Quilt*, a counterinsurgency exercise conducted during May

at Camp Pendleton. The 12th Staff Group of Los Angeles manned the regimental headquarters, and maintained tactical command of the landing force. The 2d Battalion combined with the Regular 1st Battalion, 1st Marines—with supporting tank, artillery, and antitank units from the 1st Marine Division—as RLT 24. The 2d Battalion, 1st Marines, provided aggressor forces and the 3d Battalion, 1st Marines, enacted the roles of villagers and irregulars. The regimental-size field exercise was umpired by 37 officers and NCO's from various Reserve units. As Marines moved into the mythical land of Fresco, they were confronted with rebel action and were forced to wipe out guerrilla strongholds in the hills. The exercise provided realistic experience in pursuit of a poorly-organized but hard-fighting band.

Reserves Instructed Aboard Cruiser

A visit aboard a Navy guided-missile cruiser highlighted annual field training for the 95th Rifle Company of Oshkosh, Wisconsin, during its summer drill at MCRD, San Diego. Host organization for the 73-man Reserve company was the Depot Sea School, which provided instruction in naval gunnery, communications, firefighting, and security duties aboard ship. Members of the 4th Force Reconnaissance Company, San Bernardino, Calif., made a simulated reconnaissance of the Camp Pendleton area, reaching the reservation by parachuting into remote areas, swimming to beaches along the 20-mile length of the camp, and paddling ashore through the surf in rubber boats. In several days of clandestine movement, they collected assigned intelligence data.

For the Marines of the 3d Engineer

Company of Youngstown, Ohio, annual field training meant return to the hilly island of Vieques. Working alone, or with segments of Camp Lejeune's 8th Engineer Battalion, the Youngstown unit was involved in nearly a dozen projects— including construction of roads, culverts, fences, and a swimming pool. They also worked on plumbing and roofing projects and constructed a grenade range. Marines of the 16th Rifle Company, Wilmington, Del.—also training at Vieques—found the problems of field living somewhat different from those of the previous year's AFT. Then, they had spent 2 weeks at the Marine Corps mountain warfare training site in California's chilly High Sierras. Now they were hard-pressed to make 2 canteens of water last a day in the island's intense heat as they undertook guerrilla warfare problems and weapons training.

One of the most meaningful training periods for Reserves was *Silver Lance*, a fleet exercise of the Regular forces involving more than 80 ships and 70,000 Navy and Marine Corps personnel. The maneuver, which encompassed strike warfare, antisubmarine warfare, mine and countermine warfare, antiair warfare, electronic warfare, peacemaking in a counterinsurgency environment, 2 major amphibious landings by sea and air, and ancillary amphibious operations, was held during late February and early March. Three Class II Reserve units, 1 VTU, and more than 130 Class II and III Reserve officers participated. *Silver Lance* was conducted at sea off southern California; on the offshore islands of San Clemente, San Nicolas, and San Miguel, and ashore at Camp Pendleton. Lieutenant General Victor H. Krulak, Commanding General, FMF, Pacific, as commander of the 2d Marine Expeditionary Corps, directed

operations ashore. Included in the supporting Reserve elements were the 96th Rifle Company of Milwaukee; 1 communications company from the 6th Communications Battalion, Fort Schuyler, N.Y.; and the 4th Civil Affairs Unit (VTU), Washington, D.C., under Colonel (Judge) David F. Condon.

The Marine Reserve tradition of community service continued to grow during 1965. Twice in 3 months, members of the inspector-instructor staff of the 6th Engineer Battalion of South Bend answered calls for assistance in the wake of a storm. The 4th Engineer Battalion of Baltimore built a footbridge over nearby Gunpowder Falls. And Marine reservists of the 3d Battalion, 24th Marines, pitched in to aid victims of Hurricane Betsy which left the traditionally carefree city of New Orleans in shambles late in 1965. The reservists, working their normal jobs by day, reported for duty at night to the local naval station. They stood security guard, acted as messengers, and assisted in the housing, clothing, and feeding of 12,000 evacuees of the storm-wracked area. On the individual side, Reserve Sergeant Robert J. Dimery, was awarded the Navy and Marine Corps Medal for his "heroism in saving the life of an individual at great personal risk" at the scene of an auto accident near Edmond, Okla. And, 2 members of the inspector-instructor staff of the 38th Rifle Company of Montgomery, Ala., were honored by Montgomery's city commissioners with resolutions citing their contributions in civic affairs.

Silver Anvil Award to Toys-for-Tots

The Marine Corps Reserve won the Silver Anvil Award of the Public Relations Society of America for its 1964 Toys-for-

Tots program. Throughout the country upwards of 3½ million toys were given to more than 1,145,000 children as a result of the 1964 campaign. The Award, presented annually for outstanding public relations programs carried out during the previous year, was given to the Marine reservists who competed with all other Government and military agencies in the Public Service and Public Affairs Programs category. But Marine Reservists did not rest on these laurels. The 18th annual drive in 1965 was the most productive yet, as a broader range of promotional material was made available earlier than in previous years.

The Women

Women Marines on active duty numbered approximately 150 officers and 1,600 enlisted in 1965. Serving at every major post and station in the United States, they were also assigned to district headquarters and recruiting billets in major American cities, and to overseas duty in Hawaii, London, Naples, Paris, and Santo Domingo. Approximately 660 women were being carried on the rolls as reservists, serving with Organized units as members of Class II or as Volunteers (Class III).

Although the number of Regular Women Marines is relatively small (the legal limit is 2 percent of the overall strength of the Marine Corps), their selection and training has provided the Marine Corps with a continuing source of well-trained, professionally minded women ready to meet any mobilization need such as that which occurred with rapid expansion of the Marine Corps in June 1950 during the Korean War. Since 1943 nearly 37,000 women have been trained as

Marines, both enlisted and officer, Regular and Reserve, for service during and following World War II.

Mindful of the important service the Women Marines had rendered during 3 wars, the Commandant, General Greene, convened a Woman Marine Program Study Group in August 1964. The purpose of this special review board was to determine what modifications of current policy and practice might enable the women to perform still more valuable service to the Corps.

After 4 months of investigation by the Study Group (popularly called the "Pepper Board" because it was headed by retired Lieutenant General Robert H. Pepper, USMC), a report of the Woman Marine Program was issued in the first months of 1965. It contained more than 80 separate recommendations. These touched on practically every aspect of the Woman Marine Program—from training, job classification and duty assignment, housing, and recruiting needs, to the sharply increased need for more women on active duty in a national emergency.

The report also focused attention on the increasingly important role of women reservists in event of either partial or full-scale mobilization. Specific recommendations about the latter included:

> That greater utilization of women reservists be planned at posts and stations in the initial phases of mobilization;
>
> That recruiting efforts for the Reserve program stress recruitment of prior-service personnel;
>
> That, insofar as possible, the difference between the increased number of women required at the time of initial mobilization beyond those already on active duty and in Class II (the Organized Reserve) be made up by members of Class III (Volunteer Reserve, or nonpay drill status).

According to the Director of Women Marines, Colonel Barbara J. Bishop, USMC, action on the recommendations of the "Pepper Board" is expected to improve the current Woman Marine Program, affording better career opportunity to the individual Woman Marine, and bringing increased benefits to the Corps by having women better equipped to perform more diversified and important assignments.

Among other moves designed to further streamline and give more administrative flexibility to the present-day Woman Marine Program, was the authorization and appointment of a Deputy Director of Women Marines. The first Deputy Director, assigned by midsummer 1965 to this new billet in the Office of Director of Women Marines, was Lieutenant Colonel Jeanette I. Sustad, USMC.

Marine Reserve Aviation

The Marine Air Reserve Training Command established an all-time aviation safety record on 30 June with an accident rate of 1.07 for fiscal year 1965. This rate translated into slightly more than one accident per 10,000 hours of flight—considerably less than the predicted all-Navy accident rate of 1.26 or one and one-quarter accidents per 10,000 flight hours. The Commandant said in a message to General Elwood:

> By establishing an all-time low accident rate, while flying a record number of flight hours with high-performance aircraft, your squadrons have furnished ample evidence of their readiness.

A St. Paul, Minn., Marine Reserve aviator who died a hero during World War II was given special honors when a South St. Paul airport was named for him. The ceremony included the unveiling of a stone memorial, officially dedicating the site to the memory of Captain Richard E. Fleming who was killed during the Battle of Midway in June 1942 and was posthumously awarded the Medal of Honor.

Reserve Civic Action Program

As Marine reservists looked to the future, they also looked to their responsibilities as Americans and as world citizens. Late in 1965, they launched a new effort in behalf of the people in Vietnam—the Marine Corps Reserve Civic Action Program. This project gave each Marine reservist a direct and personal means of supporting United States efforts in Vietnam. Additionally, it afforded an excellent means of placing the Marine Corps and its Reserve before the public in a favorable light.

The fund, nationally authorized and locally implemented, was designed to assist the Regular forces who already were compassionately helping the poor in Vietnam through donations of personal services, funds, and supplies. Fighting the Communist aggressor is hard enough, but securing the confidence and support of a people who have lived under the terror of communism for years is an even bigger job, the Marines noted.

"This national program will provide an economical and practicable means of support," the implementing Marine Corps Order announced.

> Inasmuch as the Commandant does not plan to ask that the Reserve be called to active duty before a specific mission exists, it is considered that the conduct of a joint Marine Corps Reserve/CARE program is a task short of mobilization for which the Reserve is singularly well-qualified.

All reservists were notified of the opportunity for organized action through the CARE organization, and procedures were established through which contributions to CARE would be credited to the individual Reserve units. Whenever possible, materials and supplies were to be purchased in Vietnam, thereby improving that country's economy.

Marine Corps Reserve Officers Association

Through its history, Marines had received support from many quarters, but seldom had any group offered such vital backing as the Marine Corps Reserve Officers Association. As the Marine Reserves approached their 50th year, MCROA entered its 41st year with a paid membership of 4,150 in 93 chapters across the country. Its function was to foster the advancement of technical and professional skills of Reserve officers, to promote the Marine Corps in the broadest and most liberal manner, to best preserve the security of the United States.

Marines paused momentarily in May to look back on one of the greatest of all military careers—that of General Thomas Holcomb, 17th Commandant, who died at New Castle, Del. It was under General Holcomb that the tiny 16,000-man Corps of the 1930's grew to 350,000 in the early days of World War II. He was the last of the Major General Commandants, and the first to hold three-star rank in the Marine Corps. Upon his retirement, he also became the first Marine to hold four-star rank. To many present-day Marines, he was one of the last remaining links with the "Old Breed."

As the war intensified in Vietnam, Marine reservists prepared for mobilization, confident of their readiness. But this very readiness acted as a deterrent to the expected callup. The Commandant planned to commit the Reserves only when the chips were down, when a Reserve division/wing team in combat would be needed. The Reserve had a unique responsibility—to be trained and ready to respond. It was a traditional role. From the time of the Revolutionary War, when farmers had dropped their plows, grabbed their muskets, and walked to war, to the conflicts in Korea and the Caribbean, when a strong force in reserve backed up America's battle to keep the peace, the country had relied on the strength of its citizen soldiers.

Should mobilization be ordered, the process would be an orderly one—a process that was well-rehearsed. Battalions of the 4th Marine Division would immediately begin movement to bases of initial assignment. The Commandant would select his commanding general who would, in turn, select his regimental commanders. Staffs would be formed with personnel from Reserve staff groups. Marine air groups and supporting elements would mobilize in place at the home air stations until ordered out. Force Troops units would report as directed to support the 4 division/wing teams. Other units, not previously assigned, would be employed as units or would provide individual augmentation through personnel processing centers at designated bases.

But should the call to arms not come, the task would not diminish, because continued readiness is hard work. The primary job of the Marine Reserve is not to fight—but to be ready to fight. Its first task is not to man the front lines, but to give depth and flexibility to the Nation's military force. Today, throughout the

Marine Reserve Establishment, every element of command, administration, and training is dedicated to that end.

Late 1965—Early 1966

During 1965 an effort was made by the history writing committee to summarize the winners of the various trophies available to Reserve Aviation units yearly. Interestingly enough, MARTCOM knew only the names of the winning squadrons over the period from 1949 to 1964 when the first trophy was awarded, but had no complete record of squadron commanding officers. Thanks to the cooperation of Brigadier General Hugh M. Elwood and the ingenuity of Informational Services Officer, Lieutenant Colonel Samuel C. Oliver, and his NCO-in-charge, Master Sergeant Louis F. Nadolny, all commands were circularized and a complete list (Appendix I) was compiled. Where 2 C.O.'s are listed, it indicates the outgoing skipper on top and the incoming one beneath.

The Trophies include the granddaddy of them all, the Herman Ridder Marine Air Reserve Trophy first made available in 1949; the Pete Ross Safety Trophy, which originated in 1950; the Chief of Naval Operations Safety Award, first given in 1955, and the "baby" Marine Air Reserve Helicopter Trophy, available since 1959 and never won by the same unit twice until last year when Seattle broke the record.

MARTCOM also did a quick check on "outstanding enlisted Marine reservists—air" and supplied a dazzling list of top pay grade Reserves, most of whom answered "yes" to both WW II and Korea as might be expected. Included were First Sergeant James W. Casey who heads up the safety education section for the Chicago Police Department; Gunnery Sergeant Michael Churille, a school teacher; and Master Gunnery Sergeant Wilbert A. Detty, a salesman. All were from Chicago. Master Sergeant Alfred G. Johnson of Lockport, Ill., is a stationary engineer; First Sergeant Michael W. Lindstrom of Palatine, Ill., is a material damage adjuster; and Gunnery Sergeant Prentice E. Trimble of St. Louis, Mo., is a teletype repairman. Commissioned Warrant Officer Thomas W. Quigley, Jr., of VMF–321 holds some kind of record for continuity. He joined the squadron in August 1946 as a technical sergeant and served as ordnance chief until December 1957. He is presently the avionics officer and hasn't missed a day of service with the unit since joining. He will have been a member 20 years when the 50th Anniversary flies by! This small part of a much larger listing is merely the visible part of the larger iceberg which gives the Marine Reserve its large, solid base.

The year 1965 was actually a great deal like many previous years, except with the ever-present overtones of Vietnam. These very overtones may have accounted for the ruggedness of the training. The *Roundup*, monthly newspaper of the 8th Marine Corps District, featured summer training in its October edition. Some significant quotes from a variety of unit stories highlight the emphasis on readiness:

> The 40th Rifle Company, Lubbock, Tex. . . . practical exercises aboard ship included fire fighting, damage control, and survival swimming . . . at San Diego's Sea School.
>
> The 13th Engineer Company, Midland, Tex. . . . for the first 3 days found themselves in water survival training, wet and dry net training, landing vehicle exercises, helicopter training, and vehicle waterproof-

ing school . . . at LFTU, Coronado and San Clemente, Calif.

The 3d Battalion, 24th Marines of Louisiana . . . specialized training included firing the M–79, use of the sniper scope, a chance to field test the new radar detection equipment against infiltrating aggressors. Tactics were emphasized from fire team to battalion . . . at Camp Pendleton.

The 2d Battalion, 24th Marines from Dallas, Fort Worth, and Wichita Falls . . . unit fired more than 400 rounds of howitzer ammunition . . . 100 percent qualifications in the Physical Readiness Test on the last day of ATD . . . at Pendleton.

The 4th Reconnaissance Battalion out of San Antonio and Corpus Christi . . . at 0430 in the morning there is little that can compare with running a few miles in crisp, thin mountain air. Or later taking a swim in an icy mountain stream. Or crossing a rapid mountain river on a single strand rope . . . at Mountain Warfare Training Center in northern California.

The 6th Rifle Company of Little Rock . . . learned to climb nets, worked with amphibian tractors and helicopters, learned to breach beach obstacles, and journeyed to historic Fort Story for the practical application phase of a counterinsurgency course . . . at Little Creek.

In late fall, some 2,000 Reserves took part in *FEX–1* which included air, mobile artillery, naval gunfire, and parachute drops in the quiet countryside around West Point, N.Y. Ten Marine units, including 4 aircraft squadrons were joined by the USS *Parker* (DD–1) in a 36-hour exercise. The destroyerborne reconnaissance Marines and those dropped by parachute on recon missions added the dash of the unusual to an imaginative problem aimed at routing guerrillas.

In November a joint Navy-Marine Reserve aerial inflight refueling exercise, *Ready One*, proved the ability of Washington-based reservists to fly non-stop their F8B "Crusader" jet fighters to the Caribbean. Major Thomas R. Moore, operations officer of MARTD at Andrews AFB led Captains Landon R. Jones, Jr., Allen Amsbaugh, and Jared M. Huebel of VMF–321 to a rendezvous with 2 tankers. The mission was supported by a NARTU SP–2E patrol plane.

An unusual set of awards from the National Recreation Association, first ever given to a military unit, went to 2 Marine air units in 1965. The 2d Engineer Squadron and Sub Unit 1 of MARTD, South Weymouth, Mass., were honored for "more than 4,000 hours of work in constructing and developing recreation areas for children of Saugus, Mass." In 2 years they cleared, graded, and filled 40 acres of timberland and 20 acres of swamp!

Vietnam came to 12th Street between the Kansas City Courthouse and City Hall on 7 December at 1 p.m. as part of the "Pearl Harbor Day Reminder Zone" sponsored by the Southern Jackson County Chamber of Commerce. Troops poured into the area, set up barricades and emplaced field pieces as Marine and Army reservists took over an area which featured the grim sign ". . . better to fight now for freedom in VIETNAM than to fight for freedom later in the streets of Kansas City."

And, in December 1965, the Marine Corps Reserve Ribbon went the way of the M–1 rifle and leggings: it was no longer issued. Officers and enlisted persons who have served a 10-year period of satisfactory service will, instead, be issued a new award. This is the Armed Forces Reserve Medal (a narrow light blue center stripe, flanked by buff, blue, buff and blue side stripes) which supersedes the Reserve Ribbon. Organized Reserve personnel who have attended training duty with an

OMCR unit for 4 consecutive years and maintained a drill attendance record of 90 percent or better continue to be eligible for the Organized Marine Corps Reserve Medal.

Stewart to Hines to Drake

There was also a change of command late in 1965. Brigadier General Joseph L. Stewart retired on 1 November and turned over the Reserve to his Deputy, Colonel Hines. Commenting on his busy and fruitful 18 months as Director, General Stewart made this valedictory:

> As I have stated many times, the Marine Corps Reserve today is the finest in history. It has never been better trained, organized, and equipped. I personally consider it the finest Reserve force in existence today. This high and unique state of readiness can be attributed to each of our predecessors whose foresight provided the objective and much of the means for securing it. The refinements, the polish, the professionalism, the devotion to duty and loyalty—the esprit de corps—are yours.

His "successor" on 3 January 1966 was Brigadier General Clifford B. Drake, then the Director of the Command and Staff College at Quantico. However, until the Regular general came aboard the first week of 1965 the Reserve had another Director who was himself a Reserve. Colonel Hines' 2-month tour was a busy one before he stepped down to the deputy desk. He attended various District Reserve conferences as principal speaker, carried on the daily functions of the Division of Reserve, and even had to announce deactivation of 10 Marine Reserve units at Naval and Marine Corps Training Centers and movement of 4 additional units to new locations.

The Reserve Conference in New Orleans was one of the highlights of this period.

Colonel Hines was given an Honorary Citizen's Certificate and the keys to the city by Colonel James Moreau, a career reservist who was recently elected to the New Orleans City Council. Also on board were Reserve Brigadier Generals Sidney S. McMath and Charles F. Duchein and MARTCOM's General Elwood. The 8th District *Roundup* reported the session in part as follows:

> The Marine Corps Reserve is the topic of much conversation and thought today in Washington, according to Colonel Owen M. Hines, Director of the Corps' Reserve forces.
>
> Colonel Hines made the statement in his remarks to the more than 100 Marine officers from the District who gathered in New Orleans, December 8–10, for the Annual Reserve Conference.
>
> The colonel, who recently took over from Brigadier General J. L. Stewart as "boss" of the Corps' Reserve Organization, went on to say that at no time in its 49-year history has a high state of readiness been more important to the Reserve. Also, he added, there has never been a time when the Reserve had the opportunity it now has to train itself into the necessary state of efficiency and preparedness in advance of any contingency that may arise. Colonel Hines urged that all commanders and members of the Reserve take full advantage of the opportunity.
>
> "I would also like to say," the colonel continued, "that there are 2 programs concerning the Reserve establishment which the Commandant is now personally interested in. These are: (1) the Marine Corps Reserve Civic Action Program, which the Commandant feels is one of the finest programs going to help the South Vietnamese people; and (2) the place of the Woman Marine in the Reserve Program. It is hoped that in the future, Woman Marines will become members of all Reserve units, both ground and air. . . ."

Four Vignettes

Four vignettes and a 190-year Birthday
message completed the year 1965. For the
first time since Korea, Women Marines
were authorized for billets in the Organized Marine Air Reserve, but minus any
"6 months' training/active duty program
for new, untrained recruits."

Reserve General William H. Klenke,
Jr., retired after long service which, among
many other distinctions, gives him credit
for being the "only Marine who ever graduated from Pensacola as a buck private."
He was assigned to flight training as a last
minute substitute and never promoted to
corporal like others at school. He was a
NAP in the first Marine Carrier Squadron
(VS–14) aboard the old *Saratoga* and in
1934 requested a Special Order Discharge
to accept a Reserve commission as a second
lieutenant for activity at Floyd Bennett
Field.

Twenty-one years after his final WWII
air battle, a rugged character named
Gregory Boyington turned up in Vietnam
late in 1965 to inspect and evaluate electronics gear supplied by an equipment firm
for which the fabled "Pappy" works.
The MARTC *Digest* reported the story in
its October issue in part as follows:

> In the MAG–11 compound, he talked about
> his visit. "The Department of Defense
> wanted someone to come to Vietnam and
> evaluate the gear. They thought it might
> be a good idea if I made the trip . . . and I
> jumped at the chance to see these guys
> again."
>
> He was visiting with the MAG–11 Com-
> mander Colonel Robert F. Conley, formerly
> commanding officer of MARTD Glenview.
> Colonel Conley had arrived immediately
> after hearing Pappy was in the area.
>
> "I've known this guy for 23 years," the
> colonel said, "and he hasn't changed a bit.
> We used to spend all of our spare time either
> playing cards or fighting each other."

> Pappy was asked about his observations on
> flying in Vietnam. "It's a lot different
> from the old days. These boys really must
> know their stuff. We never had to worry
> about things like missiles or SAM sites and
> I thank the Good Lord for that."
>
> Then the controversial hero spoke about
> the young Marine flyers of today. "You
> know, someone asked me if I was coming
> over here to take a hand in this action. I
> just looked at the guy and said, 'I hope they
> have a lot better help over there than I can
> offer.' "
>
> When I got here I saw the Corps still had
> real pilots. They look just as they always
> did, the talk doesn't change and the faces are
> the same. They get the job done. The only
> thing different I can find is the names of the
> guys."
>
> Colonel Conley took his friend on a tour of
> the MAG–11 flight line and their first visit
> was the Phantom jets of VMFA's 513 and 542.
>
> As they approached the line the colonel
> commented, "We're a little bit crowded here
> Pappy. Everything we have had to be bor-
> rowed or scrounged from the Air Force."
>
> The Medal of Honor winner turned a little
> and smiled as he answered, "So after all
> these years . . . what's new?"

And, another Reserve made news of a
different sort. Twice decorated for personal bravery by the Vietnam Government, Major Dick Kriegel, a civilian
provincial representative for AID, was the
subject of an editorial in all the Scripps
Howard papers late in October. It was
the same Kriegel who had devoted almost
half a year to research and writing on
this history. The *Cleveland Press* headed
its editorial with the words "Decorate
Him." The editorial follows:

> Bravery is not a rare thing these days in
> Vietnam.
>
> But for special citation as one of the
> bravest of the brave a young American AID
> officer out there, Richard Kriegel, should get
> a medal. But he won't.
>
> Kriegel had the laudable gall to put it

straight to visiting Senator Edward M. Kennedy and his party. Kennedy has asked, as most VIP's from back home do, what Kriegel's major problem was.

"To be blunt, sir," Kriegel replied, "if we had fewer people coming out here. In the last 45 days, we have had 35 groups. Each of them demands the 25-cent tour. It takes up my time. It takes the province chief's time."

Kennedy protested that he hadn't asked for the lavish treatment his group had been receiving. But regardless of type of treatment, Kriegel's point was eminently valid and needed to be made.

A large number of Congressional delegations are en route or planning to go to Vietnam despite efforts by Defense Secretary Robert McNamara to hold down on these junkets. Maybe Kriegel's remarks will cause a few to stay home—and thus be of great help to our war effort.

And, Commandant Greene, himself a vignette in action at home and abroad, had these words in his 1965 Birthday message to close out the Regular-Reserve year:

While we cannot foresee what the future may hold for us, we do know that whatever demands are imposed, whatever mission is assigned, we will be ready. For that has been the way of Marines past; that is our way; and that is part of the heritage which we will pass to the Marines who follow us.

To all Marines everywhere—Regular, Reserve, Retired—and to their families, I send personal greetings and best wishes on the 190th Birthday of our beloved Corps.

EPILOGUE

Neither the Marine Corps nor the Marine Corps Reserve has ever had much preoccupation with the past, except to build upon it for the future. The story of these past 50 years has had a certain sameness, but always a newness. It has been in the discarding of a part and a retention of another part that resulted in progress through the years.

Although this has been the story of the Reserves as a part of the larger Marine Corps family, an equally interesting story could have been written of these same Reserves as part of the civilian community. One part of that community is the veteran organizations and the professional guilds or groups made up of officers or of enlisted or of both. Much of this story had to be ruled out because of space. The activities of the Marine Corps Reserve Officer Association were such that they impinged in larger measure upon the Corps and its Reserve than any other group and hence could not be denied. The Marine Corps League also gave many reservists an opportunity to serve their community, their State, and their Nation.

Marine Reserves have held every rank from national commander down to post welfare officer in almost all of the veterans organizations, in the Reserve Officers Association, the Retired Officers Association, and the Military Order of the World Wars. Obviously, they have contributed leadership to the 1st, 2d, 3d, 4th, and 5th Marine Division Associations. The Navy League of the United States has also drawn upon Marine Reserves for leadership and today Brigadier General Charles Duchein is both a national vice president and chairman of the Navy League's Marine Corps Affairs Committee.

The Marine general officers in the Ready Reserve today are called upon by the Commandant for duties throughout the year. They have served as Deputy Commander of troops or as Assistant Commanding General for a 2-week summer period. Or, they have represented their Corps as principal speakers at cities across the land to explain current Corps policies and programs. They visit Organized Reserve units and make official inspections, or they review troops on special occasions. One of the favorite stories about General Maas following his retirement and blindness was the way he handled such inspections of honor guards which suddenly seemed to spring up at airport or train depot as he traveled the country for the President's Committee on Employment of the Handicapped. He would reach out and grab a rifle from the hands of a young reservist standing at "present arms," whip the butt end skyward in best approved DI fashion, place an unseeing eye to the hole in the barrel and say so all could hear, "looks clean to me" or "I don't see any dirt." Most spectators didn't know whether to laugh or cry.

The Ready Reserve generals also handle the routine duties as members or presidents of various boards, attend conferences, and represent the Corps on the Reserve Forces Policy Board. Similarly, Reserve officers in all ranks serve on boards and panels and handle other duties closer to home, particularly since the casualty lists from Vietnam are lengthening.

In February of 1966 the Reserve Officers Association *Washington Newsletter* reported that there were 160,486 Reserve officers on active duty. The Army's 59,875 amounted to 59 percent of current Army officer strength. The Navy had 28,420 Reserve officers on duty, a total of 36 percent of Navy active officer forces. The Air Force, with 66,882 Reserve officers on duty, had a Reserve percentage of 51. The Marines had 17,650 officers on active duty, 5,309 being Reserves. The Marines had 3 Reserve officers on duty out of every 10 officers for a 30 percent figure. A comparison of these figures probably would prove nothing, for each service has a variety of different missions. The total figures, however, are quite revealing. Almost every other officer on duty today is Reserve. If asked to guess how many Reserve officers were on active duty, the average informed American today would probably miss the true percentage by a country mile.

By the end of 1965 several Marine Reserves had been decorated for actions in Vietnam. A ground and an air Reserve officer had each won the Silver Star. Two platoon leaders had received the Bronze Star. Seven aviators from the Reserve had won the Distinguished Flying Cross. Purple Hearts, some presented to next of kin, and Air Medals were becoming more and more routine.

Early in 1966 the Corps announced, as it had many times before, a new realignment of the structure of the Organized Marine Corps Reserve. Eleven units in 12 communities found themselves with new names and new missions, names and missions shaped toward the future and away from the past.

The Corps also found itself with 2 new Reserve brigadier general selectees in Colonel Leland W. Smith, long a Federal executive and a standout in aviation, and Colonel Arthur B. Hanson, the 1964–66 President of MCROA and a practicing Washington attorney. Within a week after the selection, Hanson was on his way to Vietnam on a special mission. At the same time, both Generals McMath and Duchein were selected for two-star rank.

Going into its 50th year, the Reserve had a full agenda of training on its hands. Some 208 units were scheduled for 2 weeks annual field training. The usual air-ground exercises will be scheduled during the summer for large maneuvers with air and ground training meshing more and more during the entire year in their respective community areas. In another move, the Corps was endeavoring to get more Volunteer Reserve enlisted into the Class II Organized units and more Reserve enlisted, Class III or II, into the active duty Corps in many scarce military occupation specialties.

The Commandant put it this way: "The international situation is creating an ever-increasing demand on the services of our Corps. To meet this challenge we are engaged in a personnel buildup effort unequalled in recent times . . . . We need trained Marines, yet training entails time. Time is our shortest commodity."

In 50 years things hadn't changed so much for the Reserves, for time had always been a short commodity for them since they were citizens of 2 worlds, one civilian and one military. And seldom did the demands of one coincide with the other.

Whatever lies ahead in the next 50 years, one thing is certain. The Regular-Reserve team is welded-melded into a team that is READY and is pointed toward the future with all that it may hold in automation, computerization, atomic and solar energy. With God's Grace and in His own good time, the Regular-Reserve of tomorrow will continue to be Semper Fidelis, always faithful to God, Country, and Corps.

Born 4 days before the Armistice of the War to end all Wars, the current Director of Reserve, General Drake, had this to say in his first "Reserve Report" in the *Marine Corps Gazette*:

> It is a real privilege to be permitted to serve in the capacity of Director of the Marine Corps Reserve, particularly so as we enter its Golden Anniversary year. The acknowledged position of leadership among all Reserve forces which the Marine Corps Reserve enjoys today stands as a marked tribute to those thousands of Marine Reservists who, during the past 50 years, through tireless and selfless efforts, have made it what it is today . . . truly, the READY RESERVE. Needless to say, what has been accomplished during the years 1916 to 1966 also stands as a marked challenge to all of us to further enhance this proud and enviable record.

The "record" of the past half century has largely been written, but General Drake has his sights on the years ahead. The Reserve which he heads and the Corps which General Greene leads today and which others will lead tomorrow may do more orbiting than marching, more pioneering in space and under the oceans than on the traditional land, but, whatever they do they will do together.

The Division of Reserve (1965)

March, 1965

(Adapted from an article in Leatherneck Magazine, written by Staff Sergeant Harvey Hall and reprinted with permission of the Editor)

If a dozen key words were suddenly removed from the English language, the Division of Reserve at Headquarters Marine Corps would cease all activity. These words name and describe the activities of personnel who work in the Division of Reserve, and how can one work without a program? Program! There's one of those words, and since we let one of 'em slip we might as well throw in the rest.

Plans, projects, programs, procedures, coordinate, develop, prepare, formulate, expedite, designate, review, and administer are words which the Division couldn't do without. The first four name the major products of the Division and the remaining eight describe the activities necessary for the production.

No synonyms are used lest there be confusion in the "development and coordination of certain programs and projects essential to the expeditious mobilization of designated Marine Corps Reserve units in the event of a national disaster or when so directed by proper authority," or words to that effect.

The phraseology undoubtedly would become second nature to anyone who works in the headquarters offices of the Reserve Establishment for a short while, but to anyone who is merely passing through, the jargon of the trade makes each person's job sound exactly like all the others.

In a broad sense, everyone in the Division of Reserve does have the same job; that of continuing the development of what is already the "world's most ready military reserve force." But in the practical, everyday working arrangement, each person's work entails something different. This ensures that every detail is properly attended.

There are testimonials to the effect that details are properly attended. During a recent meeting of government officials in which Reserve organizations were discussed, a legislator remarked that, "If you want to know how to operate a Reserve Organization, ask the Marines. They have a good one."

Brigadier General J. L. Stewart, Director of the Division of Reserve, is responsible directly to the Commandant of the Marine Corps, whom he keeps up-to-date on Reserve programs, mobilization procedures, training plans, cost estimates, legislation which pertains to the Reserve Establishment, and other matters which concern reservists.

On the other end of the chain of command, Brigadier General Stewart controls ground Reserve units through Directors of Marine Corps Districts, and controls the Marine Air Reserve through the Commanding General, Marine Air Reserve Training Command, in Glenview, Ill.

The Division "formulates plans and policies for the Marine Corps Reserve," according to the orders which govern the Division's activities, "and is responsible for the execution of training and the administration of the Reserve program." In addition, the Reserve headquarters maintains liaison with higher echelons of command as well as agencies of other armed forces, the National Guard and State Militias.

The Director is assisted by a Deputy, an Assistant Director, and by an Assistant to the Director in addition to the seven branch section heads.

Between the staff officers and the branches of the division, there is an adjutant section and a research officer. The Adjutant Section's chores include processing mail, coming and going, which pertains to Reserve units as well as "general" mail. "General" mail files contain correspondence about nearly everything—including letters from youngsters who would like to join the Reserve—when they come of age.

The Adjutant Section also provides information about Reserve units to inspecting officers and notifies units when they are to be inspected. Funds for temporary additional duty are controlled by this office.

The Research Officer has the responsibility of answering inquiries from officials of the government. Since every reply has to be thoroughly researched, it is likely that he stays on the job late many evenings and reports to work early many mornings. In his spare time he performs "such other duties as the Director of Reserve may direct."

Branches of the Division of Reserve include the Administrative; Plans, Programs and Training; Logistics; Fiscal; Manpower; Aviation; and the Liaison and Information Branches. The name of each branch aptly describes its activity, so we'll touch only the highlights or jobs which are unique within these offices.

The Administrative Branch prepares orders for the activation, deactivation or redesignation of Reserve units and handles requests from Regular Marine unit commanders for extra personnel to help with the summer training program. The office also monitors the program for assigning Standby Reserve officers to Civil Defense activities and takes a hand in establishing or changing the tables of organization for Marine Corps District headquarters and Inspection-Instructor staffs.

In handling the huge volume of paper traffic concerning personnel and personnel policies, the Admin Branch works closely with Manpower Branch, especially regarding the assignment of Reserve officers who are assigned duty with the Selective Service Program.

Screen, process, originate and prepare are the key words for the Personnel Section of the Admin Branch. This is the office which makes all the points with reservists by approving requests for recreation funds for Organized Reserve units.

And this is the section with the kingsized mail baskets. Nearly anything a reservist wants or needs is requested by him through this office. If he has a small physical defect he wants a waiver on, this is the office which sees his letter first. If he wants to remain in the Reserves, even though he has too much time in grade, this is the office which will process his request. If a command asks for extra personnel to help with the chores during the time in which Reservists will be training, this office handles most of the paperwork.

The Manpower Branch plans the income and outgo of personnel so that the two ends come out even. One of the biggest problems which upsets well-laid plans is that many of those who enter the Reserve Program enlist in the Regular Marine Corps upon graduation from recruit training, or before their 6 months of active duty are finished.

It becomes hectic when a Reserve unit enlists six men into the 6-month program with the expectation that they will return to fill the openings in the home town unit, only to discover 5 months later that only three are coming home. The other three shipped over for a 4-year tour with the Regular Marine Corps. But as long as there are still Marines, no one minds the extra work involved in enlisting three more men. Most units have a waiting list anyhow.

In order to keep the in's and out's even, or uneven, depending upon appropriations, the Manpower Branch works with a lot of figures on population trends of the past, present and future. A city which is growing might be able to support another Reserve unit while a town which is losing people might not be able to support the one it has. Helping to justify the budget requests with estimates of the personnel strength is one more of its many duties.

No one needs to tell reservists what the Plans, Programs, and Training Branch does. This is the place where decisions such as where units will go for summer training are made. One section plans for the training units, while another plans for the training of individuals and assigns them to active duty for specified lengths of time.

The third section makes tentative plans for long-range programs. This same section keeps the Marine Corps informed as to which military skills, or how many of each, would be available to the Corps when and if the reservists are called to active duty. There are many other activities in this branch, but you get the idea. They really do plan ahead.

The Logistics Branch consists of the Facilities Section and Supply Section. Estimates of the costs of maintenance and operation, major repairs, and minor construction, are handled by the Facilities Section. Nearly everything which pertains to facilities for the training of reservists is handled by this section, provided that the cost of a single job does not exceed $10,000. Projects costing more than that amount are forwarded to the Assistant Secretary of the Navy (I&L) for funding authority.

The Supply Section reviews the tables of organization of units and recommends changes when needed. Requests from Marine Corps Districts, I–I staffs, and Reserve units are also reviewed by the section, which then makes recommendations as to the disposition of the requests. Of course, the section is involved in the preparation of budget requirements, and it helps coordinate the transportation of Reserve units to and from Annual Field Training.

Aviation Branch is divided into the Personnel Section and Plans and Programs Section. Each of the sections does what its name implies. Personnel Section spends most of its time with matters which concern or affect reservists, while the Plans and Programs Section plans how best to use the resources of the Marine Air Reserve. Air Reserve units figure prominently in any plan to mobilize ground units, and there is a constant search for better ways in which to employ all available aircraft.

Finally we come to the people who handle the money, or, more correctly, the people who handle the numbers which represent the money. The Fiscal Branch prepares the budget, and the figure which is requested in appropriations has to be justified to the Department of the Navy, Office of the Secretary of Defense, the Bureau of the Budget, and Congressional committees. This causes those who work in Fiscal Branch to examine each figure carefully.

To make things really interesting, if they are not already, the Branch must provide data on financial programs several years in advance, and be reasonably accurate in their calculations.

The Liaison and Information Branch tells the Marine Corps Reserve story in such a manner that young men will want to enlist. Recruiting Aids Section prepares information which is designed to help I–I staffs keep their units up to authorized manning levels with as little expense as possible. The Information Section publishes a newspaper entitled "Reserve Marine" and performs public relations functions. One of its most interesting and rewarding jobs is planning and coordinating public service campaigns, such as the "Toys-for-Tots" program, which is conducted every year to give needy children a better Christmas. The Section also prepares information for public release.

Directors, Marine Corps Reserve

Major General Ben H. Fuller, USMC
Officer in Charge, Marine Corps Reserve
14 September 1928–9 May 1929
Colonel Julius S. Turrill, USMC
Officer in Charge, Marine Corps Reserve
10 May 1929–30 June 1932
Brigadier General James J. Meade, USMC
Officer in Charge, Marine Corps Reserve
1 July 1932–1 September 1934
Brigadier General Richard P. Williams, USMC
General Officer in Charge of Reserve
2 September 1934–15 May 1937
Brigadier General William P. Upshur, USMC
Director, Marine Corps Reserve
16 May 1937–18 August 1939
Colonel William C. James, USMC
Director, Marine Corps Reserve (Acting)
19 August 1939–15 May 1940
Colonel Joseph C. Fegan, USMC
Director, Marine Corps Reserve
16 June 1940–6 January 1941
Brigadier General Samuel M. Harrington, USMC
Director, Marine Corps Reserve
4 February 1941–16 June 1941
Brigadier General Ralph S. Keyser, USMC
Director, Marine Corps Reserve
17 June 1941–14 March 1942
Major General Philip H. Torrey, USMC
Director, Marine Corps Reserve
16 April 1942–30 September 1942
Brigadier General Littleton W. T. Waller, Jr.,
USMCR
Director, Marine Corps Reserve
1 October 1942–1 May 1943
Colonel Clark W. Thompson, USMCR
Officer in Charge, Division of Reserve
2 May 1943–23 September 1945
Brigadier General Franklin A. Hart, USMC
Director, Division of Reserve
25 September 1945–16 January 1946
Colonel Randolph McC. Pate, USMC
Director, Division of Reserve
17 January 1946–31 March 1947

Major General William T. Clement, USMC
Director, Marine Corps Reserve
1 April 1947–2 May 1949
Lieutenant General Merwin H. Silverthorn,
USMC
Director, Marine Corps Reserve
3 May 1949–30 March 1951
Major General Edward A. Craig, USMC
Director, Marine Corps Reserve
31 March 1951–31 May 1951
Brigadier General Harry B. Liversedge, USMC
Director, Marine Corps Reserve
1 June 1951–13 November 1951
Major General Randolph McC. Pate, USMC
Director, Marine Corps Reserve
14 November 1951–15 August 1952
Major General John C. McQueen, USMC
Director, Marine Corps Reserve
16 August 1952–1 June 1954
Major General Joseph C. Burger, USMC
Director, Marine Corps Reserve
2 June 1954–3 January 1956
Brigadier General William W. Stickney, USMCR
Director, Marine Corps Reserve
4 January 1956–11 March 1956
Brigadier General Thomas G. Ennis, USMC
Director, Marine Corps Reserve
12 March 1956–28 February 1957
Brigadier General William W. Stickney, USMCR
Director, Marine Corps Reserve
1 March 1957–21 July 1957
Major General Alan Shapley, USMC
Director, Marine Corps Reserve
22 July 1957–5 November 1959
Major General William W. Stickney, USMCR
Director, Marine Corps Reserve
6 November 1959–31 December 1959
Brigadier General William T. Fairbourn, USMC
Director, Marine Corps Reserve
1 January 1960–11 June 1962
Brigadier General Ronald R. Van Stockum,
USMC
Director, Marine Corps Reserve
12 June 1962–3 March 1964

Colonel Owen M. Hines, USMCR
 Director, Marine Corps Reserve
  4 March 1964–7 April 1964
Brigadier General Joseph L. Stewart, USMC
 Director, Marine Corps Reserve
  8 April 1964–31 October 1965

Colonel Owen M. Hines, USMCR
 Director, Marine Corps Reserve
  1 November 1965–2 January 1966
Brigadier General Clifford B. Drake, USMC
 Director, Marine Corps Reserve
  3 January 1966–

Mobilization—World War II Marine Corps Reserve Battalions and Air Squadrons

Unit	Home station	1st duty station	Date assigned
BATTALION			
1st USMCR_____	New York (including Rochester), N.Y__ CO: Major George W. Bettex	MB, Quantico, Va___	9 Nov 40
2d USMCR_____	Boston (including Portland, Me.), Mass_ Major Joseph T. Crowley	MB, Quantico, Va___	8 Nov 40
3d USMCR_____	New York, N.Y_____ Major Bernard S. Barron	MB, Quantico, Va___	8 Nov 40
4th USMCR_____	Newark, N.J_____ Major Otto Lessing	MB, Quantico, Va___	9 Nov 40
5th USMCR_____	Washington (including Rockville and Alexandria) Lieutenant Colonel Harvey L. Miller	MB, Quantico, Va___	7 Nov 40
6th USMCR_____	Philadelphia (including Glenside), Pa___ Major Edward P. Simmonds	MB, NYd, Phila____	7 Nov 40
7th USMCR_____	Philadelphia, Pa. _____ Major Joseph R. Knowlan	Quantico, Va_____	7 Nov 40
6th USMCR_____	Toledo, Ohio_____ Lieutenant Colonel Iven C. Stickney	Quantico, Va_____	9 Nov 40
9th USMCR_____	Chicago (including Hammond), Ill_____ Major Harold M. Keller	MCB, San Diego, Calif.	8 Nov 50
10th USMCR_____	New Orleans, La_____ Lieutenant Colonel Alfred A. Watters	MCB, San Diego, Calif.	7 Nov 40
11th USMCR_____	Seattle, Wash. (including Tacoma)____ Major Clarence H. Baldwin	MCB, San Diego, Calif.	7 Nov 40
12th USMCR_____	San Francisco, Calif_____ Captain Wallace T. Breakey	MB, NYd, Mare Island	7 Nov 40
13th USMCR_____	Los Angeles, Calif_____ Major John J. Flynn	MCB, San Diego, Calif.	7 Nov 40
14th USMCR_____	Spokane, Wash_____ Major Edwin D. Partridge	MCB, San Diego, Calif.	8 Nov 40
15th USMCR_____	Galveston (including Texas City and Houston) Lieutenant Colonel Clark W. Thompson	MCB, San Diego, Calif.	6 Nov 40
16th USMCR_____	Indianapolis, Ind_____ Captain William C. Smith	MCB, San Diego, Calif.	8 Nov 40

Unit	Home station	1st duty station	Date assigned
17th USMCR	Detroit, Mich Major Burdette Hagerman	MB, Quantico, Va	9 Nov 40
18th USMCR	St. Paul (including Duluth) Major Eugene B. Hanson	MCB, San Diego, Calif.	8 Nov 40
19th USMCR	Augusta, Ga Major Walter W. Barr	MB, NYd, Portsmouth, Va.	8 Nov 40
20th USMCR	Portland, Oreg Major Albert G. Skelton	MB, PSNYd, Bremerton, Wash. (Puget Sound)	7 Nov 40
21st USMCR	Charlotte, N.C Major George E. Golding	MB, NNYd, Portsmouth, Va. (Norfolk)	7 Nov 40
22d USMCR	Los Angeles, Calif Major Woodbridge S. Van Dyke	MCB, San Diego, Calif.	7 Nov 40
23d USMCR	Roanoke, Va Major Carleton Penn	MB, NNYd, Portsmouth, Va.	7 Nov 40
AIR SQUADRONS			
(MarResScout Sqdn) VMS–1R	NRAB, Squantum, Mass CO: Captain N. S. Clifford	Quantico, Va	16 Dec 40
VMS–2R	NRAB, Brooklyn, N.R Major S. A. McClellan	Quantico, Va	16 Dec 40
VMS–11R	NRAB, Brooklyn, N.Y Major Karl S. Day	Quantico, Va	16 Dec 40
VMS–3R	NRAB, Anacostia, D.C Captain John B. Jacob	Quantico, Va	16 Dec 40
VMS–4R	NAS, Miami, Fla Major Bernard L. Smith	Quantico, Va	16 Dec 40
VMS–5R	NRAB, Grosse Ile, Mich Captain Charles E. Adams	Quantico, Va	16 Dec 40
SS–2MR	NRAB, Grosse Ile, Mich Captain George E. Congdon	Quantico, Va	16 Dec 40
VMS–6R	NRAB, Minneapolis, Minn Colonel Melvin J. Maas	San Diego, Calif	16 Dec 40
VMS–7R	NRAB, Long Beach, Calif Major William J. Fox	San Diego, Calif	16 Dec 40
VMS–8R	NRAB, Oakland, Calif Major Raymond W. Conroy	San Diego, Calif	16 Dec 40
VMS–9R	NRAB, Seattle, Wash Captain Joseph P. Adams	San Diego, Calif	16 Dec 40
SS–3MR	NRAB, Seattle, Wash Captain Valentine Gephart	San Diego, Calif	16 Dec 40
(MarResServ Sqdn) VMS–10R	NRAB, Kansas City, Kans Major Alton N. Parker	San Diego, Calif	16 Dec 40

Naval Vessels Named for Marine Corps Reservists Killed During World War II

U.S.S. *Agerholm*	PFC Harold C. Agerholm, USMCR
U.S.S. *Ahrens*	PFC Edward Henry Ahrens, USMCR
U.S.S. *Alvin C. Cockrell*	1stLt Alvin Chester Cockrell, Jr., USMCR
U.S.S. *Joseph E. Connolly*	Cpl Joseph Edward Connolly, USMCR
U.S.S. *Cook*	2dLt Andrew Fred Cook, Jr., USMCR
	Sgt Dallas Harry Cook, USMC (brothers)
U.S.S. *Daniel*	PFC Hugh Spencer Daniel, USMCR
U.S.S. *Cecil J. Doyle*	2dLt Cecil John Doyle, USMCR
U.S.S. *Dyess*	LtCol Aquilla J. Dyess, USMCR
U.S.S. *Epperson*	PFC Harold Glenn Epperson, USMCR
U.S.S. *Fleming*	Capt Richard E. Fleming, USMCR
U.S.S. *Frybarger*	PFC Raymond Frybarger, USMCR
U.S.S. *Gentry*	2dLt Wayne Roy Gentry, USMCR
U.S.S. *Gilligan*	Pvt John Joseph Gilligan, Jr., USMCR
U.S.S. *Hanson*	1stLt Robert Murray Hanson, USMCR
U.S.S. *Hawkins*	1st Lt William Deane Hawkins, USMCR
U.S.S. *Willard Keith*	Capt Willard Woodard Keith, Jr., USMCR
U.S.S. *Richard E. Kraus*	PFC Richard Edward Kraus, USMCR
U.S.S. *La Prade*	1stLt Robert M. La Prade, USMCR
U.S.S. *Everett F. Larson*	PFC Everett Frederick Larson, USMCR
U.S.S. *Maurice J. Manuel*	PFC Maurice Joseph Manuel, USMCR
U.S.S. *Jack Miller*	1stLt Jack Miller, USMCR
U.S.S. *Oliver Mitchell*	2dLt Oliver Mitchell, USMCR
U.S.S. *Melvin R. Nawman*	2dLt Melvin Rollie Nawman, USMCR
U.S.S. *Thomas F. Nickel*	Pvt Thomas Frederick Nickel, USMCR
U.S.S. *Ozbourn*	Pvt Joseph W. Ozbourn, USMCR
U.S.S. *Robert I. Paine*	Pvt Robert Ignatius Paine, USMCR
U.S.S. *Power*	1stLt John Vincent Power, USMCR
U.S.S. *Pratt*	LtComdr Malcolm Lewis Pratt, USNR/USMC
	1stLt John Lester Pratt, USMCR (father and son)
U.S.S. *McCoy Reynolds*	Pvt McCoy Reynolds, USMCR
U.S.S. *Charles H. Roan*	PFC Charles H. Roan, USMCR
U.S.S. *Stafford*	Capt Richard Y. Stafford, USMCR
U.S.S. *Lawrence C. Taylor*	2dLt Lawrence Coburn Taylor, USMCR
U.S.S. *Herbert J. Thomas*	Sgt Herbert J. Thomas, USMCR
U.S.S. *Leland E. Thomas*	2dLt Leland Evan Thomas, USMCR
U.S.S. *Thomason*	Sgt Clyde Thomason, USMCR
U.S.S. *Tweedy*	2dLt Albert William Tweedy, Jr., USMCR
U.S.S. *Witek*	Pvt Frank P. Witek, USMCR

List of Congressmen Supporting Marine Bill

REPRESENTATIVES

John J. Allen	California	Donald Jackson	California
Victor Anfuso	New York	Henry M. Jackson	Washington
William H. Ayres	Ohio	Benjamin F. James	Pennsylvania
Walter S. Baring	Nevada	Walter Judd	Minnesota
George Bender	Ohio	Bernard W. Kearney	New York
Charles E. Bennett	Florida	Thomas J. Lane	Massachusetts
J. Caleb Boggs	Delaware	James F. Lind	Pennsylvania
Joseph R. Bryson	South Carolina	Gordon L. McDonough	California
Thurmond Chatham	North Carolina	Clinton D. McKinnon	California
Robert B. Chiperfield	Illinois	Mike Mansfield	Montana
Robert J. Corbett	Pennsylvania	Chester E. Merrow	New Hampshire
Paul B. Dague	Pennsylvania	George P. Miller	California
James C. Davis	Georgia	Hugh B. Mitchell	Washington
James P. S. Devereux	Maryland	Albert P. Morano	Connecticut
James I. Dolliver	Iowa	Thomas E. Morgan	Pennsylvania
James G. Donovan	New York	Walter Norblad	Oregon
Joe L. Evins	Tennessee	Joseph P. O'Hara	Minnesota
Gerald R. Ford, Jr	Michigan	Harry P. O'Neill	Pennsylvania
Tom B. Fugate	Virginia	James Patterson	Connecticut
James G. Fulton	Pennsylvania	John Phillips	California
Myron V. George	Kansas	Norris Poulson	California
Thomas S. Gordon	Illinois	Prince H. Preston, Jr	Georgia
Louis E. Graham	Pennsylvania	L. Mendel Rivers	South Carolina
William T. Granahan	Pennsylvania	Hugh D. Scott, Jr	Pennsylvania
Edward J. Hart	New Jersey	Hubert B. Scudder	California
Louis B. Heller	New York	Lawrence H. Smith	Wisconsin
William Hess	Ohio	Clark Thompson	Texas
Patrick Hillings	California	James Van Zandt	Pennsylvania
Clare E. Hoffman	Michigan	Alvin F. Weichel	Ohio
Allan O. Hunter	Ohio	Clement J. Zablocki	Wisconsin

SENATORS

George Aiken	Vermont	Zales Ecton	Montana
Owen Brewster	Maine	Homer Ferguson	Michigan
John Bricker	Ohio	Ralph E. Flanders	Vermont
Hugh Butler	Nebraska	William Fulbright	Arkansas
Homer E. Capehart	Indiana	Walter George	Georgia
Francis Case	South Dakota	Guy Gillette	Iowa
Dennis Chavez	New Mexico	Robert Hendrickson	New Jersey
Everett M. Dirksen	Illinois	Bourke B. Hickenlooper	Iowa
Paul Douglas	Illinois	Hubert H. Humphrey	Minnesota
James Duff	Pennsylvania	Irving M. Ives	New York

Edwin C. Johnson_____ Colorado

Olin D. Johnston_____ South Carolina

Estes Kefauver_____ Tennessee

Herbert Lehman_____ New York

Pat McCarran_____ Nevada

Joseph McCarthy_____ Wisconsin

Burnet R. Maybank_____ South Carolina

Wayne Morse_____ Oregon

Karl E. Mundt_____ South Dakota

James E. Murray_____ Montana

Matthew M. Neely_____ West Virginia

Richard M. Nixon_____ California

Willis Robertson_____ Virginia

Andrew F. Schoeppel____ Kansas

George Smathers_____ Florida

H. Alexander Smith_____ New Jersey

John J. Sparkman_____ Alabama

Edward J. Thye_____ Minnesota

Charles W. Tobey_____ New Hampshire

Arthur V. Watkins_____ Utah

Alexander Wiley_____ Wisconsin

House Report No. 666, (82d Cong., 1st Sess.)

FIXING THE PERSONNEL STRENGTH OF
THE UNITED STATES MARINE CORPS,
ADDING THE COMMANDANT OF THE
MARINE CORPS AS A MEMBER OF THE
JOINT CHIEFS OF STAFF

June 30, 1951—Committed to the Committee of
the Whole House on the State of the Union and
ordered to be printed

Mr. Vinson, from the Committee on Armed
Services, submitted the following Report (to accompany S. 677).

Report of the National President, 1951 Conference of Chapter Presidents, Marine Corps Reserve Officers Association, May 19, 1951, Washington, D.C.

Much has happened since we met a year ago. For one thing, during the year we have been officially proclaimed as the most famous police force in the world, although our propaganda department has been put in question as being only second rate. Seriously, the whole outlook has drastically changed for the Marine Corps and its Reserves.

The Corps, with the help of its Reserves, has written a gloriously new and dramatic chapter in its history and has added a new foreign name to its long list, beginning with Tripoli through Montezuma, Belleau Wood, Guadalcanal, and on to Okinawa. Now Korea joins the global record of the Marines. As I make my last report to you, I do so with mixed feelings. Little in my career can ever mean as much to me as MCROA. I step aside without regret and with pride in my association with the finest group of Americans I have ever known. I had the privilege of being MCROA's first president when the association was formed in 1926. No group was ever organized with a more unselfish purpose or conducted through the years with loftier ideals. MCROA has never fought for reservists for any selfish benefit to the reservists but only so that the reserves could be better prepared to aid the Marine Corps in the accomplishment of the Corps' mission and obligation to the nation. I believe that in a quarter century of MCROA's existence, the association has left its imprint on the Marine Corps, for we have really developed a very fine partnership through these years between the Regulars and the Reserves.

The Marine Corps has been the first of our military forces to adopt the attitude that its Reserves are an integral part of the forces and that the Corps is composed equally of Regulars and Reserves, and is not complete without both. This relationship has become a pattern for the

Reserves of the other military services to aim at. It is just another in the long list of Marine Corps "firsts."

Their Reserve organization and training program has become the model for the other services. None will contend, not even the top command at headquarters, that our system was perfect, nor that it couldn't be improved, but the acid test of Korea, which came without warning, proved that our Marine Reserve system worked and worked well, and under the most extremely extenuating circumstances.

Just a few years after a war and during the traditional American postwar letdown period, the Marine Reserves were suddenly and most unexpectedly called upon for a gigantic task and quickly. The Marine Corps and its Reserves were equal to the task, to the astonishment and marvel of the world. I think we even surprised ourselves.

Outside of the Inchon landing the Marines in Korea are performing a task not normally contemplated nor specified as one of the missions of the Corps. However, just as Iceland and Guadalcanal were not really Marine Corps missions, except perhaps the initial landing, but since no other service was ready to do the job when it had to be done, the mission was assigned to the Marines as in the present crisis. Thanks, in large part, to the readiness and the spirit of the Marine Reserves, the Corps in each case nobly and successfully accomplished its task. For this, you of MCROA can take a just measure of credit and I am sure that the leaders of the Regular component of the Corps will ungrudgingly give you your full share of the credit.

MCROA was formed, in fact, to work for a training program. Congress, in 1925, provided for an organized Marine Corps Reserve but little was done about it since virtually no appropriations were available. Upon its formation, MCROA organized a campaign to get the then leaders in the Marine Corps to take a more active interest in creating and maintaining an active reserve force. We obtained directly from the Congress, without budget support, the small appropriations that provided the beginnings of an organized Marine Corps Reserve. Each year the budget limited the Marine Corps' request for reserve appropriations to the amount appropriated the previous year. Each year we appealed to the Appropriations Committee of the Congress to increase the amount and won congressional support by proving that the Marine reservists were accomplishing more with fewer dollars than for any other military expenditures being appropriated. This continued until the emergency was declared in 1940.

At the same time, MCROA worked diligently with the leaders in the Marine Corps to establish a definite system of reserve policies, and I think it is safe to say that in the twenties and most of the thirties, almost every progressive Marine Corps Headquarters policy affecting the reserves had its origin in MCROA.

MCROA also sponsored the various legislative proposals that became the law for the Reserves, including their basic Reserve Act of 1938 under which we still operate. The leaders in MCROA played an active part in the movement that led to the establishment of the Civilian Components Policy Board, soon to be renamed the Reserve Forces Policy Board, in the Office of the Secretary of Defense.

The whole Marine Corps—Regulars and Reserves—form an unbeatable team and both are dedicated only to the security of our beloved Nation.

I leave the high office of president of MCROA with full confidence that this association will always fulfill its obligation to our country by aiding the Corps through assistance in the development and maintenance of the finest Reserve of any military service. I shall always maintain my active interest in MCROA as I do in the Corps itself, but I know that the time has come when the leadership of this association must be turned over to younger officers who are more representative of the modern age of Marine reservists, and who are in closer touch with them. Never has the Nation needed a strong and vigorous Marine Corps more than it does now. Never

has the Corps needed its Reserves backed by a virile, potent and strong association more than now.

Not only does the state of this Nation require, but its very ability to survive as a nation, depends upon its ability to maintain an adequate citizen military reserve. Without a proper sized and competent Reserve to back its Regular Forces, this Nation has only two choices, both equally disastrous ones. It can relapse into a state of dangerous unpreparedness. To do so will inevitably invite and result in an attack that will succeed in destroying us; or it can attempt to maintain permanently full wartime military forces.

This course, in addition to being repugnant to every American tradition, would defeat its own purpose; for the enormous size required of the standing forces would entail such staggering costs that soon they would accomplish what no external enemy ever has—our defeat—through internal collapse of our economic system. Therefore, the only alternative is to adhere to the long-accepted United States policy of a relatively small highly skilled professional force and a large well trained semiprofessional force—the Reserves.

As I told you before in previous years, there will always be a United States so long as there is a U.S. Marine Corps and there will always be a Marine Corps so long as there is an effective Marine Corps Reserve. I now tell you that there will always be a Marine Corps Reserve so long as there is a strong Marine Corps Reserve Officers Association. You are leaders in your communities. You understand the language of the professional Corps, yet you speak the language of the citizenry, and you can and must translate the needs of the Corps into effective public opinion in order to adequately support the Corps. This must be done so that we may jointly fulfill our obligation to the United States, which now symbolizes all of the freedom-loving people of the whole world. Therefore, you leaders of MCROA—the chapter presidents and the national council—have a tremendous responsibility transcending that of most other citizens in this country.

Since the Marine Corps sets the pattern for the latest in tactical developments in the military art, and it is charged by law with leadership in developing amphibious warfare, it is essential for our preservation that the Marine Corps not only be preserved but strengthened and expanded. Modern warfare has reemphasized the dependence upon seizing, securing, and holding advanced bases of operation. Even the mighty airplane must start from bases and return to them. As a war progresses, bases must be steadily advanced toward the heart of the enemy. Bases for operation of the Navy, the Army, or the Air Force must first be taken from the enemy. Without advancing bases the war cannot advance to a successful conclusion. Upon the shoulders of Marines rests the burden of obtaining advanced bases.

As the Marine Corps must depend upon its Reserve for its complete ability to fulfill its mission, so too the other services must depend upon effective reserve components. Since the Marine Corps Reserve set the pattern for the development and training of the other Reserves, Marine reservists, have a great responsibility. The leaders of the Marine Reserve officers, through their association, have the unique and challenging responsibility of aiding the Corps by seeing that such a Reserve is provided first for the support of the Marine Corps and secondly, as a pattern for all services.

I hand this challenge and this responsibility on to those who shall be selected today to carry on the direction of the Marine Corps Reserve Officers Association. As I say goodby to you as your President, I wish to paraphrase, but slightly change, a recent farewell of a great American. Old Marines, unlike old soldiers, do not die; we don't even fade away; we only step a pace to the rear. So as an old Marine, I do not "fade away" from you, but only step back so that I may better help from now on by pushing. So as I step back to the ranks, I assure you that I shall always be in there backing up the younger Marines in the common job of preserving these magnificent United States, by always having a loyal fighting U.S. Marine Corps to lead the task force in our preservation.

A rising vote of thanks and appreciation was tendered General Maas.

Sequence of Post-Korea Woman Marine Reserve Platoons

Boston, Mass.: WM Classification Platoon, 1st MCRRD
    Activated: 13 January 1952
    Attached to: 2d Infantry Battalion, USMCR
St. Louis, Mo.: WM Administrative Platoon, 9th MCRRD
    Activated: 13 February 1952
    Attached to: 3d Infantry Battalion
Detroit, Mich.: WM Administrative Platoon, 9th MCRRD
    Activated: 6 March 1952
    Attached to: 5th Infantry Battalion
Los Angeles, Calif.: WM Classification Platoon, 12th MCRRD
    Activated: 25 March 1952
    Attached to: 2d 105mm Howitzer Battalion
New York, N.Y.: WM Classification Platoon, 1st MCRRD
    Activated: 17 April 1952
    Attached to: 1st ANGLICO (Air and Naval Gunfire Liaison Company), Fort Schuyler, N.Y.
Chicago, Ill.: WM Classification Platoon, 9th MCRRD
    Activated: 24 April 1952
    Attached to: 9th Infantry Battalion
Philadelphia, Pa.: WM Supply Platoon, 4th MCRRD
    Activated: 24 April 1952
    Attached to: 2d Depot Supply Battalion
Seattle, Wash.: WM Classification Platoon, 12th MCRRD
    Activated: 1 May 1952
    Attached to: 10th Infantry Battalion
Philadelphia, Pa.: WM Disbursing Platoon, 4th MCRRD
    Activated: 22 May 1952 (by 1954 consolidated into WM Supply unit)
    Attached to: 2d Depot Supply Battalion
Tampa, Fla.: WM Disbursing Platoon, 6th MCRRD
    Activated: 27 May 1952
    Attached to: 1st Amphibian Tractor Battalion

Baltimore, Md.: WM Classification Platoon, 5th MCRRD
    Activated: 12 August 1952
    Attached to: 1st Engineer Battalion
Dallas, Tex.: WM Administrative Platoon, 8th MCRRD
    Activated: 30 August 1952
    Attached to: 1st 4.5'' Rocket Battalion
Minneapolis, Minn.: WM Administrative Platoon, 9th MCRRD
    Activated: 5 September 1952
    Attached to: 4th Infantry Battalion
Cleveland, Ohio: WM Supply Platoon, 9th MCRRD
    Activated: 2 December 1952
    Attached to: 11th Infantry Battalion
San Francisco, Calif.: WM Supply Platoon, 12th MCRRD
    Activated: 28 February 1953
    Attached to: 1st AAA–AW Battalion
Denver, Colo.: WM Disbursing Platoon, 9th MCCRD
    Activated: 28 April 1953
    Attached to: 1st 155mm Gun Battalion
Washington, D.C.: WM Disbursing Platoon, 5th MCRRD
    Activated: 28 April 1953
    Attached to: 5th Special Infantry Battalion
Brooklyn, N.Y.: WM Communication Platoon, 1st MCRRD
    Activated: 19 November 1953
    Attached to: 2d Signal Company
Worcester, Mass.: WM Disbursing Platoon, 1st MCRRD
    Activated: 1 December 1953
    Attached to: 1st Communication Company
Kansas City, Mo.: WM Supply Platoon, 9th MCRRD
    Activated: 7 March 1954
    Attached to: 2d Weapons Battalion
Miami, Fla.: WM Administrative Platoon, 6th MCRRD
    Activated: 31 July 1955
    Attached to: 2d 155mm Gun Battery

285

Marine Air Reserve Trophy Winners

Herman Ridder Marine Air Reserve Trophy

Year	Squadron	Detachment	CO's name
1949	VMF-142	Miami (Jax)	LtCol Rolland F. Smith
1949	MACS-19	Grosse Ile	Capt Kenneth Mudey
1950	VMF-451	Willow Grove	Maj Henry S. Miller
1950	MACS-15	Atlanta	LtCol Leland W. Smith
1951	VMF-132	New York	LtCol Jonathan D. Mendes
			Maj Thomas S. Ferdinand
1951 [1]	MACS-15	Atlanta	LtCol Henry W. Branson
1952	VMF-141	Oakland (Alameda)	LtCol William L. Bacheler
			LtCol Leon Sparrow
1952	MACS-18	Los Alamitos	Capt Ralph J. Clabb, Jr.
			LtCol Robert C. Schmid
1953	VMF-216	Seattle	Maj Charles G. Carr
1953	MACS-17	Willow Grove	Maj Crawford Venn
1954	VMF-236	Denver (Olathe)	LtCol Leslie C. Reed
1954	MACS-21	South Weymouth	LtCol Thomas H. Murphy
FY-56	VMF-351	Atlanta	Maj Robert C. Smith
FY-56	MACS-17	Willow Grove	Maj William H. Marks
FY-57	VMF-231	Akron (Grosse Ile)	Maj Herbert Jennings
FY-57	MACS-24	Anacostia (Andrews)	Maj Robert Young
FY-58	VMA-216	Seattle	LtCol Rolland N. Rinabarger
FY-58	MACS-31	South Weymouth	Maj Robert L. Smith
FY-59	VMF-511	Willow Grove	Maj Frank L. Moister
FY-59	MACS-19	Grosse Ile	LtCol James R. Mallon
FY-60	VMF-541	Seattle	LtCol Merle A. Kime
FY-60	MACS-26	New York	LtCol Francis P. Paterno
			LtCol David B. Fisher
FY-61	MACS-18	Los Alamitos	Maj Donald F. Davis
FY-61	VMF-511	Willow Grove	LtCol John T. Graver, Jr.
FY-62	VMF-313	New York	LtCol Russell Hunchar
			LtCol J. M. P. Morin
FY-62	MACS-19	Grosse Ile	Maj Julius R. Karsten
FY-63	VMF-321	Andrews	LtCol Carol W. Morris
FY-63	MACS-15	Atlanta	LtCol J. A. Hook
FY-64	VMF-215	Olathe	LtCol J. B. Giberson
FY-64	MACS-23	Denver (Olathe)	LtCol John D. Frisk
FY-64	VMA-233	Norfolk	LtCol Russell F. Fiske
FY-65	VMR-234	Twin Cities	LtCol Lyle S. McCabe
FY-65	MACS-23	Denver	LtCol R. W. Mitchell

[1] All MACS on active duty in Korea.

Chief of Naval Operations (CNO) Safety Award

Year	Squadron	Detachment	CO's name
FY–55	VMF–123	Los Alamitos	LtCol David M. Williams
			LtCol James F. Coleman
FY–56	VMF–215	Olathe	LtCol Frank P. Barker, Jr.
FY–57	VMF–221	St. Louis (Memphis)	Maj Frederick G. Armstrong
FY–58	VMF–141	Oakland (Alameda)	LtCol James A. Leckie
FY–59	VMF–218	Willow Grove	Maj Lynford S. Walters, Jr.
FY–60	VMA–213	Twin Cities	Maj John H. Wastvedt
FY–60	VMA–233	Norfolk	Maj Delmar L. Dee
			Maj Jack W. Campbell
FY–60	HMM–767	New Orleans	LtCol Joseph E. Givens
FY–61	VMA–231	Grosse Ile	LtCol Edwin Piotrowski
FY–61	VMA–233	Norfolk	LtCol J. W. Campbell, Jr.
FY–61	HMM–772	Willow Grove	LtCol Gordon C. Hart
FY–62	VMF–313	New York	LtCol James Ireland
FY–62	VMR–222	Grosse Ile	LtCol Charles Witacre
FY–62	HMM–773	Grosse Ile	Capt Erich Kilmer
FY–63	VMF–511	Willow Grove	LtCol John J. Quinn
FY–63	VMA–141	Alameda	LtCol Robert F. Harvey
FY–63	VMR–234	Twin Cities	LtCol Dale E. Thorne
FY–63	HMM–768	New York	LtCol Donald G. Clarke
FY–64	VMF–611	Glenview	LtCol Jack G. Harrington
FY–64	VMA–322	South Weymouth	LtCol Thomas W. Conlon
FY–64	VMR–234	Twin Cities	LtCol James O'Neil
FY–64	HMM–772	Willow Grove	Maj Robert C. McGee
FY–65	HMM–770	Seattle	LtCol Dexter A. Dimick

Pete Ross Safety Trophy

Year	Squadron	Detachment	CO's name
1950	VMF–541	Birmingham (Atlanta)	Maj John H. McEnery, Jr.
1951	VMF–351	Atlanta	LtCol Leon L. Clark
1952	VMF–142	Miami (Jax)	LtCol Chauncey M. Laughlin
1953	VMF–141	Oakland (Alameda)	LtCol Leon Sparrow
1954	VMF–215	Olathe	LtCol Floyd E. Beard
FY–56	VMF–215	Olathe	LtCol Frank P. Barker, Jr.
FY–57	VMA–231	Akron (Grosse Ile)	Maj Herbert Jennings
FY–57	VMF–141	Oakland (Alameda)	LtCol James A. Leckie
FY–58	VMA–216	Seattle	LtCol Rolland N. Rinabarger
FY–58	VMF–236	Denver (Olathe)	Maj Howard Armstrong
FY–59	VMA–233	Norfolk	Maj Delmar L. Dee
FY–59	VMF–112	Dallas	LtCol Robert J. Irwin
FY–60	VMA–213	Twin Cities	Maj John H. Wastvedt
FY–60	VMA–233	Norfolk	Maj Delmar L. Dee
			Maj Jack W. Campbell
FY–61	VMA–231	Grosse Ile	LtCol Edwin Piotrowski
FY–61	VMA–233	Norfolk	LtCol Jack W. Campbell, Jr.
1962	VMF–112	Dallas	LtCol Robert J. Irwin
1963	VMA–322	South Weymouth	LtCol Thomas W. Conlon
1964	VMA–133	Alameda	LtCol John Kapowich
1965	VMA–134	Los Alamitos	Maj Ronald Trepas

Marine Air Reserve Helicopter Trophy

Year	Squadron	Detachment	CO's name
FY–59	HMM–767	New Orleans	LtCol Donald G. Clark
FY–60	HMM–766	Twin Cities	LtCol A. O. Hellerude
FY–61	HMM–774	New York	LtCol Edwin J. Cartoski
FY–62	HMM–768	New York	LtCol Donald G. Clark
FY–63	HMM–771	South Weymouth	LtCol John W. Lincoln
FY–64	HMM–770	Seattle	LtCol Vernon Clarkson, Jr.
FY–65	HMM–770	Seattle	LtCol Dexter A. Dimick

Bibliographical Note

In preparing this History of the U.S. Marine Corps Reserve, writing team members of the Public Affairs Unit 4–1 have relied on a variety of source materials, including Congressional records. In addition to official Marine Corps documents, staff memoranda, and releases, publications such as *The Marine Corps Gazette*, *Leatherneck*, *The Reserve Marine*, and District newsletters have furnished colorful accounts of Reserve units and personalities. Historical Archives of Headquarters Marine Corps provided an almost endless amount of authentic material.

Personal letters with their wartime reminiscences from some 80 reviewing officers of the History contributed facts about the Reserve that, in many cases, have never before appeared in print. Books, published and unpublished research studies, and non-Marine publications also lent valuable sidelights to the growth of the Reserve.

A fully documented copy of "The Marine Corps Reserve—A History" is available for researchers in the Archives of the Historical Reference Section, Historical Branch, G–3 Division, at Headquarters Marine Corps.

Index

U. S. GOVERNMENT PRINTING OFFICE: 1966 O - 217-733

359.96
U.S. Marine Corps.   Div. of
Reserve.   The Marine Corps
Reserve; a history.....